Once upon a City

New York from 1890 to 1910

as photographed by Byron

and described by GRACE M. MAYER

Museum of the City of New York

with a foreword by Edward Steichen

Once upon a City

The Macmillan Company

New York 1958

First Printing

Printed in the United States of America

Library of Congress catalog card number: 57–10777

NOTE

The photographs reproduced in this book are from

The Byron Collection
Museum of the City of New York

Applications to reproduce any of the photographs,
except for review purposes, should be addressed
to the Museum of the City of New York.

PERMISSIONS

Permission to quote copyrighted material is gratefully acknowledged to publishers, authors, and authorized representatives as follows: AP Newsfeatures—Dispatch dated May 16, 1949; Annmary Brown Memorial, Brown University—*The Wagnerian Cult* by Rush C. Hawkins, copyright, 1904, by Rush C. Hawkins; Appleton-Century-Crofts, Inc.—*Appletons' Dictionary of New York and Its Vicinity*, copyright, 1902, by D. Appleton and Company, *Old Bowery Days* by Alvin F. Harlow, copyright, 1931, by Alvin F. Harlow, *A Backward Glance* by Edith Wharton, copyright, 1934, by D. Appleton-Century Company, Inc., *The Age of Innocence* by Edith Wharton, copyright, 1920, by D. Appleton and Company, *The Reminiscences of Augustus Saint-Gaudens* edited and amplified by Homer Saint-Gaudens, copyright, 1913, by The Century Co.; *The Architectural Record*—"Architectural Appreciations," copyright, 1902, by Architectural Record; Broadcast Music, Inc.—"The Columbia Song" by John Tempest Walker, Jr., copyright, 1925, by Alumni Federation of Columbia University, copyright renewed, 1953, by Alumni Federation of Columbia University; Brooklyn Institute of Arts and Sciences Brooklyn Museum—*An American Genre Painter, Eastman Johnson 1824–1906* by John I. H. Baur, copyright, 1940, by Brooklyn Institute of Arts and Sciences Brooklyn Museum; Coward-McCann, Inc.—*All Our Lives: Alice Duer Miller* by Henry Wise Miller, copyright, 1945, by Henry Wise Miller, *The White Cliffs* by Alice Duer Miller, copyright, 1940, by Alice Duer Miller, and Methuen & Co., Ltd., London, for the British edition; Thomas Y. Crowell Company—*Famous Painters of America* by J. Walker McSpadden, copyright, 1907, by Thomas Y. Crowell Company; Doubleday & Company, Inc.—*The Four Million* by O. Henry, copyright, 1906, by Doubleday & Company, Inc.; E. P. Dutton & Co., Inc.—*Pinocchio* by C. Collodi, translated by M. A. Murray, copyright, 1911, by E. P. Dutton & Co., and Ernest Benn, Ltd., London, for the British edition, *My Years on the Stage* by John Drew (1922); Francis, Day & Hunter, Ltd.—*Florodora* by Leslie Stuart and Owen Hall, reproduced by permission of Francis, Day & Hunter, Ltd., 138–140 Charing Cross Road, London, W.C. 2; Mrs. Zane Grey—*Old Well-Well* by Zane Grey (1910); Harcourt, Brace and Company, Inc.—*Steichen The Photographer* by Carl Sandburg, copyright, 1929, by Harcourt, Brace and Company, Inc., *The Manner Is Ordinary* by John LaFarge, S. J., copyright, 1954, by John LaFarge; Harper & Brothers—*Here Is New York* by E. B. White (1949), *A Musician and His Wife* by Mrs. Reginald de Koven, copyright, 1926, by Harper & Brothers, *After All* by Elsie de Wolfe, copyright, 1935, by Elsie de Wolfe Mendl, *Memories: An Autobiography* by Ethel Barrymore, copyright, 1955, by Ethel Barrymore, *The Last Resorts* by Cleveland Amory, copyright, 1948, 1952, by Cleveland Amory, *With Sabre and Scalpel: The Autobiography of a Soldier and Surgeon* by John Allan Wyeth, copyright, 1914, by Harper & Brothers; Harvard University Press—*This Was America* by Oscar Handlin, copyright, 1949, by The President and Fellows of Harvard College; Henry Holt and Company, Inc.—"Fire and Ice" from *New Hampshire* by Robert Frost, copyright, 1923, by Henry Holt and Company, copyright, 1951, by Robert Frost, "Cool Tombs" from *Cornhuskers* by Carl Sandburg, copyright, 1918, by Henry Holt and Company, copyright, 1946, by Carl Sandburg, by permission of the publishers; The Jewish Publication Society of America—*The Melting Pot* by Israel Zangwill, copyright, 1909, by The Macmillan Company; Alfred A. Knopf Inc.—*How I Discovered America* by The Marquis Boni de Castellane, copyright, 1924, by Alfred A. Knopf Inc., *My Mortal Enemy* by Willa Cather, copyright, 1926, by Alfred A. Knopf, Inc.; *Ladies' Home Journal*—"The Girlishness of Ethel

Barrymore" and "John Drew and His Daughter" by Gustav Kobbé, reprinted by special permission of the *Ladies' Home Journal*, copyright, 1903, by the Curtis Publishing Company; The Laymen's Club of The Cathedral of Saint John the Divine—*A Guide to The Cathedral of Saint John the Divine* by Edward Hagaman Hall (Tenth Edition), copyright, 1931, by The Laymen's Club of The Cathedral of Saint John the Divine; J. B. Lippincott Company—*The Etiquette of New York To-day* by Mrs. Frank Learned, copyright, 1906, by Frederick A. Stokes Company; The Macmillan Company—*The Battle with the Slum* by Jacob A. Riis, copyright, 1902, by The Macmillan Company, *The Diary of George Templeton Strong* edited by Allan Nevins and Milton Halsey Thomas, copyright, 1952, by The Macmillan Company; Music Publishers Holding Corporation—lyric of "Come Down Ma Evenin' Star" by Robert B. Smith and John Stromberg, copyright, 1902, by M. Witmark & Sons, copyright renewed, reprinted by permission; *The New Yorker*—"A Lady Who Writes" by Harvey O'Higgins, copyright, 1927, by The New Yorker Magazine, Inc.; Northwestern University—*Baron Klinkowström's America* translated by Franklin D. Scott, copyright, 1952, by Northwestern University; Random House, Inc.—*Lillian Russell: The Era of Plush* by Parker Morell, copyright, 1940, by Random House, Inc., *Curtain Time* by Lloyd Morris, copyright, 1953, by Lloyd Morris; Charles Scribner's Sons—*The House of Mirth* by Edith Wharton, copyright, 1905, by Charles Scribner's Sons, and John Lehmann, Ltd., London, for the British edition, *Trail of an Artist-Naturalist* by Ernest Thompson Seton, copyright, 1940, by Ernest Thompson Seton, and Christy & Moore, Ltd., London, for the British edition; the Estate of Louis C. Tiffany— *The Art Work of Louis C. Tiffany* by Charles de Kay, copyright, 1914, by Doubleday, Page & Co.

My thanks are also due to the following institutions and publishers who have allowed me to quote brief extracts from the files, brochures, periodicals, or issues of their publications: The American Federation of Arts; *Collier's;* Macfadden Publications, Inc.; The Pierpont Morgan Library; Popular Publications, Inc.; Press Publishing Company; The Public Record Office of Northern Ireland; The *New York Herald Tribune;* The New-York Historical Society; The *New York Sun,* Inc.; *The New York Times; Scientific American;* The Society of American Magicians; *Sports Illustrated.*

Finally, I should like to acknowledge my indebtedness to the individuals who have courteously allowed me to quote their statements, correspondence, or other material in their possession and who have helped in providing valuable information: Mr. John I. H. Baur; Mr. Percy C. Byron; Mr. Erich Hartmann; Mr. Wallace Irwin; Mrs. Robert H. Kridel; Mr. Thomas A. Larremore; Mrs. Reginald Marsh; Mr. Peter Mason; Miss Phyllis Neilson-Terry; Miss Georgia O'Keeffe and the Estate of Alfred Stieglitz; Mr. Maxfield Parrish; Mr. Charles Johnson Post and Miss Phyllis Bradford Post; Mr. Berry Rockwell; Mr. Carl Sandburg; Miss Rose Schneiderman; Mrs. Gallatin Seton; Mr. Ben Shahn; Mr. James Thrall Soby; Miss Madeleine B. Stern; Mr. E. B. White.

To my parents
Who also looked upon this City

Foreword

By Edward Steichen

THE NEW photographic techniques, processes and paraphernalia for photography that science and industry have placed at our disposal have opened up doors previously closed to the photographer. In photographing people what began as an ordeal of sitting still for several minutes in the glaring brightness of the sun can today be photographed in a split second and under almost any conditions of light. "If you can see it you can photograph it." This book tells the story of a family that began staining its fingers with chemicals and became familiar with the smell of hypo in the very early days of photography.

Just before and after the turn of the century the name Byron appeared regularly on a parade of timely photographs. Prodigious is the word for the quantity of photographs produced under the imprint of "Byron." To the Byrons, father and son, photography was a profession, a business. They were among the earliest to realize that the camera used for visual reporting opened up an endless field in photography. It became a good business because of their enthusiastic and tireless energy, their uncanny instinct for finding timely newsworthy aspects in almost everything, whether photographed on the basis of a commission or on shrewd speculation of what would be saleable. Their only specialty was making photographs, photographs without opinion, comment, slant or emotion. If the word objective has any meaning in relation to photography here it is. There is no pretense or artifice, no willful accent or suppression. Composition is based on including everything within the camera's angle and photographing so that everything is plainly visible. These photographs are objective because the places, the things and the people photographed have a chance to speak for themselves without interference.

From this formidable mass of work covering several decades, Grace Mayer here gives us a selection of prints of a quality that today take on an importance and a significance far beyond what may have been originally intended or even suspected by the photographer. Photographs that were made as records, as reports for news or for publicity have in the intervening years become historic evidence, unique documents of a period. The simple directness of the photographs in this book are now statements open to this and future generations for a variety of interpretations, uses and services.

The value of the Byron collection has a certain importance because of the quantity of pictures they made in their daily professional routine wherein all sorts of jobs and assignments led them into so many and such varied directions and situations. Here in this book this quantity of facts has been reduced, distilled and made into an important and beautiful document of an earlier New York.

There is here also a valuable lesson for today's photographers, for these prints that were once regarded by some as senseless and trite have become a visual slice of Americana that without the Byrons would have been lost and without the Museum of the City of New York might so easily have been overlooked.

The Byrons, father and son, as well as you and I who now hold this book in our hands are indeed indebted to Miss Mayer for the patient scholarly research and warm understanding she has given to this legacy and more particularly for her sensitive selection and the juxtapositions that bring the images to life and us face to face with a bygone New York and New Yorkers and does it with a real bang. The events and locations, the things and the people that have been recorded with this brassy impersonal kind of realism, here and now vividly evoke a nostalgia mixed with fun and frolick, contempt and laughter and these so often tied up into a bundle of deep affection for a time and a place from where we have emerged and where so much of us still lingers.

Edward Steichen

The Byron Company

In the year 1844, in an ancient city in an old world, a young family entered a new profession, to follow photography for five generations, even unto today.

It was in Nottingham on the Trent, when Victoria had been seven years a Queen, that Percy C. Byron's great-grandfather founded the firm. That very year Percy's father, Joseph, was born—the son and grandson of photographers. The family name, Clayton, was legally changed to Byron when the more enterprising clansmen decided to expand the business, against the timid judgment of a reactionary member, who retained the original surname and soon found himself left far behind. Thus it came about that Joseph, the child of the third generation, matured with a growing chain of studios in four English cities. The field of endeavor included posters and other forms of advertising. So up-and-coming were the seceders that the backs of tramcar tickets served as their tradecard, carrying an untitled likeness of "Boz" alongside one of Byron, as a play on the popular question, "Who the Dickens is [Byron]?", the reply in this instance being "Why, The Photographer." The Byrons took advantage of the mid-Victorian mania for *carte-de-visite* portraits, and actually employed salesmen to peddle reduced rate coupons to working people, who queued up outside the Nottingham headquarters, where a uniformed doorman gave out numbered tickets, requesting the eager overflow to return for sittings the next morning. Joseph Byron was always interested in the camera's ability to seize upon what Mr. Steichen has called "The Exact Instant," and interpreted the news for *The Graphic* (of London), preparing and developing his wet plates in a hansom cab, its windows suitably veiled for protection from the light at once the glory and the curse of his craft. Among other noteworthy assignments, he undertook a documentation of coal mines for the British Government. One day in 1885, in his atelier in Nottingham, he came upon his seven-year-old son, Percy, wasting sheets of sensitized paper by printing images of fern leaves, and knew that he had a partner.

In 1888, Mr. and Mrs. Joseph Byron came to America with their first-born, Maude Mary, and established a New York studio. At October's end of the following year, the four remaining children crossed the Atlantic in their grandmother's care. At eleven, Percy was a full-blown photographer, just three years short of his initial sale of a news picture—a view of Grant's humble temporary tomb (reproduced on page 463)—to Arthur Brisbane, at that time Managing Editor of *The World*. In fledgling confusion, the young lensman erroneously sold a print from this self-same negative to the *New York Recorder*. Ten days later, *The New York Herald* purchased his shot of Edwin Booth's casket being sorrowfully borne from The Players. After that commissions piled up with such furious fastness that they have become blurred in his memory.

An early employer was P. F. Collier, for whose budding magazine *Once A Week* the Byrons took a series of photographs of the homes of "the 400." *The Illustrated American,* too, carried reproductions of the firm's first local fruits. In 1891, Joseph Byron pioneered in the new field of stage photography, which, with the subsequent addition of stem to stern coverage of ships, formed their basic business. It has been said with some truth that for many years Percy Byron photographed every transatlantic liner to enter the port of New York. Then there were the news events, the banquets and the balls, the weddings and the funerals, the parties and the parades, the people and the buildings, the hospitals and the hotels, the parks and the beaches, the gilded and the sordid—a ceaseless range of subject matter (recorded for newspapers, Sunday supplements, magazines, books, industries and individuals) that in the aggregate became the portrait of a city and a period. Thus the Byrons photographed New York—sometimes as a vocation and sometimes as an avocation, but always lovingly—achieving a documentation comparable with the work of Jean-Eugène-Auguste Atget, who was so tenderly depicting his adored city of Paris at about the same epoch. Atget worked alone and lonesomely, but with the Byrons it was a family affair that at one time or another involved all seven members. At first the father managed the business and took all the photographs. His wife supervised the printing department with the aid of their second daughter, Florence Mabel, who headed a staff of a dozen girls engaged in making contact prints from the cumbersome, fragile 8 x 10 and 11 x 14 glass negatives—this by sunlight, or, on dark days, in a huge suspended cabinet with a thirty-five ampere arc lamp at its center. Maude Mary busied herself in all capacities, while her husband, Jack Ferris, served as Percy's assistant, along with Tom Lunt. Georgiana took charge of the office. Louis Philip, less dedicated than his siblings, shared their labors for several years. Then there were two expert retouchers in constant attendance, and three or four young women who toned, fixed, washed and dried the rich, glossy, chocolate-hued Solio prints (printing-out paper). It was a happy, free-lancing crew, working day and night, Percy Byron tells me, "like an orchestra without any noise," and it exposed a sum total of almost 30,000 negatives during the twenty years of our present concern. Even carrier pigeons played a part in the firm's activities, for when the Byrons, *père et fils,* covered the *America's* Cup Races for Joseph Pulitzer in 1895, cut-outs made from line drawings based on their photographs were wing-borne from Sandy Hook to a Frankfort Street loft, near the gilded dome of the World Building, and delivered to the City Desk in record time. Percy absented himself to serve as a Spanish-American War camera-correspondent for *The Journal,* and again from 1906 to 1916, when—for reasons of health—he went to Edmonton, Alberta, Canada, where he started the first photo-engraving plant between Winnipeg and the Pacific. Returning to New York in 1917, he resumed specialization in ship photography, making a record-breaking 650 prints on the maiden voyage of the ill-starred S. S. *Normandie* in 1935. After Joseph Byron's death in 1923, his widow and Percy C. carried on together until 1930. Elizabeth Byron served as her father's secretary for a considerable span (1928–1935) and her brother, Joseph M., as his assistant from 1932 to 1934, bringing the count of the generations up to five. The beginning of the Second World War brought an end to civilian photography on the high seas, and in 1942 the ninety-eight-year-old firm closed its books. But withal there had been time for the design of a camera that was a precursor of the Speed Graphic, and the winning of "Ten Gold Medals and Diplomas from Principal Exhibitions of Europe and America" and "First Prize International Exposition 1931 and 1932" (to quote from the Company's letterhead).

In 1942 Percy C. Byron presented a good part of the labor of two lifetimes to the Museum of the City of New York—a collection of over 10,000 prints and negatives. From this great and well-nigh inexhaustible treasury three major exhibitions have been drawn, the answers to literally hundreds of research problems found, and this book evolved.

Two years after his "retirement," Percy C. Byron became the commercial photographer of the Art Photo Engraving Company, which in 1954 combined with the Essex Engraving Company to become the Essex Art Engraving Company of Newark. Today, over seventy years a photographer and still actively engaged in the field, he is busy with new experiments and fresh inventions. "Whether this job I will ever finish, I know not," he wrote to me in 1956, "but it is progressing. . . . I would like to leave a few more things to a profession that has given me so much, and for so long. . . ."

"Joseph Byron's Children, Present and Future Company Workers"
The members of the fourth generation in the firm photographed by their father in 1895, at 128th Street and St. Nicholas Avenue

Left to right: Louis Philip (active in the firm from 1906–1909); Georgiana (in charge of the office from 1900–1905); Florence Mabel (who assisted her mother, Julia Lewin Byron, in the printing department from 1898–1905); Percy C. (who entered the field in 1885, at the age of seven); Maude Mary (who worked in various departments from 1895–1902)

Once upon a City

"ITS FRONT is lifted to the future. On the past its back is turned." This extraordinarily perceptive statement about the Flatiron Building appears in an essay by Edgar Saltus, which sparkles in the pages of *Munsey's Magazine* (July, 1905). "Of what has gone before it is American in its unconcern. Monstrous yet infantile, it is a recent issue of the gigantic upheaval that is transforming the whole city, and which will end by making it a curiosity to which people will come and stare as they do at cataracts and big caves and great trees and fat women and whatever else is abnormal. Yet the changes, however disconcerting, are but tokens of others to be. In certain aspects New York still preserves its old colonial squalor. In others it presents the hasty hideousness of boom towns. In the lingering streets of brownstone fronts it is embryonic still. Near the rivers it has thoroughfares and avenues which, in ruthless atrocity and shuddersome ugliness, are nightmares in stone. But these are as measles and mumps to a child. They are not definite conditions. Nor is there, nor will there be, anything definite here until, from the Battery to the Plaza, the buildings one and all are so huge that nothing huger is possible."

The triangulated Fuller Building which Saltus uses as the pivot of his impressions in this article (entitulated "New York From The Flatiron.") inherited its nickname from the smoother-like shape of its site, and from the beginning resisted nominal association with its general contractors, the George A. Fuller Company. To D. H. Burnham & Company fell a unique obligation in the design of covering a site once described as "a stingy piece of pie." *The Architectural Record* of October, 1902, granted that the 20-story edifice (with its 3,680 tons of structural steel work designed by the consulting engineers Purdy and Henderson—also responsible for the foundations—and manufactured by the American Bridge Company) was "quite the most notorious thing in New York" attracting "more attention than all the other buildings now going up put together," but the magazine was for the most part adversely critical. "Either of the principal elevations," the writer of "Architectural Appreciations" asserted, "taken in conjunction with the edge upon which they converge, has not the aspect of an enclosing wall, so much as of a huge screen, a vast theatrical 'wing,' which conceivably rests upon Titanic castors and is meant to be pushed about, instead of being rooted to the spot." With congratulations on the effective monochromic matching of "the warm yellow-gray of the limestone base in the tint of the terra cotta above," and successful "surface enrichment," the critic found the fenestration denoted "want of thought," and expressed sympathy for the tenant of the wedge, provided with "a mere bird-cage," allowing "perhaps . . . wall space within for one [lightstruck] roll-top desk. . . . But suppose he needed a bookcase? . . ." In any consoling event, "Undoubtedly he has a highly eligible place from which to view processions." The *New-York Tribune Illustrated Supplement*, on June 29, 1902, was more generous: "Since the removal last week of the scaffolding . . . there is scarcely an hour when a staring wayfarer doesn't by his example collect a big crowd of other staring people. Sometimes a

1

hundred or more, with heads bent backward until a general breakage of necks seems imminent, collect along the walk . . . and stay there until 'one of the finest' orders them to move on. No wonder people stare! A building 307 feet high presenting an edge almost as sharp as the bow of a ship . . . is well worth looking at." Reaching thirty-five feet underground, it was capable of sheltering seventeen hundred office workers—more than the population of "a respectable suburban village." Commenting on its giant verticality, the amateur architectural dissertator calculated that "if it fell over to the eastward it would almost reach Madison-ave.," which, some uninformed viewers thought, was a very real danger. The *Tribune* writer parleyed: "The Flatiron is not the tallest building in New-York, but it is the slenderest—as a bright girl expresses it, 'the most aquiline.' 'It's the sharpest thing any architect ever perpetrated,' according to another authority." Sidney Allan (that is, Sadakichi Hartmann) in "An Esthetical Dissertation" in *Camera Work*, October, 1903, found the Flatiron trendful and exulted that "never in the history of mankind has a little triangular piece of real estate been utilized in such a *raffiné* manner. . . . It is a building without a main façade. . . . And we would not be astonished . . . if the whole triangular block would suddenly begin to move northward through the crowd of pedestrians and traffic of our two leading thoroughfares, which would break like the waves of the ocean on the huge prow-like angle." Appended is a hosanna by "S. H." (probably again the writer called by Amy Lowell "the most mysterious man in American literature") ending

> "Well may you smile over Gotham's vast domain
> As dawn greets your pillars with roseate flame,
> For future ages will proclaim
> Your beauty
> Boldly, without shame."

Sir Philip Burne-Jones (artist son of the more famous Edward) in the *Dollars and Democracy* (New York, 1904) account of his 1902–1903 visit to these rebel shores, commenting on the "fever-heat" construction of the young, specifically American architectural idiom, singled out the Flatiron Building for special condemnation: "One vast horror, facing Madison Square, is distinctly responsible for a new form of hurricane, which meets unsuspecting pedestrians as they reach the corner, causing them extreme discomfort. . . . When its effects first became noticeable, a little rude crowd of loafers and street arabs used to congregate upon the curb to jeer and gloat over the distress of ladies whose skirts were blown into their eyes as they rounded the treacherous corner. Hanging about this particular spot soon became a recognised and punishable offence." *The New York Herald* of January 31, 1903 (the 30th having been a particularly flawy day) reported an afflicting case: "After the young woman had been unwound from the lamp post and her hat had been rescued from under the heels of a cab horse she was escorted to the lee side of the HERALD's Twenty-third street office. 'Well, this is awful!' she exclaimed through her tears. 'I will never pass that hateful old Flatiron Building again. Somebody ought to arrest the man who built it!'"

The aeolian currents carry the thoughts to the motion of a swirling canvas by John Sloan— the *Dust Storm* of 1906 (in The Metropolitan Museum of Art); into the quiet mistiness of Edward Steichen's great nocturnal photograph (exhibited at the London Salon in 1905 and today with the Metropolitan's masterworks); toward the angularity of the building's shiplike prow in the starkness of the Berenice Abbott photograph of 1938—for a site and a city live forever in the affectionate touch of the artists who have sought them out with love. Then back again full circle to the Byron document below and swiftly to the Flatiron's summit to survey with Edgar Saltus "The Most Extraordinary Panorama In The World":

" 'What do you know of New York?' said one wanderer to another.

" 'Only what I have read in Dante,' was the bleak reply.

"Dante told of the inferno. He told, too, of paradise. Manhattan may typify both. It represents other things also. The latter, mainly, are superlatives. From the top floors of the Flatiron you get an idea of a few. On one side is Broadway. Barring trade routes, Broadway is the longest commercial stretch on the planet. On the other side is Fifth Avenue. Barring nothing, Fifth Avenue is the richest thoroughfare in the world. From the top floors of the Flatiron each looks meager, almost mean. In them are things that you would take for beetles, others that seem to you ants.

"The beetles are cabs; the ants are human beings . . . hurrying grotesquely over the most expensive spot on earth. They hurry because everybody hurries, because haste is in the air, in the effrontery of the impudent 'step lively,' in the hammers of the ceaseless skyscrapers

General view looking south from Madison Square, about 1905

ceaselessly going up, in the ambient neurosis, in the scudding motors, in the unending noise, the pervading scramble, the metallic roar of the city.

"Beyond is the slam-bang of the Sixth Avenue Elevated. . . . Parallelly is the Subway rumbling relentlessly. Farther east are two additional slam-bangers. To the west is a fourth. Beneath them are great ocher brutes of cars, herds of them, stampeding violently with grinding grunts, and, on the microbish pavements, swarms such as Dante may indeed have seen, but not in paradise.

"In the morning they are there, scurrying to their toil; at high noon to their food; at evening to their homes; at night to amusements more laborious than their work. . . . Save at night, when the crowd moves elsewhere, always are there compact throngs, . . . human streams which the Flatiron cleaves indifferently, rearing its knifish face with the same disdain of the ephemeral that the Sphinx displays. . . .

". . . as you lean and gaze from the toppest floors on houses below, which from those floors seem huts, it may occur to you that precisely as these huts were once regarded as supreme achievements, so . . . from other and higher floors, the Flatiron may seem a hut itself. . . .

". . . It will be demonstrable that as buildings ascend so do ideas. It is mental progress that skyscrapers engender. . . .

"Meanwhile, on those toppest floors, the eager sun, aslant, shuttles the mounting roar. In the noise and glare you need but a modicum of imagination to fancy yourself contemplating a volcano in active operation. . . .

"Above . . . indifferently, the Flatiron looms. Semi-animate as the motor is, superhuman, vibrant with a life of its own, from its hundred eyes it stares. . . .

". . . Indifferently on these things the Flatiron stares."

Through its windows, Saltus prophetizes on the physical and spiritual future of the city:

"Sooner or later . . . where now are, say, eighty or a hundred buildings to a square there will be but one. . . ." He saw indications "that emporiums of the future will cover two squares—three, perhaps; that no hotel, no apartment house or office-building will be really content with less than one, and that however it may be elsewhere, on the thirty-five streets between Twenty-third Street and the Plaza, Fifth Avenue will contain not many more than seventy structures, about one to each square, structures extending back on the west to Broadway or Sixth Avenue, on the east to Madison, with, on these arteries, similar structures, similarly extending, repeating themselves to the river fronts." (It might be mentioned that in 1935, as stated in his *Quand Les Cathédrales Etaient Blanches*, Paris, 1937, it was Le Corbusier's turn to say of New York "The skyscrapers are too small.")

". . . It will be horrible; but analyze the horrible, and sometimes you find the sublime, again the unique, occasionally the commercial. The three derivatives present here will provide a spectacle shameful and superb."

. . . . The world is mine!

WITH THE characteristic northward surge of geographical inevitability, New York's "Rialto"—which into the 1890's had centered around Union Square—moved up Broadway's Golden Mile and along the side-street capillaries to the Forty-second Street area even before the new century was welcomed by some on the hilarious midnight of December 31, 1899, and denied admission by the contentiously correct until a full year later. The "Crossroads of the World" or "Diamond Jim" Brady's "Street in the Midnight Sun" did not receive its present magic name until 1904, when the cornerstone of the Times Building was laid at its feet.

Long Acre (now Times) Square, November, 1900
Looking south from Forty-fifth Street

Here—by one of those strange concatenations of a usually perverse destiny—on October 16, 1888, on the third floor of the Hotel Cadillac (then known as the Barrett House, a family hotel) Eugene O'Neill was born, at a time when his handsome matinée idol father James (perennially starring in the Charles Fechter adaptation of Dumas' magic tale, *The Count of Monte Cristo*) was hurling the ringing second-act curtain line—"The world is mine!"—across the footlights at his New England audience. Later, this triumphal cry could have been echoed by the younger O'Neill in connection with his success as a dramatist in the spiritual and topographical zone of his birth.

A block north of this hallowed spot, the legend known as Rector's opened on September 23, 1899—its main dining room all green and gold, its great mirrors sparklingly reflecting the beauty and elegance and glamour of the Gibson era, chiefly in the matutinal hours after curtain-fall, when the fashionable *haut monde* and *demimonde* and the stranger in Manhattan gathered night after incandescent night.

. . . . *The great fighting-ground of the city*

"It would take an idle man half an hour to read the signs on the front of one block of lower Broadway, and the face of each building is a small directory." This pithy observation appears in "Broadway"—Richard Harding Davis' brilliant curtain-raiser to *The Great Streets Of The World* (New York, 1892).

Arresting is the wooden statue of Peg-Leg Peter, in front of the Stuyvesant Insurance Company's 157 Broadway office, three blocks above The Wall that marked the northern extent of the little Dutch city whose gable-shadowed streets echoed with his stomping gubernatorial irascibility. Close by is the trade sign of The Obrig Camera Co., to prosper and remove to 147 Fulton Street in 1906. Familiar firm names are not infrequent: Crouch & Fitzgerald, already sixty years in the luggage business, are established at No. 161, and a placard urges Waterman's Fountain Pens on volunteers answering President McKinley's call for 125,000 men to serve in the Cuban affray. The building at block's end bears the name of Benedict, according to advertisement "Jewelers and Keepers of the City Time" extending back to 1821 in chronology and chronometry. On the left the eye travels past the Western Union Building (created by George B. Post, previewed by *The Daily Graphic* of June 3, 1873 as "A Telegraphic Palace," and altered by Henry J. Hardenbergh, following an aerial fire in 1890) to the elevated pinnacle of the home of *The Mail & Express*. Marginally, on the east side, one comes against the St. Paul Building, Post's 1896 triumph, south of the frozen horror of the many-columned Post Office completed in 1878 under the misguidance of Alexander B. Mullett.

The New Metropolis (edited by E. Idell Zeisloft, New York, 1899) found the immediate foreground not too versicolorous: "From here onward Broadway becomes a street of retail stores, with occasional banks and insurance offices and a large element of miscellaneous offices. Business in general—jewelers, restaurants, hatters, clothiers, and shoe dealers—is represented, and it continues so for many blocks." Therefore, we return to Richard Harding Davis' more polychromatic dissection: "The business man knows Broadway as a street . . . with pavements which move with unbroken lines of men. . . . It is a place where no one strolls, and where a man can as easily swing his cane as a woman could wear a train. Pedestrians do not walk steadily forward here, or in a straight line, but dodge in and out like runners on a football field. . . . The man who stops to speak to a friend, or to gaze into a shop window, is jostled and pushed and shouldered to one side. . . . So intent are they on their errands that they would not recognize their own wives if they passed them by." Lower Broadway "is the great fighting-ground of the city, where the battle of business goes on from eight o'clock in the morning . . . until five, when the armies declare an armistice for the day and march off uptown to plan a fresh campaign. . . . The armies begin to arrive before eight, and gather from every point of the compass. . . . It is one of the most impressive sights the city has to offer. The gathering of the clans was less impressive and less momentous. They do not all meet on Broadway at once, but before the business day is over they will have passed up or down it, and will have contributed at one time to the hurrying crowds on its two pavements. . . . There was a great trade parade in the city two years ago [on May 1, 1889, as part of the centennial celebration of Washington's inauguration], and it gave New Yorkers a pleasing idea of their prosperity; but its theatrical display and bands of music were but a pageant to the grim reality of the great trade parade which forces its way up and down Broadway every morning in the year. There is a narrow turn in Cheapside, of which Londoners boast that the traffic is so great as to block the street for half an hour at a time; but on Broadway, for a mile, there are over four long lines of drays and wagons, with the tongue of the one behind touching the back-board of the one in front. That is the trade parade with which New Yorkers are too familiar to fully appreciate. It represents, in its loads and burdens, every industry and product of the world."

Let us find an islet or a window from which we can study the passing specimens along with Cleveland Moffett, who makes apology for the title of his article—"Is New York Degenerate?"—in *The Illustrated American,* June 22, 1895: "I use the word degenerate merely because it happens to be in vogue." Then he limns a tenebrous portrait: "In the first place, let us examine New Yorkers physically and see if we can detect any signs of bodily deterioration. I am afraid we can. . . . In your next stroll down Broadway or along Wall street, fancy yourself for a moment a student of hygiene. . . . You will be surprised . . . to see so few . . . in fine physical condition, so many with bloodless faces, rounded shoulders, waddling or shuffling gait, apoplectic necks and bloated stomachs. . . . Is all this of the imagination, or have we here signs that we are drifting toward a condition of physical degeneracy? If so, the explanation is not hard to find. Think of the constant strain under which New York men live—the never-ceasing tension of money-getting, the daily jostle of hurrying crowds, . . . the bolted meals and lunches, the maddening noise . . . the pernicious treating habit, . . . the absence of simple, sensible pleasures—is it any wonder that these evils, which exist in New York as in scarcely any other city, have a harmful effect upon the bodies of New Yorkers? Living always in a fever-laden atmosphere—the fever of money-making—is it strange that the vital forces of these men are prematurely exhausted . . . ? And what sort of fathers can they make, these thin-faced, weak-legged, big-bellied, dyspeptic citizens of New York? What sort of children can they expect to breed? Where is the use or glory in being 'smart' and amassing fortunes for enfeebled sons to spend in getting paresis?"

For anodyne, let us look into the all but unbroken barrier in the center of the millrace:

Broadway, 1898
North from Liberty Street

"The cable cars come down Broadway as the waters come down at Lodore." This master stroke of simile springs from an essay written about 1895 by Stephen Crane of the promise-kept, too little time (two years dead at 29, when Digby, Long & Co. of London published *Last Words* in 1902). Even the chapter heading tingles as it tells—"In the Broadway Cars. Panorama of a Day from the Down-town Rush of the Morning to the Uninterrupted Whirr of the Cable at Night. . . ." In word painting, his picture ranks with the unexcelled: "Years ago Father Knickerbocker had convulsions when it was proposed to lay impious rails on his sacred thoroughfare. At the present day the cars, by force of column and numbers, almost dominate the great street, and the eye of even an old New Yorker is held by these long yellow monsters which prowl intently up and down, up and down, in a mystic search. In the grey of the morning they come out of the up-town, bearing janitors, porters, all that class which carries the keys to set alive the great down-town. Later, they shower clerks. Later still, they shower more clerks. And the thermometer which is attached to a conductor's temper is steadily rising, rising, and the blissful time arrives when everybody hangs to a strap and stands on his neighbour's toes. Ten o'clock comes, and the Broadway cars, as well as elevated cars, horse cars and ferryboats innumerable, heave sighs of relief. They have filled lower New York with a vast army of men who will chase to and fro and amuse themselves until almost night-fall." He writes of swift descent: "It [the cable car] passes Madison Square and enters the gorge made by the towering walls of great shops. It sweeps around the double curve at Union Square and Fourteenth Street. . . . Meanwhile, the gripman has become involved with countless truck drivers, and inch by inch, foot by foot, he fights his way to City Hall Park. On past the Post Office the car goes, with the gripman getting advice, admonition, personal comment, an invitation to fight from the drivers, until Battery Park appears at the foot of the slope, and as the car goes sedately around the curve the burnished shield of the bay shines through the trees."

. . . . *All that flams is not Flamboyant*

"THE LINE of men at midnight" sometimes stretched several blocks above the elbow of Broadway and east on Tenth Street. Here, often far in advance of the turn of a new day without promise, they waited in the desperate, patient anonymity of misery, to reach for the brief comfort of bread and the transient warmth of coffee, before they turned home to their homelessness. In the blanching cold they shivered; in the searing heat they shuffled wearily in their shabbiness toward the dole. Charles Dana Gibson (in a drawing reproduced in *Scribner's Magazine* for November, 1898, and now owned by the Cincinnati Art Museum) turned aside from glamour, to sketch them in their gauntness and despair—grim, gray, attenuated, careworn opposites of the insouciant heroes of his high romance. Organized charity found the methodology medieval, but Louis Fleischmann maintained, "If a man will stand on the curb for two or three hours for half a loaf . . . or a few rolls he's hungry." They stood in respectful line on the day of his funeral, too. There was dignity in his giving and in their taking, and some of the hundreds of thousands of men (professional mendicants, down-and-outers, bums, and in times of depression the unemployed, even the impoverished student

Fleischmann's Vienna Model Bakery, 1898
Northeast corner of Broadway and Tenth Street

and the ill-paid white-collar worker) who partook of it under the friendly supervision of "Captain Henry" and his special corps, later achieved dime novel-like success. The length of the queue was a gauge of economic fluctuation, and the compassionate darkness a protective covering from the prurient eyes of slummers, nocturnal revelers, and banqueters at the St. Denis Hotel across the way. Hospitals, too, profited from the millionaire baker's beneficence.

By day all was quite different, for of an afternoon there was a true *Gemütlichkeit* as prominent Germans and Austrians (among them such virtuosi as Anton Seidl and the stars of the opera company) gathered at the continental coffee hour to linger and chat and read the homeland papers—outdoors in summer behind the leafy trellis, indoors in winter. Here fashionable patrons of Wanamaker's and other neighborhood retail emporiums paused to enjoy the aromatic coffee and chocolate, the crisp rolls, and the succulent pastries.

Back of this New York institution stood a former officer in the Austrian Army, with two medals for bravery at the battle of Sadowa. In 1875 he had joined his brothers, engaged in the manufacture of yeast in this country, and a year later, when the firm of Gaff, Fleischmann & Company faced failure, he staged a handsome exhibit at the Philadelphia Centennial Exposition, where fair-goers could watch the manufacture of the product, see the rising of the dough and the baking of the bread, and then savor it at the adjoining restaurant. So popular and successful was this large-scaled advertisement that the firm flourished, and Louis Fleischmann established his Vienna Model Bakery on Broadway. In response to the age-old cry, he soon instituted his bounty; and before his death on September 25, 1904, he asked that the distribution of the loaves be continued during the life of the ovens he had lighted. One of his sons, Raoul H. Fleischmann, publisher of *The New Yorker,* spent four years (1907–1911) in this milieu of delectation and charity.

The bakery stood beside the unpolished marble walls—lit within by stained glass glory—of Grace Church. ". . . all that flams is not Flamboyant," paraphrased *Putnam's Monthly,* in describing Renwick's Gothic *coup d'essai* in September, 1853. Formerly a neighbor of the mothering Trinity, in 1846 the congregation moved north on Broadway to its present commanding location, once a section of the Brevoort farm, just above the side-stepping wedge of the Randall property that became part of the inheritance of Sailors' Snug Harbor and the Vienna Bakery corner. In 1905, just short of Grace's centennial, the vestry, ever mindful of responsibilities aesthetic and spiritual, protectively purchased the ground on which Fleischmann's stood and, leveling the building three years later, covered its basement with the green peace that since 1911 has been known as "Huntington Close" in honor of the beloved sixth rector. So the landmark of the "midnight supper" (to be discontinued in 1910) moved across Broadway to the northwest corner of Eleventh Street, still near the church about which Philip Hone speculated in his diary entry of February 5, 1846, shortly after the auctioning of the pews: ". . . the word of God as it came down to us from Fishermen and Mechanics will cost the Quality who worship in this splendid temple about $3 every Sunday, this may have a good effect, for many of them tho rich, know how to calculate, and if they do not go regularly to church they will not get the worth of their money."

It would be possible to write an entire book without leaving the frame of this photograph. One could tell of the "El" that vanished in 1939; of the two great newspapers that gave their names to the bounding squares; of the McKim, Mead & White *palazzo* (with its famed clock and the bronze figures of Minerva and the Bell Ringers—nicknamed "Stuff and Guff"—by Antonin Jean Carlès) that housed *The New York Herald,* and of the triangular Times Building designed by Eidlitz and McKenzie; of Macy's, seven-years-new to the neighborhood; of the "Seeing New York" rubberneck bus, which started from the Flatiron Building; of the wheeled and pedestrian traffic along the Broadway blocks then nearing the end of their turn as New York's Rialto; of the theatres along the stretch from Thirty-fourth to Forty-second Street: the Herald Square, the Knickerbocker, the Casino, the Empire, the Broadway, and the Metropolitan Opera House. A chapter could be devoted to the hotels that lined the way: among them the very much surviving Astor (dating from 1904) in the distance; the Knickerbocker (see page 402), the Marlborough (1888–1923), favored by stars of the stage and famous because there Anna Held took her milky bath; and the Normandie (1884–1927) where Samuel Gompers held many labor conferences, where Kid McCoy presided over the Rathskeller and where the woman's suffrage movement had its headquarters. It would take pages to list even the possibilities, but I have decided to focus on what seems to me the most arresting part of the picture—the large electric sign atop the Normandie.

First, I must confess to you that the Byron camera—always the soul of truth—tells a pardonably white lie in this instance. The marquee on Lew Fields' Herald Square Theatre announces that the beloved vagabond comedian Jefferson De Angelis is playing there in *The Beauty Spot.* It is history that this musical comedy, in which he acted the role of General Samovar, opened on April 10, 1909 and closed on August 7th of that year; also and forever it is history that the electric sign was first illuminated on June 18, 1910—a date given over to Theodore Roosevelt's return from his African safari (see page 17). In the Byron folder relating to the "spectacular" there is a print showing a legend in lights—"Welcome Colonel Roosevelt Welcome Home"— which may have been the first words "spoken" by this Broadway phenomenon. It therefore becomes apparent that the Byron Company in 1910 superimposed the sign on one of their earlier views of Broadway, taken in 1909, to show prospective customers of the Rice Electric Display Company of Dayton, Ohio (with a New York office at 1328 Broadway), how their money would burn.

Electric signs were not new to this man-made Milky Way, for back in 1891 the first one ("Buy Homes on Long Island Swept By Ocean Breezes . . . .") had told the town of the coolth of the Oriental and Manhattan hotels on the near-by Atlantic strand, where Gilmore's Band played and Brock's Fireworks flared. O. J. Gude (who christened "The Great White Way") set this brief literature alight on the north wall of the Cumberland apartments, on the present Flatiron site; others followed in hasty multiplication. The *New-York Daily Tribune* of September 22, 1906 ran an article under the headlines *An Electric City. New*

Broadway, 1909 and 1910
North from Thirty-fourth Street

York's Sky Illuminated at Night by Thousands of Signs.: "The number of signs . . . has increased fully 60 per cent, . . . within the last year. Over the twenty-two square miles in Manhattan Island there are some three thousand electric signs of all sizes and descriptions. To make up their glaring talk and to voice with illumination signs and windows that formerly lay dark and dead, no less than one hundred thousand lights are set sparkling each night all over the island."

Four years later, "The Fiery Chariot Race in New York" (inspired by the popularity of *Ben Hur*) was to account for 20,000 collective gleams—chiefly of two candle-power—consuming about 600 horsepower and flashing 2,500 times per minute. Half a million feet of wire, 70,000 separate electrical connections, and 2,750 electric switches (automatically operated) were involved in this 60-by-90-foot sign, supported by a 60-ton steel structure rising 72 feet above the hotel roof. The letters were 4 feet high; the chariot wheel in the foreground, 8 feet in diameter; and the curtain tassels over 6 feet long. These impressive statistics are from the *Scientific American* of July 9, 1910, which described this "Animated Scene In White And Colored Lights" as "overshadowing all others, not only in point of size, but as a spectacular display. It represents a Roman chariot race . . . in which the horses appear to be speeding around an arena at a mad gallop. The main theme . . . is represented by the words placed at the very top of the sign, namely, 'Leaders of the World.' One of the chariots . . . is represented as being well in the lead of the other two. . . . Above the arena is a large curtain on which advertisements are displayed of various concerns whose goods mark them as the leaders of the world in their special lines. These announcements are flashed out every few seconds, the entire series occupying a period of about nine or ten minutes, after which the series is repeated. . . . The aim of the sign is not merely to attract the attention of passers-by, but to hold them and impress them with a splendid and magnificent spectacle, and to cause the public to make special excursions to see it. In this respect the sign is a decided success. A most careful study of the motions of a running horse has been made, so as to make the display as realistic as possible. . . . One of the cleverest features . . . is the production of the dust whirls under the horses and the chariot wheels. . . . Not the least effective feature . . . are the torches . . . at each side. The flames appear to be belching forth out of the braziers as if they were real fire, and they cast a lurid glare over the whole scene." Millions stood and marveled at the galloping horses, with ". . . their tails and manes . . . waving in the breeze, and the drivers' garments . . . fluttering, and the wheels of the chariot . . . revolving at such a speed that the spokes . . . [are] invisible."

And so it does not seem lacking in sequacity that when the English man of letters, G. K. Chesterton, came here on a lecture tour in 1921 (an experience he later reviewed in *What I Saw In America*, published the following year) the Broadway signs "advertising everything from pork to pianos, through the agency of the two most vivid and most mystical of the gifts of God; colour and fire . . ." brought forth the exclamation: "What a glorious garden of wonders this would be, to any one who was lucky enough to be unable to read. . . ."

"NEVER IN the history of Wall street was the country more at the mercy of bears than it is to-day." This statement, from *The New York Herald* of November 4, 1906, has no financial implications whatsoever; on the contrary, it deals with the productivity of Margarete Steiff, "a little old woman" in Germany, "commanding a company of more than two thousand workers whose busy fingers fly from early morning till late at night cutting out, stitching up and putting together plush bears for the American market." The article—titled "The Teddy Bear Craze in New York"—credits "Young America" with the christening of these cuddlesome toy animals (of adult popularity, too), for "Isn't the President the hero of every boy who longs to grow big enough to hold a gun to shoot bears and some day do just the very same things that 'Teddy' Roosevelt does? So Teddy the bears are named, and as Teddy they are known now the length and breadth of our country, as well as on the other side of the Atlantic. . . . Stuffed plush Teddies are fairly rampant." Subsequent research, however, strips the little paralytic toymaker of the Black Forest of this imaginative creation. For once, the icy truth is more attractive than the embroidery. It seems that on November 16, 1902 Clifford Berryman, in the *Washington Post,* cartooned T. R.'s refusal to shoot a captive bear cub thoughtfully provided by his hosts in the absence of big game. The original caption—"Drawing the line in Mississippi!"—was changed to "Teddy's Bear" by the editor of one of the many newspapers and magazines that reprinted this classic. The avalanching vogue was on its way. According to Mrs. Marie Matheson of the International Doll Collectors, Inc.—as told by Lesley Gordon in *Peepshow Into Paradise A History of Children's Toys* (London, 1953)—Morris Michtom, a Russian immigrant, gave the new favorite plush three-dimensionality in his store window, and found a boom market ready-made. While duplication multiplied, he sent his original to Washington, to plead for presidential permission to be called "Teddy Bear." T. R. replied: "I don't think my name is likely to be worth much in the bear business, but you are welcome to use it."

On March 4, 1909, Theodore Roosevelt turned away from The White House and on the 23rd a world watched him set forth on his African safari. Here in New York, at the Jardin de Paris (New York Roof) audiences vibrant with affectionate laughter attended the 64 performances of the *Ziegfeld Follies of 1909* (the third of the series that made local summers

The Building of Charles Scribner's Sons
155 Fifth Avenue (east side, between Twenty-first and
Twenty-second Streets)
decorated for Theodore Roosevelt's homecoming, 1910

17

scintillant with a new glorification of the American girl) which included a riotsome skit entitled "African Jungle," with Sophie Tucker as "The Jungle Queen" in "Moving Day in Jungle Town," and Harry Kelly playing the role of "T. R., a Mighty Hunter." In the more factual existence, after a grand total of 512 wild creatures had less cheerfully laid down their lives for Nimrod and his son Kermit, there were Continental crowned heads to be visited, and the funeral of King Edward VII of England to be attended in official capacity. For fifteen months and 30,000 miles, "Always the sovereigns of the great West, the people who make and unmake Presidents, walked with Colonel Roosevelt," wrote Walter Wellman in his article "Lo! the Conquering Hero," in the July, 1910 issue of *The Metropolitan Magazine.* "They were ever in his mind. He has them, as no man ever had them before, but he intends to keep them. They, and not the denizens of the royal palaces of Europe, were the real audience he was playing to as he walked and preached and promoted his own publicity and projected his personality into peopled space down history's great highway from the White Nile to the Hudson."

He reached the last named stream on June 18, 1910 and his welcome home ". . . began off Sea Gate, when the Kaiserin Auguste Victoria shot out of the fog like the ex-President diving forward to greet a friend, and lasted all the way up the North River to the turning point of the naval parade, back to the Battery and up the island again to Central Park—fifty miles of cheers seven hours long." The *New-York Daily Tribune* of the 19th continues: "It took the cannon of two forts and three warships to welcome Mr. Roosevelt. It required a naval parade and a harbor full of merchant craft and excursion vessels and pleasure yachts. It needed the shores of two states lined with cheering crowds. It took a land parade five miles long with a guard of honor lining both sides of Fifth avenue. . . . It called for fifty thousand persons in Battery Park and some hundreds of thousands along Broadway . . . and on Fifth avenue from Washington Square to 59th street. . . . It gathered the Roosevelt Rough Riders for their first reunion in four years. . . . It even held up the weather. . . . 'He may be somewhat of a demagogue, but he's a high class one,' said one man in the crowd at Madison Square Park, with a kind of grudging admiration. 'Oh, but he's grand!' returned his feminine companion, and a minute later both man and woman were shrieking their plaudits and the man had his hat waving and was yelling, 'Oh, you Teddy!' . . ." This affectional salutation appeared on many lettered signs along the decorated line of march, intermingled with the toothy Rooseveltian trademark—"Dee-lighted"—and the more hackneyed but heartfelt "Welcome Home." Animal masks and the little make-believe Ursidae were everywhere on display. "Sitting on the coping of a toy house was a life-size Teddy bear . . . [with] legs . . . wav[ing] wildly by means of strings as Mr. Roosevelt drove by and he laughed out loud at the grotesque sight." At 155 Fifth Avenue, part of the façade designed in 1893 by Ernest Flagg for Charles Scribner's Sons (whose imprimatur has appeared on many books by and about the figure more than any other epitomic of his era) was hidden by a two-story-length portrait of Roosevelt in safari attire.

While Professor A. Alonzo Stagg, director of athletics at the University of Chicago, promulgated the theory (as faithfully reported in the *Tribune* of June 19th) that "Sweat Makes Roosevelt," a poet set about celebrating the modern Odysseus in "The Teddysee," which first appeared in *The Saturday Evening Post* (October 8, 15, 22 and 29, 1910) and was published in book form in the same year. (Antecedent was Otho Cushing's cartoon series—"The

18

Teddyssey"—which sprang from the pages of *Life* in 1907.) Of the cacophonic homecoming of his hero, Wallace Irwin versified:

> "Muses, lend me an earthquake
>   To rattle the big blue dome,
> Or a dynamite bomb,
> Or a fierce tom-tom,
> Or a bugle-call,
> Or Niagara's fall—
> Full justice to do
> To the hullabaloo
> Which roared New York and the Country through
>   When Teddy came sailing home.
> Thunder and smoke, how the Patriots woke
>   From Kalamazoo to Nome!
> Your Uncle Sam fell off o' the porch
> And the Statue of Liberty swallowed her torch
>   When Teddy came sailing home."

. . . . *Charms of The Boulevard*

"Dove" luncheons, as some of the bachelor members called them, were an exceedingly popular innovation at the Colonial Club, a West Side neighborhood institution organized in April and incorporated in May, 1889. The 1890 plans filed by the architect Henry F. Kilburn for the gray limestone and gray brick, terra cotta-trimmed retreat at the southwest corner of Broadway and Seventy-second Street, made conscious provision among the brave for the fair— an advanced gesture soon followed by the Metropolitan and other men's clubs. A separate entrance, through the shallow side street porch, gave elevator access to the set-apartness of the third floor, with its special reception and dining rooms, particularly favored on the Sabbath. "It is the custom of many families in this city to dine away from home on Sunday evenings," stated the *New-York Daily Tribune* of May 5, 1895. "One cause for this is that many servants insist on having . . . [that] afternoon and evening 'out,' and would rather give up their places than cook an elaborate evening meal. So it is the part of prudence to give them all possible liberty after the dishes of the noonday repast have been washed. A second consideration is the delight of a dinner away from home. . . . Restaurants as well as clubs profit." Wives and daughters, too, patronized the basement bowling alleys of winter mornings and shared in the enjoyment of cultural and social functions in the 62-by-32-foot assembly or ball room on the second floor. The consequent—though unfortunately temporary—prosperity of the Colonial overcame the last lingering doubts of even the Club hermits. The building (sold in 1903) still survives as an apartment house.

The *New-York Daily Tribune* on May 6, 1894, eloquently discursive of the "Charms of The Boulevard," commented on the "driveway . . divided for its full length by a strip of green flanked on each side by trees, . . . the only street that does not depend upon the

buildings for its beauty," and pronounced one of its "finest views" the segment here preserved by Byron. From the axial Columbus (or Grand) Circle, with its new central column, the Boulevard (Broadway) swept past the Hotel Empire of the "quaint towers," "one of the finest structures to attract attention," to the Marie Antoinette, three blocks above at Sixty-sixth Street, nearing completion opposite the Tecumseh. Advancing into the upper sixties and lower seventies, one first came upon the 22nd Regiment Armory and the Bloomingdale Reformed Church, flanking the eastern side, with the Nevada and the Sherman Square Hotel on the west—"all new buildings and all attractive and of superior architecture." South of the Colonial Club, at the northwest corner of Seventy-first Street and Broadway, is seen Christ Church, going back in worship to 1794, but a newcomer to this part of town, whence a series of northward migrations propelled it in 1890, with C. C. Haight as architect.

"But the development of the Boulevard is only in its incipiency," the *Tribune* gave assurance, quoting a delighted resident as saying: "It is the ideal large apartment-house street . . . its pavement of the noiseless kind." These advantages for settler and transient and solid house-holder—a local "population equal in numbers to that of Albany or Rochester, and . . . daily growing"—made the need for "the large drygoods department stores" in the area obvious; and great possibilities awaited a "West Side theatre and hall for high-class musical entertainments."

North of Seventy-second Street, in 1895 (again we are indebted to the *New-York Daily Tribune*, this time the issue of June 9) there were "no less than eighty excavations for buildings" (mainly private houses) west of Central Park. Citing the "El," the extension of the cable-car lines, and the more leisurely horsecars, the paper added: "It would not be easy to find anywhere a better illustration of the powerful influence of transportation facilities upon the material evolution of a locality than has been afforded here. That this section is possessed of natural advantages superior to any other part of Manhattan Island is no new discovery." And "the unequalled views, pure air, solid foundations and proximity to the city's pleasure grounds . . . substantial inducements for residential settlement" had merely waited on locomotive improvements.

At least three newspapers—*The New York Herald*, the *New-York Daily Tribune*, and *The World*—even chronicled the social life of the "West End"—known as "Bloomingdale," or the "Vale of Flowers," from Dutch village days on down—in a segregated column, apart from gleanings about the more fashionable province to the southeast and east.

Sherman Square, about 1897
Looking southwest from Broadway and Seventy-second Street

OF A sunshiny day, two young women are walking into the first summer of the new century, totally unconscious of the hovering ghostly presence of William Allen Butler's "Miss Flora M'Flimsey, of Madison Square," forever engaged in the utterly feminine lament that ". . . she had nothing whatever to wear!" They have probably been replenishing their own considerably less lavish wardrobes and may even have been extravagant to the point of investing in silk stockings, of which 150,864 pairs had been sold in the United States in 1900. Before making this astounding purchase at Arnold Constable & Co.'s Broadway and Nineteenth Street emporium, they might have stopped by at Brentano's on Union Square to order the latest Gibson Book—*Americans*—as a wedding present for a bride in their circle, in preference to a romantically illustrated *Rubáiyát*. Both had been disturbed by *Sister Carrie* and shared the opinion of J. P. Kerfoot (as expressed in *Life,* March 7, 1901) that Theodore Dreiser, in this ". . . story of middle-class immorality and crime . . . written with an honest desire to draw a true picture of real life . . . utterly lack[ed] . . . the master-touch which can create from a repulsive scene a work of art." They had noticed another Doubleday, Page and Company imprint —*Up from Slavery, An Autobiography*, by Booker T. Washington—on the counter, and this title, they remembered, had received Kerfoot's commendation (in *Life*, April 25, 1901) as an "important, deeply interesting volume . . ." by a writer whose every word on "the race problem" merited "careful study." However, it was *The Crisis*, a Civil War romance by Winston Churchill, newly published by The Macmillan Company in a first edition of 100,000 copies—a "phenomenal seller," the clerk told them—that they were planning to take on their vacation trip to the "Rainbow City," as the Pan-American Exposition at Buffalo was called. Although they were as "bargainivorous" as the best (irresistible adjective extracted from the *New-York Tribune Illustrated Supplement* of March 17, 1901) they had waved aside the "sidewalk flower merchant's" ten-cent bunch of putrefying double violets, as they were on their way to a meeting called to discuss fund-producing plans for their favorite charity. They had decided to suggest philanthropy's new "wind raiser," as the same Sunday feature (on January 13) categorized the rummage sale. Untroubled by such matters as the faraway Boer War (although they had been intrigued by accounts of Winston Spencer Churchill's Pond-promoted lectures on his imprisonment at Praetoria) and our own involvement in the Philippines, they are probably gossiping about last night's party and the memory of those beefsteak dinners that had become so popular during the past winter. They agreed that it had been a good theatrical season, too. They had seen Julia Marlowe several times in *When Knighthood Was In Flower* (it had been a great year for the dramatized novel)—a play that had cast a romanceless aura on their comparatively unchivalric swains. Their parents had felt it far more suitable entertainment than the forbidden burning *Sapho* of 1900, although several daring young friends—heedless of *Life's* effort (on March 15 of that year) to spare its readers the "mortification and expense" of attending this unclean play, "at which no self-respecting woman should be seen"—had actually applauded Olga Nethersole, the target of the yellow journals. They had souvenirs of the 100th performance (on May 1) of *Under Two Flags*, with Miss Blanche Bates as Cigarette. They hummed songs from *Florodora* (see page 247) as they passed the line of hansom cabs shadowed against the background of that Republican stronghold—the Fifth Avenue Hotel. The high-perched jehus are completely disinterested in the strollers, for according to a cartoon by Gray Parker (in *Life*, May 3, 1900) they could not expect any tips from lady shoppers. O. Henry—in "From The Cabby's Seat" (*The Four Million*)—described the *Gestalt* of this lofty "cock-of-the-roost," ". . . more single-minded, perhaps, than that of a follower of any other calling . . . he looks upon his fellow-men as nomadic particles, of no account except when possessed of migratory desires. . . . Be you President or vagabond, to cabby you are only a Fare. . . . Helpless, ridiculous, confined, bobbing like a toy mandarin, you sit like a rat in a trap—you before whom butlers cringe on solid land—and must squeak upward through a slit in your peripatetic sarcophagus to make your feeble wishes known. Then, in a cab, you are not even an occupant; you are contents. You are a cargo at sea. . . ." The young women were well aware that even this lurching world had its etiquette. "There is one inflexible rule . . ." insisted *The New York Herald* of May 5, 1901, "that is not generally understood. It is that the lady . . . [ascending to Paradise ahead of her escort] shall . . . immediately seat herself at the side nearest the curb. The man must then pass her . . . and take the other side." The paper had it ". . . on good authority that nothing marks so sharply one's social standing as the way in which one enters a hansom."

Madison Square, 1901

AT THREE o'clock on the brisk, windy afternoon of St. Patrick's Day, 1899, when Fifth Avenue was bright with flags, alive with holiday crowds, filled with the echoing music of bands and the measured footsteps of marching men, the famous twenty-six-wintered Windsor Hotel, an "old pile of moth-eaten rubbish and creaking floors . . . was burnt down as quickly and spectacularly as if it were . . . a frame house in the middle of a Kansas plain." So the May issue of *The Illustrated American Magazine* relates, with insinuative reference to six similar tinder boxes about town "to which no man should go except for the purpose of committing suicide."

On June 21, 1900, the *New-York Daily Tribune* announced that plans had been drawn up for a fireproof structure on this seared site, "to be of an imposing style of architecture, and especially designed for a gallery of fine arts and displays by merchants in glass and china. It is to consist of arcades, along which the wares of these dealers will be exhibited . . . its chief qualities . . . [being] those of affording large air and light privileges to its occupants." Commodore Elbridge T. Gerry, since 1896 owner of the property and famed for his philanthropies and his affectation of sealskin headgear, employed Charles I. Berg to design the $300,000 Beaux-Arts monument which advanced the northernmost boundary of retail trade on Fifth Avenue to Forty-seventh Street. Pach Brothers, photographers since 1867, had already contracted for a duplex studio; Steinway & Company set up elaborate showrooms; among other tenants were the Windsor Trust Company and Fraser & Company, Pharmacists. Randall Blackshaw in *The Century Magazine* of August, 1902, hailed the three-story newcomer to "The New New York" as "A notable structure . . . [that] emphasizes the fact that height is not indispensable to striking architectural effects." The Windsor Arcade was truncated when W. & J. Sloane took over the upper end of the block for its present establishment, opened on April 8, 1912, while the obstinately surviving southern section held out until Warren & Wetmore raised the S. W. Straus Bank Building there in 1920–1921.

The somewhat untidy traffic is in the transitional phase, for among the equine-drawn vehicles—private and commercial—one can spot an electric. The rather precariously perched people are inspecting the Windsor Arcade from atop a horse-drawn "Public Coach" of the type "built for The Fifth Avenue Transportation Co., of New York, by E. M. Miller & Co., of Quincy, Ill.," (according to a tradecard in the Museum's collection), and in use from the beginning of the system in 1886 until the summer of 1907, although the first of the electric omnibuses took to the Avenue with the dawn of 1900. The next objective awaiting the passengers' passing curiosity is the house on the north corner of Forty-seventh Street, which played a merciful part in the parade-interrupting Windsor Hotel fire, for Helen Gould (later Mrs. Finley J. Shepard) converted it into a temporary hospital and shelter, providing 5,681 meals for firemen and victims of the catastrophe. Her mansarded brownstone, of which S. D. Hatch was the architect, dated from 1868, and in 1881–1882 became the home of her father, Jay

The Windsor Arcade, 1902
East side of Fifth Avenue
Forty-sixth to Forty-seventh Streets

Gould (who had moved onto Fifth Avenue, across the street at No. 580, in the year of the famous financial "Black Friday"—September 24, 1869—largely of his making). In 1942 the mansion was leased to Gimbel Brothers for the use of the Kende Galleries as an auxiliary evening auction room; and at the time of its demolition to make way for an office building ten years later was virtually the residual last of the Avenue's private domiciles below the Central Park stretch.

North of the succeeding chocolate reaches, on the site occupied by Saks Fifth Avenue since 1924, the contrasting red-colored selectivity of The Belgravia, overshadowing a smaller similarly hued apartment house, the brownstone Democratic Club and the aristocratic Buckingham (a family-favored hotel built by George Kemp in 1875) were neighbors to St. Patrick's. While the cornerstone of this Renwick-designed Cathedral was laid on August 15, 1858, and its dedication took place on May 25, 1879, it was not until 1888 that its twin spires— joining the steepled heights of the Church of St. Nicholas, St. Thomas's and the Fifth Avenue Presbyterian Church—brought to the gilded territory a freshly dominant, piercing new skylinity.

. . . . *The face filled with a tired restlessness*

"IT APPEARED at all events, on the late days of spring, just a response to the facility of things and so much of their juvenile pleasantry, to find one's self 'liking,' without more ado, . . . the heterogeneous, miscellaneous apology for a Square marking the spot at which the main entrance . . . to the Park opens toward Fifth Avenue." So this "most jovial of all the sacrifices of preconsidered composition," this evidence "of the brave New York humor," captivated Henry James upon his visitation following nearly a quarter-century of self-elected literary exile. In the first of a series of articles in the *North American Review* (beginning in January, 1906 and later appearing between boards in *The American Scene*, published by Harper & Brothers the following year), he went on: "The best thing in the picture, obviously, is Saint Gaudens's great group, splendid in its golden elegance." The "dauntless refinement of the Sherman image" impressed him, although he would have preferred "a Sherman of the terrible March (the 'immortal' march, in all abundance, if that be the needed note), not irradiating benevolence, but signifying, by every ingenious device, the misery, the ruin and the vengeance of his track," to the "Destroyer" as "messenger of peace, with the olive branch too waved in the blast, and with embodied grace, in the form of a beautiful American Girl, attending his business."

William Dean Howells, too, deplored "the introduction of the ideal" into the composition; but the sculptor himself wrote that this symbolic figure (drawn by strange contradiction from a young southern woman) was "the grandest 'Victory' anybody ever made." To Saint-Gaudens—who believed always that "You can do anything you please. It's the way it's done that makes the difference."—William Tecumseh Sherman had ever been of the highest stuff of heroes; and out of his reverence and admiration he had modeled a bust of the aging soldier from life in 1888, "in about eighteen periods of two hours each," the face filled with a tired restlessness. This head was later virtually copied as the basis of the Plaza monument, which

The Statue of William Tecumseh Sherman, about 1905
Fifth Avenue between Fifty-ninth and Sixtieth Streets
Against the background of Park & Tilford's (at this site 1884–
1915); and the Hotel Netherland (1892–1925)

was ten years with him, he tells in *The Reminiscences Of Augustus Saint-Gaudens*, Edited And Amplified By Homer Saint-Gaudens (New York, 1913), a tracery of moments of agony and of triumph. He created the figure "from an Italian model very much of the General's build"; and Ontario, "the famous high jumper," became the nervous, swift-moving charger stepping close to the pine branch on the base, "placed there to typify Georgia." He began the actual work in New York in 1896, and carried it along to his Paris studio, at the outset of his long last illness. When it was exhibited in the Champ de Mars of 1899 he wrote to his son Homer on May 2: "I have got a swelled head for the first time in my life, for the 'Sherman' really looks bully and is smashingly fine. It's in the place of honor . . . and from a screeching maniac I have become a harmless, drooling, gibbering idiot, sitting all day long looking at the statue. Occasionally I fall on my knees and adore it. And there you are!" The cast next appeared in the French Exposition of 1900, where (with his Shaw Memorial and *Amor Caritas* of the Luxembourg) it carried off the highest award. "I'm very cocky about the 'Sherman', which has turned out well," he informed his brother Louis by letter. And still he labored on, in his hill-framed Cornish, New Hampshire studio, making change after change to be incorporated in the casting in progress in Paris. And at creation's end, his son tells us, "he set up the bronze itself in the field back of his house, to the delight of the farmers, that he might experiment with the pedestal and supervise the application of the patine. He had always spent much time over the color of his productions . . . and in the case of the 'Sherman' he explained, 'I am sick of seeing statues look like stove pipes.' Hence he longed for the unusual combination of a gilded bronze on a cream-colored base. The plan was not wholly feasible, as he failed to obtain the stone he desired. . . . But at least he covered the 'Sherman' with two layers of gold-leaf." He failed, too, to secure the background of Grant's Tomb, or the straight passage of the Mall, which he coveted, and after seeing the statue placed to such happy advantage at the Pan-American Exposition of 1901, had to accept the confining Plaza in discontent. Here, "Erected By Citizens of New York [whose streets were familiar to the old warrior] under The Auspices Of The Chamber Of Commerce Of The State Of New York," the heroic equestrian statue was unveiled on Decoration Day, 1903. The polished granite pedestal was the work of Charles Follen McKim—to Augustus Saint-Gaudens "Charles the Charmer," many-time collaborator and long-time friend, of whom he wrote, "A devouring love for ice-cream brought us together."

. . . . *Good air, drainage and social propinquity*

THE "HABITAT of this monstrous aristocracy"—so the Irish patriot, James Stephens, here to raise funds and recruit volunteers for the Fenian Movement, described the Fifth Avenue of 1858, in a manuscript in the Public Record Office of Northern Ireland and available in photostat at The New York Public Library. "Most of the houses denote wealth; some of them are sumptuous; but, with few exceptions, they are but the monstrous offspring of barbarizing expenditure. But now this display of the almighty dollar, has, like almost everything else in America, something both uppish-sham & cheap about it. I had previously observed that the fronts of stone or marble (dirt-colored stone & . . . streaked marble) were mere *facings* . . . forming

28

The west side of Fifth Avenue, about 1892
North from Fifty-first Street

an outward coating to the . . . walls of brick! Indeed everything here is done as if no man had any faith in the stability of things—as if each & all were engaged in a rough-&-tumble scramble, & recklessly grabbed at whatever chance threw in his way. The general taste . . . is barbarous; and the exceptions (I am now speaking of the buildings—the *private* ones, for there are no public buildings in New-York!) are but servile imitations, or exact fac-similes, of European dwellings."

Thirty-five years later, Paul Bourget made similar allegations, in one of his articles published simultaneously in *The New York Herald* and *Le Figaro* from August, 1893 to April, 1894, and issued in book form under the title of *Outre-Mer* (New York and Paris, 1895). He found that "it is but too evident that money cannot have much value here. There is too much of it. The interminable succession of luxurious mansions which line Fifth Avenue proclaim its mad abundance. No shops,—unless of articles of luxury,—a few dressmakers, a few picture-dealers—the last froth of the spent wave of that tide of business which drowns the rest of the city—only independent dwellings, each one of which, including the ground on which it stands, implies a revenue which one dares not calculate. Here and there are vast constructions which reproduce the palaces and châteaux of Europe. . . . The absence of unity in this architecture is a sufficient reminder that this is the country of the individual will, as the absence of gardens and trees around these sumptuous residences proves the newness of all this wealth and of the city. This avenue has visibly been willed and created by sheer force of millions."

"Finest of all are the Vanderbilt palaces," maintained Richard H. Titherington in *Munsey's Magazine*, November, 1891, corroborating the adulatory statement of Hans Knickerbocker in *Collier's Once A Week*, February 9, 1889: "The Vanderbilts have come nobly forward and shown the world how millionaires ought to live." In the photographs here reproduced Byron has conserved the unfortified castles ebulliated by the most prominent dreamers-in-stone of the day for the New York dynasty so definitely dealt with by Wayne Andrews in *The Vanderbilt Legend* (New York, 1941).

First comes the tripartite group erected by William Henry Vanderbilt (1821–1885), son of the Commodore: a block-long sequence of "That warm-colored brown freestone whose healthy surface constitutes the armor of so many American homes," placed, so Edward Strahan (that is, Earl Shinn) opines in his four-volume, ten-section monograph *Mr. Vanderbilt's House and Collection* (Philadelphia, 1884), "in one of the finest situations of New York [the southern part reserved by it until 1947] for good air, drainage, etc., to say nothing of social propinquity. . . . This house is a box, if you will, but there is a finish and a style about it that shows it is a jewel-box." It took many dollars (an estimated million and three-quarters) and the minds and hands of many men to fashion the "cubical simplicity" of an "edifice [which] would not look out of place among the *palazzi* put up in Northern Italy. . . . The architects, both for the external and internal work, including designs for most of the upholstery, were Herter Brothers . . . assisted for the building details by J. B. Snook [with mention of C. B. Atwood in the plans as originally filed in 1879]. . . . Sixty [imported] foreign sculptors and carvers were in employ for two years. . . . Upon the interior decorations were engaged between six hundred and seven hundred men, for a year and a half. . . . The external bronze railings were cast by Bureau Brothers and Heaton of Philadelphia. The internal wood-carving . . . was executed by some two hundred and fifty workmen from the designs of Mr. Christian Herter." The year after their labors ended, *Artistic Houses* (New York, 1883) devoted seventeen pages and eleven illustrations to the $800,000 interior of this decorator's extravaganza, the twin sections of which were connected by an "outer vestibule or *atrium*, . . . which serves as a link between Mr. Vanderbilt's house and that of two of his sons-in-law, Messrs. [Elliott F.] Shepard [husband of Margaret Louisa] and [William D.] Sloane [who married Emily Thorn]." In the drawing room of the paternal domicile (which superseded the A. T. Stewart mansion as the finest in town) "The effect is gorgeous in the extreme: everything sparkles and flashes with gold and color—with mother-of-pearl, with marbles, with jewel-effects in glass—and almost every surface is covered, one might say weighted, with ornament." The art gallery, an "honorable retreat" to which the public was admitted by card on Thursdays, contained "one of the most notable private collections of modern pictures in the world," and was "an important element in cultivating the artistic taste of the metropolis."

Across Fifty-second Street (from 1882 until 1925) was the home built by Mr. and Mrs. William K. Vanderbilt (son and daughter-in-law of William Henry), about which *Collier's Once A Week* (February 9, 1889) tells "People talked . . . for at least twenty-four hours after it was thrown open to the world." Richard M. Hunt's masterpiece—a singing marriage of the Château de Blois and the Jacques Cœur house at Bourges—was the setting for the splendiferous Fancy Dress Ball of March 26, 1883, to which Mrs. Astor (according to Henry Clews, in *Fifty Years In Wall Street*, New York, c. 1908) was forced to gain admission by genuflection. *The World* (March 27, 1883) appraised the total expenditure involved at

30

$250,000, of which $155,750 went into costumers' hands. The kinetic hostess—née Alva Smith and mother of the future Duchess of Marlborough—was metamorphosed into a Venetian Princess, dove-surrounded in the set of photographs by Mora, which includes the risible image of Miss Kate F. Strong (later Mrs. Arthur N. Welman) crowned with a stuffed cat, and, for the benefit of the literate, her nickname ("Puss" or "Pussy"—the angle of vision interferes) spelled out on her neckband. P. F. Collier's publication proclaimed the house "Undoubtedly the handsomest mansion in this country, and perhaps in the world. . . . Both exterior and interior are monuments to the architect's skill and taste. What is called the dining-room is a vast banqueting hall, with two enormous fireplaces, whose huge chimneys, settles, mantels and carvings remind one of the old castles which date back to the Middle Ages. . . . The great feature of the house . . . is the staircase, which is in marble. . . . The hall is large enough to accommodate a whole row of 'brown stone fronts.'" In 1906, William K. Vanderbilt II and his wife (née Virginia Graham Fair) moved into a mansion designed by Stanford White in the tradition of the paternal palace, relieving part of the tediousness north of the fabled 660.

Just above St. Thomas's Church, and out of the camera's reach, one passed the comparatively modest dwellings at Nos. 680 and 684, fashioned by J. B. Snook for Mrs. W. Seward Webb and Mrs. H. McK. Twombly, daughters of W. H. Vanderbilt. Strolling up the Avenue into the photograph on pages 32–33, one came upon another family castle—a red brick and white stone château, built in two sections (the unseen Fifty-seventh Street part in 1881–1882 and visible upper end in 1892–1894) by George B. Post, with the helping hand of Richard M. Hunt in the northeast tower. Its owner was Cornelius Vanderbilt II, inheritor of the sceptor on the death of his father, William H., in 1885. If we are to give credence to *The New York Herald* of February 20, 1898, he and his wife, the former Alice Gwynne, stood "well up at the head of families possessing great retinues of 'help.' They have something like thirty servants, an army for a city house." The schedule of a few of the privates in this legion is given: "It is at an early hour in the morning that the staff in these great houses gets at its work. In the Cornelius Vanderbilt mansion, for example, when the family is at home, the parlor maids must start in at six o'clock, and have the entire drawing room floor and the halls swept, and garnished, and every ornament and bit of bric-a-brac dusted and rubbed clean before nine o'clock. On the stroke of nine . . . they must vanish and leave the parlors ready for the day. The Vanderbilts are somewhat of an exception in this regard, however. The rule of New York swelldom [or gigmanity, to use a pet period term] is to give the parlor maids until twelve o'clock for their 'redding up,' a day of fashion in this city not commencing until noon."

To the northwest of this feudal domain (demolished in 1927, and now represented by the splendor of its gates guarding the Conservatory Gardens at Fifth Avenue and 105th Street) is the Plaza Hotel, the second of that name to occupy the site. Erection of the first one, begun in 1881 by the firm of Fife & Campbell, was interrupted by litigation over the estate of the milliardaire tobacco merchant John Anderson, former owner of the land. The New York Life Insurance Company, mortgage holders, set 1,400 men to work on the project during the summer of 1889, and on October 1st of the following year (the *New-York Daily Tribune* of September 30—in its account of the previewing dinner on the 29th—relates) "another great house [under the management of F. A. Hammond] has been added to the host of New-York's splendid hotels. . . . The elegance and beauty of the decorations . . . are such that a volume

Fifth Avenue and West Fifty-eighth Street,
1908

would be required to describe them fully." All this magnificence was short-lived, for in a seventeen-day sale ending with an auction on June 29, 1905, the $500,000 furnishings were disposed of for about one-tenth of that impressive sum, "ten vanloads of goods" (according to the *Tribune* account of the following day) being purchased for renewed lease on life in the fashionable Hotel Marie Antoinette, at Broadway and Sixty-sixth Street.

Whether by chance or sentiment, the present Hotel Plaza—with Henry J. Hardenbergh as its architect, the George A. Fuller Construction Company as the builders and Fred Sterry as the Managing Director—opened on October 1, 1907, the seventeenth anniversary of its predecessor's day of glory. A carefully timed feature of the inauguration was the "Parade Of The New Taxicabs." According to the *Tribune* twenty-five of these four-cylinder French-made motor vehicles, "bright red, with green panels," and equipped with odometers, were piloted down Fifth Avenue by uniformed drivers, to "take their place in line at the Plaza Hotel." According to *The New York Times* reporter, the Belmont shared in this innovative service. These vehicles, operated by the New York Taxicab Company, were in the vanguard of a fleet of 600 to be allocated the following day to stands in front of the St. Regis, the Imperial, the Netherland, and the Knickerbocker, as well as Rector's.

The new "home hotel"—with its 753 rooms for occupancy by about 600 guests, staffed by "hundreds of servants"—opened (the *Tribune* relates) "under unusually auspicious circumstances, for among the persons who have engaged suites for the year are some whose names are well known in social and financial circles, many of whom have heretofore always occupied their own houses. Among these are Alfred G. Vanderbilt, George J. Gould, Mr. and Mrs. Oliver Harriman, Mrs. James Henry Smith . . . and John W. ["Bet-a-Million"] Gates, whose apartment consists of sixteen rooms."

At the dinner tendered to the press on September 30, Samuel P. McConnell (counsel for the Plaza Operating Company), according to the account in *The New York Herald* of the next day, called attention to the wonderful vista from the hotel windows, rivalling "an outlook from the Alps."

. . . . *A complete architectural meal*

"IT IS a solid mile and a half of millionaires' residences, practically without a break, except where a vacant spot awaits the coming of still another Croesus," elated *The New York Herald* on February 13, 1898, surveying the bullionated eastern borderland of Central Park, from Sixtieth Street to Ninetieth. The present "Court End of Town," Wilson Chambers (in an article in the *Metropolitan Magazine* for April, 1899) called the purple purlieu bounded on the south by the Metropolitan Club and extending about as far as Byron's perspective here. The writer described it as "the richest neighborhood in New York . . . a sort of first-class Midway Plaisance," where "nearly every one of the sixty or seventy houses in the line is a place of entertainment of the continuous performance sort," with "so many breakfasts, luncheons, receptions, teas, dinners, balls, and suppers . . . in one day that no one society matron can attend them all. . . . Every style of architecture is represented, in barbaric confusion," with some façades embodimental of what Edith Wharton, in *The House of Mirth*, was later

34

Fifth Avenue north from Sixty-fifth Street, 1898

35

Fifth Avenue south from Seventy-eighth Street, 1901

to label forever as "a complete architectural meal." Mr. Chambers opined: "To describe one of these mansions would be the same as describing all; for in all there are the same old tapestries and the same new decorations, the same antique furniture and the same modern improvements . . . differ[ing] only in respect to certain individual oddities." Among the diversities he cited "that famous two-ton bathtub of Mrs. John Jacob Astor, . . . cut out of a solid block of marble," tucked away in Hunt's glorified bi-family mansion at the right of the photograph on page 35; "that superb law library in Elbridge T. Gerry's house" (out of the picture, at the south corner of Sixty-first Street); "that costly group of old violins in Henry O. Havemeyer's house" (set down by C. C. Haight at the north corner of Sixty-sixth Street) which also sheltered the works of Old Masters beside the sunlit Impressionist canvases selected with the aid of Mary Cassatt and now part of the angelic taste at The Metropolitan Museum of Art; and "that twenty thousand dollar rug which ornaments Mrs. George J. Gould's music room," a block north at No. 857. "But why is this preserve . . . called the 'Court End of the Town'?" Mr. Chambers answers his own question: "It is really because the queen of society lives on the corner of Fifth avenue and Sixty-fifth street. She is Mrs. William Astor. Some New Yorkers call her the dowager queen, looking upon her daughter [by courtesy of the in-law], Mrs. John Jacob Astor, as the reigning queen. Among the great ladies of the Court are Mrs. Ogden Mills, who lives on the corner of Sixty-ninth street, near William C. Whitney; Mrs. Elbridge T. Gerry, Mrs. W. Watts Sherman [residing just south of the Sovereign], and Mrs. O. H. P. Belmont," of No. 677. After listing the *petite noblesse*, the author propounds: "If all these people had a title consistent with their wealth, not one man would rank below a prince, and not one woman below the rank of duchess."

An article in *Munsey's Magazine* of June, 1898, entitled "Two Miles of Millionaires"—covering the stretch from Murray Hill to Eightieth Street along this grand canal of Mammon, soon to elasticate as far as Andrew Carnegie's "Highland" home ten blocks north—vouches that "The repaving of Fifth Avenue with asphalt last fall made it at once the delight of the bicyclist and the parade ground of the pleasure driver, and, in fact, of every one who can command a hansom." Therefore, let us ride past "the palaces that stir the passion of the socialist to envy," and rejoin Byron a few steps above Seventy-eighth Street. Just within his focus comes the home of Henry H. Cook, the vitalizing point of "the bric-à-brac block" bounded by Seventy-eighth Street and Seventy-ninth, Fifth Avenue and Madison, so called, the *New-York Daily Tribune* of April 12, 1903, explains, by some facetious real estate operators "on account of the extraordinary rise in the value of its ground within the last few years and the great demand among wealthy men for home sites in this choice parcel," astutely acquired by Mr. Cook in 1884, for about $500,000. "It can be truly said that to-day the block holds a unique position in the realty market. Beyond a question of doubt it is one of the most valuable residential blocks in the city." With the improvements, its estimated worth was about $19,000,000. Mr. Cook had exercised great selectivity in his choice of neighbors. Among them were numbered the social leaders Mr. and Mrs. Stuyvesant Fish, at 25 East Seventy-eighth Street; Isaac D. Fletcher, unrelated to the Charles H. Fletcher for whose palatable Castoria little children cried so piteously, at 2 East Seventy-ninth Street; and Frederic Gebhard at 6 East Seventy-ninth Street. "The house of Mr. Cook . . . [on the site occupied by the Duke mansion since 1909] is considered by many architects to be one of the best types of architecture in dwelling houses," said the *Tribune* in tribute to the work of W. Wheeler Smith. At this time The J. C. Lyons Building and Operating Company was engaged in erecting costly habitations for sale in this sacrosanct square—a practice not uncommon at the period when many men of means contented themselves with being the architects of their own fortunes and bought ready-to-wear homes.

Across Seventy-eighth Street, on the south corner, is another R. M. Hunt contribution to this avenue of millionaires, occupied by Mr. and Mrs. William V. Lawrence (No. 969); and, down the line, the newly arrived No. 967–968, followed by the residences of Dr. George H. Butler (No. 964); Charles F. Dieterich (No. 963); and Rowland A. Robbins (No. 962).

The dominator of this streetscape is Temple Beth-El, on the south corner of Seventy-sixth Street, described on the morning of its September 18, 1891 dedication by the *New-York Daily Tribune* as being "massive and striking in its architectural beauty," and, in the opinion of its congregation, unsurpassed "among the synagogues of the world." To stand until 1947, "the most conspicuous feature" of this Indiana limestone, generally Romanesque edifice— the inspiration of Messrs. Brunner and Tryon—was the "immense central structure, half dome, half tower, fifty-one feet in diameter at the base and rising to a height of 140 feet . . . flanked by two smaller towers . . . built of iron and covered with copper, with tracery of gilded copper."

To be reared on the basis of a fortune rising from this same metallic element was the white granite, one hundred and thirty-chambered palace home of Senator William A. Clark of Montana, here seen in early constructive upheaval at the north corner of Seventy-seventh Street, and destined to be shelter for his young family and growing collection. The model and plans by Lord, Hewlett & Hull and K. M. Murchison, with a well-paid nod from H. Deglane of Paris, were "closely scrutinized," uncritically stated the *New-York Daily Tribune* of February 12, 1899, "at the exhibition of the Architectural League . . . last week in the league's rooms in Fifty-seventh-st." Upon the completion of the pile—to remain eye-irritant until 1927—Norman Hapgood, in *Collier's* for January 28, 1905, was less noncommittal: "The only way it could be deemed good art is that it correctly represents the personality and taste of the Copper King who owns it." In the vein of what Ludwig Charell once paraphrastically called "*Chacun à son degoût,*" the forthright editor, in his "Readings and Reflections," declared: "This house would have seemed the ideal dwelling to the late Mr. Barnum. It is as flamboyant as he could wish—an airy fantasy in granite blocks. If, as Schelling said, architecture is frozen music, this edifice is frozen ragtime discord." In the issue of March 11, the weekly returned to the attack on the "Regal Taste" of the Gentleman from Montana with unveiled imputations on his probity and vengeful verse by Wallace Irwin (whose *Letters of a Japanese Schoolboy* were to become the literary talk of 1909):

> "Senator Copper of Tonapah Ditch
> Made a clean billion in minin' and sich,
> Hiked fer Noo York, where his money he blew
> Buildin' a palace on Fift' Avenoo.
> 'How,' sez the Senator, 'can I look proudest?
> Build me a house that'll holler the loudest—'
>
> . . .
>
> Forty-eight architects came to consult,

Drawin' up plans for a splendid result;
If the old Senator wanted to pay,
They'd give 'im Art with a capital A,

. . .

Pillars Ionic,
Eaves Babylonic,
Doors cut in scallops, resemblin' a shell;
Roof wuz Egyptian,
Gables caniptian,
Whole grand effect, when completed, wuz—hell."

. . . . Breathing-places to the inhabitants

"UNION PLACE, at the northern termination of Broadway, is in an elliptical form, enclosed with a fine iron fence, having a public fountain in the centre with ornamental jets, and is a delightful breathing-place to the inhabitants." So the stranger in Manhattan—wandering through one of the city's finest residential sections—oriented himself as he perused *The Great Metropolis; Or Guide To New-York For 1849*, issued by H. Wilson.

In early September, 1887, the Square was much in the news. On the 4th the *New-York Daily Tribune* was moved to lyricism: "No dream of the tropics, and such visions far exceed the sober reality, could be more enchanting than the display of water plants in the fountain of Union Square Park." Here in profusion were Indian lotus flowers, and American pond lilies, dominated by a "great Zanzibar lily . . . blue and huge." A note of another color, closer to the present-day concept of the locale, appeared on the editorial page: "The painters will parade on Labor Day. They ought to leave their red paint at home." And it was announced in Monday's preview of the workers' celebration that "The Socialists are determined to carry their red flags, but all the organizations in sympathy with the United Labor Party will carry only their trade banners and the American flag." The "new holiday of Labor" was saluted in the early morning hours with "bonfires, skyrockets and a din of fishhorns and steam whistles," prior to the climactic pageant organized by the Central Labor Union. Twenty thousand men and women, to the music of bands playing "The Marseillaise," marched past the reviewing stand on Union Square, "where Henry George and leading men of the labor movement were gathered together." The various trades demonstrated their skills from atop a series of horse-drawn floats, including one on which "a squad of bricklayers built a chimney and stopped to drink beer out of a 'growler,'" the *Tribune* of the 6th recalls.

At a less dramatic moment, Richard Harding Davis—who was charged with the Broadway chapter in *The Great Streets Of The World* (1892)—paused at what he called the "second break" in the pathway which "means so many different things to so many different people." Union Square, he found in the day so very much his, a "gayer and more metropolitan pleasure-ground" than City Hall Park, "much more popular, as one can see by the multitude of nurse-maids and children, and in the number and cared-for beauty of the plants and flowers, and in the general air of easy geniality of the park policemen. . . . Union Square is bounded

40

on the south by that famous strip of pavement known to New Yorkers . . . as the Rialto. This is the promenade of actors. . . . It is said it is possible to cast, in one morning, any one of Shakespeare's plays, to equip any number of farce companies, and to 'organize' three Uncle Tom's Cabin combinations . . . from this melancholy market of talent that ranges about the theatrical agencies and costumers' shops and bar-rooms of lower Union Square."

Byron, more heavily laden than the "Soldier of Fortune," followed a few years in his wake. The photograph on pages 42–43, selected partly because of its compositional value, just cuts out the Fourteenth Street side (deserted by the Thespians since the mid-nineties, in favor of the Herald Square stretch) as the camera swings in a north-easterly direction from Broadway, looking toward the Washington Statue's backdrop, now institutionally occupied by Klein's; then the purlieu of the Hotel Hungaria, the Union Square Bank, and, at the southeast corner of Fourth Avenue and Fifteenth Street, the Union Square Hotel (where Richard Canfield had served as night clerk in the 1870's, before he found more gamblesome ways of spending the dark hours). In the photograph on page 44, the moppetude dismissed by Richard Harding Davis with a single clause has been ousted by more potent factors, but it comes into its own in the Byron's-eye view of Madison Square (page 45) and by way of *The New York Herald* article of September 18, 1898. This feature admonished that a revolution in the baby carriage trade was brewing; that the *vieux-jeu*, Frenchified child conveyance "with its pillows, lace and satin, its flounced parasol and its ribbons" was about to be superseded by a restrained Anglicized variant in black (replacing the formerly preferred "baby tints") with a buggy-like top, needing "little more than shafts and a small horse in front to actually make it a miniature wagon." By 1900, *The New York Herald* of April 8th of that year pointed out that the up-to-the-minute perambulator had "little in common with the baby carriage of ten years ago," bringing the once costly antiquated version "within the reach of even quite poor people. . . . The aristocratic baby of to-day goes out for his or her baby airing in great state, and most picturesque are some of the scions of America's noble houses," in imitation of the "swell [Brewster-built, no doubt] turnout" of their seniors, even to miniature rubber tires, handles of silver plate or baser nickel, and springs. For the nautically minded mater "There is one style [with an adjustable awning] that looks like a boat." Some mothers, however, puristically favored "polished white wood, with gilt or gold trimmings." Popular with all classes was the push cart or go-cart, "In reality . . . a low chair with wheels and a high bar at the back to push it." Only the perennially fashionable wicker and rattan models retained the saucy parasols, "now made more often of dotted or plain swiss muslin and lace" than of the costly openwork of other days. In winter, tiny feet rested on a fur rug, and dimpled knees were protected by lap robes of pelts, while elaborately stitched flannel or woolen coverlets and matching pillows with "bands of ribbon across them painted by hand or embroidered" came out in benign weather. "Picturesqueness," so we are told, "reigns supreme in the costuming of the children. 'The smaller the child, the larger the hat,' seems to be the rule, and the little faces look very cunning under the overhanging brims of silk or satin or chiffon. As in the blankets, white is the prevailing color." The *Herald* expert in juvenility was particularly fascinated by one pampered poppet, facing, I warrant, an unfortunate future, since even at the malleable age of two or three, it was "apparently perfectly conscious of its fine appearance." This poor little victim of parental aberration was swathed in sealskin, and wore an ensemble of dark brown, with muff and collar of the same breed of marine carnivores, "and

Union Square, 1898

"Sun Dodgers," Union Square, 1898

a huge poke bonnet of brown velvet, with two brown ostrich tips and a cluster of tiny pink rosebuds at the side." The *Herald* proclaimed that "the fashions in [baby] carriages can be seen to best advantage" in Washington and Madison squares, up and down Park Avenue between Thirty-fourth Street and Forty-second, and latterly along Central Park West and East.

By 1907 some of these baby parade grounds were suffering from the blight of cities. *Leslie's Weekly* on November 7 captioned a view of Union Square (preempted by what O. Henry called "Bed Liners" in discouraged benchdom) with the caption "Central Recreation Space In A District Containing Hundreds of Sweat-Shops And Other Factories," and earlier that

44

The Baby Carriage Trade in Madison Square, 1898

year (on April 7) *The New York Herald* ran an article on the "deplorable deterioration of the parks and squares of this city," commenting on "the riffraff of humanity" in Washington, Union, and Madison squares, as well as Central Park, "which has its full quota of . . . tramps these days. . . . Many a tract intended as an oasis where self-respecting working men or tired toilers might find rest . . . and women and children might go for outings and exercise, is now practically in the possession of the idle and the vicious . . . [and] the air is tainted by diseased and filthy vagrants who have almost driven away those for whom the parks were intended." Employing a designation he labelled the delight of sociologists, the writer suspired that these whilom peaceful preserves had lost caste as "breathing places."

" 'GOD BLESS Billy McGlory!' exclaimed a temperance orator last Sunday evening. 'God bless Billy McGlory! He has a great soul.' In the prayer-clause of this speech we all concur. We do not wish Billy McGlory to be damned, and we hope that God will bless him and everybody else." This from an editorial in the *New-York Daily Tribune* of February 5, 1884, which continues: "But the statement that the proprietor of Armory Hall has a great soul seems to have been made upon scanty evidence. There is no reason to think that he was in possession of that article when his place was pulled last week, or even up to the moment of his conviction; and if he has acquired it in the Tombs the transformation in his character must be one of the most marvellously rapid changes on record. . . . He insists that he has not been very bad. He has been anxious for some time to get away from the deadly traffic in 'table beer' and the society of young ladies accomplished in 'the high kick act'; but he has been entangled, as he declares, by capitalists and respectable members of society who would not let him reform. . . . Nobody questions the duty of Christian sympathy and help for the wicked who propose to reform; but the haste of some goody-goody people to begin coddling McGlory before he has exhibited any higher feeling than self-commiseration is silly and disgusting."

It is not my intention to coddle this fine gangster product of the Five Points, but I have chosen him as the center of my piece, foregoing the duller delights of enlarging upon other themes evoked by the deceptive innocence of the photograph on pages 48 and 49. The Byrons have given me every chance to discourse on the beginning supersession of the slow four-footed by the swift four-wheeled, since a large livery stable is near neighbor to a garage; I have been offered rich opportunity to tell of the Tin Woodman and Scarecrow fame of Montgomery and Stone, for even myopia could not overlook the poster promoting *The Wizard of Oz*, which attraction opened the nearby Majestic Theatre on January 20, 1903, ("Curtain Rises on A Kansas Cyclone 8 sharp," the newspaper advertisements insisted throughout the long run). The *New-York Daily Tribune Index* offers me many a reference to the "Grand Circle" traffic problems of the period. Certainly the seventy-five-foot Columbus Monument, unveiled on October 12, 1892, should be good for pithy paragraphs about the days when Gaetano Russo's work was not dwarfed by the New York Coliseum that erased this segment of Fifty-ninth Street from the city maps in the late spring of 1954. But no, I find fascination in Billy McGlory and his Armory Hall—the most disreputable of dance halls, peopled with pickpockets, pimps, panderers, homosexuals, men and women of the half-world—where soon the dubious delights of "elephant hunting" (as "slumming" came to be called while the Seventies blended into the Eighties) were fraught with danger. All this was at 158 Hester Street, remote from Byron's scene, but the distance is easily bridged by an article in the *New-York Daily Tribune* of November 17, 1899, headlined " 'Billy' M'Glory Bobs Up Again." We read on: "It is reported that the notorious 'Billy' McGlory, who for years kept one of the most infamous dives in the

46

city, is about to open a concert garden and dance hall in Fifty-ninth-st., between Central Park West and Columbus-ave., not far from the Church of the Paulist Fathers. 'The Paulist Fathers are opposed to this whole enterprise,' said the Rev. Father Alexander P. Doyle yesterday, 'and will fight it by every legal measure possible.' . . . The men connected with the Holy Name Society of St. Paul the Apostle's Parish, numbering 1,347, met on Sunday night last and resolved to enter a most emphatic protest with the Board of Police Commissioners." The offending building (its birthdate, 1899, pedimentally proclaimed) at Nos. 313–15 West 59th Street, is described in the *Tribune* of the 20th as "rather a pretentious one for a place of the kind, being built of white stone, three stories high, with stone balconies and balustrades on the second floor." The controversy went on, with invocation of the Raines Law (see page 400) and other statutes, but the news in the *Tribune* of January 4, 1900 was disheartening: " 'Billy' McGlory's new bar, ball and concert room . . . was open last night 'for inspection' only—that is to say, there was no performance on the stage, not even music. 'Billy's' friends and a few strangers who had heard of his new venture through the publicity given to it by the efforts of the Paulist Fathers to keep it from being licensed, visited the place from time to time in the evening, ordered a few drinks and went away. An air of suspense hung about the hall. 'Billy's' friends conversed in low tones, a policeman was stationed just outside the door. . . . In spite of this guarded way of opening the new hall, one unmistakable evidence was given of the kind of place it is intended to be if it is not suppressed. Though only open 'for inspection,' at least 25 per cent of the people present at 11 o'clock last night were women, unescorted, who sat drinking beer at the small tables."

Action was under way to revoke the license that had been issued to Frank J. Campbell (a nephew of the illustrious "Billy," evidently serving as a blind) and arrest followed, with August Ruck, the owner of the building, standing bail. Arraignment, parole, raids, police and court actions, and opening and shutting of doors, all enter into the interminable record. However, a passage in the *Tribune* of March 21, 1900 may be found amusing: " 'Billy' McGlory, in a coat of clerical cut [his favorite fashion] and with an air of injured innocence, went before the Grand Jury yesterday of his own volition, and told how harshly and unfairly his nephew . . . had been treated in being arrested and fined $100 for having music in his new saloon and hall . . . 'just because,' as he says, 'the Paulist Fathers are agin me nephew.' " On Tuesday, October 23, the *Tribune* told of another frustration: "Announcement was made in the Tenderloin and Bowery resorts recently that 'a ball would be given in McGlory's dance hall . . . on Monday evening. . . .' The carpets were removed and the floor was waxed, and other preparations made for the ball. Early last evening the crowd, headed by 'Joe' Burke [one-time conductor of "The Idle Hour," a resort at No. 161 Bowery], wearing a silk hat, began to arrive. They were met by McGlory. An attempt was made to light the gas, and it was found that the gas company had neglected to turn it on . . . [alleging] that a former bill had not been paid. . . . At 11 o'clock the band was dismissed and the people told that there would be no ball. . . . McGlory has been seen near the hall quite frequently of late. When asked last night concerning the story that the place was to be turned into a church McGlory said: 'A guy came to me and said he wanted to run it as a church, but if there's any graft in this thing, I want it.' " A sequel to this news appeared in the *Tribune* of December 31, 1900: "Evangelical services [instituted by S. H. Pratt, who had been conducting tent meetings in the neighborhood] were held yesterday in the building . . . which the notorious 'Billy'

West Fifty-ninth Street, 1903
North side, between Ninth Avenue
and Columbus Circle, looking east
(Part of the site now occupied by
the New York Coliseum)

McGlory erected for a concert hall. . . . Rev. R. S. MacArthur, of Calvary Baptist Church . . . said that it was delightful to think that a building that had been used for such purposes should finally be used for the worship of God and the reclamation of sinners. He hoped that McGlory himself would attend one of the meetings, and if he did he would probably have glory in his heart and soul as well as in his name." The *Tribune* of October 23, 1901 announced that the structure had been secured for "undenominational" religious services; but on December 1, 1902, it stated that a Boston theatrical manager, intent on launching "a high class vaudeville show" in the newsworthy edifice, had abandoned the project because of the renewed opposition of the Paulist Fathers.

And this brings us close to the moment at which Byron brought his heavy equipment to bear on this apparently pacific street; and also to an incident reported in the *Tribune* of June 1, 1903 proving that the central figure in this lurid tale had moments of minor nobility: " 'Billy' McGlory, the reputed proprietor of the saloon at No. 2,451 Third-ave., was arraigned in Morrisania court yesterday, charged with selling liquor without a license, and held for examination. At the Harlem prison McGlory found a young man . . . bemoaning the fact that he had only $2 and would have to be locked up in default of a $3 fine . . . imposed for intoxication [due to understandable grief, as he had come to New York to bury his mother]. . . . McGlory offered to pay the fine, but Adams would take only a dollar to add to his two. . . . 'I'll send it back to you,' said Adams. 'Well, if you do,' answered McGlory, 'I'll get drunk, because it will be the first dollar that ever came back to me.' "

. . . . Avenue to the Gods

"THE TIFFANY house in Madison Avenue is the one that pleased me most in America," said Edmund Gosse, in an interview recorded in *The Critic* (January 24, 1885). "I think it the most beautiful modern domestic building I have almost ever seen." He felt about it "a sort of vastness, as if it had grown like a mountain."

Commissioned, but by obstinate choice never occupied by Charles Lewis Tiffany (whose stationery and notion store—with sales aggregating $4.98 during its first three business days in 1837—burgeoned into a name synonymic with jewelry), this Romanesque apartment mansion bore the impress of McKim, Mead & White. Stanford White brought to it the benefit of his recent training under H. H. Richardson, and out of his collaboration with his patron's artist son, Louis Comfort Tiffany (designer of the roof with its two superimposed stories and decorator of the whole) evolved the inspired originality of this house, superb in its many improvisations, its ornamental use of terra cotta, and the long, narrow bricks of the upper floors, with their soft, broken color gradations in light brown and muted yellow. This "realization of an architect's dream," as Gosse called it, was completed in 1884, its portcullised entrance facing the white frame simplicity of the Lenox farmhouse, sole occupant of the block to the immediate south, with the Hunt-designed Presbyterian Hospital at Seventy-first Street and the notable Marquand home just below, at Sixty-eighth. Madison soon became second only to Fifth as a residential thoroughfare, and was also termed "the Avenue to the Gods,"

The Tiffany House, about 1900
27 East Seventy-second Street
At the northwest corner of Madison Avenue

because of the splendid ecclesiastical edifices dotting its length, including the pink Milford stone St. James' Lutheran Church with its brownstone trim and Tiffany Company interior, erected at the southwest corner of Seventy-third Street in 1890. The Tiffany house, passing into the ownership of Lewis Cass Ledyard about 1895, continued to shelter, among others, its original family (overlapping into the connecting No. 898 Madison Avenue) until the death of Louis C. Tiffany three years prior to the demolition of its exotic unreality in 1936.

The other-worldly beauty that was the vast studio interior of the four central fireplaces has been distilled by Charles de Kay (his anonymity betrayed by the careful penciling of Rodman Gilder on the title pages of several copies of that extravagantly exquisite monograph, *The Art Work of Louis C. Tiffany*, written for and at the request of his children and published by Doubleday, Page & Company in 1914 for "private distribution" to a favored five hundred and two). "As one enters the studio the vestibule is like a bit from the palace of an Indian Rajah. . . . Entering thence the lofty high-peaked studio, one sees lamps of Japanese bronze and unique favrile glass"—Mr. Tiffany's most widely known *Art Nouveau* creativity—"suspended from on high, each adding a new note of color or quaint shape. Great windows of dull greenish-yellow glass in the sloping roof give a general tone by daylight. . . . Colored tiles and the cinnabar red so much loved by the Japanese, iridescent glass and shelves full of keramics in subdued tones meet the eye in every direction. . . . At night the glow from the hearths round the central stack [a shaft earlier described as "easy of line as the bole of a great tree"] lights up the brightest of the vases and bowls and plaques, gleams with dull rich notes on copper and bronze and throws broad spaces of the irregular apartment into deep shadow. The suspended lamps of many shades of red, rose, yellow and creamy white are foiled against the blackness of the high roof-ceiling. If at that moment a skilled hand touches the keys of the organ the great studio merges into fairy-land."

The rest of this "house of many mansions," all on different planes and levels, was in accord with the ramifications of its creator's enveloping genius, for Louis Comfort Tiffany was a painter, an inventive master of glass and stained glass, a designer of jewelry, of enamels, of textiles, of rugs, of interiors; an architect in landscapes and in beauty, a fashioner of tastes— a man who, while so much of and ahead of his time, would have been at home in the days of the Medici.

. . . . *A multiplication table of elegant adaptabilities*

"MADISON SQUARE was then at the parting of the ways; had a double personality, half commercial, half social, with shops to the south and residences on the north," in the newborn 1900's, when the young narrator of Willa Cather's *My Mortal Enemy* (New York, 1926) saw the city for the first time, in provincial wonderment. "It seemed to me so neat, after the raggedness of our Western cities; so protected by good manners and courtesy—like an open-air drawing-room. . . . The snow fell lightly all the afternoon, and friendly old men with brooms kept sweeping the paths. . . . The trees and shrubbery seemed well-groomed and sociable, like pleasant people. The snow lay in clinging folds on the bushes, and outlined every twig of every tree—a line of white upon a line of black. . . . I lingered long by the intermittent fountain. Its rhythmical splash was like the voice of the place. It rose and fell like something taking deep, happy breaths; and the sound was musical, seemed to come from the throat of spring. . . . Here, I felt, winter brought no desolation; it was tamed, like a polar bear led on a leash by a beautiful lady."

The Byron tripod was set up after a later snowfall had lightly dusted the Square (see pages 54–55). With an incidental glance at the statue of Roscoe P. Conkling by J. Q. A. Ward, N.A., presented to the City in 1893, and the drinking fountain (the 1880 work of W. W. Smith, commissioned by Miss Olivia Egleston Phelps Stokes, and standing until February, 1957, with its two basins for horses and one for less polydipsic mortals) the eye follows the camera to the Metropolitan Life Building, at One Madison Avenue. Early outgrowing the original structure erected in 1890–1893 from designs by N. LeBrun and Sons, the insurance company had already launched the seventh of thirteen building operations and physical expansions at the time of this recorded instant, which exposes the site just vacated by the first Madison Square Presbyterian Church, at the southeast corner of Madison Avenue and Twenty-fourth Street. From here was about to spring the famous Metropolitan Life Tower, begun in 1906 and completed three years later. The lens, lacking prescience, could not envision the steps that led to the ninth addition—the D. Everett Waid replacement (1919–1921) of Dr. Parkhurst's second pulpit on the Square (to be described in the next paragraph) or the subsequent changes involved in the development of the great Home Office plant.

Stanford White's masterpiece and swan song was happily completed in 1906—just before his assassination within sight of the lantern of the green-tiled dome surmounting its yellow brick beauty, accented by cornices of his favorite colored terra cotta, with green granite columns supporting the H. Siddons Mowbray pediment modeled by A. A. Weinman. All this unorthodoxy—"in the manner of the early Christians," the architect said—was severely criticized at the time, but John Jay Chapman, writing in *Vanity Fair*, September, 1919, expressed elegiac admiration at the period of its passing: "It was like a Byzantine jewel. . . . It was a little princess of a building." Fortunately, the gemlike whole—which "brought you to a full stop of admiration"—has been twice reproduced in California and West Virginia, and segments of the beauty are corporate in the home built by Donn Barber for the *Hartford Times,* as well as in The Brooklyn Museum and The Metropolitan Museum of Art.

Beyond, still standing at the northeast corner of Twenty-fifth Street, indistinctly seen against the overshadowing Madison Square Apartments, is the Appellate Division of the Supreme Court, which—as revealed in *The New York Herald* on March 12, 1899—was "rapidly nearing completion. . . . Mr. James Brown Lord is the architect, and American sculptors and mural painters are enjoying the first great opportunity ever offered to the allied arts by the municipality of New York. . . ." Among the sculptural talents recruited were Charles H. Niehaus, F. W. Ruckstuhl, Thomas Shields Clarke, Maximilian M. Schwarzott and a decemvirate (George Bissel, J. Scott Hartley, E. C. Potter, Herbert Adams, Augustus Lukeman, Charles A. Lopez, John Donoghue, Philip Martiny, H. K. Bush-Brown and William Couper) responsible for the "ten 'decorative architectural' figures," which, supplementing "The two principal groups, that of 'Justice,' by Daniel C. French, and 'Peace' by Carl [sic] Bitter . . . will serve to break the sky line of the building. . . ." The ten painters engaged in the mural decorations (Edward Simmons, E. H. Blashfield, H. O. Walker, Kenyon Cox, Alfred Q. Collins, Joseph Lauber, H. Siddons Mowbray, Robert Reid, Willard L. Metcalf, and C. Y.

Madison Square, about 1907
Looking northeast from Twenty-third Street

Outside Madison Square Garden during the Horse Show,
1899
Looking north on Fourth Avenue from Twenty-sixth Street

Turner) "formed themselves into an association, accepting Mr. John LaFarge as adviser and arbiter of all professional differences."

The hidden mansarded mansion, on the southeast corner of Twenty-sixth Street, built in 1859 by J. B. Snook, while least significant of the early twentieth century physiognomical aspects of the locale, had the greatest influence on the chronology of our times, for here Jennie Jerome, the mother of Winston Churchill, spent two childhood years (1865–1867).

The transcendent glory of a plaza which in all equity should be renamed in honor of Stanford White—its genius in architecture—was his Madison Square Garden of many uses, a multiplication table of elegant adaptabilities and gaieties. The great amphitheatre, which opened on June 16, 1890, "with its tremendous concourse of spectacles made a magnificent picture," according to the *New-York Daily Tribune* of the 17th. "There is something tremendously imposing in its vast dimensions, and . . . something exceedingly agreeable in the excellence of its proportions and the impression of combined strength and gracefulness in its constructive details." Entertainments and presentations and exhibitions of all kinds exceeded each other in spectacular—if sometimes financially unsuccessful—frenzy, noteworthy among them the perennial equine pageant so favored and flavored and savored by Society that Charles Dana Gibson pointed his finger at it twice in a single "Sporting Number" of *Life* (November 18, 1897). The double-page spread "Wild Enthusiasm At The Horse Show During A Critical Event In The Ring" deals with a handsome girl cheerfully enduring worship, while the other drawing shows a silent beauty with a sheaf of roses, to the left of a short, fat, stocky man and an elegantly elongated companion engaged in conversation: "Will you make an exhibit at the horse show?" "My daughter is going." An earlier version, in the issue of November 16, 1893—"How The Animals Appear From The Boxes"—depicted the arena swarming with "brave men and fair women."

The New-York Times of September 28, 1890, declared that "no fault can be rationally found" with the Garden Theatre, which had opened the previous evening with "The Laughing Success Of The London Season," *Doctor Bill,* by Hamilton Aide, starring Wilton Lackaye without too much initial success. As for the interior of the new house: "The tone of the decorations is delightfully refreshing to the eye. The striped silk hangings and the pure white of the pillars, proscenium arch, and ceiling, which is relieved by cream color and gilding, do not produce a dazzling effect, but are continuously agreeable and restful. . . . The lighting arrangements are excellent. . . . The painted act drop, [a reproduction of Boldini's *The Park at Versailles*] by Mr. [Henry E.] Hoyt, is much better than such works of art generally are." Byron's photograph (see page 59) of the arcaded exterior was taken some time during the five prosperous weeks between April 25 and May 21, 1898, when Richard Mansfield was playing in *The First Violin,* which (under pseudonym of Meridan Phelps) he had dramatized from Jessie Fothergill's tenderly romantic novel, with the aid of J. I. C. Clarke.

On November 2, 1891, the Giralda-like Tower (see pages 54–55) opened. At ten o'clock that evening, according to *The New York Herald* of the next day, "a succession of explosions outdoors announced the beginning of the fireworks. From then on till eleven Diana of the Tower was in a blaze of glory, and a huge crowd of people in adjoining streets enjoyed the charming effects of different colored lights on the perfect architecture." After it was over, Stanford White met "the chrysanthemite," Adolf Ladenburg, organizer of the Autumn Flower Show, which began its Madison Square Garden run concurrently. "White was grimy and hot, having been

. . . directing the pyrotechnics about his girl. Ladenburg was dapper and cool, having been coaching his Japanese girls" (costumed beauties borrowed from behind local retail trade counters). " 'Well, Ladenburg,' says White, 'mine had more brass than yours.' 'That's all right,' was the quick reply, 'but mine were better Japanned.' "

A hyalescently veiled description of a festive evening in the architect's alpestrine apartment appears in Anna (Mrs. Reginald) de Koven's novel, *A Sawdust Doll* (Chicago, 1895), later validated in *A Musician and His Wife* (New York, 1926): "Mr. White . . . often gave parties in his rooms in the tower of the Madison Square Garden. To one of these we were invited [in 1895]. A crescent table was covered with old golden damask and spread with orchids, lights twinkled in surrounding bay trees, a mandolin band shed music like a sprinkling fountain, and about the table were women as lovely and varied in type as he ever assembled."

Eleven years later and a few stories lower, on the night of June 25, 1906, three shots from Harry K. Thaw's revolver rapped out to the comedy music of *Mamzelle Champagne,* and Stanford White lay dead on the Garden's Roof.

Far removed from the tabloidal melodrama of the "unwritten law," and the defense's plea of insanity, a huntress all in gold veered with the winds. "The tower is surmounted with a statue, in whose outlines I recognize the Diana of . . . St. Gaudens," wrote Paul Bourget at the time of his August, 1893, arrival. "The slender figure of the goddess stands out finely against the blue sky. It is the first evidence of beauty that I have seen since I set foot outside of the ship." In *The Reminiscences of Augustus Saint-Gaudens* (New York, 1913) the editor, Homer Saint-Gaudens, tells that this inspiration of his father's "was purely a labor of love. Stanford White originally suggested that . . . he consent to give his work upon it, provided White pay the expenses; and Saint-Gaudens eagerly grasped the opportunity since . . . all his life he was anxious to create ideal figures, with scarcely an occasion to gratify his desires, this indeed being the only nude he ever completed. Unwittingly, however, the two men drew upon themselves a more expensive effort than they were prepared to bear. The Diana was first modeled eighteen feet high, according to White's estimate, and finished in hammered sheet copper, only to be found too large when hoisted into place." So—the primogenous daughter having been driven into Chicago exile, for appearance at the World's Fair there— "both sculptor and architect were forced to empty their pocket-books" to substitute a figure thirteen feet high. Since 1932 (seven years after the razing of the Madison Square Garden) the second Diana has stood, like a latter-day Victory bereft of wings, in the Philadelphia Museum of Art. The "gold Diana" that Willa Cather's young narrator saw "against a green-blue sky" or as she "stepped out freely and fearlessly into the grey air" was a controversial goddess: Price Collier wrote in *America And The Americans* (New York, 1897) that this undraped vision "caused much criticism on the score of its indecency; and yet at several of the public balls, one of which I attended for an hour or two, women appeared in costumes, and behaved in a manner, that made my youthful memories of the Mabille seem sombre and saltless."

There was a Diana incarnadine—Julia ("Dudie") Baird, according to *The New York Herald* of November 21, 1897, "one of the striking figures" of the Sherwood (that artists' Bohemia at

The Garden Theatre, Spring of 1898
Southeast corner of Madison Avenue and Twenty-seventh Street

58

58 West Fifty-seventh Street), "a favorite model" whose fair face and form appears in lovely repetition in the works of such painters as Edwin Austin Abbey, T. W. Dewing, Kenyon Cox, Robert Reid, Edward Simmons, and Edwin H. Blashfield. "The thrones that I haven't sat on," she told in an interview published in the *Herald* on December 5, 1897, "are so few that you could count them on your fingers. For a person who is not royalty I have reigned on more than probably any other woman in this land. . . . I suppose there are about one hundred artists' models in this city. . . . A model receives fifty cents an hour, or $3 for a day of six hours. No model gets a cent more from a serious worker. . . . There are a lot of society fellows in town who like to pose as artists, whose 'studios' are usually gorgeously appointed, but whose paintings are enough to make Rome howl. Now these 'duffers,' as we call them, may pay models $10 a day, but it's the kind of engagement which means 'come any old time,' and a case of luncheon or supper." Miss Baird scorned such assignments, as well as offers from art schools ("I don't care to pose at wholesale"), from women artists ("they are less considerate . . . than men"), and from the ungifted. "I think I can say that I have engaged myself . . . only to the very best in this country. There is a certain amount of reciprocal art feeling between painter and model, and I don't think there is any doubt that a good model will deteriorate if she poses too often for a mediocre painter." Of the goddess atop the Tower she said: "To hear other models talk you'd think that the originals of the 'Diana' were as plenty [*sic*] as huckleberries, but, as a matter of fact, I am the only model who posed for Mr. St. Gaudens [for that particular work]. I'm the 'Diana of the Garden' in more senses than one, for the figure . . . was modelled from a plaster cast which was actually taken from my figure. The plaster was put around me as I posed. B-r-r! I can feel it now. It was so cold at first it made me shiver. For the first Diana I simply posed, just as I would for a painter, and Mr. St. Gaudens made a small model from my figure. This model was then sent to the foundry and enlarged to the requisite size. . . . But for the second Diana the modelling was very different. It took six workmen three-quarters of a day to get the plaster cast of my figure. Of course, you mustn't think that I was plastered all over at once. . . . I was, so to speak, cast in sections. . . . Remember that the Diana is poised on the toes of one foot. The other leg is extended backward. Now, of course, it would have been impossible for me to stand on the toes of one foot all day long. I probably couldn't have done it for five minutes. . . . To meet this difficulty Mr. St. Gaudens had two ladders placed in such a position that I could be propped up on them. To begin with, I at once took the full pose— arms in position, just as if I was going to send the arrow whizzing from its bow, the toes of one foot lightly touching the floor, the other leg extending back. . . . The slight bit of drapery which in the finished statue you see floating gracefully back from the figure . . . Mr. St. Gaudens must have modelled . . . afterward." And "in getting the 'torse' ["the hang of it"] on this occasion I at the same time propped myself up on the ladder by running my arms over two of the rungs. . . . It was a ticklish moment, in more senses than one. . . . I didn't dare move, for the slightest motion would have spoiled the mould. I suppose it required from four to five minutes . . . for . . . [the plaster] to set. Then they cut it with a thread and took off the mould in two sections. In this way they went over my entire figure, section by section, and the cast [5′6″, the model's height] was sent to the foundry to be enlarged . . . to its present size—thirteen feet. . . . Did I object to posing for Mr. St. Gaudens for the 'Diana of the Garden?' Not at all. I have often posed for artists in the 'toot and scramble,' if you choose to call it that."

60

. . . . *Hackman's poorhouse*

"The 'Hackman's Poorhouse,' that portion of Sixth avenue and Broadway between Thirty-second and Thirty-third streets known [since 1894] as Greeley square, is carrying a heavy hoodoo, according to the 'cabbies' who take their station there and wait all day for the elusive 'call.'" This made Sunday reading in *The New York Herald* of November 13, 1898. "The difference between the 'Hackman's Poorhouse' at noon time and at midnight is the difference between day and night. Dressed in yellow top coats and shiny silk hat, the cabmen of the day, with their spick and span hansom cabs, are the 'real thing,' but at night . . . the polite coachman of the afternoon is succeeded by the real Tenderloin 'night hawk' watching for his prey. It is at night that the 'Night Hawk's Poorhouse' is most often spoken of under that name, for when the Poorhouse Quartet assembles at the foot of the 'L' station and raises its combination of voices to the midnight air hard luck is stamped upon every face. The gaudy top coat and silk hat of the hansom cab driver are succeeded by the shabby old coat, slouch hat and ancient shawl of the night hawk, and fares to them are few and far between [and often high in alcohol content and low in funds]. . . . 'Sure, the name was given to the place by "Poorhouse Bill" when he used to hack around here,' said a cabby late last night. 'He was always in hard luck. . . . He called the place "Hackman's Poorhouse," and the name has clung to it ever since, although Bill went to Potter's Field many years ago. It is a poor house, anyway, and there is little but scrapings to be picked up now, although years ago it was a good stand.'"

Wilbur F. Fauley, writing on "Types of People in Greater New York" in *The Illustrated American* December 25, 1897, describes these landlubbing Charons: "The cabmen . . . are a type to themselves. We see them everywhere; no matter how early in the morning or how late at night, they are to be seen, hugging a favorite street curbing or darting hither and thither among the labyrinth of cable cars, vehicles and people. Their hours for sleep are few and far between. . . . They are always characterized by a brilliant red nose and cheeks, but as to whether the coloring comes from within or without we have our suspicions. That they have souls above the whip we can surmise by the occasional glimpses we catch of them, piloting visitors to the metropolis with the diplomacy of a European guide." One of their number, all rubefaction and undoubtedly possessed of a spirit behind the lash, posed for George Luks in 1921, and earned the immortality of great canvas for his today all but vanished breed.

"Poorhouse Bill's" confrères and their patient nags were evidently inured to pandemonium, for William Dean Howells, in "New York Streets," (the grandly final essay in his *Impressions and Experiences*, 1896) brings the quick hand to the tortured ear: ". . . no experience of noise can enable you to conceive of the furious din that bursts upon the sense, when at some corner two cars encounter on the parallel tracks below, while two trains roar and shriek and hiss on the rails overhead, and a turmoil of rattling express wagons, heavy drays and trucks, and carts, hacks, carriages and huge vans rolls itself between and beneath the prime agents of the uproar. . . . The noise is not only deafening, it is bewildering. . . ." He grants, how-

61

Greeley Square, 1898

Cabby at Battery Park (South Ferry Station of the El),
about 1895

ever, that "The ["El"] stations, though they have the prevailing effect of over-use, and look dirty and unkempt, are rather pretty in themselves; and you reach them, at frequent intervals, by flights of not ungraceful iron steps." This archeological beauty was wasted on *The Illustrated American* of May 16, 1896, which saw only that the accesses to the higher locomotion were "sickening with expectorations. A lady's skirt cannot touch those boards without gathering a harvest of bacilli. The eye is not able to find a square yard free from the hideous excrement, and the nausea is sometimes unendurable. . . . It is not at all necessary to use a smooth floor or stairs for a spittoon—there is always a gutter." These overhead islands of alightment along the Sixth Avenue Elevated were designed by Jasper F. Cropsey of the Hudson River School, and in their pristinity were considered objects of utilitarian beauty. An article in *Frank Leslie's Illustrated Newspaper* of April 27, 1878, anticipated the opening on

64

June 5: "The depot pavilion . . . affords a pleasant promenade in front of the track for passengers. The general style . . . of the buildings, with their many gables, ventilators, finials, etc., might be properly classed as a modification of the Renaissance and Gothic styles . . . presenting somewhat the appearance of a Swiss villa. . . . The interior of both the ladies' and gentlemen's waiting-rooms are to be very tastefully furnished and finished throughout, in what is known as the Eastlake style of decoration."

Since the Greeley Square hackmen were experiencing hard times, it is doubtful that they were depositors in the Union Dime Savings Institution (in the left background of the photograph), although that bank—since its founding in 1859—has always cheerfully countenanced the small account. It had moved into this palace of white marble (its third home, designed by S. D. Hatch) the year after the century passed the three-quarter mark, there to remain until 1910.

Of later vintage is Alexander Doyle's heroic statue of Horace Greeley, presented to the City in 1890. "The Printer," as he was fondly known to his *Tribune* staff, is seated in solid bronze comfort, holding a copy of the newspaper that was his life.

It is hoped that cab fares were forthcoming from among the audiences of the Manhattan Theatre (on Gimbel's present site). There on September 3, 1898 had opened *La Tortue*— a "Farcical Comedy" of bedroom implications, including a "Disrobing Act," adapted by Joseph W. Herbert from the French of Leon Gandillot. Despite a two-year titillant run at the Théâtre des Nouveautés in Paris and current success in Berlin, the critic of *The New York Times* (of the 4th instant) commented on ". . . its lack of wit," of which he found it had "as little as a lamp dealer's catalogue."

. . . . The peace of Broadway in their arms

"ALL DAY each Broadway sidewalk to the north and south of Fulton Street is densely thronged; it is a hurrying, jostling neighborhood, for Fulton Street is the great artery leading to the chief ferry connecting Manhattan borough with that of Brooklyn, and a few feet farther Park Row joins Broadway and becomes the gangway to the East River Bridge. Traffic flows fast and in opposing tides. The passage of the street is perilous, for every class of vehicle known to a civilized city competes for headway here; the cable cars increase the confusion, and at intervals occur seemingly hopeless blockades. But the tall policeman of the Broadway squad, at the Fulton Street crossing, has become a master in the art of straightening out the tangle of cars and wagons, carriages, trucks and people." This passage appears in *The New Metropolis*, edited by E. Idell Zeisloft (New York, 1899). "A czar of New York is the man of the 'Broadway Squad' [organized in 1860, abolished in 1896, reactivated in 1898 and disbanded about 1905]. From Bowling Green to Forty-second Street, at every important corner—sometimes two and three at a corner—these men are placed, sixty-four in all. They must be at their posts from early morning until half past six at night. They are physical giants, each individual man. . . . These are the brave fellows the visitor to New York sees most frequently and most admires. They are the pick of the force, not only physically but mentally, for each man has daily to answer scores of questions and give unlimited advice. Their daily work is full of danger.

65

More than one of the 'Broadway Squad' has been maimed for life in a jam, or caught between two cable cars. Yet they have no fear. They hold the peace of Broadway in their arms."

On the north side of Fulton Street—where, according to one account, wheatfields are said to have flourished in the mid-eighteenth century, and in the memory of another "small houses of wood" were standing (both of which statements, according to I. N. Phelps Stokes, may be approximately correct)—is seen the vine-covered south wall of St. Paul's Chapel, today the sole ecclesiastical building of the Colonial period still extant on Manhattan Island. Erected by Trinity Parish, its foundation stone was laid on May 14, 1764, and its dedication took place on October 30, 1766. Its architect was Thomas McBean, a pupil of James Gibbs (the genius of London's St. Mary-le-Strand and St. Martin's-in-the-Fields). Here, on April 30, 1789, George Washington—"the soul, look, and figure of a hero united in him," as the Comte de Moustier, Plenipotentiary of France, wrote home—knelt in prayer following his inauguration. The steeple at the west end—where the grounds sloped to meet the Hudson River—dates from 1794. *The New-York Magazine; or, Literary Repository* of October, 1795 pronounced the church "the most elegant in the city . . . generally esteemed preferable to most of the kind in the United States."

On Wednesday November 9, 1831, Philip Hone, strolling along Broadway near his home at No. 235, noticed that "A Marble Obelisk 30 feet in Height and weighing 27 Tons has been brought from Westchester and now Incumbers the street opposite St Pauls church, in the Yard of which it is to be erected. . . . This monument to the memory of the eloquent and amiable Thomas Addis Emmet is to be paid for by his countrymen and other Citizens. I have not had an opportunity of seeing it, as it is boxed up, and secured with Iron clamps, but I fear it is not appropriate to its Location." Hewn out of a single block, designed by the eminent artist Charles C. Ingham and executed by the sculptor John Preece, the tall white shaft, with its profile likeness of "the old man eloquent" in bas-relief near the top, was "nearly or wholly completed" according to *The Evening Post* of December 24. A native of Cork, Thomas Addis Emmet (1764–1827), Doctor first of Medicine and then of Law, and national idol of Ireland, came to New York in 1804, was admitted to citizenship and the bar, achieved great distinction, and commanded great love. As the voluminous four-sided inscription on his cenotaph says in part: "An orator of the first order, clear, copious, fervid, Alike powerful To Kindle the imagination, Touch the affections, And sway the reason and the will; Simple in his tastes, Unassuming in his manners, Frank, generous, kind-hearted And honorable, His private life was beautiful, As his public course was Brilliant."

A Policeman of "The Broadway Squad"—"Directing a
Stranger." About 1898
Scene at Broadway and Fulton Street

Trucks on West Street, 1898
Along the waterfront, north from Hubert Street (Showing the
Pennsylvania Railroad and Star Union Line Piers at the left)

"A HEAVY dray laden with big boxes of drygoods has just tied itself up in a hopeless mess with an empty truck returning from taking a load of coffee to the freight warehouse at Chambers-st. . . . The curses and cries of the drivers filled the air, the horses brought their steel hoofs down on the pavements with resounding beats as they tried to answer the urgings of the drivers to loosen the load behind them from its predicament. . . . In a moment a long line of horses and drays was wedged in hopelessly, and one of those blockades had happened which every driver through the lower streets of the city dreads as he does the worst misfortune that can befall him." This impasse (no newer to the New York of the Nineties than is its mechanized analogue a problem of today and tomorrow) served the *New-York Daily Tribune* of December 20, 1896 as subject for a Sunday piece, under the headline "An Hour On A Truck," with an illustration captioned "A Daily Occurrence In West-St."—verbal and linear version of what Byron's camera caught.

This photograph merited full-page reproduction in E. Idell Zeisloft's abecedarium of New York, *The New Metropolis* (1899). His description of the marginal thoroughfare tempts quotation: "On the river side the street is occupied with the freight and ferry houses of the great railroad and steamship lines, which receive and discharge their cargoes and passengers here. This makes an enormous amount of trucking and cab trade. . . . The buildings on the east side . . . are storage and cold-storage warehouses and large commission houses, and on the sidewalks are frequent booths for the sale of refreshments . . . [giving] a human touch to the base of the warehouses, which, with closed iron shutters, otherwise look gloomy and forbidding. . . . This is a lucrative locality for 'Raines Law' hotels which cater to the longshoremen and other workers on the docks. The large crowds of loungers noticeable on South Street . . . are missing here, because odd jobs are not usual, most freight being handled by regular employees of the different lines. Miscellaneous shipping is also absent, for the piers are owned and protected by the large companies which monopolize them. Much of the wholesale selling of the commission houses is done on the piers."

While we have been orienting ourselves, the *Tribune* reporter has accepted an invitation from one of the truck drivers heading for this milieu, "a jolly sort of a fellow, with a rotund figure and a face which spoke for . . . good nature and amiability," who hailed him: "Want a ride, did you say? All right; jump on." So they shared deceleration as "the truck joined in the procession of other trucks, loaded and unloaded, which were taking their way toward the western part of the city. As the truck turned into Duane-st. the noise of the traffic became almost deafening; emphatically so as the load approached Greenwich-st., where the roar . . . on the elevated road added to the din and confusion. In the mean time the jolly driver had been telling . . . that he was a public truckman [a breed lacking the prestige of the express wagon charioteer] and was helping out a large wholesale shoe house in getting a big shipment off. It seemed as if all the trucks and drays in the city had let themselves loose in the locality through which they were passing. By the time Washington-st. had been crossed

69

it certainly looked as if the limit of further progress had been reached. Here there was a wait of at least ten minutes while a load of waste paper bundles was separated from a coal cart with which it had linked itself as if for all time. . . . Then the way was cleared, and the procession moved on, reaching at last its destination, which was the Erie freight house at the foot of Chambers-st. The driver, although kept busy guiding his truck through the intricate situations which had made the journey one of excitement and interest, had found time to go into many detailed accounts of the life he led and the accidents which were constantly besetting him and his fellows. West-st. is conceded . . . to be the worst street in the city, especially at that point near Cortlandt-st. . . . Scudder—that was the friendly driver's name— was able to make this dangerous ground without delay, owing to the fact that he struck it at a lucky moment . . . but as he looked ahead he gave vent to a full yard of profanity, seeing the mass of wheels, boxes, whips, horses and drivers which stood before him. 'Look at that! I'll bet there are nearly two hundred of those fellows in there now, and I won't have to do a thing but wait for my turn.' . . . There were drygoods, hardware, candy, wool, rags, stoves, boxes and barrels containing nobody could tell what, tobacco, produce, bales and bundles without end. In that space there certainly must have been $500,000 worth of merchandise, all in charge of the waiting truckmen who were lying idly on top of their loads or standing near by discussing some topic of interest. . . . Meantime Scudder chattered on at a brisk rate. 'Some days we get along without a block, and then for two or three days at a time it seems as if we couldn't dodge 'em. All of these crosstown streets below Canal are bad.'" Speaking of the situation in the drygoods district around Worth and Thomas streets, he continued: ". . . and when them fellers get to rushing it there's always bound to be trouble. They pile on mighty big loads, and then their carts are as big as a whole house and lot, and it don't take more than one or two to block up a street in great shape. Hudson-st.'s a peach, and so is Greenwich and Washington. It's a kind of toss-up between 'em. Broadway? Oh, we don't go much for that. It's always too crowded with streetcars and carriages to please us, and then the police are too all-fired smart and think they own the earth. Besides, the cable-car gripmen run a man down every chance they get, and when it comes to investigating and finding out whose fault it is, why, it's always us; and there you are." And, at afternoon's end—for it sometimes took over six hours from warehouse to point of shipment and return, what with the costly blockages and line-ups and interminable turn-waiting at unloading platforms "under the glare of the electric lights"—Scudder bade his human freight farewell, with a cheery "Hello; I'm next!"

"WELL, I would rather be wet than gawky," declared Mrs. Walker Whiteside, who evidently shared a subcutaneous sorority with the lady Mr. Byron caught strolling down Broadway (see pages 72–73), one hand dedicated to raising her sodden skirt and ahead the tiresome prospect of soon replacing weather-worn "brush binding." Mrs. Whiteside had expressed her preference at the first meeting of the Rainy Day Club, held in the 146 West Twenty-third Street studio of Bertha Welby on the afternoon of November 5, 1896, during a cooperative squall. The *New-York Daily Tribune* of the next morning, covering this historic occasion, surveyed the situation: "The average woman abroad on business or pleasure bent was soaked to the knees. It was only a gown many inches from the ground, light of weight and without frill, that could see its wearer home fresh, dry and happy, and it was the object of the women of the Rainy Day Club to set the seal of their approval on such a costume and pledge themselves to adopt it. . . ." The hostess and secretary took the chair in the presidential absence of Mrs. Emma Beckwith, and placed the first question before the forty-odd charter members present: "Shall the club, in toto, adopt a skirt a given number of inches from the ground, or shall each woman use her own discretion in regulating her skirt, not making it less than five or more than eight inches from the ground?" In the impassioned debate that followed, Miss Emma Fielde favored as a minimum the maximum clearance proposed by the chair. An "exceedingly pretty" lady "in a moderately short gown" argued, "I don't believe in a woman wearing anything that makes her ridiculous," to which Miss Fielde made prompt retort: "A woman never looks so ridiculous as when her gowns are soaked and dripping with mud." And here Mrs. Whiteside made her Hobsonian choice. A majority vote favored "the 'sliding scale'" with a three-inch leeway, and the "rainy-day jacket" optional as well. Footwear was next on the agenda, Mrs. Harriet Hubbard Ayer holding for "strong leather shoes, lacing snugly to the knees." Mrs. Gertrude Andrews advocated the adoption of the common-sense attire for schoolgirls, and Mrs. Y. B. Merrill, taking a broader view, proposed "that the members of the Rainy Day Club should not be content with achieving their own well-being, but should do all in their power to induce saleswomen and factory women to join them and don the costume. The suggestion was received with applause, and the club members pledged themselves to wear the skirt and advocate its adoption by all women." *Experientia Docet* (Experience teaches)—with ignorant or purposive deletion of the conventional ending, "even fools"—was advanced as the adorning motto on the riband to which the club pin—in the shape of a furled silver umbrella—was to be fastened.

Miss Ida Van Cortlandt appeared at the December meeting in what the *New-York Daily Tribune* of the 3rd described as "rainy-day costume" at once ". . . graceful and artistic. It was made of dark-blue waterproof cloth, with a silk-lined skirt, high boots, silk knickerbockers lined with flannel, a short military jacket, braided, and accompanied by a round hat of the cloth, with pompons and quills at the left side."

Herald Square, about 1900

As it is obviously impossible for you to sit in on all the business and cultural meetings until 1918 (when the Club disappears from the city directories) we will eavesdrop occasionally through the courtesy of the *Tribune* of the day following each session mentioned (unless another source is cited).

On March 3, 1897, Miss Chapman of Montclair, New Jersey, read a most effective paper, "Clothes Are Our Friends or Our Foes," in which she urged: "I do not recommend the male attire, but let our dress be as wings and not as weights." The Reverend Phebe Hanaford then delivered a secular sermon, "All Hail to the Club, Though It Is Rainy." On May 5 recommendation was followed to appoint a delegate to the W.C.T.U., then in convention at the Broadway Tabernacle, and announcement was made that the 5th of August had been designated as "a Rainy Day Club day at the Point o' Woods, Chautauqua." On October 6, proselytizing vacationers "were pleased to report that much interest was shown, and that the fame of the 'Rainy Daisies' had gone abroad over the land." Mrs. Beckwith orated: "The day of the clinging vine has gone by, partly because of lack of strength in the strong oak, and partly on account of this very ambitious unrest. In fact, a recent philosopher has dubbed us the 'unquiet sex.' Considering all these things it was in the natural course that woman should grow dissatisfied with her clothing. . . . As her life broadened from the four walls and the three d's—dresses, diseases and domestics—she beheld the urgent necessity of a better use for her strength than carrying about so much clothing and cloth."

Helen C. Candee maintained in *The Illustrated American*, November 6, 1897, that in this respect "the general woman of the public is slow at throwing aside prejudice in favor of good sense. . . . In our unwritten prejudices, the ways of wealth are the ways we desire to exhibit in our daily conduct. Especially is this true of women, no one of whom likes to advertise herself before her sisters as being less well off than they. It is patent to all that the woman of wealth with her brougham at hand can dress the same on rainy days as on fair, and the woman of lesser means can call a cab and still retain her elegant sweep of skirts. Behold, then, how poor is she who can afford no means of transportation save her own energetic feet or a five-cent tram. Is she willing to advertise her impoverished condition by her shortened gown? . . . Fancy the relief to tired women if all skirts worn out of the house were shortened to six inches above the ground, and fancy the tons of bedraggled, germ-filled drygoods of which their delicate frames would be relieved."

Munsey's Magazine for March, 1898, stooping to an equivoke—"The Rain of Fashion"—was all admiration for the well tailored, stormproof, abbreviated skirt; found "the high boots, reaching presumably to the boundaries of remote bloomers" possessed of "rather a swashing, high spirited, attractive air"; and granted to "the heavy masculine gloves . . . an aspect of social knowingness." On the debit side, "The only thing one has to resent about . . . [the wearer] is the expression of her face. She has struck a good thing and she knows it, and the knowledge sits impertinently on her eyelids, nose, and chin. . . . Many who would heartily approve of the Rainy Day clothes are antagonized by the Rainy Day face, and fear to adopt the one lest the other should be an inevitable feature of the movement."

At the May 4, 1898 meeting, Mrs. A. M. Palmer, the president, appeared in a black cravenette effectuation of her own design. "The garment had eight pockets, which was the only immodest and mannish thing about it, the wearer stated." The chary Mrs. Jane Croly (Jennie June) apologetically justified her sartorial defection with the excuse that "she had not yet succeeded in getting rid of the clothes she always wore on rainy days, and could not get over the idea that it was 'awfully extravagant' to wear new clothes in rainy weather." By December, 153 members had been enrolled locally; clubs in other cities had long since followed the movement of the ground-scorning skirt in emancipated copycatination.

"Miss Dora Goldthwaite created something of a stir" on December 5, 1900, when she suggested a member's uniform "for evening wear . . . either black or white, with a bunch of violets at the corsage, which will combine the club colors." This formative notion was referred to committee, although one recalcitrant Daisy was heard to murmur: "I hope it will be more generally adopted than the rainy day skirt has been."

On October 6, 1901, *The New York Herald* injected a disturbing note: "It would seem as though the trim short skirt, so often to be seen on rainy days, would be out of the race this coming season among New York women; there is such a violent fancy shown for the rain coats that every one is buying one. A showerproof cravenette or a long, loose coat of rain-proof quality is the fashionable garment. . . . The straight back affairs seen last year are not to be worn at all." Alarm was premature, however, for on December 24, 1905, the Magazine Section of the *Herald* alluded to the club's following as "constantly augmented by fresh recruits to the belief of the members—'sanity in dress.'" On September 2 of the following year the same Sabbath supplement, complete with an illustration, urged "All the members of the Dolls' Sewing Circle" to get to work, as "Miss Dolly really needs a separate skirt for rainy days, so as to save her best skirts from getting soiled around the bottom and wearing out too soon."

But all this is by way of divarication and I make amend by providing for your attendance at the meeting of May 14, 1902, on the gala occasion of "a 'cocoon tea' that was to develop, it was announced, into a butterfly dance. Mere man came, as expected, in hordes, to see the Rainy Daisies emerge in airy butterfly costume. All their expectations, however, were blasted at one fell swoop. The Rainy Daisies resembled butterflies only in the brilliancy of their gowns, and the dance was seen upon the programme alone." Arrangements for a performance by children of members had been abortive, and a solitary professional was imported to redeem the day. However, there had been a sad oversight: "The Butterfly looked witheringly" at the promoters, "evidently thinking that even an unsophisticated Daisy might know that no right minded butterfly would dance without music. Then she folded her costume and silently stole away. . . . Behind a partition of screens, in the [Carnegie Hall] chapter room . . . were the four cocoons that gave name to the entertainment, and there several young women instructed undeveloped talent in the art of putting paint on cardboard in such a way as to suggest butterflies to a gifted imagination. Japanese napkins, deftly twisted into huge butterfly forms, dangled from strings attached to the ceiling, and gorgeous things of tinsel and crêpe paper were sold to the charitably inclined. The animated hum of conversation was likened by one poetic soul to the murmur of bees and leaves in the springtime."

THAT "THE messenger boy is travelling a very sorry road," was the conclusion reached by Miss Helen Marot, in charge of an "investigation of his life by the Child Labor Committee," as paraphrased in the *New-York Daily Tribune* of February 15, 1903. The young scholar at the right, however, seems to be surveying Mercury—at pause for refreshment in his flight—with envious admiration.

Gotham's courier service is described in *Appletons' Dictionary of New York And Its Vicinity* (in its twenty-fourth year when the edition quoted went to press in July, 1902): "There is a District Telegraph Company, which will place an instrument in your house contained in a miniature iron box, having a small crank on the outside. By means of this you can summon at will a policeman, a fireman with an extinguisher, and notify the Fire Department, or a boy-messenger in uniform, who will execute any commission you desire. The offices are never more than 5 minutes' walk from the point where the instrument is located. These instruments are to be found at the disposal of any person in the offices of all first-class hotels and restaurants, and are very convenient for the delivery of notes, invitations, circulars, the carrying of parcels or hand luggage, etc. The charge for messenger-service is based upon a standard rate of 30 cents per hour, but a tariff book is furnished . . . with each instrument. . . . An additional 5 cents is charged for bringing an answer to a note, and at the rate of 30 cents per hour for any detention of the messenger. There are also three or four companies known as 'City Dispatch Companies,' which deliver letters or circulars in quantities, as well as singly."

Some of these juvenile bearers of tidings—like the one here shown in a foot-weary moment— walked the uneven pavements; others rode gloriously on shining wheels. *Collier's Weekly* of May 25, 1901, extolled "The Bicycle Messenger Boy" as a sort of unsung paladin: "The visitor to New York—and, in fact, the citizen—gives but a passing thought to the gray-uniformed messenger who is to be seen at all hours . . . dodging a truck or cable-car here, an automobile or Victoria there, and taking his puny life in his hand at almost every corner with a degree of indifference to consequences which no competitor in a bicycle race ever felt. The bicycle mounted messenger boy of New York combines characteristics that should . . . win him distinction in after years—intrepidity and determination of character, honesty of purpose, physical bravery, and independence. . . . The idea of equipping its messenger boys with bicycles occurred first to the Postal Telegraph Company [a statement open to question]. . . . About the same time the A. D. T. service [American District-Telegraph Company, incorporated in 1873, and affiliated with Western Union the following year] was inaugurated, and these two great corporations to-day employ thousands of boys. . . . In the crowded sections of great cities, the wheel, for obvious reasons, is not employed in this service, but in the residential and suburban districts it has become almost invaluable. . . . It is a comparatively easy matter to cover a prescribed distance on a bicycle track in competition . . . but when the rider is called upon to cover miles upon miles of crowded city thoroughfares the mes-

Forty-second Street, looking west from near Fifth Avenue,
1901
During the construction of The New York Public Library

senger boy displays daily a degree of courage that the racing man is rarely called upon to exhibit. There is as keen a spirit of rivalry between these lads for honors in their calling as exists to-day among any class of public servants or officials. New York enjoys many and varied branches of public service, but every metropolitan citizen knows . . . that it is indebted to no class to a greater degree than the messenger boy of New York, particularly the boy who renders such service a-wheel."

A considerably less exemplificative specimen of dispatch bearer is revealed when "The calcium light of scientific investigation" was turned on the local Hermes in an effort to secure passage of legislation designed to "keep youngsters under fourteen years out of the checkered service"—in which, according to the *Tribune's* calculation, some "two or three thousand" children were employed in 1903. "The New-York messenger boy is just about what one makes him," reads the account. "In the first place, he is a boy—an intensely human boy, with the imp side of him a little accentuated, perhaps. His wits are sharpened by the constant brushing which the world gives him, and when it comes to morals—well, he is no Sunday school youngster. He is honest if one makes him so. . . . If he smokes cigarettes and drinks when he gets the chance he is doing what other boys of his station . . . are likely to do." Workers from twenty-three settlement houses made home visits and turned in case reports. Fred ———, for instance [whose mother complacently declared, "Oh, he don't care to go to school"], so loved his work that he was "at it regular from 8 a.m. to 7 p.m.," and—out of pure devotion—generally put in extra hours. This affection for his calling was not dictated by economic necessity, and his weekly wage of $4 plus tips and "overcharges" was spent according to the dictates of his fancy. James ———, at fourteen an old soldier backed by two years in the service, termed himself a "drifter," changing his headquarters frequently. "Some offices are much more desirable than others," the newspaper explains, "and a boy does not remain long in the business until he finds out the best paying. The offices are named according to the sort of work which predominates. For instance, the offices about Grand Central Station are known as 'express wagons,' because the boys have to 'tote' so much hand baggage. 'Tenderloin' offices are considered the 'snaps' in the service, because of the tips." Before being warned by one of his colleagues to "shut up," James volunteered that he had once spent a month in the Broadway and Thirty-second Street office. "Gee, but that's a warm one! Learned more there than I ever learned. You ought to get John to tell you when he was in the 'Tenderloin,' hey, fellows! He was night-clerk at the office, and he's got some warm ones." Another lad, "called to a house where a woman was entertaining two men and sent out for drinks . . . [which he was asked to serve] became frightened at their language and fled home in terror" at the end of an hour, to resign his commission in favor of work in a civil engineer's office and night school at Cooper Union, much to parental displeasure. His hyposensitive brother, " a veteran of 'the Tenderloin,' " returned to headquarters with $65 after answering a call from a female who dispatched him for a bottle of champagne, which they shared before touring the town in a cab, "having drinks and spending money like kings and queens." A Charles Dana Gibson drawing ("Going Home From The Theater," *The Century Magazine*, February, 1895) gives a gentler version, showing one of the fraternity serving as respectful escort to a timid lady. There were stories of gratuities withheld from family knowledge, but sometimes under compulsion divided with the office supervisor, himself often a graduate of this tough school. The turnover, according to the *Tribune*, was tremendous: "One company employing 1,000 boys at a time works through a list of 6,000 during a year." In most instances, the boy's own overstatement of his age—a chronic, pathetic fourteen—was accepted by the employer, and the law imposing an annual eighty days of school attendance slackly enforced. And the future? Some of the alumni became drivers of "night hawk," or "owl," cabs (see page 61); but, on the more roseate side, others learned telegraphy or found positions in brokerage houses.

One speculates about Byron's young lemonade stand patron, and wonders on what errand he is bound after quenching his thirst at this unsparkling source. *The New York Herald* of May 26, 1901, discourses on "The pushcart in its various phases" and the part it played in the lives of East Side children in particular, second only in entertainment value to such profitless pastimes as "the excitement of a fight or an arrest in one of the tenements," or the healthier "joyous diversion of a hand organ. . . . A puzzling circumstance to the outsider," the Sunday feature tells, "is that these forlorn, ragged, dirty, pasty complexioned, bony youngsters seem almost without exception to have an abundance of pocket money. As early as seven o'clock in the morning they are seen crowded around the hokey-pokey cart or the soda water stand. . . . Their only substitute for the necessities of life being the luxuries thereof, they welcome the pushcart. . . . From morning until night the children stuff themselves. Perhaps they do not all stuff, but to the observer they seem to live in a perpetual gingerbread fair. Where does the money come from? . . . Thriftless, but affectionate, is the lower class parent. Shoes the child must do without, for the father has not quite enough money to purchase them. But here is five cents to buy hokey-pokey. That much he can afford."

. . . . *A little music*

"THE STREET musician, with his heavy hand organ on his back, endures many a hardship. He is often driven away from a block by policemen, and servant girls insult him, and often while he looks up to the windows of a handsome house and grinds out 'America' or 'Annie Rooney' the butler comes out and gives him ten cents to play on the next block." A victim of this bribeful back-handed benevolence earned the sympathy of the author of an article on "Everyday Sights About The City," in which he introduced "An Organ Grinder With Feelings . . . [and] an Ear for Music as Well as a Pocket for Dimes" to the readers of *The New York Herald* of Sunday, March 29, 1896. "You might think this was what he wanted. It may be so in some cases, but the particular organ grinder of whom I write is not altogether pleased. Although the ten cents is a welcome acquisition to his funds, the fact remains that he has the true Italian love of music. To his taste the hand organ produces more beautiful sounds than are heard in the finest Wagnerian opera. When people drive him away from their houses he feels like returning to the sunny land where everything is music, love and poetry, macaroni and Chianti. But there are times when the organ grinder's life is happy. If he gets an encore he considers the place where the applause was sounded as the most beautiful spot in the city. Unfortunately, his audience at this time is not critical, the hand clappings and the pennies coming entirely from children. But the old organ grinder does not mind that. His music has been appreciated. He removes his hat, bows, his corrugated face breaks into a broad smile and he grinds out the notes of 'Annie Laurie' with the ache gone from every muscle in his body."

79

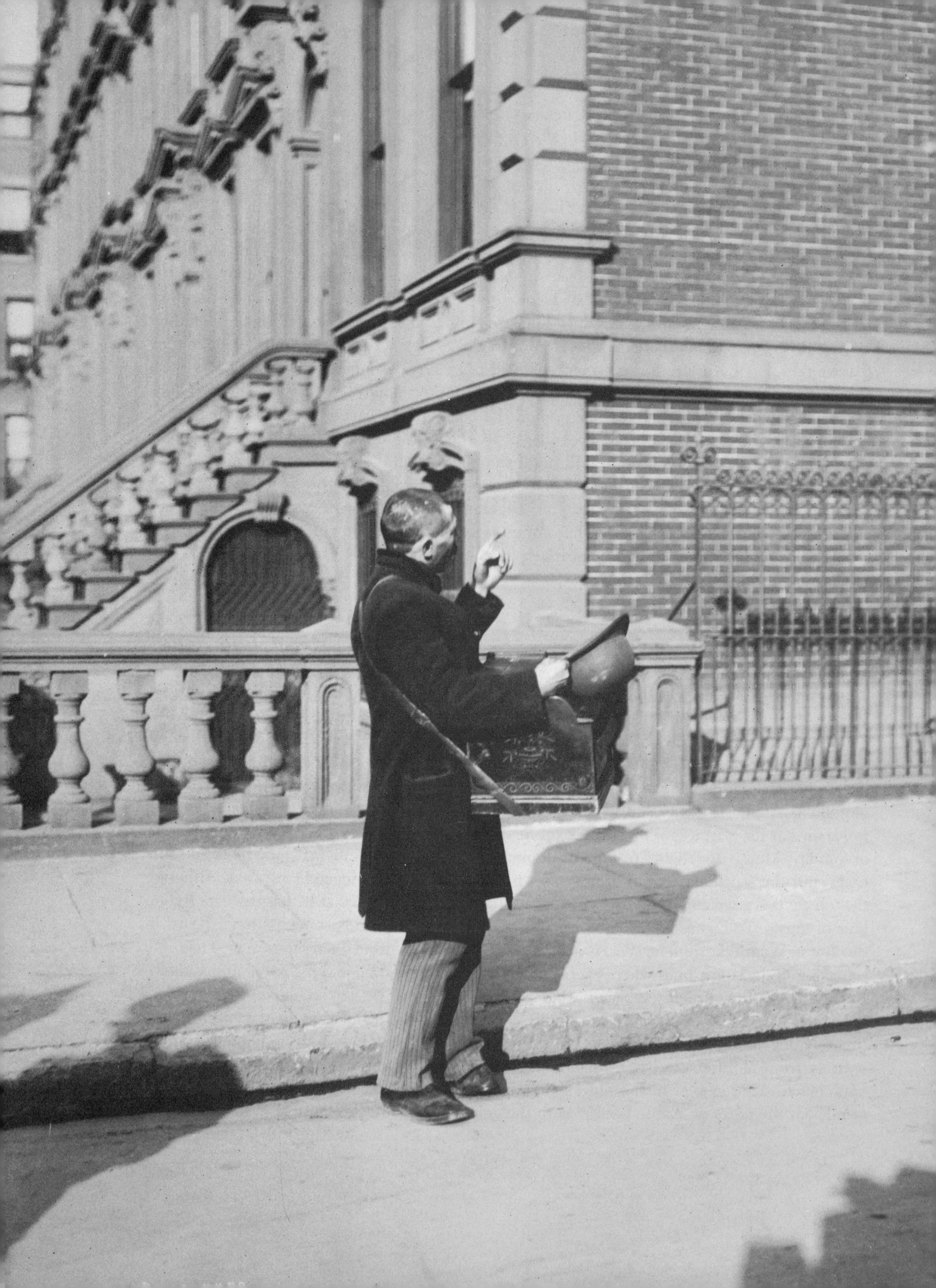

Back in 1856 (on July 24, to be exact) George Templeton Strong made fretful diary entry about "One of our civic scourges, an organ-grinder," and on April 26, 1879, *Harper's Weekly* found "The German bands . . . becoming a feature here . . . a great improvement on the Italian hand-organ." The nineteenth century weekly, *Time,* complained on November 16, 1889, of civic tyranny and unionization: "Municipal life would be dreary indeed without the reformers. In New York, wires spilling high-tension currents are strung over everybody's head, the pavements are so bad that driving resembles a penitental [*sic*] pilgrimage, . . . and the harbor is ornamented with fleets of garbage scows; but Mayor Grant, ever mindful of the interests of the Metropolis, has succeeded in clearing the streets of little German bands, Italian organ-grinders, hurdy-gurdy players and fugitive cornetists. The reason is not that a majority of the residents . . . want these players suppressed, for at least three fourths of the people approve them to such an extent that voluntary contributions makes [*sic*] the avocation of strolling minstrel profitable. In the poorer quarters of the city, particularly, these musicians serve a purpose as useful, if not quite so high as—let us say the Thomas Orchestra [of so many favored seasons]. . . . The players have been banished because they do not belong to the musical union. This is a free country, and its citizens are not going to be enthralled by pauper-made Italian and German music. It matters very little, if a large percentage of theater goers of the male sex have been driven to drink by the scraping, wheezing and pounding of members of musical unions between the acts; the musicians do their best and ought not to be shot. Possibly, if the public approved them as highly as it does the itinerant musician and saved its pennies for playhouse orchestras, the musical union would find better talent to translate into sound the written music in its possession." George J. Manson, in his *Harper's Weekly* series on "The 'Foreign Element' in New York City," wrote of vanishing pavement melody in the issue of October 18, 1890, "There are not one-third the number of organ-grinders that there were a few years ago," attributing the decline to legislation against the use of the soliciting costumed monkey and the rising demand for Italian laborers. "Organ grinding a few years ago was an industry of which the Italians had the monopoly. A certain organ maker on Chatham Square says that during the last twenty-seven years . . . he has supplied 5000 Italians with hand-organs . . . cost[ing] from $25 to $225, and the ordinary instrument is capable of inflicting eight tunes. Aside from that prejudiced class of persons to whom the hand-organ is never welcome, it may be said that a tune on this instrument remains popular with the public for six months." Of this phase of the industry, twenty-seven-year-old Theodore Dreiser (his sensational *Sister Carrie* two years short of publication) wrote in the *Metropolitan Magazine,* November, 1898: ". . . very few know of the important part played by the hand and street organ and by the phonograph in familiarizing the masses with the merits of a song. Nearly all the piano-organs so numerously dragged about the city are controlled by an Italian padrone, who leases them to immigrant Greeks and Italians at so much a day. This business is quite an extensive one, involving . . . hundreds of organs and organ grinders, a large repair shop, and a factory where the barrels, upon which the melodies are indicated by

Street scene, about 1898

81

steel pins, are prepared. . . . With the organ-master-general the up-to-date publisher is in close communication." The *New-York Tribune Illustrated Supplement* appears to have been late in unearthing a local monopoly, for on July 24, 1904, it reported an amazing discovery: "A trust is said to have invaded recently the mysterious realm of the organ grinder, and laid hands on his scanty coppers. Certain charity workers, bent on other investigations, the other day wandered into a rear tenement in Fifty-ninth-st., and suddenly they realized that they had traced the hand organ man to his habitat. From numberless tenement stories and endless rooms there suddenly emerged a vast swarm of grinders. Unterrified, the charity workers pursued their clew, and soon discovered that they had hit upon a distributing centre of a real hand organ trust, a corporation even more soulless than usual, and that every inhabitant of this rear tenement world was fast in its clutches. To be sure, others might regard this trust as a mere ramification of the padrone system, familiar wherever the Italian is found. . . . The two Savoyard brothers, who operate this hand organ trust, own hundreds of organs . . . and they employ Italians, who . . . turn over all but a pittance of their pennies for the rent of the organ. In this tenement they house their employees like cattle, feed them like animals, and regularly send them forth on various routes." In the poorer sections of these circuits, "as extensive and intertwining as those of a trunk system," the mendicant musicians turned the gray pavements into bright, open-air ballrooms for tenement waifs. In *The Illustrated American's* column "As Seen Through Women's Eyes," January 18, 1896, J. H. N. found reason for rejoicement: "I am glad to see that the superintendent of police has not thought it necessary to prohibit the street children from dancing to the strains of the perennial hand-organ. There is so little of pleasure that comes into their poor little lives that it would be cruel to begrudge them this—and the joyous grace with which many of them respond to the music as expressed by the wheezy street organs, indicates the something in them which has never before had the incentive to develop. I confess I often watch them with pleasure, but never without wondering why they should be considered 'indecent 'and 'objectionable' in their dancing." The cover of *Leslie's Weekly* for July 7, 1897 consisted of a Photo-Drawing by L. L. Roush, entitled "Sidewalk-Dancing In New York," over the following brief text: "The hand-organ musician is ubiquitous, but he flourishes in great numbers in the metropolis, where he delights or worries the people, according to their individual temperaments. The children in some parts of the town, notably where tenement-houses are most numerous, get great amusement to the music ground out by these unwashed sons of sunny Italy. What may be particularly observed any day is the grace with which these little girls take their steps and the great interest excited in the passers-by who stop to watch with smiling amusement these unconventional Terpsichorean feats. Only churls complain of the interruption of traffic." Among other artists who found a theme in this pattern of refugeful rhythm was Jerome Myers, the canvas bard of "The Children of the Poor," who memorialized these vanished steps in such paintings as his *Pursuit of Pleasure*, *The Tambourine* and *O Sole Mio*.

The street musician—often malapropishly called the "hurdy-gurdy" man—found his anonymous poetaster, too, in *The New York Herald*, December 24, 1905:

> "The organ grinder hustles on apace,
>   And upward gazes with a mute appeal,
>   For in his aching palm he longs to feel

The magic coin that never fails to chase
The wolf away with swiftness and with grace.
   And while he grinds the very latest reel,
   And sees the child awhirl on toe and heel,
The witching beauty of his glad grimace
Is like the scent of the anemone
   That 'broiders springtime's zephyr on the fly—
   It is so subtle that it makes elate
The spirit of his purple 'monk,' till he
   Soars swiftly coinward, with his cheering sigh:—
   'They always win that never stand and wait.' "

. . . . *Piquant sensuousness spicily wafted*

" 'ONLY VERY, very rarely,' explained a charming girl" (to the Editor of "Current Topics of Interest to Women," in *The Illustrated American*, June 27, 1891), " 'does one ever meet in this country either divan, or divan lounger with the vaguest knowledge of correct uses for that ideal piece of furniture. Broad, low, deeply and softly tufted, draped with a heavy rug of smooth surface and heaped with fluffy pillows, it is the apotheosis of physical comfortableness.' " It seems that this "widely travelled young beauty" had been indoctrinated at a soirée in Stamboul, when she "approached a great divan of glowing colors, and proceeded to seat herself. . . . Drawing her skirts primly about her, she sat gingerly upon the very edge, with two neat little toes carefully balanced to touch the floor." Her "beautifully handsome young Turco-Greek" escort lost his "Eastern dignity . . . in amusement; he laughed, and begged permission to give a few lessons in the art of using a couch. 'Sit on your foot' [a vulgar violation of Victorian postural etiquette], he commanded; 'curl it comfortably under you, so. Now be seated, far back, build a wall of cushions about your shoulders, and know true happiness.' "

One has but to read the files of *The Decorator and Furnisher* (New York, 1882–1898)— that "golden treasury" of the taste and tastelessness of two decades—to follow the fashionable *Drang nach Osten* that swept all before it. In April, 1884, for example, we learn from an article on "The New York Casino" (see page 245) that "The Moresque form of decoration has, of recent years, gained steadily in popularity. . . . Nor is the Moresque confined to public buildings. . . . Many private houses, dwellings, and clubs have made use of its eccentricities to ornament and adorn their interiors." In July, 1892, we gain uninvited admission to the "Finest Bachelor Apartment in this Country,"—that of Lewis G. Tewksbury, banker and connoisseur, in The Wilbraham, at Fifth Avenue and Thirtieth Street. There we behold "An Oriental Divan That Recalls The Fabled Splendors of The Arabian Nights. . . . The furnishings include Damascus tables, on which stand nargilehs and pots of incense, cigars, pipes, cigarettes, etc. Beside the door stands a life size nude statue in bronze of an Odalisque, holding in one arm a tray. . . . This odoriferous retreat is an epitome of all the languorous charms of the Orient. . . . It is an Aladdin's cave filled with costly treasures." In the November, 1893, issue James Thomson stated: "In every magazine and daily paper catering

Oriental room, decorated in
the late 1880's or early 1890's
and photographed in 1904

to the interests of womankind, we are confronted with schemes for the fitting up of cozy corners and odd nooks. It is a fad in furnishing that has certainly taken hold among the fair sex, and judging from present indications will show no diminution in the immediate future." The stores were willingly eager to give abetting aid—for instance (as relayed in the November, 1894, number): "The seven Oriental interiors illustrating Persian, Japanese, Indian, Chinese, Moorish and the high class Japanese curio room, recently constructed by Messrs. A. A. Vantine & Co. on the fifth floor of their [877–79] Broadway warehouse, are in themselves complete object lessons in the study of the home furnishings of the Oriental people. . . . In the Moorish room will be seen an illustration of almost any type of the ever graceful inlaid Damascus table, including a Cairene folding stand for supporting a brass tray, painted in the brightest of enamel colors. Five o'clock tea tables of Eastern production, support vases of chiseled brass and porcelain. The ceiling of the apartment is decorated with Moorish banners. . . . A considerable portion of the walls of the apartment are constructed of screens of Cairene lattice work, or are filled with Moorish cabinets filled with costly bric-a-brac. Divans are prevalent. The entrance contains the inevitable horse shoe arch of the Moors, on either side of which stand two enormous incense burners of repoussé brass work. This scheme of decoration is admirably suited to the requirements of a hall, den, or smoking room. . . . The great sense of rest [not to say dust] that impregnates Moorish belongings in particular is very grateful to our Western people, who are driven by steam in their daily life and must have a chamber specially furnished for wakeful rest." In January, 1894, Emma T. Kaye went at full blast: "The busy American, when he reaches home, weary with the rush and worry of commercial strife, naturally desires, most of all, to sink into a luxurious retreat, where, rested and soothed by soft carpets, upholstery, hangings and embroideries, illuminated with lamps and lit with the gleams of art metal work and porcelain, [he] can rest and refresh himself for the next day's battle. With regard to decorative furnishings, the question arises: Do we receive most value for our money in surrounding ourselves with orthodox furnishings of Western manufacture? Does the Italian Renaissance and French styles of the eighteenth century, the starveling Chippendale and Colonial styles give us that peace of mind and repose that we most crave for at home, the luxuriant restfulness of Oriental furnishings? Emphatically, they do not. Why a man who sits bolt upright in his office chair . . . should come home to sit bolt upright in a chair of the Empire or Chippendale order, is past our comprehension. . . . But why should a man live uncomfortably for the sake of fashion? If he will not dare to go the length of furnishing his house outright . . . in luxurious Eastern style, there certainly should be . . . one room . . . whether we call it library, divan, den, boudoir, salon or snuggery, wherein a man may find peace, and where his heated nerves will be soothed and cooled to the proper temperature. There are at present at least three different styles for furnishing interiors in Oriental effects. For example, we have a room in the Moorish, Japanese style or Indian style, all individually distinct, and all equally charming." She advised a visit to Vantine's, but we have anticipated her wisdom.

The whole trend was unfrocked by Edith Wharton and her Boston architect collaborator, Ogden Codman, Jr., in *The Decoration of Houses* (New York, 1897). Damning was the dismissal: "The smoking-room proper, with its *mise en scène* of Turkish divans, narghilehs, brass coffee-trays, and other Oriental properties, is no longer considered a necessity in the modern house; and the room which would formerly have been used for this special purpose now comes rather under the head of the master's lounging-room, or 'den'—since the latte word seems to have attained the dignity of a technical term."

Evidently the *New-York Daily Tribune* was unfamiliar with this now standard work (to which the novelist subsequently referred with pardonable pride of honesty as fashion's "touchstone of taste") for on November 27, 1898 a three-column cut of a décor astoundingly similar to the Byron photograph on pages 84 and 85 appeared with the following explanation: " 'Turkish rooms' which are almost as elaborate as even the palaces of the Sultan himself exist in New-York. . . . In a house [evidently that of H. S. Favshanjian] in West Seventy-second-st., in this city, is an Oriental parlor containing $25,000 worth of Turkish rugs and carpets, and it does not look crowded at that. The rugs are gems of Eastern art in weave and color. The growth of appreciation of such treasures in America has been most notable since the Centennial Exhibition in Philadelphia. . . . Last year, the dealers say, the sales of these Oriental rugs were larger than ever before."

The New York Herald, too, ignored the Wharton-Codman manifesto, in an April 26, 1903 dissertation on " 'Period' Rooms The Fashion in Furnishing": "Orientalism plays no small part in the everyday furnishing of modern houses. Its charm lies partly in the unconventional atmosphere which it breathes and partly in its restfulness. After the clean cut pilastered beauty of a classic room or the magnificently gilded delights of a Louis boudoir the luxury of the East is soft and soothing. Human nature craves variety, even in its daily setting, and when grandeur palls and daintiness grows a bit wearisome, the piquant sensuousness spicily wafted from some Turkish seraglio or an East Indian zenana, if it suits the individual mood, is above the price of rubies. Oriental rooms are by no means reasonably furnished. If they are to be genuine in detail much time is required to gather together the thousand and one different pieces which the habitué of the East would insist upon having. . . . One of the best and handsomest models of a Turkish apartment is that seen in the Waldorf [decorated in 1893]. Here luxury reigns supreme. . . . Canopied couches, bristling with guns and spears, are a feature of rooms of this style, while soft rugs, heavy hangings and countless cushions and stools give an air of real Turkish voluptuousness." The *Herald* then allows itself a *volte-face* (although admitting that "Each mode has its adaptabilities . . ." and place, for even the most erratic schizophrene would not tolerate a Gallic den or an Oriental parlor): "We are all more or less familiar with the style adopted by nearly every fashionable hostess for her drawing room furnishings. There is a certain amount of dignity and conventionality about any of the French period rooms that cannot but appeal to lovers of the beautiful, and such apartments will retain their charm long after the convert to Orientalism has grown weary of the languor of the East."

Elsie de Wolfe in a "Cosy Corner" of her New York home,
1896,
122 East Seventeenth Street, at Irving Place

"THE MEEK candle of her mimetic talent"—a phrase used in *The Illustrated American* of September 15, 1894 to describe Elsie de Wolfe's qualifications as a "society amateur"—did not burn any more brightly during the period of her professional stardom, which extended from the economic necessity of her 1891 début as Fabienne in Victorien Sardou's *Thermidor* to her voluntary retirement in 1905 after the failure of *A Wife Without a Smile,* by Arthur Wing Pinero. Through these years languid drama critics monotonously applauded her as "the one exponent of . . . [the] peculiar art of wearing good clothes well" on the somewhat long-suffering boards of the American stage.

Miss de Wolfe (who died in 1950 as Lady Mendl) had a talent for taste. When she and her friend Elisabeth Marbury (already on the way to preëminence as impresario, play broker, literary agent and political force) took over the dwelling somewhat apocryphally associated with Washington Irving, the alchemy which was to make her famous in the field of interior decorating created an advanced setting of functional beauty. In *The House in Good Taste* (New York, 1913) and her autobiographical *After All* (1935), she describes the metamorphosis of this "favorite love" of hers—the "sleepy, shabby but adorable little house," to be theirs from 1887 to 1911:

"It was not a pretty house. But it was good. . . . Outside there was little to be changed. . . . The dining-room was pure joy because it was so well spaced. It was an octagonal room with cut-off corners forming closets. . . . Around them and the doors I arranged mirrors in a way of my own—like frames. . . . It was such a perfect room that it needed little coaxing to put its best foot forward. A precious old Chinese rug . . . with a rose ground and blue-and-gold flowered medallions graced the floor. . . . The table was painted a deep ivory, and the chairs to match with cane seats and backs. For every chair there was a yellow-velvet footstool, and when not in use they were ranged in a row beneath the deep yellow-velvet window seat where so many people sat on Sunday afternoons. . . . Few were the celebrities who visited our shores without entering our doors . . . and our New York friends often spoke laughingly of the . . . house as the 'Immigrant's Home.' It was a brilliant group that flocked to our simple little Sundays" at the call of the genius for hospitality that was to make Miss de Wolfe a famed international hostess to the end of a long social career which began with sedate presentation to Queen Victoria and carried through to the unorthodoxy of her great-grandson's court in exile.

But let Miss de Wolfe walk in memory through the archway with a yellow marble column on each side (like those giving the dining room "an air of unaccustomed grandeur") into the drawing room, with its here unseen marble-floored and fountained conservatory (resulting from the slimming treatment of "an austere and paunchy bay window," around the top of which were set boxes matching the ivory color woodwork, "from which trailed long tendrils of ivy forming curtains"). "We wanted the furniture to be on good terms with the room,"

Dining room in the home of Elsie de Wolfe and Elisabeth
Marbury, 1896

The dining room after re-decoration, 1898

reasoned Miss de Wolfe: therefore—since the "Early American" house was "an aristocrat by inheritance," to be lived in and peopled with cosmopolites, and as the two Francophile careerists had already assembled good pieces of furniture in their travels—it was decided that the drawing room should be French. "One of our treasures was a Louis XIV sofa, and it fitted quite happily beneath a paneled wall . . . under the bronze wall clock. The chairs were Louis XVI, and Louis XV. . . . The decorative portrait by Nattier . . . was set into the panel above the mantel. . . . The floor was covered by an old Persian rug, from which I took the color scheme of the room—rose, yellow, and old ivory. The hangings were deep rose, as was much of the upholstery. There were graceful little tables with girandoles and bowls of flowers. For lighting we had two crystal chandeliers and even then many candles. The curtains throughout the house were of fine white book muslin."

Each sleeping room had what the then amateur decorator considered two indispensabilities—a couch or *chaise-longue* and a bedside table—and in these "secret gardens" (as she called them), furnished and re-furnished "bit by bit, need by need," like the rest of the

Elsie de Wolfe's bedroom, 1898

Elisabeth Marbury's bedroom, 1898

house ever changing, was presaged the revival of the Age of Chintz, which became a de Wolfian trademark.

So it was that when in 1905—not long after Miss de Wolfe sent out a professional announcement with the sign of "a little wolf with a flower in his paw"—Stanford White called on her to decorate the building he had designed as the first home of the Colony Club at 120–124 Madison Avenue, she was ready to meet her new career face to face, with experience, cumulative knowledge, and love. In this proving ground, readied for the opening reception on March 14, 1907, "the keynote" (wrote Anna McClure Sholl in *Munsey's Magazine,* the following August) was "perhaps an aristocratic reserve. . . . Lovers of magnificence or of mere costliness, the 'yellow rich,' or even the unworthy poor, might find this house, with its chintses [*sic*], its tinted walls, and its unobtrusive, comfortable furniture, a very plain affair. . . . Here is no erysipelas of ornament."

93

"AT PRESENT in this city," wrote Eliot Gregory, confessedly "An Idler," in one of his urbane essays in *The New York Post*, collected between covers in 1898 under the title *Worldly Ways & Byways*, "I know of but two hospitable firesides where you are sure to meet the best the city holds of either foreign or native talent. The one is presided over by the wife of a young composer [Mrs. Reginald de Koven], and the other, oddly enough, by two unmarried ladies [Elisabeth Marbury and Elsie de Wolfe]. An invitation to a dinner or a supper at either of these houses is as eagerly sought after and as highly prized in the great world as it is by the Bohemians."

The bracketed asides are not surmisals, for Anna Farwell de Koven gladly gives the key in *A Musician and His Wife* (New York, 1926), in which she dwells on six years—1891 to 1897—in the life of this room. It even figures in her first novel, *A Sawdust Doll*, (1895), for within the Aubrey Beardsley-like format of this little volume she sees it as "charming . . . not over-crowded with furniture, but . . . warm and comforting and shadowy," with an "infinite variety of photographs, small and great," scattered about, and by way of over-mantel decoration "a very remarkable collection of blue china" and a portrait of her faintly Ibsenesque heroine by Carolus-Duran (she herself sat for his pupil, Harper Pennington). The two ailing specimens of *Ficus elastica*—the "rubber plants" so patently part of the décor of the day—were left unsung, which may account in some measure for their asthenic tendencies. Although Eleonora Duse is not mentioned in the lion-studded pages of the tale of two lives, the burning tragedy of her pictured eyes looked down (from the far end of the wall at the left) on a great company. This house was filled with sound—sound from Paderewski's fingers; from the casta-nets of Mme. Calvé as she danced the *Habanera* in an impromptu performance of *Carmen;* from the throats of Schumann-Heink, the brothers de Reszke, Sembrich, and endless others; sound of the talk of Max Beerbohm and Ellen Terry. Here, too, were held some of the Monday morning meetings of "The Browning Class" organized by Mrs. de Koven as "her own con-tribution to the knowledge of English poetry"—readings by Mrs. Sarah Cowell LeMoyne later digested by sixteen of the eager and faithful in the pattern of cultural regurgitation epitomic of the period.

The host and hostess, by fortunate endowment and happy accomplishment, fitted inher-ently into the joint hemispheres of society and the arts that made up their world. They brought to this house their young success. Anna Farwell de Koven (1862–1953), daughter of a Republican Senator from Illinois, valedictorian of her class at Lake Forest University, had passed from a triumphant first season in Washington to competent journalistic achieve-ments in belles-lettres and the position of literary editor of the Chicago *Evening Post*, with the added luster of a sensitive translation of Pierre Loti's *Pêcheur d'Islande*. Reginald de Koven (1859–1920) to whom she was married in 1884, had also served the same paper on the first

94

Drawing room in the home of Mr. and Mrs. Reginald de
Koven, 1897
83 Irving Place

term of his long career as music critic, had initiated the era of light opera in America with
The Begum in 1887 and reached his apogee in *Robin Hood*, first produced three years later.
The hymeneal "Oh promise me" was interpolated in this score, the music of which has been
best described in Mrs. de Koven's loving and apt simile—"Like a little boy whistling in the
morning. . . ."

. . . . Twenty-five servants—none too many

ON JANUARY 24, 1895 Peter Fenelon Collier's *Once A Week* (a forerunner of the long popular lately defunct magazine) gave its readers a glimpse of Mrs. Theodore A. Havemeyer "At Home And In Society." Her portrait appeared on the cover, bearing out Gilson Willets's description of one dressed "with artistic taste . . . a woman tall and commanding of figure, a face equally commanding, but not cold—a full, round, good face, with two very black eyes full of both dignity and fun flashing in a frame of glossy black hair . . . one of those of whom some one has said that all men who would feel noble ought to see, every day—a beautiful woman." A full-page spread of reproductions of seven photographs by Byron (including the one here shown) served to illustrate a two-column article about her *modus vivendi* and her residence, first occupied by the family in about 1867–1868, but lately (about 1891–1892) remodeled by Society's architectural darling, Richard Morris Hunt. "There is something about the exterior of this [red brick] house which makes it seem particularly home-like," pondered the cicerone. "It may be its great number of windows with the sunshine streaming through them; it may be the strip of green lawn, or that inviting entrance, not at all common to New York houses—the porte-cochere."

Following Mr. Willets, the readers vicariously attended an afternoon reception, driving "through the high wrought-iron gates." He leads the way far better than can I, so I turn you over to him: "The horses' feet ring and echo upon the stone pavement of the courtyard, and you step directly from the carriage into the house. You are now in a great hallway, the walls of which, like the floor, are all of white marble, though the floor is covered with soft thicknesses of crimson velvet." Pausing to rest in this floreal bower, you seat yourself on one of the "massive golden chairs upholstered in crimson," to listen to the "sweet strains" of an invisible orchestra. "To give life to this scene, to-day—perhaps it is about four o'clock—imagine a sprinkling in twos, threes and larger groups of 'smart' men and women—the men in frock coats with boutonnieres, the women resplendent in fashionable frocks. Many of the fairer sex are young and beautiful; some of the sterner ones are strong and well-groomed, and both men and women are good to look at. . . . At five o'clock electric lights [which had first come into domestic use in 1881, in the J. Pierpont Morgan mansion two blocks to the south] spring into being everywhere, in the most unexpected places, and then the scene becomes literally brilliant . . . and now you enter the Louis Quatorze drawing-room . . . with its many-mirrored sides and lights, to pay your respects to the hostess 'At Home' to-day. . . . On the right are the reception-rooms, the salon and the dining-room; on the left is the ballroom. Upstairs [mounting the "grand staircase, flanked by broad and heavy tapestries"] you stumble into the conservatory with an open way in the centre looking down into the salon. Next to this is what Mrs. Havemeyer calls the antique room, and quite rightly, for it is filled with all sorts of rare and costly antiquities. . . . At the further end of the hall are the bed-chambers, *en suite*. The prevailing color is crimson. . . . In her town house alone [one of four establishments] Mrs. Havemeyer has probably twenty-five servants—and this number

The "Chinese Room" in the home of Mr. and Mrs. Theodore
A. Havemeyer, 1894
244 Madison Avenue, at the southwest corner of Thirty-eighth
Street

is none too many when the size of the house and the frequent entertainments are considered.
The *chef* must have his understudies, the coachman his grooms, the butler his assistants, the
housekeeper her maids, not to count the body-servants of lord and lady."

The master of this ménage (active member of a dynasty long preëminently and ever pros-
perously identified with sugar refining, amateur violinist, breeder of blooded cattle, and
sportsman—driving enthusiast as well as one of the first in this country to take up golf) in
an interview recaptured in the *New-York Daily Tribune* obituary of April 27, 1897, told of

his younger days, when by election "Pilot bread and cheese made . . . many a meal," and a "canvas suit was . . . [his] daily apparel." He recalled, with the special pride of his generation: "For twenty-five years I was at work at 7 a.m. and did not leave the refinery until 7 p.m. . . . Many times I worked all night long. While I was a single man [that is until October 12, 1863, when he married Miss Emily de Loosey, who was to bear him twelve children] my expenses never exceeded $50 a month."

. . . . *Left to her bank-book and her past*

". . . THERE WAS a weird fascination about her [Lola Montez]; the fascination bred of the camp and the coulisse . . . ; a gipsy beauty of mere wantonness and furious desire that made self-indulgent men forget her harsh and uncomely face, and women whose passions swayed their senses envy her her freedom. . . . Among the loose-girdled sisterhood this pinchbeck monarch gathered into her realm of license and abandon was a young woman [the far-in-the-future Mrs. Frank Leslie, née Miriam Florence Follin, her first marriage to David Charles Peacock, a jeweler's clerk, already annulled] whose reluctant decency had long been at war with the respectable poverty that forced her to be honest. . . . Her youth [she was 21 in 1857] and beauty touched the sensual heart of the seeress herself, and the pair elected themselves sisters. . . . The public scoffed at them as actresses, but the audacity of the one and the loveliness of the other touched its heart. . . . The time came when . . . the minion began to contest the laurels of the mistress. . . . Then the elective affiliation was broken and the acolyte was turned loose to make her own way . . . mounting the rising wave until the glitter of the upper sunlight dazzled the eye to the darkness out of which she had emerged. It was the gift of her husband's doting adoration, and true to her own nature she repaid it with treason. He [E. G. Squier, the eminent archaeologist] made her the wife of an honest man, of a scholar and a genius; she made him the husband of a wanton. They . . . returned from foreign wanderings . . . and settled down in New York, where he assumed control of a great business [the Frank Leslie Publishing House] whose master confided its interests wholly to him. . . . [Leslie] made the home of his prime minister his own. . . . When the explosion came it was a terrific one. . . . [E. G. Squier finally] was cast into a madhouse; [and later divorced] and his successor [Leslie] sat down to enjoy life and love at the hearth he had polluted, with the woman who had helped him to defile it. They lived as man and mistress for some years. . . . The pair were married [on July 13, 1874, at St. Thomas's Church]. . . . Her lusts . . . succumbed to her ambitions. She set to work to completely establish her supremacy at home. . . . His business [in which she was an active participant], which was at the time [of his death on January 10, 1880] deeply involved by his and her extravagances, was still a splendid fortune. By his will he left it all to her [cutting off his sons, who contested unsuccessfully]. . . . Lais, grown *passée* and with her ruder passions blunted, . . . clamored at society's gates in vain. . . . Then she took up with a shabby, greased and whiskered foreign adventurer [who went by the polysyllabic name of William Redivivus Oliver de Loncourt, Marquis de Leuville]. . . . This little extravaganza . . . kept the town grinning for a twelvemonth. Then it ended . . . and she was left to her bank-book and her past, to her Bohemian parasites whose venal flatteries wearied her. . . ."

We are indebted to Madeleine B. Stern, whose definitive biography, *Purple Passage   The Life of Mrs. Frank Leslie* (University of Oklahoma Press, Norman, 1953), gives the sesamic bracketed clues to the above quoted No. 4 of *Tales Of To-day* (subtitled *From Puddle To Palace*) which brought this latterday Lais' career up-to-date in diaphanous disguise for the titillation of the readers of E. D. Mann's scandal mongering *Town Topics* on March 27, 1886. Eight years earlier, the July 14, 1878 issue of the *Territorial Enterprise* of Virginia City, Nevada, had devoted its entire front page [reprinted in pamphlet form as that collector's item, the *Territorial Enterprise Extra*] to retaliative excoriation of Mrs. Leslie, who had made unfortunate references to that "God-forsaken" town in her book, *California: A Pleasure Trip from Gotham to the Golden Gate* (New York, 1877).

The object of these calumnitous assaults had since 1863 successfully edited certain of the House of Leslie publications, with ingravescent participation in its expanding empire, and from 1881 on became in point of name and fact Frank Leslie—not as a case of mistaken identity, but by way of a court of law. Her subsequent career included a transcontinental lecture tour; a transient 20-month marriage—her fourth—to William Charles Kingsbury Wilde (dissolute, bibulous brother of Oscar), terminated by divorce in 1893; other unsuccessful *affaires de cœur;* the augmentation of her literary output by the publication of a diversity of books and articles on subjects serious and amatory, with such title as *Rents in Our Robes* (a compilation of her views on relations between the sexes—tonic and platonic), *Beautiful Women of Twelve Epochs* (its title page showing the authoress's likeness surrounded by medallionated pictures of an historic galaxy of pulchritude), *Are Men Gay Deceivers? And Other Sketches, Which Is Woman's Happiest Hour?* . . . (the palpitant one preceding the arrival of her lover); and, terminally upon her death on September 18, 1914 as the Baroness de Bazus (the resurrection of a claimed family title), the bequest of her residual estate—finally amounting to $977,875.02—to Mrs. Carrie Chapman Catt for "the furtherance of the cause of Woman's Suffrage," a substantial factor in bringing about the Nineteenth Amendment.

In the portrait of a room in Mrs. Leslie's apartment (pages 100 and 101), amid the newly opened elegance of Sherry's, the Byrons have preserved the emanation of her perambulant salon, which found successive backgrounds in one New York hotel after the other. In these sanctuaries her diamonds and her polyglottic conversation vied in dazzlement, during the Thursday evening receptions at which, among others, such diverse talents as those of Joaquin Miller and the Italian baritone, Signor Giuseppe Del Puente, were displayed at her possessive and beckoning command. At one of these Bohemian *soirées* in 1887, Ella Wheeler Wilcox, authoress of *Poems of Passion,* clad in a high-belted "white satin Empress Josephine gown" (shown in all its unpressed, home-madish naïveté in her autobiographical *The Worlds and I*) monotonously recited "The Birth of The Opal," a phenomenon resulting from the mystic marriage of the Moonbeam ". . . so shy—so shy," and the Sunbeam ". . . his heart . . . afire with mad desire. . . ."

Byron
5874

A room in Mrs. Frank Leslie's apartment at Sherry's, 1899
522 Fifth Avenue (southwest corner of Forty-fourth Street)

. . . . Pale silvery blue brocade

ON AN early April day in 1885 a broken sword with hilt of gold was found on the battlefield of Chalchuapa; in 1891 Joseph Byron entered a stately dark red brick mansion, with gray stone trimming, on Fifth Avenue between Sixty-sixth and Sixty-seventh Streets, walked up a carved staircase, took a photograph by flashlight, and subsequently tucked it away without ado or annotation in an envelope marked "New York Drawing-Rooms."

More than half a century later these seemingly disparate events slipped back into their inevitable logical sequence as, routinely leafing through a file of *The Illustrated American*, my eye caught the unmistakable combination of "conversation seat" and conservatory, and in a single happy instant the unidentified print regained "a local habitation and a name." "Mme. de Barrios' Drawing-Room," I read beneath this reproduction in the issue of August 8, 1891, and delightedly sought the accompanying text: "Nothing is more eloquent of the mistress of a house than the drawing-room, set apart as a social shrine where . . . its owner's best and highest energies are expended in adornment and elaboration. . . . The grand drawing-room, of which a picture is here given, is an elegantly proportioned apartment, hung in pale silvery blue brocade. The wood-work is of inlaid satinwood, while the ceiling is tinted in delicate colors, showing garlands of flowers, fluttering ribbons, and delicate scrolls. All about are bits of artistic bric-à-brac, heavy but graceful draperies, luxurious furniture, and interesting personal souvenirs. It is through a broad door-way to the right, spanned above by an arch of jewelled glass, that one looks away into a big conservatory from whence come the songs of many birds."

But what of "the gracious Spanish-American lady who dignifies these spacious apartments," and what of the shattered sword? Fascinated, I traced the story and, bit by bit, learned the romance of a room. It seems that in the highlands of Guatemala, Francesca de Aparicio, a schoolgirl from the Convent of the Sacred Heart at Quezaltenango, met the President of her country in her father's house, and, at the age of scarce fifteen, became his bride. Ten years later, in a war he had instigated to unite the five republics of Central America under his dictatorship, Justo Rufino de Barrios fell on the battlefield of Chalchuapa, leaving his young widow with children to the number of seven and a count of only two less in millions of dollars. The cultivated Madame de Barrios ("a woman of pure Spanish type," to quote *The Illustrated American* of April 16, 1892, "with long, lustrous dark eyes under delicately arched black brows, warm creamy skin fine in texture as a rose-leaf, . . . abundant dusky hair . . . and a handsome throat and bust . . . modest as a flower") came to make her home in New York, where her "physical loveliness, inherent personal charm, and princely riches" imparted an almost legendary ambiance.

Through this very drawing room, on the evening of April 21, 1892, passed Francesca de Barrios, leaning on the parental arm, clad (according to the *New-York Daily Tribune* of the following morning) in "a superb gown of pale apple-green satin trimmed with emerald-green

102

jet passementerie" to wed with José Martinez de Roda, a member of the Spanish Parliament from Grenada, resplendent in the full regalia of a nobleman of the Queen's household. "Now," expatied the awed *Illustrated American* writer, "those who have met the successful suitor confess his worthiness of the rich prize he has won. . . . He himself is a man of personal distinction . . . straight, muscular and graceful, has big brown eyes, dark hair and beard, a clear brunette skin, and winning, dignified manners. He is rather reserved, is quiet, with intellectual tastes, and [oh, omniscient journalism!] gentleness yet fire in his nature."

"Grand Drawing-Room" in the home of Mme. de Barrios,
1891, 855 Fifth Avenue

CELIBACY IS often a question of creature comfort. "The peculiarity of living in boarding-houses . . . is one of the most distinguishing features of society in New-York. . . . The advantages derived from this mode of life to unmarried men are unquestionable . . . but the disadvantages are also great; for the habit of finding all that they need without much cost or trouble, and the enjoyment of female society besides, lessens the necessity of marriage." This pronouncement was made by James Silk Buckingham, the English delight of the lyceum movement, whose *America, Historical, Statistic, And Descriptive* (London, 1841) records a biased British impression of New York in 1837–1838. A good sixty years later, *The New Metropolis*, edited by E. Idell Zeisloft (New York, 1899), dealing with the habitats of a "very notable class [bachelors] which is housed with a comfort quite unknown in the olden time," notes that "Some observers of manners and fashions have ventured to express the opinion that fewer men will be driven into matrimony for the sake of a home than was formerly the case." We will return to these antisocial abodes after pondering a statement on the "Only Woman's Page" of the *New-York Daily Tribune* of September 8, 1899 (when the Empire State had a 26 per cent surplus of unmarried males over nubile maidens): ". . . It has been claimed by many men that the extravagant taste of women in dress is one of the chief obstacles to matrimony. Every man has a laudable desire to see his wife as well gowned as those with whom she mingles, and when bicycle, golf and tennis suits [not to mention "Rainy Daisy" outfits, for which see page 71] are added to the regular wardrobe a discreet man will think twice before assuming such an obligation. . . ." Mr. Zeisloft describes the *modus vivendi* of the cautious and uncaptured: "We used to think of these men as lonely and rather uncomfortable. They may be a trifle lonely still, but they are no longer uncomfortable. Quite the contrary. Considering their deserts, and their capacity for usage, they are better housed than any other class of persons in the town. Allusion is not made to bachelors of such limited means or circumscribed taste that they must or can find some measure of content in an ordinary lodging or boarding house; but we refer to the bachelors who have five thousand dollars a year and upward, and who can afford to live in one or another of the splendid bachelor apartment houses which during the last decade have been erected for them. . . . These apartment houses are divided into apartments of from five to three rooms. . . . The three-room apartment (six hundred to twelve hundred dollars a year) will generally consist of a sitting room, a bedroom, and a bathroom. The rental for these usually includes heat and light, and sometimes attendance; it always includes a general attendance. . . . But in one of these apartments a man can provide himself with excellent service."

The *New-York Daily Tribune* of February 20, 1900, pointed an editorial finger at the lack of "true civic pride" exhibited by "certain wealthy investors in real estate on Manhattan Island [who] have evidently made up their minds that the number of the obstinate unmated in this town is certain to expand. This is clear from the fact that these investors are now building on various parts of this borough handsome and costly structures reserved for the narrow minded foes of matrimony. These homes for bachelors are so attractively designed that they are likely to bring about a marked reduction in the wedding statistics. . . . When over and above the fascinations of the clubs in Fifth-ave. and elsewhere bachelors find it easy to rent apartments so sumptuous and so cunningly contrived as to shut out all thoughts of family life, is it not plain that the outlook is somewhat dispiriting?"

James L. Ford, in an eleven-page article on "Luxurious Bachelordom," (*Munsey's Magazine*, January, 1899) goes into the interior decorating aspects: "The bachelor of the hall bedroom period accepted meekly whatever his landlady chose to give him. . . . Now, he not only furnishes his own room, but also devotes a great deal of time, ingenuity, and good taste to the task, feeling that he is making a permanent home for himself, and not merely fitting up temporary quarters. . . . The young man who knows his business will try to make his rooms interesting rather than costly and gorgeous. . . . By covering his walls with original drawings and photographs, or with dinner cards signed by well known names, the bachelor of artistic tastes can make his little home far more . . . attractive to the average clever woman of society than the . . . costly establishment of the man who is engaged in humdrum commercial pursuits." He takes us into what he describes as "the ideal bachelor home": "The walls of the parlor are covered with sage green denim, and are hung with pictures that do credit to the occupant's taste. The furniture is chiefly of old mahogany, and one end of the apartment is occupied by a divan, hung with gorgeous embroidered eastern stuffs [not to overlook a neat disarray of cushions pyrographically embellished or otherwise embroidered by wishful hands]. The diningroom is somewhat smaller . . . and contains a round table, a side board, and a corner china closet, all of old mahogany. The walls are covered with dark red paper, and the curtains of the same warm shade. One side of the room contains a handsome mantelpiece over an open fireplace."

An article by John Gilmer Speed in *The New York Herald*, December 4, 1898, explains the compulsion (an inverse variety of "*Cherchez la Femme*-ism") behind all this effort: "Ladies, both young and old, by the way, are responsible for much of the conceit in which bachelors hold their rooms. No entertainments seem so alluring to women as those bachelors give in their own apartments." The *New-York Daily Tribune*, September 22, 1901, gave sage counsel: "The women guests are always specially delighted at the midnight [after theatre] feast in bachelor quarters, and if it be a chafing dish supper, where the host is the chef, it is all the more appreciated. The unmarried man is always sought for as a guest during the summer season as well as at the dinners and dances of the winter. While it is well known that some of the most sought . . . men never think to repay any of the courtesies . . . that are showered upon them, it is considered a graceful act of the man thus fêted to plan one of these informal evenings for his hostesses. . . . A party of three or four men and an equal number of girls with the chaperon and the host himself constitutes a pleasant gathering. . . . In the case of married guests the party may be less formally arranged. Separate cabs may be sent for the women, but a pleasanter fashion is the hiring of a carryall. . . . Lace or embroidered doilies on a polished table are more effective than the large white table cover. . . . In selecting dishes for the supper it is pleasant to introduce novelties and club dishes, highly seasoned grills and other dainties that are rarely placed before women, who often get tired of the ribbon tied pates and ices that are invariably placed before them." Other suggestions include an oyster cocktail (a "bachelor delicacy" counted in multiples of

The bachelor apartment of "Mr. Fox, Tailor," 1904

ten!), partridge and quail, rolled and club sandwiches. However, "Welsh rarebit is seldom chosen as a supper dish when the bachelor entertains his women friends, as it does not allow of the addition of other dishes."

Margaret E. Sangster's column, "Round The Hearth," in *Collier's Weekly* (the wisdom quoted being from the issue of April 14, 1900) suggests less sophisticated entertainment: "Perhaps during her Easter vacation the girl just at home from college may be allowed to accompany her mother and her débutante sister to a bachelor's tea, in a studio or elsewhere. She will have a glimpse of a very interesting interior . . . filled with curios and objects of interest brought from many lands. The modern bachelor lives in such independence of feminine administration that his need of a womanly presence and wifely care is far less than that of a man in more primitive society. . . . That he misses something of the Benedict's dignity, and much of the Benedict's joy in living, he probably acknowledges, since one man cannot have everything. . . . We are sometimes afraid that the bachelor apartment is a foe to domesticity. . . ."

. . . . And the prattle just as infantile

IN 1897, into their new five-story white limestone American basement home (still standing today) moved The Hon. and Mrs. Theodore Sutro: he, one of New York's leading German-born citizens, a prominent member of the bar and Commissioner of Taxes and Assessments; she (née Florence Edith Clinton) twenty years his junior, versed in the law, an accomplished musician—the first of her sex in the United States to bear the title of Doctor of Music—and an inveterate clubwoman. The *New-York Daily Tribune* of November 14, 1896, listed her affiliation in "a formidable array" of no less than twenty organizations, adding that she did not attempt to attend every meeting of each of these groups, as so doing "would occupy all her time, and she would have none left for her 'Home Club,' which, she says, interests her more than any of the others." Less than a year after the appearance of this amazing inventory of her multifarious activities, her husband admonished her (in one of the epistles to be found in the privately printed *Milestones on Life's Pathway*—a rather one-sided compilation of his love letters to her, and other sidelights on a successful marriage, assembled by Mrs. Sutro as a wifely tribute on their twentieth wedding anniversary in 1904): "Do not try to be a 'new' or a 'strong minded' or 'progressive' or 'aggressive' woman, or a woman of too pronounced a type of any kind. The world may admire and praise such an achievement; but for me 'the spell which has bound me' will be gone." This same congratulatory missive, at once redolent of the times and of his Teutonic origin, opened with the mollifying statement: "Your cheeks are just as round, all the dimples are there, the smile is just as sweet and the prattle is just as infantile as when our anniversary was I [back in 1885]." A close study of this intimate apotheosis of two happy decades takes one through the courtship which began in 1883 in true summer resort fashion (*vide* his entry in her autograph album: "The Harmony of your magic touch/ The whole world doth inspire!/ The harmony of your guileless soul/ I equally admire!") past the fifth anniversary celebration (called for half past five, at Delmonico's, Madison Square—"You will pardon the 'wood'/ If the dinner be good!"); into a *catalogue raisonné* of his gifts to her after the swift passage of thirteen

108

Kitchen in the home of The Hon. and Mrs. Theodore Sutro,
1899
320 West 102nd Street

blissful years—"the potted plants (the nucleus of our conservatory), the flowers, bonbons, and trifles . . . a tiled jardinière . . . [the] wherewith[al] to procure a covering for your lovely head (nothing could adorn it)," tokens augmented in later years by *objets d'art* and works from the now almost forgotten brushes of Paul de Longpré, Thomas Sidney Moran and others. So the chronology goes merrily on—a period piece if ever one was set forth in all its minutiae—with a facsimile of the invitation to the Crystal Anniversary reception, carefully worded "from half after three until six o'clock or from half after eight until eleven o'clock," at which event Mr. and Mrs. Sutro—she clad in her wedding dress, cut décolleté for the occasion—received five hundred distinguished guests under a canopy of blossoms. If the *Home Journal* of October 4, 1899 can be believed, "Garlands of flowers were caught back in loops to wires strung across the bay windows, and trailed to the floor, completely encircling the couple, and on each side, reaching from floor to ceiling, were growing plants and Autumn leaves. Columns of flowers were placed at the entrance and intertwined roses and smilax formed portières."

It was in this house (redecorated in 1903) so often gay with friends and good music, that on April 30, 1906, a private funeral service was held for Mrs. Sutro—to be buried at forty-one in her bridal gown—followed by public obsequies at near-by St. Michael's Episcopal Church. Floral tributes filled the chancel, many of them in the shape of musical instruments, the most conspicuous being "a large harp of roses with a broken string."

Vista in the home of The Hon. and Mrs. Theodore Sutro, 1896

. . . . *Cold tea, hot Apollinaris, and bad music*

"Madame Sans-Gêne of New York" they called her—"the interesting woman who for many years was one of the most potent and bizarre figures in the modish life of the metropolis." "As in the case of the Duchess of Dantzic [delight of the Napoleonic court and delicious heroine of Sardou's 1893 comedy]," continued *The Illustrated American* of April 20, 1895 in post mortem evaluation, "the eccentricities of the late Mrs. Paran Stevens [who died on April 3], her indifference to the stiff and starched conventionalities of over-nice fashion, her brave, almost frantic opposition to what hinted of social cant, her disregard of 'form' when principle or right was at stake" made her "in many ways, the most notable figure in the fashionable world of this generation." *Harper's Weekly* (April 13, 1895) gave her the accolade of "great courage, great energy, great force" and pronounced her "very tough, very game, very able, very enterprising, exceedingly interesting, . . . impulsively generous and kind." She had, they said, "an abundance of fun," contributing largely to the enjoyment of the populace as it followed her on the street, at the opera, in frequent courtroom litigation, affectionately regarding her "as the greatest social spectacle that New York afforded."

This gallant lady was born Marietta Reed in 1827 in the town of Lowell, Massachusetts, the daughter of a locally prominent merchant, and early bellehood presaged her brilliant future in the role of mistress of salons on both sides of the Atlantic. As the second wife of Paran Stevens, many years her senior, she abjured her triumphs as one of the most prominent young matrons of Boston for the broader and at first more challenging conquest of Manhattan, where her husband's Bonifacial interests in Boston, the Quaker City and New York's first Fifth Avenue Hotel finally proved surmountable barriers. Mr. Stevens died in 1872 at his 244 Fifth Avenue home—"an exceedingly quiet and amiable old gentleman," *The New York Herald* informed by way of resurrection in its April 4, 1895 columns, "who attended strictly to business, never went into society and had decided tastes only for fast horses, pictures and statuary."

His marmoreal yearnings doubtless led to the acquisition of Giovanni Benzoni's greatly admired narrative masterpiece—*The Flight from Pompeii*—executed in Rome in 1868 and destined to bring $1,650 at the November 25, 1895 auction of Mrs. Stevens's effects, when it passed into the hands of a Dr. Cooke. Tell-tale repairs, evident on the photograph, identify this as the selfsame group later to become a feature of the old Waldorf-Astoria's cultural *mise en scène* and currently a part of the Park Avenue *décor*. In 1893 this poem in stone went on a journey that made front page news in the *New-York Daily Tribune* of May 28: "Two statues belonging to Mrs. Paran Stevens—one by Benzoni and the other representing Cleopatra [the work of William Wetmore Story]—valued at many thousand dollars, were successfully moved yesterday from her old home, No. 244 Fifth-ave., to her present house, No. 1 East Fifty-seventh-st. Eight men were needed for each statue. For nearly three

112

Parlor in the home of Mrs. Paran Stevens, 1894
One East Fifty-seventh Street

days the contractor had his men at work on the valuable group. They used jackscrews and hydraulic jacks to remove the statues." The Benzoni conception is here seen in the setting to which Mrs. Stevens—in retreat from the northward plunge of retail trade—removed in 1892, when she leased the mansion at the south end of the "Marble Row" Robert Mook had built (1867–1869) at the behest of Mary Mason Jones. This house and its original occupant figure in the family and fiction of Edith Wharton, in whose novel *The Age of Innocence*, Marietta Stevens also found a place, thinly disguised as Mrs. Lemuel Struthers—heroines of fact and phantasy alike noted for the entertainments that contributed to the amusement of the Four Hundred "on Sunday evenings, when the whole of New York is dying of inanition." In this context the witty enfant terribilism of William R. Travers once led him to affectionate chiding of Mrs. Stevens. "My dear lady," he is said to have said, "it is impossible for me to resist the magnetism of your charming society, although I know that it only draws me back to cold tea, hot Apollinaris, and bad music."

. . . . *The people may be divided into seven classes*

"ON THE island of Manhattan the people may be divided into seven classes: the very rich, the rich, the prosperous, the well-to-do comfortable, the well-to-do uncomfortable, the comfortable or contented poor, and the submerged or uncomfortable poor." Thus categorized E. Idell Zeisloft, editor of *The New Metropolis*, published in 1899. According to his differential those in the first two orders of the descending hierarchy had annual incomes ranging "from one hundred thousand dollars to any amount exceeding that sum"; and there were roughly ten thousand New Yorkers in this bracket at the century's end.

The several succeeding early owners of 871 Fifth Avenue had a common denominator other than extraordinary wealth, and that was more than ordinary misfortune. Robert L. Stuart, sugar refiner and philanthropist, who purchased the rocky uptown terrain in 1880, did not live to see the completion of the mansarded brownstone palace he commissioned William Schickel to build; his relict occupied it for nine years before the infirmities of age took her to "more stately mansions." Amzi L. Barber, president of the Asphalt Paving Company, paid $562,000 for it in 1894, and, without passing a night in its substantial shelter (which ultimately was to require two months of wrecking crew time) leased it to Levi P. Morton and then sold it to William C. Whitney in November, 1896, for about $650,000. In 1899 the second Mrs. Whitney died a lingering death as the result of a hunting accident before the three-year-long renovation readied the house for occupancy. Her husband (financier, one-time Secretary of the Navy, sportsman and father of Pauline Whitney) (see page 206) was to succumb in 1904 to the then fashionable and at that time frequently fatal disease—appendicitis. James Henry ("Silent") Smith, who had taciturnly inherited $50,000,000 from a delightfully eccentric uncle, was the next lord of the manor, and kept his appointment in Samarra (it happened to be Kyoto, Japan) on his global honeymoon in 1907. This apparently broke the spell, for Harry Payne Whitney (son of William C.) in an access of costly sentiment bought the house and its furnishings for almost $3,000,000 on January 4, 1910, just four days before it was to be sold at an elaborately catalogued auction, and enjoyed it for twoscore years. Destiny overtook his widow, Gertrude Vanderbilt Whitney (well known as hostess and sculptress, and founder of the Whitney Museum of American Art), on April 18, 1942, a bare eleven days before the auctioneer's hammer knocked down the contents (exclusive of the French ballroom) for a wartime $295,411. The strange history of the house was terminated by the greedy hand of demolition that very November, and a Fifth Avenue tenement erected on its expensive site.

Byron's photograph is one of a series taken after the completion of the extensive $150,000 alterations made by McKim, Mead & White, including the addition of a one-story ballroom—sixty-three feet long with a forty-five-foot ceiling—generally considered one of the handsomest in the United States. *The New York Times* writer, describing the mansion on February 18, 1900, said of the interior: "Mr. Whitney's house [with the exception of the ballroom] is a consistent example of the art of one period—that of the Italian Renaissance . . . as near an approach to a Venetian or Florentine palace of the days of Leonardo da Vinci and Michel Angelo as it is possible to obtain." On the same Sunday the *New-York*

The main staircase in the home of William C. Whitney, 1899
871 Fifth Avenue, at the northeast corner of Sixty-eighth
Street

Tribune Illustrated Supplement also highlighted it in a double-page spread, and devoted more than a paragraph to the vista here shown: "The grand staircase, which, from an architectural point of view and because of its beauty, is one of the chief features of the building, begins at the back of the grand hall. Stairs, balustrade and rail are chiselled out of massive blocks of Istrian marble. The balustrade is a Renaissance pattern, the design for which was suggested by a section of sixteenth century carving brought by Mr. Whitney from Italy. . . . The steps are joined in such a way that they support themselves and the balustrade without other support in the way of columns or braces, and the staircase is probably the largest of its kind in the country."

As a matter of casual interest it might be noted that, according to *The Dictionary of American Biography*, Mr. Whitney died possessed of at least ten residences, and that "in spite of great wealth he remained a Democrat through life."

. . . . *A different set of intellectual muscles*

THE NEW YORK city directories, issued annually (with very few lapses) under various private auspices from 1786 until 1933–34 (when it became evident—even to their dismayed publisher—that the more demanding telephone book had become almost standard household equipment), make excellent reading. They trace many a man, if not from the cradle, often to the grave, and far from being impersonal, sometimes give surprising insight into behavior patterns. For instance, it may be deduced from Dr. William A. Hammond's listing in the 1873–1874 volume ("162 W. 34th until November 1st, after that at 43 W. 54") that he was a man of more than ordinary vision. It is to be hoped that his new thirty-two-room red-brick-and-brownstone—the façade of which reproduced that of an old house in Nuremberg which had pleased the physician to such an extent that he had ordered a drawing made of it, thus anticipating any latent eclectic ideas his architect may have entertained—was ready in good time to receive his family and his practice. While *Artistic Houses*—a luxurious set of folio volumes "Printed For The Subscribers By D. Appleton and Company" in 1883–1884—gives only this brief hint of the externals, it fulfills the majesty of its subtitle ("Being A Series of Interior Views of a number of the Most Beautiful and Celebrated Homes in the United States With A Description of the Art Treasures contained therein") with merciless vengeance through more than eight florid pages and three illustrations. We learn that the library was "decorated in the style of the wise Egyptians"; that the doctor's operating room was a "cozy retreat"; that he had a predilection for oak, "perhaps for the same reason that Virgil liked it"; that Mr. Engel of Reynolds & Engel, who had adorned the dining-room ceiling—above a run of gustatorial quotations—"with golden butterflies and dragon-flies moving around stars within an elliptical border of conventional wild-growths," devoted three months of concentration to the drawing-room overhead of turquoise blue "divided by Celtic bands . . . into squares filled with Celtic ornaments" and a frieze based on the Bayeux tapestry; that there was a "Japanese bedroom"; that Mrs. Hammond's Renaissance chamber, encircled with quaintly lettered legends in Latin, was "a fresh, cheerful apartment . . . not too nicely calculated in its chromatic balances," in contrast to the "sober magnificence" of the master's sleeping quarters.

In 1888 Dr. Hammond (Civil War Surgeon-General of the United States Army, pioneering figure in the teaching and treatment of nervous and mental disorders, with the temerity of collecting a $10 fee, author of a treatise announced as the first textbook in English bearing on the young specialty, playwright, and novelist) transferred his orbit to Washington. On June 16 of that year Chauncey M. Depew acquired this hybridous mansion, apparently unfurnished. To it, he added such hardware as a suit of late Gothic German armor and a railroad mantel clock, all manner of presentation pieces, bric-a-brac, paintings and his own portrait in marble complete with sideburns (seen in the photograph below).

He evidently did not find it difficult to live with another man's mottoes, for he retained this domicile until his death in 1928, just short of his ninety-fourth birthday. His only and overshadowed son (by his first marriage) succumbed three years later, and in 1933 the great high-stooped mansion, sharing the common destiny of so many of its unwieldy genus,

A corner of the salon in the home of The Hon. Chauncey M. Depew, 1899
27 (formerly 43) West Fifty-fourth Street

Library in the home of The Hon. Chauncey M. Depew, 1899

was broken up into one- and two-room suites, to make way for the present-day apartment house in 1938.

To the Honorable Chauncey M. Depew (A.B., LL.D.) it was given to live up to his own village boyhood expectations of becoming a United States Senator (Republican, from New York, 1899–1911) and president of a railroad (the Vanderbilt-controlled New York Central and Hudson River Rail Road). His popularity, on from student days at Yale, suffered only one brief eclipse—during the Armstrong Committee investigation of the great life insurance companies of New York (see page 217)—and he ranked as one of the best known Americans of his long time. By dint of abstemiousness, he was able to weather an endless chain of banquets, to which he contributed the witty after-dinner speeches that became synonymous with his name. In them he found recreation from his business life, for they involved the use of "a different set of intellectual muscles." Sometimes as many as five late afternoons a week, he would shut himself up pre-prandially in his reference library (his "mental laboratory" here shown) and "walk up and down gathering ideas and allusions to the topic of the evening." Why he elected to do this under the sheltering pinions of a mounted albatross

118

has eluded me. However, armed with information from the Plaza Art Galleries' catalogue of the sale of his effects, I can pass on the comfortable assurance that as late as 1931 this remarkable specimen—though it brought only $5 in a falling market—was still in "excellent condition," its noble "wings outspread."

. . . . *With fresh spoils from the London and Paris markets*

"MRS. EDWARD BRANDUS [née Julie Berthe Henry] is among the passengers who arrived on the Fuerst Bismarck Friday," according to a note in "The Week In Society" column of the *New-York Daily Tribune* of Sunday November 13, 1898. "She will give a number of social entertainments in the coming winter at her new house, No. 16 West Eighty-eighth-st." Her tenure there was brief, for the city directories do not list the family at that address after July 1, 1904. The white, five-story American basement dwelling with its protective iron gates still survives somewhat sadly through the chastening years.

Edward Brandus (born in Paris on August 31, 1857, of the union of Gemmy Brandus, music publisher, of 9 rue de Trévise, and his wife, Betsy Davis) had been christened Charles Louis Edouard. He evidently came to New York about 1885 and engaged in a variety of occupations during his early years here (the descriptive entries following his directory listings being "artist"; "panoramas"; "publisher"; "plater" and "advertising" simultaneously). In 1895 he settled down as an art dealer, a vocation he was to pursue locally until about 1917, with punctuating visits to his native city, where he maintained a residence, and where he died in retirement on February 16, 1939, a widower and a Chevalier de la Légion d'Honneur. I can furnish only a few oblique glimpses of his career. According to an interview recorded in the *New-York Daily Tribune* of November 8, the warm months of 1891 must have been busy ones for him: "Edward Brandus, representative of the French authors in this country, who arrived in New-York a few days ago, met personally many of the great French writers during his sojourn in Paris last summer. Most of them, however, were old friends, as Mr. Brandus is the son of the well-known Parisian publisher, . . . and lived for many years in the capital of the great transatlantic Republic. . . ." Among the names that figured intimately in his conversation were those of Emile Zola, Paul Bourget, Georges Ohnet, Alphonse Daudet and Alexandre Dumas fils. The entrepreneur showed equal catholicity of taste in the field of art, as evidenced in the catalogues of periodic preprimaveral auctions —apparently clearance sales—of a vast stock of ". . . valuable Paintings By The Masters Of The Ancient and Modern Schools," the first of which (including *objets d'art*) was conducted by Thomas E. Kirby at The American Art Galleries in 1896. Subsequent sales through the years were under the celebrated hammer of J. P. Silo of the Fifth Avenue Art Galleries at No. 366 Fifth Avenue. On March 9, 1904, for instance, we learn of misfortune through *The New York Times:* "The colony of art dealers on Fifth Avenue is about to lose one of its members. Mr. Edward Brandus, who has imported many remarkable paintings by recent and old masters for his well-known gallery on that avenue, near Thirty-seventh Street, has met with an accident and determined to close his business, preparatory to a trip abroad to recover his health. Mr. Brandus has made many friends who will regret his departure and

A young girl's room, 1902. In the home of Edward Brandus,
16 West Eighty-eighth Street

look for his return next year with fresh spoils from the London and Paris markets." The
following day the *Times* informed: "In the grand ballroom of the Waldorf-Astoria last night,
James P. Silo sold at auction sixty-seven paintings from the collection of Edward Brandus"
for $22,790. "The [three session] sale was originally scheduled to be held at the Fifth Avenue
Art Galleries, where the entire Brandus collection has been on view for the last few days.
So many people visited the galleries during that time and signified their intention of being
present at the sale that it was determined to hold it in the larger place. Almost every seat
in the ballroom was taken when Mr. Silo began the sale. Dealers were few in number,"—a
statement open to various interpretations. The 1906 sale, a triple-header under the same
auspices, to the music of $227,355, brought a large and fashionable gathering to the Thirty-
fourth Street hostelry, the final séance on March 14 yielding $150,645 for a crop of seventy-five
canvases. An Alma-Tadema, *The Sculptor's Studio,* fetched the highest price, $23,000;
Isabey's *Return of the Fishermen* changed hands for $7,800; Schreyer's *Walachian Horses*
found a new owner for $7,500; there was active bidding for the works of Corot—$2,300 for
Italian Girl, $5,600 for *Landscape* and $2,250 for *Ideal Landscape (The Ruins)*—while
a small LeBrun (not in the catalogue) netted a mere $25. The sale on March 12 and 13,
1914, totaled $79,320, with Hoppner's *Portrait of Mrs. Penrose* leading the field at $2,400
on the opening night, and Drouais' *Portrait of Madame Sophie* at $8,100 crowning the
second evening; an Old Crome went for $5,000; Corot's *Ville d'Avray* for $3,100, while
the highest bidder paid $110 for Sarah Bernhardt's painting—*Her Pet Dog*. So much for
Brandus' traffic in canvas.

By way of collateral, little did little Miss Brandus—so demurely seated at her desk, so

Bathroom in the home of Edward Brandus, 1902

very definitely and dreamily the *jeune fille* of the early years of the twentieth century—realize the future of the photograph on page 120. In 1954, long after the smoke of Byron's flashlight had floated away, Miss Lili Cassel, a young artist, came to the Museum of the City of New York for guidance, and with her feeling and skilful pen translated this study in adolescence (along with details from other Byron subjects) into book illustrations for *The House Next Door,* by Virginia Sorensen. In this wise Miss Brandus unwittingly became "Gerry McGill," a sixteen-year-old Virginia-born heroine, who in 1890 traveled all the way to the Territory that six years later became the State of Utah, and, as recorded in her diarized description of the train trip, while en route—as prelude to adventure—met "a real Indian" and conversed with a Mormon.

. . . . The "Wagner face"

"PERSONALLY I feel that *Aïda* is about as far in the Wagnerian direction as any composer ought to venture. That composition is both understandable and enjoyable, and has never needed the strenuous efforts of intolerant partisans to maintain its meritorious position among the greater operatic compositions. It has neither the sweet tum-tum of the old Italian compositions nor the brain-worrying and tympanum-splitting of all that is dreary and repulsive in the Wagnerian masterpieces." This statement by the eminent collector of incunabula, Rush Christopher Hawkins, terminates the central essay of his strangely assorted trilogy, *Corlears Hook in 1820 The Wagnerian Cult, And Our Manners* (New York, 1904). It explains the *avant-garde* aura of this risible corner of a room. A skit by Margaret Johnson, in the January 16, 1902 issue of *Life,* entitled "The Enjoyment Of Wagner. (One Way.)" reflects further on the document in deification.

I.

"*Scene:* Dress-circle of the Cosmopolitan Opera House. Enter Fanny and Julia, accompanied by the rustle of silk and the scent of violets, Herbert following meekly in their wake.

FANNY (*brisk, breathless, and smiling* . . .): There, you sit between us, Herbert, and then we can tell you about it as it goes along, so that you will have *some* idea what it is all about. Here's the book. . . .

(Herbert reads, under difficulties, picking up the librettos and handkerchiefs which the ladies on either side drop occasionally as they struggle with veils, hatpins, wraps, etc.)

JULIA: You must hurry, because the overture will begin in a minute. . . . You see, it gives a sort of *résumé* of the whole opera,—all the principal *motifs* are in it. . . .

HERBERT (*skeptically*): How do you know so much about it?

FANNY (*triumphantly*): O, we've been reading it up! Just as soon as you telephoned about the tickets we sent down to the Library. . . . You see, everything depends, in Wagner, on being *perfectly* familiar with the opera beforehand. . . . O, Herbert, I do hope you'll enjoy it! . . .

HERBERT (*diffidently*): O yes; and the—the Meistersinger is rather—rather musical, isn't it?

FANNY (*horrified*): Musical? . . . It's exquisite! There, don't bother with that libretto any longer. . . . Here's Lavignac—perfectly charming—and *so* clear; you just feel as if you knew exactly what Wagner meant by it all when you've read that [*The Music Dramas of*

A shrine to Wagner, photographed in 1908

Richard Wagner . . . , by Albert Lavignac. . . . Translated . . . by Esther Singleton, with illustrations and diagrams. New York, 1898].

HERBERT (*floundering helplessly in the Lavignac*): Hold on a minute . . . till I find out who the old Meistersingers were, anyway! . . .

(Overture begins. Both ladies settle back in their seats with sighs of rapture.)

II.

FANNY: . . . . Julia! (*in an ecstatic whisper across Herbert*) There's the 'Meistersinger' *motif!* . . .

JULIA (*also whispering*): Yes—glorious! . . . And that's the 'Banner.'

FANNY: Yes—no— . . . . I think that's the 'Assembly.' . . .

HERBERT (*growing uneasy*): Say, what does it matter, anyway, whether it's the Banner or the Assembly or the—House of Representatives? . . .

JULIA: . . . . Fanny! 'Waking Love!' . . .

FANNY: Herbert, what makes you frown so?

HERBERT (*pensively*): Was I frowning? . . . It's the Wagner face, I suppose. . . . There, the curtain is going up now. . . . Now they're *playing!* That thing's got a tune to it—regular psalm-tune. . . .

FANNY: . . . . Julia! 'Waking Love'! . . . . Don't you see, Herbert? You can tell exactly what Sir Walter is thinking about by the music!

HERBERT: . . . . Pshaw! Anybody could tell by the way he acts. . . . He's smitten with that girl in pink in the front pew. I don't need any music to tell me that!

JULIA: But see how exquisitely the music expresses his emotions! It seems to understand them even better than he does himself!

HERBERT (*with sarcasm*): Hardly possible, I should think. . . . What did you say this *motif* was—Making Love? . . .

III.

HERBERT (*at the Chorus of Apprentices, with animation*): Say, that's pretty! What d'ye call it? Regular 'rag-time'! . . .

JULIA: Doesn't sound a bit like Wagner, does it?

HERBERT: Not a bit. It's first-rate! Pity Wagner didn't know enough to hold on to a good thing when he'd got it. The tunes don't stay long enough for a fellow to get 'em into his head.

. . . .

IV.

. . . .

(Herbert, left to enjoy it in his own way, proceeds to do so. An expression of deep peace takes the place of the 'Wagner face.' His breathing becomes suspicious.)

FANNY (*suddenly*): Herbert! . . . You were asleep!

HERBERT: No, I wasn't! At least, if I was, I haven't missed anything. Old Sachs was sitting there talking to himself just like that when I last saw him, and he hasn't got through yet. Bet you he's been asleep too! . . . Talking in his sleep!

. . . .

JULIA: You're just making fun of everything! I don't believe you appreciate it one bit!

HERBERT (*earnestly*): Yes, I do; the trouble is, I appreciate it so much I can't enjoy it. . . ."

"A TENEMENT back yard in New York is delivered through a photograph, alive with a hundred pages of O. Henry." So wrote Carl Sandburg, with the reverence of an artist for an artist, in *Steichen The Photographer*—that "little record of data, opinion and whim, as between friends" (New York, 1929). Seldom in the entire, more than century-long range of Photography has the summital eloquence of *Laughing Boxes*—the document the poet so tenderly describes in tributary perfection—been even approximated by another eye and mind and heart and camera. It is one of the myriad gages flung before all those who skepticize about the place of the lens in art, for it is creativity incarnate, passionate imagination unleashed in the pure nobility of compassion. The genius that conceived it—today the foremost figure in many flowering fields—was one of the chief founders of the trajectory Photo-Secession movement launched by Alfred Stieglitz in 1902, with its inspirited quarterly voice (*Camera Work*, 1903–1917) and its spiritual home, the legendary demesne—dedicated to progress on November 24, 1905—known as the "Little Galleries," or "291" (after its Fifth Avenue address). Here (well ahead of the Armory Show) among other *avant-coureur* miracles was germinated in white excitement and great moments the introduction of modern art to America, in such Steichen-promulgated exhibitions as the drawings of Rodin (1908), followed by the work of Matisse; the lithographs of Toulouse-Lautrec (1909); the drawings and Sunday paintings of Henri Rousseau, *le Douanier* (1910), together with lithographs by Cézanne, Renoir, Manet and Toulouse-Lautrec; watercolors by Cézanne, and the early innovations of Picasso (both in 1911). Nor was native talent overlooked: here the American-born genius of John Marin received its initial recognition in 1909, and the works of Marsden Hartley, Arthur G. Dove and many others were given first showing. Here Photography battled and won its place in the aesthetical concept, with Edward Steichen (a painter, too) as one of its young immortals. "To ramble through fifty or a hundred of his photographs," says Sandburg, "is to come in touch with something of the world of art and the world of science and then some thing else beyond these worlds, for which we do not have words. . . ."

So, though expressed with less economy than *Laughing Boxes*, does the personal difference of this earlier Byron portrait (pages 126 and 127) of a similar subject tell its wordless tale—an integer in itself and of itself, isolate in silence while saying all that can be said.

Tenement backyard, 1897

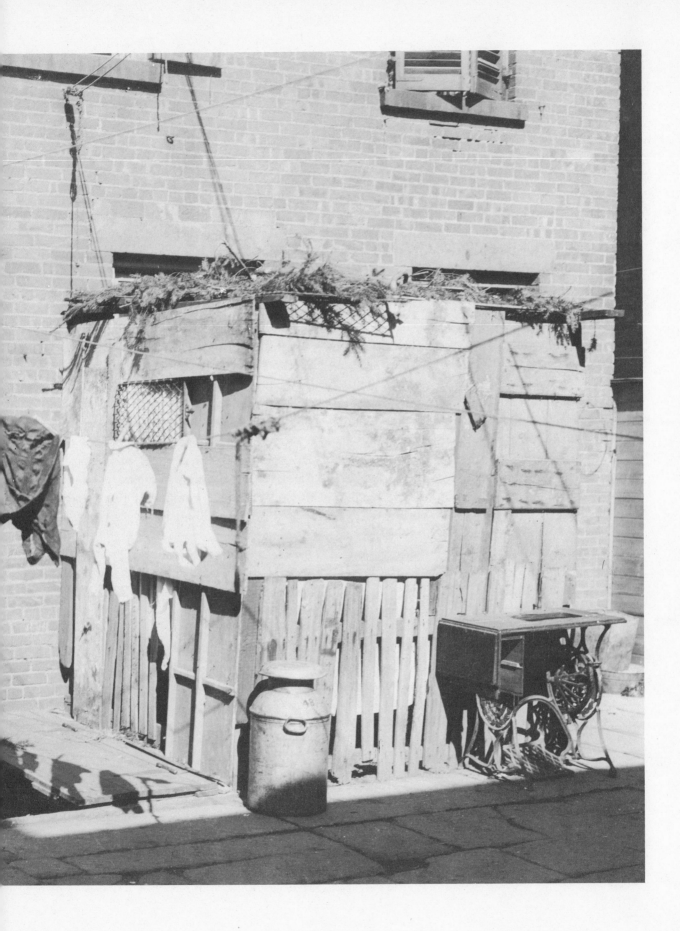

ONE OF America's greatest social reformers was also her first journalist-photographer; and his unparagoned documentary photographs—taken between 1887 and 1897—were the ammunition he used in his war against the slum, his crusade for the underprivileged. As a police reporter, Jacob A. Riis penetrated New York's lower depth and sought for a means of bringing to public attention the conditions under which what he called "The Other Half" lived and worked. He found that when he spoke his words went unheeded or were thought to be a magnification of the truth; his writings went unread or were considered overstatements. He concluded that the answer lay in a pictorial approach, but "that charlatan, Light" (to use a phrase of Corot's) stood in the way of the lens he brought into the tenement gloom. One morning in 1887 a press dispatch describing a method of recording images by flashlight (which he immediately realized would illuminate the darkest corners of the foulest lodging) showed him the way, and before very long he set forth armed with his camera and pistol, for the early flashlight powder was contained in cartridges fired from a revolver. He later substituted a frying pan for this terrifying device, and thus equipped took the shots that were to aid him in his spectacular achievements. His priority in the field of photographic journalism was established by Alexander Alland, and partly through the efforts of this specialist in minority groups the historic Jacob A. Riis Collection was generously presented to the Museum of the City of New York in 1946 by the late Roger William Riis, to serve again the cause for which his father's life was given.

This Byron print (used as an illustration in *The New Metropolis*, edited by E. Idell Zeisloft, New York, 1899) follows in the logical succession that found grim reflorescence in the new-century documents of Lewis W. Hine, Charles Frederick Weller (while a social worker in Washington, D. C.) and other photographers of seeing pity. It is a chronicle of child labor in the tenements and shows a poor little flower maker shadow-weary, with a box of gay artificial petals and bright unrealistic leaves and lifeless stems beside her, waiting to be assembled into a semblance of nature after the restless sleep of starvation was too early over. The speaking derby above the boarded-up fireplace seemed meant for three pages of dissertation, but a detailed length of letter from Percy C. Byron has spared me great effort and you endless torment. It came in response to my inquiry as to whether flash or existing light had illuminated this racking document (for often the firm's use of brief artificial brilliance was so skilled as to defy detection, even by presently practicing professionals). Here is my question's answer:

"I remember it [the interior here reproduced] distinctly for I was with my father when he took this photo and the mistake in that picture is that my dad's hat is on the mantel, he was that kind of gentleman that took off his hat no matter how lowly a room he entered. We always carried flashlights with us when out on such assignments but cannot recall whether it was used or not, I know there was plenty of light from one side and a little flash either direct or bounce might have been used to soften intensity. If my memory serves me rightly this picture was made . . . [in the] East Side Slum Section . . . for St. John's Guild Floating Hospital. . . . My! You ask for a *Yes* or *No* on a question and look what I let you in for."

Tenement interior, 1896
Lower East Side

. . . . One of the age-old scourges

RESEARCH, EVEN as many another goddess, is fickle: like Carmen, she refuses to come at your bidding; as is the way of a child, she pulls insistently and makes furious demand on your wandering attention. The Jacob A. Riis Collection, in the Museum of the City of New York, includes—among some documentary shots by Lewis W. Hine, Jessie Tarbox Beals and others—the tantalizing photograph here reproduced. Through the years it defied identification with that archly roguish "Find me if you can" which is the torturous instrument and the haunting challenge to all would-be historians. Students, in quest of source material relating to the master sociologist, have speculated on this print he treasured, toyed with its hidden narrative: some have theorized that the young woman in white was a "do-gooder," a "slummer"; others have woven tall tales about the prodigal daughter—dressed in her idea of the best—paying a visit to her pathetically grateful progenitors; nobody could explain this pictorial *roman à clef*. I made up my mind that one day I would break the obsession, but the relief came in the nature of a sort of intellectual extra dividend, for, while searching for something quite disparate, that Venetian scene—all by itself—leapt and laughed at me from a page of the *New-York Daily Tribune* of Sunday June 28, 1908. This is the story the reporter had to tell:

ANTI-PLAGUE POSTERS
Charity Organization Society Starts
Novel War on Tuberculosis.

To fight tuberculosis by means of an attractive poster is a scheme of the Charity Organization Society [now, with the A. I. C. P., known as The Community Service Society of New York] committee on the prevention of tuberculosis, and so far many Italian homes on the East Side have these pictured warnings against faults which may lead to the ill nourished, poorly housed getting the disease which to them seems one of the age-old scourges which cannot be avoided.

A brightly colored view of a part of a canal in Venice is surrounded with advice, in English, and those who receive the posters are, of course, first attracted by the colored bit of scenery representative of their native land. Then they scan the printed matter [which tells them that "A COUGH MAY LEAD TO CONSUMPTION," and urges the sufferers to see a doctor or report to the nearest tuberculosis clinic, The New York Dispensary].

The work of distribution [of the poster] was begun on June 12 by Miss Sillenda, a young Italian, who, it was said, had been cured of consumption at Stony Wold, in the Adirondacks. She had much trouble in getting the Italians to keep the poster, as they believed that a money payment would be required. When they were convinced that it was for their benefit, without cost ["Compliments of The Committee On The Prevention

130

Of Tuberculosis of the Charity Organization Society."], they gladly accepted it as a pretty decoration. The lesson it taught was then impressed on their minds.

Lawrence Veiller, the director of the committee's work, will extend the distribution among other nationalities as soon as the Italian families have been supplied. Miss Sillenda has distributed nearly two thousand posters so far in the district bounded by East Houston, the Bowery, Spring and Crosby streets.

This work, in connection with the free open air stereopticon exhibition given by the Health Department, continuing instructions in the same line, will, it is believed, have a marked effect in the course of time in reducing the mortality from tuberculosis. The Health Department will keep a close observation on the health reports from the districts covered by the posters and the stereopticon exhibitions.

A "White Plague" Poster, June, 1908

IT WAS known as the "Pig Market" because pork was about the only unavailable commodity. One could buy everything and anything on Hester Street (extending both ways from the Ludlow Street axis) and in and out the surrounding side streets for several blocks. Of Thursday nights and Friday mornings especially, pre-Shabbos trade was brisk, and bargains and bargaining rife. "Bandanas and tin cups at two cents," wrote Jacob A. Riis in *How the Other Half Lives* (New York, 1890), "peaches at a cent a quart, 'damaged' eggs for a song, hats for a quarter, and spectacles, warranted to suit the eye, at the optician's who has opened shop on a Hester Street door-step, for thirty-five cents; frowsy-looking chickens and half-plucked geese, hung by the neck and protesting with wildly strutting feet even in death . . . are the great staple of the market. . . . Here is a woman churning horse-radish on a machine she has chained and padlocked to a tree on the sidewalk, lest someone steal it. Beside her a butcher's stand with cuts at prices the avenues never dreamed of. Old coats are hawked for fifty cents . . . and 'pants' . . . at anything that can be got. There is a knot of half a dozen 'pants' pedlars in the middle of the street. . . . The suspender pedlar is the mystery of the Pig-market, omnipresent and unfathomable . . . met at every step with his wares dangling over his shoulder, down his back, and in front. Millions of suspenders thus perambulate . . . all day on a sort of dress parade. Why suspenders . . . and where do they all go to? . . . I cannot tell. I only know that more suspenders are hawked about the Pig-market every day than would supply the whole of New York for a year." These wares—dry goods, meat, fish, fowl, and vegetable—effluvious with the staleness of dirt and decay, behind the comparative stability of glass fronts, on wagons, on human counters or improvised boards mounted on ash barrels, on pushcarts, made tenement-bordered eddies of squalor in all directions, with guttural cries in many tongues rising to a crescendo of indignation in the retreating path of health officer and policeman. Such was the market place of the Lower East Side.

While the history of Judaism in America reaches back 300 years and more—to that September of 1654 when the first group of twenty-three settlers sought religious freedom in New Amsterdam—the story of New York's Ghetto began with the assassination of Alexander II, Czar of Russia, on March 13, 1881, at the hands of a band of nihilists. Prior to 1846, almost the only representatives of the faith in the United States had been of Portuguese and Dutch origin; from this mid-century date until 1876 the Germanic Jew predominated in New York and a broad estimate placed the Russian-Polish figure at some thirty thousand, centered around Baxter and Bayard, Hester and Essex streets. However, between April, 1881, and June, 1882, more than 225,000 Jewish families fled from the tyrannous persecution of Alexander III. Affinity of worship, language, idea, and ideal drew the first of this terror-stricken band to reach New York toward Hester, Essex and Ludlow streets; several thousand swarmed into Baxter, Bayard, and Mott streets, and presently the area bounded by Rivington, Clinton

132

The Lower East Side, 1898
Orchard Street, looking south from Hester Street

The Lower East Side, 1898
Scene on Hester Street

The Lower East Side, 1898
Intersection of Hester Street (at the right)
and Suffolk Street, with Essex Street
in the background, showing the
clearance for Seward Park

and Canal streets and the Bowery thronged with the refugees. And so came about the diabolic multiplication of five- and six-story tenement houses to supplement the degraded mansions of an earlier day, and the overcrowding of lodgers, so that a two-room family apartment often sheltered an additional half-dozen boarders, and the central Pig Market became an outdoor employment agency for services of all kinds, with a preponderance of tailors to satisfy the exigent law of demand. Under the more liberal sway of Count Dmitri Tolstoi, who succeeded Ignatiev as Russian Minister of the Interior, the influx suddenly dwindled to the immigration of relatives of the earlier arrivals. Then within a few years came the Galician Jews, to settle around Willett, Pitt, Sheriff and Ridge streets. In 1891 a recrudescence of pogroms in Russia drove 63,861 adult fugitives through Hamburg to England and the United States between July 10 and the following May 21. The majority of those who crossed the Atlantic settled in New York, and out of raw misery and frenzied competition the sweat-shop was born. By the turn of the century the northern boundary of the Ghetto had been extended to Tenth Street, the southern reach was Cherry Street, and between the rivers the district stretched from Goerck Street on the east to the Bowery on the west. In the Ghetto the humblest unskilled labor and the professional man of genius and all the layers of mediocrity in between shared a common anguish and often a common misunderstanding. With the assimilative facility of the young came the inevitable clash of the generations.

In James Huneker's *New Cosmopolis* (New York, 1915) all this—with impinging national groups—represented "A vast cauldron" where "every race bubbles and boils and fuses" in "the dear old dirty, often disreputable, though never dull East Side." It too was a part of Israel Zangwill's impassioned drama—his America, "the great Melting-Pot where all the races of Europe are melting and re-forming," his "fifty groups" with their "fifty languages and histories," their "fifty blood hatreds and rivalries," passing through Ellis Island "into the Crucible," where "God is making the American."

. . . . *The stiletto is rarely brought into play here*

THE FIRST European eyes to gaze upon the "much populated" southern tip of Manhattan Island were those of an Italian, Giovanni da Verrazano, who in March of 1524—eighty-five years ahead of the belated Henry Hudson—as recorded in the Cèllere Codex (preserved in The Pierpont Morgan Library and generally conceded to be the embodiment of the explorer's famous lost letter to Francis I) described New York's westerly avenue to the sea as "a very great river," and left "the said land with much regret because of its commodiousness and beauty, thinking it was not without some properties of value."

The last two decades of the nineteenth century saw the beginning of a mass migration of Verrazano's compatriots, who because of divers political, social, economic, hygienic and agrarian pressures sought security in the haven he had so reluctantly forsaken. The natives—more inhibited than those who "clothed with the feathers of birds of various colors" had greeted Verrazano and his party "joyfully, uttering very great exclamations of admiration"—eyed the new immigrants with commingled curiosity, hostility and apprehension, as the great majority were swiftly processed (first at Castle Garden; from 1892 on at Ellis Island) and

"Little Italy in Harlem," 1890
A page from Joseph Byron's album

shipped to destinations in the interior, under the sponsorship of relatives or the exploitation of padrones. Presently, however, some of these later arrivals began to settle in New York, at first mainly in the sordor of the Mulberry Bend area, and then in Harlem, starting spottily at Ninety-seventh Street near Third Avenue and spreading intensely northward into the neighborhood which even today houses the greatest concentration of the city's Italian population. E. Idell Zeisloft, in *The New Metropolis* (1899) gives the following geographical and ethnological data: "Little Italy, one of the most flourishing and picturesque Italian colonies in New York, commences at One Hundred and Fourth Street, to the east of Second Avenue. It extends to the river and has gradually crept uptown until it has reached One Hundred and Sixteenth Street. . . . The tenements that line these streets are not much to look at in themselves, but the quaintly furnished rooms in them, the fire escapes loaded down with household goods of many sorts, the gay lines of 'wash,' the small shops and the street scenes make up a picture that never loses its interest. . . . These are peaceful Italians from the north of Italy, and the stiletto is rarely brought into play here."

A variety of differences in occupation (fruit and vegetable and ice vending, dressmaking and tailoring, stonecutting, bootblacking, manufacturing macaroni, confectionery, and artificial flowers, knife-sharpening, organ grinding, etc.) with undercurrents of maladjustment, overtones of language difficulties—all were fused in a common religious comfort. Out of a fiesta first held on July 16, 1881, to honor the Patron Saint of Polla, grew an annual festival, bright with flowers and color and the soft light of votive candles carried in procession. In the beginning a touchingly impromptu chapel was set up in a tenement room to shelter a statue of the Virgin. Three years later Father Emil Koerner of the Pious Society of Missions sought funds to build a shrine of befitting dignity, and in 1885 the Church of Our Lady of Mt. Carmel on 115th Street east of First Avenue was dedicated, later to be elevated to a sanctuary by Pope Leo XIII. This tender mystery circumfused and dominated the lives of the earlier generations of Italian-born immigrants who gave New York some of its most distinguished citizens in far-flung fields of endeavor.

. . . . *Out of the tenement furnaces*

THE MASTER sociologist, Jacob A. Riis, wrote in *A Ten Years' War* (1900): "The play pier is the kindergarten in the educational campaign against the gang. It gives the little ones a chance. Often enough it is a chance for life. The street as a playground is a heavy contributor to the undertaker's bank account."

The first of these "Roof Gardens," as the children called them, was opened at the foot of East Third Street in June of 1897. The idea that had taken seven years to germinate was executed in about an equal number of weeks, and Riis tells of the victory and the lesson: "Half the East Side swarmed over . . . [the recreation pier] with shrieks of delight, and carried the mayor and the city government, who had come to see the show, fairly off their feet. And now 'we are seven,' or will be when the one in Brooklyn has been built,—great, handsome structures, seven hundred feet long, some of them. . . . The street is far away with its noise." Strategically located along the East River at Twenty-fourth Street in the German-American

The Recreation Pier at West 129th Street, 1901

and Irish-American neighborhood, and at 112th Street for the benefit of "Little Italy," these oases—open from 8 A.M. into the moonlight at 10:30 P.M., during the brutal months starting in June until the first cold struck in November—were soon duplicated on the Hudson side, first in the Greenwich Village area, and in the summer of 1899 at West 50th Street and West 129th Street. The *New-York Tribune Illustrated Supplement* of Sunday June 4 of that year stated that if the piers "were money-making enterprises the flattering attendance that has greeted them from the first day would insure a highly prosperous financial season. As it is, the city has reason to congratulate itself upon the thorough appreciation shown for them by the tenement children—and, for that matter, by their elders, too." Here to spend the day came the waifs, in many cases unaccompanied by adults, and the "little mothers," often scarcely larger than the young siblings it was their duty to "mind," and under the guidance of matron and kindergarten teacher learned new ways of delight, good manners and cleanliness. Here in the evenings thronged the parents and young lovers, out of the tenement furnaces into the cool of the river night, to listen to the band and "walk around the pier in a constantly moving procession."

139

THIS STUDY of Street Arabia (unable to afford even a ball for impoverished and probably truant play) speaks at once in terms of Tom Sawyer and—to use a Jacob A. Riis chapter head ing—"The Genesis Of The Gang."

The emptiness of the stark plate is filled with revelatory detail. By way of instance, one of the boys has what appears to be a defiant butt in his mouth. "The cigarette," Jacob A. Riis wrote in *The Children Of The Poor* (New York, 1892), "if not a cause, is at least the mean accessory of half the mischief of the street. And I am not sure it is not a cause too. It is an inexorable creditor that has goaded many a boy to stealing; for cigarettes cost money, and they do not encourage industry. Of course there is a law against the cigarette, or rather against the boy smoking it who is not old enough to work—there is law in plenty, usually, if that would only make people good. It don't in the matter of the cigarette. It helps make the boy bad by adding the relish of law-breaking to his enjoyment of the smoke. Nobody stops him." The mud-baked playground of poverty is peopled with Street Arabs—those homeless, sparrow waifs who sold newspapers and shined shoes and gambled with their pathetic pennies, "shooting craps" in dark areaways. Riis (in *How the Other Half Lives*, New York, 1890) devotes a chapter to this segment of salvageable childhood waste. "The Street Arab," he declares, "has all the faults and all the virtues of the lawless life he leads. Vagabond that he is, acknowledging no authority and owing no allegiance to anybody or anything, with his grimy fist raised against society whenever it tries to coerce him, he is as bright and sharp as the weasel. . . . His sturdy independence, love of freedom and absolute self-reliance, together with his rude sense of justice that enables him to govern his little community, not always in accordance with municipal law or city ordinances, but often a good deal closer to the saving line of 'doing to others as one would be done by'—these are strong handles by which those who know how can catch the boy and make him useful. . . . There is scarcely a learned profession, or branch of honorable business, that has not in the last twenty years borrowed some of its brightest light from the poverty and gloom of New York's streets."

This print holds a dozen subjects for J. G. Brown (see page 422). Had Ben Shahn—contemporary artist, chiefly of palette, but of camera, too—known of the existence of this document, he might have drawn on it to some extent for his *Handball* of 1939. Of the making of this tempera masterpiece, now owned by The Museum of Modern Art, James Thrall Soby wrote in his 1947 monograph (one of *The Penguin Modern Painters* series): ". . . while Shahn's painting often records a photographically arrested reality, its impact is quickened by the most exacting and imaginative painterly means. For example, he originally photographed the scene which appears [with rearrangements] in *Handball*. The painting retains the photograph's opposition of small, dark figures to bright, looming wall; its young athletes are realistic in type and stance. . . . In brief, Shahn uses photography as other artists use preliminary sketches, and from its notations proceeds under the compulsion of a painter's inner vision."

140

This interplay has long been common to many brothers of the brush and one cannot but see that the Byrons had that "inner vision," for the frequency with which their subjects and compositions insist on comparison with recognized master works (familiar to us, but in all likelihood not in their calculations at the moment of exposure) is more than fortuitous or accidental. "Of our fine art there are the two main streams," said Ben Shahn at the Niagara Frontier Convocation of the University of Buffalo on December 7, 1951, "one humanistic, necessarily asking the question, 'to what end?' greatly concerned with the implication of man's way of life; the other, the abstract and non-objective. . . ." Sometimes the Byrons touched both. Here they have made felt the tactile absence of soft green grass beneath the bare feet; of rocks and tree shadows—the gas tank a poor substitute for the hillside. The unerring inclusion of the chalked scoreboard points up the entire arrangement. It has always seemed to me that one criterion of perfection in painting or photograph is the complete disruption that would result from the elimination of even a minute detail; and thus a personal rule has governed my selection of this particular print, which could stand without apology beside some of Cartier-Bresson's best.

A game of "Cat-Stick," 1898

Hudsonbank Gymnasium and Playground, 1898
Fifty-third Street and Eleventh Avenue

. . . . *To wrestle with the gang for the boy*

THE OUTDOOR Recreation League was founded in May, 1898, for the purpose of establishing "proper and sufficient exercise and recreation places, playgrounds and open-air gymnasiums for the people" of New York. Under its auspices, with funds contributed by sympathizers, "Hudsonbank," on the old Stryker estate, was formally dedicated on August 27, in a saloon-infested, gang-dominated neighborhood, where 3,000 people were herded in a single desperate block. The full complement of trapezes, traveling and flying rings, horizontal bars, and the organized classes had an immediate success, and the management won the instant respect of the unruly, pugnacious men and boys of this notoriously rough "Hell's Kitchen" community. The equipment and the surrounding thousand-foot wooden fence were permitted to remain intact in a region where boards commanded high values and private property—subject to constant vandalism and depredation—was held in low esteem. Similar establishments under the same banner were set up the following year in Seward Park and in the block bounded by Broadway, Amsterdam Avenue, Sixty-eighth and Sixty-ninth streets.

This was all part of a slow pattern of progress, for in 1897—as the militant Jacob A. Riis recorded in *The Battle with the Slum*, published in 1902—Abram S. Hewitt, who as Mayor had championed the Small Parks Act of 1887 (just bearing belated first fruit in the opening of Mulberry Bend Park), pondered "Everything takes ten years," as he assumed the chairmanship of the Advisory Committee on Small Parks. That body called in the police to indicate on a prepared map the areas of rowdyism, which invariably turned out to parallel districts in which the treeless slum street was the only playground, while captains of precincts with islands of greenery reported that order prevailed in their bailiwicks. This marked chart, along with a copy of Chapter 338 of the laws of 1895 (stipulating that "Hereafter no schoolhouse shall be constructed in the city of New York without an open-air playground attached to or used in connection with the same"), was sent to the Mayor, together with thirteen recommendations, Riis tells, "as to the location of parks and detached playgrounds." Then the Committee rested, its assignment complete. By 1901, Riis noted, only two of these suggestions had been acted on, one being "over at Hudsonbank." There, too, he told, "on the site of the [DeWitt Clinton] park that is coming . . . teams hired by the Board of Education are ploughing up the site of Stryker's Lane, and the young toughs of the West Side who held that the world owed them a living and collected it as they could, are turning truck farmers." In 1902, New York counted but forty-four improved and thirteen unimproved parks and squares, while condemnation proceedings were in motion in two additional spots. Yet with confident hope Riis could say: "The playground is here to wrestle with the gang for the boy, and it will win."

It is a fearsome thought that today this equation no longer has the same validity, for one of the city's greatest foci of narcotic addiction, crime and juvenile delinquency is located within stepping distance of its greatest park.

"FOR THREE years the pin awarded to the best all round gymnast has been won by Miss Clair Carter, the eighteen year old niece of the head instructor" in a "physical development institute in West Fifty-ninth street." Evidently *The New York Herald* of May 21, 1899 saw no trace of nepotism in this sustained superiority: "Miss Clair Carter has worked in the gymnasium since she was eight. . . . One of the most beautiful . . . [of her feats] is her pose of 'Flying Angel.' In this she holds the weight of her whole body in the flying ring by the support of one hand and the curved toes of one foot. This . . . requires nerve, strength, uncommon grace and untiring practice. She gets into the rings without assistance, climbs up the ropes, and, after going through a series of interesting and difficult poses she gracefully slides down the ropes into the pose of 'Flying Angel.' . . . [She] can play basket ball in a way calculated to excite the envy [and conceivably other emotions] of Harvard and Yale." Princetonians, by inference, leaned toward less sinewy seraphim. Two of her classmates gave proficient performance in a complexity known as "Crab in the Trapeze," about which the astounded *Herald* stated: "It is impossible for an onlooker to see just how it is done. The girls take hold of the flying rings, and, after a few graceful twists and turns, they become so intricately mixed up that it is hard to tell just what has happened, when suddenly they seem to develope into a most interesting figure, and both hang swinging in the rings." It must have been indeed a colorful sight, for the institute's uniform consisted of "navy blue [bloomerized] costumes with Harvard red sashes, black stockings and heelless slippers." The illustrated feature includes a statement by Dr. Watson Lewis Savage (Director of the Gymnasium at Columbia University, 1898–1903) who was of the opinion that "Every one should learn to run. . . ."

Up on Morningside Heights, Teachers College had dedicated its present Main Building on November 13, 1894. Since March, 1898, a professional school of Columbia University, this College traced its origin to the Kitchen-Garden Association (founded in 1880, and dissolved four years later to emerge as the Industrial Education Association, which in turn was replaced by the New York College for the Training of Teachers, a designation used from 1889 to 1892). As early as 1889 a Department of Physical Culture was instituted, to become the Department of Physical Training in 1893, and in 1901, under the beginning chairmanship of Dr. Thomas Denison Wood, the Department of Physical Education. The year following, thanks to funds donated by Mrs. Frederick Ferris Thompson in memory of her husband, plans were made for the construction of a still utilized building to house this unit of Teachers College. The dedication of the plant (standing between Main Hall and the experimental Horace Mann School) in November, 1904, marked the end of what *The New York Times* of the 7th played up as "The great swimming-pool controversy," arising from the guest use of the Columbia University gymnasium and tank by girl athletes. It seems that the "academic waters" were "stirred . . . to their very depths" and "The waters of the pool were affected as well, for the boys averred that the young women left the tank full of hair-pins, combs, and

Handball at Teachers College, 1904
525 West 120th Street

A gymnasium group at Christ Church House, 1905
224–228 West Thirty-fifth Street

rats, and that the dye-stuffs from their bathing suits left the water . . . all colors of the rainbow." Chivalry was reinstated with the passing of pollution, "for the girls now have a [four-story brownstone and brick] physical culture building for their exclusive occupancy, which is said to be the finest of its kind in the world." The main gymnasium hall, with its $50,000 equipment, occupied the top floor; the second and third stories were given over to "special corrective exercise rooms, including rooms supplied with rowing machines"; the entrance floor was devoted to administrative offices, "a lavishly furnished reception room" and examination and conference rooms. "But that feature . . . upon which the girls are most profuse in their encomiums is the novel hair-drying room located in the basement" adjacent to the swimming pool, the bowling alleys, and special exercise rooms, the fencing and the handball courts. The last mentioned—in addition to affording the Byron Company one of its best compositions—were, according to *The New York Herald Magazine Section* of November 17, 1907, "ventilated by a system so perfect as to give . . . the sensation of being out in the open."

Meanwhile, in another part of the city (as the saying goes) members of the Van Dyke Club of Christ Church House were receiving gymnastic instruction. This was one of many groups happily functioning in the converted tenement at 224–228 West Thirty-fifth Street that sheltered the multiple Parish House activities from 1867 until October 29, 1905. An article in *The Church Economist* for that month described the vital program: "The Church As A Guide And Friend. We reproduce in half tone . . . a remarkable series of [Byron] photographs [including the one here shown] which have just won a diploma of highest excellence at the International Exposition at Liège, Belgium. These views cover the varied social work [begun in 1857 as a Sunday School] of Christ Presbyterian Church. . . . This is one of the two branches of the Brick Church, and is located in a downtown, densely populated region in the so-called 'Tenderloin' district. The pictures speak for themselves [showing as they do such diverse projects as basket weaving at the Saturday Morning Club; the Carpenter Shop of the Boys' Club; the Kindergarten; a drill of the Lincoln Cadets; classes in sewing, embroidery, millinery, cooking and physical culture]. . . . One beauty of this work has been its success under rather severe limitations. The church has fairly earned the good fortune which has now come to it in the splendid new plant [334–344 West 36th Street, dedicated October 27–29, 1905 and still in use] erected as a joint testimony to Dr. [Henry] Van Dyke's ministry, and also as a memorial to the late Maltbie [Davenport] Babcock, his beloved successor at the Brick Church [1900–1901]."

After the many-careered man of letters, too, was named the Van Dyke Club, here shown in vigorous action and described in the fiftieth anniversary brochure (1907) as a group of "working girls from 14 to 16" which met "three evenings in the week . . . for physical exercise, profitable employment in the study of millinery, cooking and literature." One of the observers (standing) has been identified as Miss Margaret E. Kinnie, a salaried Church Visitor.

These two photographs are offered in evidence of erring journalism and a rational philosophy, for in *Mr. Dooley's Opinions,* by Finley Peter Dunne (New York, 1901) the following dialogue occurs:

" 'I see be th' pa-aper,' said Mr. Hennessy, 'th' athletic girl is goin' out, what iver that means.'

" 'She had to,' said Mr. Dooley, 'or we wud.' "

. . . . The skin you love to touch

ASPIRANTS FOR titular honors in the roped arena of the ring and the glove might do well to follow the example of the gladiatorial immortal, Robert Prometheus Fitzsimmons, who is here beheld (page 148) (according to the Advertising Supplements of the *Metropolitan Magazine* of October and November, 1895) undergoing "An Innovation in Training" preparatory to his match with "Gentleman Jim" Corbett, which, after several deferments, finally made "the Cornishman" heavyweight champion of the world in Carson City on St. Patrick's Day, 1897.

"Fighting Bob," whose muscles had had early workouts in his father's blacksmith shop in Timaru, New Zealand, soon became a celebrity in antipodean boxing circles, and in 1890 he crossed the Pacific to wrest the middleweight crown from Jack Dempsey at New Orleans on January 14 of the following year. His knock-kneed underpinnings, supporting a massive torso, caused John L. Sullivan to dub him "a fighting machine on stilts," and the "solar plexus" blow that felled Corbett became his trademark by virtue of sports writers' reiterations, although it was the same punch that Jack Broughton had used in 1730. At the ripe old pugilistic age of thirty-seven, Fitzsimmons lost his title to Jim Jeffries at Coney Island on June 9, 1899. An unscarred veteran of more than 360 fights, carrying over into his fifty-second year, he somewhat stiffly invaded the theatre and achieved his greatest Thespian success in a fisticuff vehicle entitled *A Fight for Love*, which in real life transiently earned for him the heart and hand of a singer in the company. He died an impoverished vaudevillian on October 22, 1917, with his fourth wife in dutiful attendance. When the grief-stricken widow informed her stepson that all Fitzsimmons' diamonds had been pawned, she evidently omitted mention of those he carried to the grave tastefully set in his teeth, for in 1926 she petitioned the Chicago superintendent of police for an exhumation order, to retrieve these dental adornments installed by "Painless Parker" (see page 349). One of the great boxer's empathically inclined friends insisted that she desired the embedded gems merely for sparkling keepsakes.

As an antidote to the gloom cast by this ghoulish interpolation, I return to the November, 1895 article lightly dismissed in the opening paragraph: "The . . . illustration [here serving again] . . . shows three prominent men in a corner in the electric department [of "The largest establishment in the world for the treatment of the Skin, Scalp, and Complexion, Nervous and Blood Diseases, Eczema, Moles, Warts, Freckles, Superfluous Hair, Birth-marks, Moth, Tan, Pimples, Wrinkles, Red Nose, Blackheads, Barbers' Itch, Facial Development, etc., etc.," not to mention plastic surgery]. They are Bob Fitzsimmons, the pugilist; John H. Woodbury, and John Wilson Gibbs, M.D. . . . The picture illustrates Fitzsimmons taking one of his semi-weekly electrical treatments . . . which he says did him much good. The electricity passes through his system and increases the circulation, makes the muscles supple, pliable and hard. . . . When the picture was taken Dr. Woodbury was increasing the amount of electricity, and Dr. Gibbs was applying the force to Fitzsimmons' back by means of an electrode."

147

"Bob" Fitzsimmons at the John H. Woodbury Dermatological
Institute, Summer of 1895
127 West Forty-second Street

Even President Cleveland had once submitted to apparently unsuccessful anti-obesity treatments, doubtless lured by the ubiquitous magic of the Woodbury advertisements on which the good dermatologist was spending two hundred thousand dollars a year at this time. Part of this budget was invested in "a team of elk . . . trained to drive in harness . . . a buck and a doe, four and three years old respectively," and their appearance on the streets of New York attracted admiring throngs, who marveled at the female's "natural" dimples (as distinguished from the "artificial" ones implanted *sine dolore* on the physiognomies of trusting clients of the Institute). It is reassuring to be informed that the moose were enthusiastic users of that most famous and enduring of the doctor's products, "Woodbury's Facial Soap," thus accounting for the reference to the clarity of their complexions, which had all the charm of "the skin you love to touch."

148

"ANY DENIZEN of Gotham or parts adjacent who is still so far behind the times . . . as to imagine that the cult of the 'wheel' is not to-day the cult of the commonweal" was advised by *The New York Herald* of January 21, 1896 to betake himself to the Cycle Show at Madison Square Garden, where an average of 15,000 visitors a day—talking " 'wheel' in all its moods and tenses"—milled about the "four hundred and odd stalls."

"Two lone, but not lonely, women" of "the great army of the unattached wheelers" venturesomely journeyed thither from primordial Brooklyn of an evening, and the spokesman of the pair confided to a *New-York Daily Tribune* reporter (as set forth in the issue of January 23): "One was pulled and hauled and pushed and knocked around generally. . . . We are not members of a football team, but we ride wheels and attend the gymnasium, and found our training stood us in good stead. . . . At 10:05, feeling as if we had come from the hot room of a Turkish bath, we left the Garden." Early in their round, she said, "we received our first souvenir . . . and we forthwith degenerated into seekers after spoils. . . . We did not get everything we wanted, but one of us has twelve different stick-pins, a hat-pin, two clasp-pins, two badges, a puzzle, five different buttons, two pieces of music and a bookslate, besides catalogues galore." Their outing was marred only by failure to capture other charms in the form of a star, a tiny bicycle, and a miniature saddle. Evidently the last mentioned was a particularly desirable acquisition, for it also figured in the rhyme of a forever anonymous poet in the *Tribune* of the 24th:

> "Sing a song of souvenirs, of folks and wheels a lot;
> I visited the Cycle Show, now list to what I got!"

Follows a lengthy recapitulation of "Souvenirs By The Cartload," ending with a wail of frustration:

> "But still I am not happy, tho' these my eyes do dazzle—
> I was late in finding 'Mesinger' and didn't get a saddle!"

One manufacturer, according to the *Tribune*, must have spent a "small fortune" on little mementoes of silver, "and the chances are that nine out of ten of the fair sex who have visited the Garden . . . have either secured one of these trinkets or have practically used up all their nervous and physical force in the effort."

A "well-known authority on sporting affairs," also veiled in a protective coating of anonymity, was quoted in the *Tribune* on April 5, 1896, as saying: "These bicycle manufacturers are the most persistent advertisers we have ever had in any kind of sport. . . . The average manufacturer realizes that if he wishes to get his high grade wares before the public he must reach them through the newspapers." The Fowler Cycle Manufacturing Company of Chicago (with a New York Branch at 307 Broadway) devoted a good part of its promotional budget during the show to "The Fowler Sextuplet . . . Will Race The Empire State Express One-Half-Mile, Flying Start, In The Near Future. Final Announcement Later. And What's More, We Will Wager Any Amount From $10,000 to $100,000 That The Sextuplet Wins. See It At The Cycle Show."—and in this photograph. The Stearns Exhibit also included a "sextet." These attenuated giants were only less sensational than the Pope Manufacturing Company's bellicose version of "A Bicycle Built for Two"—"the new army tandem"—and "Model No. 40, mounted with a forty-pound Colt automatic rapid-firing machine gun . . . on exhibition for the first time," described at length in the *Tribune* of January 21st. Other wheels adapted for martial use were the Wolff "Sociable"—a two-seated tricycle equipped with a Maxim Gun—and the Columbia Company's tandem, with twin guns, soldiers' kits and signal flag. In general, according to the *Herald* of the 22nd, the makers (responsible for about a thousand different brands, representing an output of over a million "silent steeds" in 1895) concentrated not on the models that "can be driven a 'century' at racing speed; but [on] the wheel that will take you fifty miles from home, over any kind of going, and bring you back." Racing cyclists and "scorchers" represented a mere 10 per cent of the buying public, to whom bicycle posters of more or less artistic execution proved undeniably attractive. The Fowler choice of subject may have lacked the attributes of Maxfield Parrish's prize-winning entry in the Pope Manufacturing Company's competition; but it showed strength in the absolute, a superman who could support "on his chest a platform holding a grand piano and a man to play it, with four more musicians standing on the top of it," according to the *New-York Daily Tribune* of December 12, 1893. This was only one of the physical *tours de force* that made the twenty-seven-year-old, 196-pound regnant Monarch of Muscle and Demon with a Dumbbell the idol of the sthenic, the asthenic, and the sculptor alike. A full page in *Frank Leslie's Illustrated Newspaper* of March 29, 1894, was devoted to his prowess, with the caption: "The Latest Society Fad. Fashion Pays Court to Sandow . . . At His Private Levees." The article begins with the withering generalization that "this is an age of extremes; of abnormal development of all the resources of the earth, and of the human body and of the mind," and goes on to state: "Sandow is the strongest man in the world—the modern Hercules, Samson, and Goliath . . . and that is what draws crowds of people . . . to see this fair-haired Teuton of the wonderfully-developed body. . . . Really the most interesting exhibition is the private one . . . after his stage performance. . . . The room in which these receptions are held is in the annex of Koster & Bial's [on the north side of 34th Street, between Broadway and Seventh Avenue, where he was currently balancing three horses on his thorax]. . . . Seats are arranged about the room, and Sandow, stripped to the waist, begins his lecture. After each muscle is described he walks about, and the ladies and gentlemen pat his biceps [as the illustration by B. West Clinedinst affirms] and try in vain to find a soft spot; all is as hard, as unimpressionable as a mass of granite." His body reminded H. P. M., the chronicler of this gladiatorial salon, "of some great, massive, gnarled oak, petrified and as relentless as stone." A reporter from *The World* (June 18, 1893) gave a glimpse of "this German bunch of muscle" in his home, at No. 210 West Thirty-eighth Street, a week after his American debut at the Casino: "With him . . . lives a friend, Mr. Marius Sieverking. . . . It is pleasant to see them together. Mr. Sieverking [a pianist] . . . practices from seven to eight hours a day. . . . While he plays Sandow sits beside him on a chair listening to the music and working his muscles. . . . Both enjoy themselves and neither loses any time."

150

His act followed the much admired performance of the popular matinée exemplar of pulchritude—Henry E. Dixey in his oft-repeated role of Adonis—and, said the *World's* vengeful scrivener, brought New Yorkers to the realization of "what a wretched, scrawny creation the usual well-built young gentleman is compared with a perfect man." We are once again taken back stage: "Five minutes after the curtain went down Sandow, clothed only in his muscular development, was found crouching in a rubber bath tub in his dressing-room, while an attendant with a rubber pipe doused him with cold water." Emerging from this martyrization "Sandow, with the fond pride of a mother displaying a large family of children, proceeded to display his collection of muscles one at a time and to dwell modestly but lovingly upon their merits"—capable of bringing in $50,000 a year. More important to the Fowler Cycle Manufacturing Company was the fact that Sandow advocated the wheel as affording "an excellent exercise." In an article in *The Cosmopolitan*, June, 1894, he stated: "my nightly exhibitions . . . supply me, together with a good constitutional every day, or a spin on my bicycle [make unfortunately not specified], with all the exercise I need. If I want more, I take it, as I sit reading or smoking, by flicking my muscles."

Scene at the New-York Cycle Show, Madison Square Garden, January 18–25, 1896

Other exhibitors, with less faith in the pictorial approach, relied on live talent. A western firm displayed—as capable of being wheel-borne on their 23-pound pride—"Baby Bliss" in all the glory of his 582 times 16 ounces, his 58-inch chest, his 66-inch waist, his 72-inch hips. From these measurements the *Herald* of January 21 deduced that Sandow's opposite was "pear shaped." "I found him yesterday," declared the reporter, "surrounded by a large number of small, wheeling citizens. . . . Mr. Bliss stood on the edge of his platform, and nothing loath let 'em gaze; but then it may be remarked that some men have no sense of shame." On the same tour of duty, the *Tribune's* scout spotted a booth devoted to electric bicycle lamps, in a dark, secluded part of the Garden: "When one approaches the stand," he wrote out of positive experience, it is to "see the form of a young girl, dim and almost indistinct," and then to "receive a glare of light in his eyes which will destroy that vision of feminine loveliness and nearly blind him as well. The woman has a [battery operated] way of throwing that reflection into the eyes of men who show a disposition to be too admiring or inquisitive."

. . . . *I wish you'd come and play with me*

READERS OF *The Evening Telegram* were kept in titillated anticipation for three whole weeks, before a sketch based on a Byron photograph (page 155) appeared on June 27, 1896, in centered two-columnar bravura with the following elucidative paragraph: "The accompanying illustration shows Mr. Maurice Aron, who won the first prize in the EVENING TELEGRAM cycle parade of June 6. Mr. Aron's picture was made in the costume in which he won the beautiful [Columbia] bicycle that was given to the best costumed gentleman rider. In the future this costume will be known as the EVENING TELEGRAM bicycle suit. It has some new and very original ideas in connection with its manufacture and has been patented in both this and foreign countries. Those who have seen the costume declare that its originality was well worth the prize that it received." Aron, a clerk residing at 58 West Ninety-second Street, was an aide in the parade and a member of the West End Cycle Club with nine enthusiastic years of handlebar experience. The details of the custom-made perfection of his crash suit had been described on June 10 as "one of the most original costumes that has been seen in New York. . . . This gentleman . . . conceived the idea of having a suit made entirely in one piece. The result was so unique that it could not fail to attract the attention of the judges, and it did."

Lest it be assumed that these arbiters—General Horace Porter, Edward Bell, Jefferson Seligman, James B. Townsend, Isaac B. Potter (in absentia), Police Commissioner Avery D. Andrews (who appeared just in time to attend the deliberative banquet at Claremont), and Chauncey M. Depew—took their responsibilities lightly, a sentence from Mr. Depew's digestant remarks, as reported on the 8th, should be carefully analyzed: "I felt when the EVENING TELEGRAM said:—'Will you be a judge of the bicycle parade?' that the time had come for me to show what I know about something I don't understand." The task accepted in such humility of spirit was not a sinecure, for, as relayed "By Carrier Pigeon" from the eighty-foot bunting-decorated grandstand at Riverside Drive and 114th Street to the waiting presses, the judges—"driven by Lawson N. Fuller, behind his six record-breaking trotters," and accom-

152

panied by a "handsomely-uniformed escort of couriers"—took their places at 2:45 P.M., to the plaudits of five thousand surrounding spectators, and it was not until well after five that the last of the armada of cyclists left this dedicated group vertiginous.

An era encapsulated had passed before their eyes in what *The Evening Telegram* of the 6th called "the greatest parade of modern times"—a glittering array of twelve divisions on wheels that had spun its way up the Boulevard from Sixty-fifth Street to 108th and thence north on Riverside Drive, encircling Grant's Tomb and Claremont. Following the military cyclers and the various clubs (up to and including the Lobster Cycling Club, fresh from a crustacean banquet, and, in more propagandistic vein, the "Junita" Cycle Club, its two hundred and more members carrying banners with the emblazonment "Cuba Libre") came the fancy-dress wheelmen. Quaint were their conceits. The entourage of the "Jewel King" consisted of five "English soldiers" and a peaceable band of feathered Hottentots with girdles of leopard skin; "Annabelle," from Madison Square Garden, represented Trilby and was accompanied by a scowling Svengali and the blond bigness of Taffy; Press Eldridge—known in minstrelsy and vaudeville circles as "Commander-in-Chief of the Army of Fun"—was "attired in a baby waist of mouseline de soie . . . and a hat . . . that looked like an escape valve for his seething fancies." ("He also wore clothes," concludes the description). "Old Hoss" Hoey—forever associated with the hit song, "The Man Who Broke the Bank at Monte Carlo"—was in kilts, playing a bagpipe as he rode with his small, bedazzled blue-eyed daughter, "all in red"; a slightly confused "turbaned Turk" was "half concealed beneath an immense Japanese sunshade"; a "properly rigged" yacht awheel, celebrated the *Defender* (which had protected the *America's* Cup from Lord Dunraven's challenger, *Valkyrie* III, in 1895); and there were tramps and "Reuben" the rustic. There was no end to ingenuity. The wheel manufacturers went in for symbolism. The Stanley Manufacturing Company, for instance, used the energy of seventy riders—explorers and Zulus all—to retell the story of the miraculously deductive man who had stirred the jungle and the world in 1871, with that most felicitous of greetings, "Dr. Livingstone, I presume." The "Rambler racing team" was represented in jockey costume by "sixty-five colored boys mounted on Rambler wheels, so arranged with horses heads and blankets as to look like racers, . . . each wheel . . . labelled with the name of some famous race horse." Seventy-five cyclists of the Pope Manufacturing Company were mounted on Columbia wheels (voted the most desirable of all makes), with two tandems supporting a large florally banked facsimile of the coveted nameplate, in advance of "Uncle Sam" and "Columbia,"—"personated by an exceptionally pretty miss."

Little wonder that the judges were left, as General Porter expressed it, "with the sensation following a ride in the merry-go-round of childhood." The crowning of their decision was witnessed by 2,000 to 3,000 spectators, at the finale of the week-long "Grand Cycle Concert and Carnival" at Madison Square Garden on June 12. *The Evening Telegram* of the 13th thus described its own munificence: "The prize winners were the gayest of the gay, and the ladies looked longingly at the gracefully proportioned, full nickeled bicycle that had fallen to Miss [Ella] Sullivan's share, while the men could not keep their eyes off the splendid wheel that had been awarded to Mr. Aron, nor off the charming prize winners that the excellent taste of the judges had selected. Hastily arranging themselves in a semi-circle about the table of prizes . . . the cyclists looked meekly at the photographer [Byron, the credit line attests] who had pointed his camera at the group. They had not long to look, when the 'old thing exploded,' as Press Eldridge [who had descended from the Garden's Roof, still in black-face] remarked, and a flash light picture was taken of the smiling faces. Over in the sections where the Century Wheelmen, the Brooklyn Bicycle Club and the Riverside Wheelmen sat [winners all] there were loud cries for 'more!' and the photographer thereupon 'shot' the group a second time." Eldridge (himself the recipient of a cup) then introduced State Senator Thomas F. Grady, who set about rewarding the successful contestants.

Withal, far less favored were they than the fortunate prize winners of the *New York Journal*-sponsored parade of September 12, 1896—a "Bicycle Fairyland." On stage, after curtain-fall, following a performance of Evans and Hoey's "evergreen" favorite *A Parlor Match* at the Herald Square Theatre on the 24th, these victors received their glittering spoils from the lovely hands of Anna Held enveloped in a "bewilderingly beautiful blue gown," fresh from the café-concerts of Paris and already twice imperishable in lithographs by Henri de Toulouse-Lautrec. There, across the footlights, with all the compelling magic of her orthography-defying accent, she extended the witchery of her pleading invitation in song:

> "I'm fond of games and romps, you see;
> I wish you'd come and play with me,
> For I have such a nice little way with me;
> I wish you'd come and play with me."

A prize winner in "The Evening Telegram Cycle Parade," June 6, 1896

. . . . The cult of the commonweal

OF A Sabbath, with the coming of spring, "trulls and brawlers" (according to *The Illustrated American* of May 25, 1895), "a strangely-hued and motley-mannered herd" of "noisy and bedizened creatures" who made "the fast set of New York . . . the ugliest institution of its kind in the world," emerged from their winter hide-outs in the "dubious tap-rooms and eating saloons" of the Tenderloin to infest the sunlit serenity of the "cosy chateaux" of Central Park (the Casino and Mount St. Vincent) and the wind-swept reaches of Claremont. The press inveighed against "the subversion of these pretty resorts" intended for the provision of "sober and economical entertainments for respectable people," and argued for the ouster of their lessees, including Edward S. Stokes—the blood of Jim Fisk still drying on his hands after twenty-three years—who presided over the historic Riverside resort patronized by the dregs of the *demimonde* and the opulent of the cycling fraternity.

For a decade New York society had forsworn even the myth of a spring season; but its twin delights of the moment—a passion for tea (in line with the Anglomaniacal trend) and a new-found fondness for that already established proletarian favorite, the "iron donkey" (as the French dubbed the bicycle)—led to a revival of pre-summer elegance, in the form of a tannic acid fête awheel, celebrated at Claremont on the 4th of May, 1895, for the benefit of the Burnham Industrial Farm, "a non-sectarian home for unruly boys" at Canaan Four Corners, Columbia County, New York. "One of the most brilliant assemblages of fashionable men and women seen anywhere," exulted the *New-York Daily Tribune* of May 5th, came by pedal, by coach, by carriage, and on horseback to enjoy "the warm, balmy air . . . tempered with a breeze . . . freighted with the perfumes of jonquils, hyacinths and mi-

The Michaux Cycle Club attending the Bicycle Tea at Claremont, Saturday, May 4, 1895
Riverside Drive, nearly opposite 125th Street

Bicycling on Fifth Avenue, 1897
Looking north from 124th Street

gnonette." Tea, chocolate and bouillon tables on the glass-enclosed veranda were presided over by ladies clad in the non-participant sports fashions of the day, like Mrs. Peter Cooper Hewitt's simple attire, catalogued as "a skirt of black moire and a waist of cream silk, thickly covered with black jet and trimmed with lace, and a large hat of purple velvet, trimmed with plumes of the same shade." Other attractions were a bicycle booth "stocked with all the appurtenances" and latest models, and a "photograph stand," while on the lawn, where Lander's Orchestra played, was a flower and fruit bazaar.

As the afternoon waned, the assemblage was swelled by the arrival of the thirsty and famished members of the newly organized Michaux Cycle Club, whose first spring meet had started with a luncheon at the Casino and paused for refreshment at Mount St. Vincent before undertaking the hot twenty-minute run to 125th Street. Ladies of this élite band, shunning the immodesty of bloomers and knickerbockers, for the most part rode in "gowns of short walking length . . . somewhat on the plan of a riding-habit, with tight-fitting waist or jacket, and skirt plain and full, short enough to show the trim little boots and leggings." The members of this association (named in honor of the French inventors of the modern two-wheeler's prototype) had opened elaborate headquarters at Bowman's Hall on Broadway at Fifty-second Street the previous December, and soon became so proficient that they were able to execute intricate cotillion figures and even perform the Virginia reel on their "silent steeds."

157

"So, LET the 'bus-drivers smile and applaud; let ladies wave their handkerchiefs from the windows as the gallant equipage thunders by; let the dainty little swells, with only vigor enough to flourish a toy-cane, burst with envy; the Four-in-hand is our latest Phœnix!" This editorial salvo appeared in the *New-York Daily Tribune* on May 4, 1876, three days after the maiden trip here of Colonel DeLancey A. Kane's coach. This event was recorded on a canvas by H. C. Bispham now in the collection of Harry T. Peters, Jr., and reproduced as an Endicott & Company lithograph. It appears resplendent on the covers of song sheets issued by William A. Pond & Co. and the American Music Publishing Co., and is celebrated in the form of a wood engraving (after a drawing by I. Pranishnikoff) for the education of the readers of *Harper's Weekly Supplement* of June 3, in which the passage of this land yacht (pioneering public coaching in the United States) is duly set forth along with the following text: "We venture to say that more genuine, healthful enjoyment can be derived from one ride out to Pelham Bridge and back on the top of Colonel KANE's coach than from the whole flying railway trip from New York to San Francisco. Colonel DeLANCEY KANE is an American gentleman of fortune and leisure who takes an enthusiastic interest in coaching. Last summer he drove a coach from London to Windsor Forest. This year, believing that Americans would take kindly to the novel amusement, he is running a regular old-fashioned English coach from New York to the above-mentioned locality." This coach—"The Tally-Ho," built by Holland & Holland of London, and owned since 1933 by the Museum of the City of New York—provided an erroneous generic name for the prides of the "Knights of the Lash." "It is elegant and luxurious. The point of departure is the Hotel Brunswick . . . [at the northeast corner of Fifth Avenue and Twenty-sixth Street] at eleven o'clock in the morning, arriving at [the Arcularius Hotel] Pelham Bridge at one in the afternoon. At half past three, the interval giving plenty of time for a dinner, a picnic, or a stroll, the coach starts on its return, and arrives at the Hotel Brunswick at five. More than railroad punctuality is observed. The fare for the round trip is three dollars, fifty cents extra each way for a box seat. Passengers' luggage up to eighty-five pounds is carried free. Parcels are taken at moderate rates, and delivered with care." The *New-York Daily Tribune* of May 3, 1876, filled in such details as the seating capacity (fifteen); the advance bookings (practically no accommodations available for the six ensuing weeks); the identity of the "English guard of long experience" (Arthur Fownes), "who looks after the comfort of the passengers, collects fares, and sounds the horn"; the number of horses used for the line (sixteen), etc. The previously quoted editorial adds a floral touch, "the spanking steeds carry bouquets at their left ears" and gives its benison: "In whatever manner the other members of the Coaching Club may follow Col. Kane's lead, they have our hearty good wishes. When young gentlemen of wealth and leisure devote themselves to a pastime which requires strength and skill, which is virile and healthy, and which at the same time enlists them in the service of the public, they deserve only encouragement."

The praiseworthy organization mentioned—formed "to encourage four-in-hand driving in America"—had been activated by the communicable enthusiasm of William Jay's talk of his encounters with the Duke of Beaufort, the motive spirit in British amateur coaching. Its first meeting was held at the Knickerbocker Club (which today still shelters the fraternity) on December 3, 1875, and the initial meet took place on the April 22 following. A romantic account of origins is found in the *New-York Daily Tribune* of March 23, 1890: "The first English Coach brought to this country was made in London for T. Bigelow Lawrence, of Boston, and he drove it in that city as early as 1860. . . . When he died, Brewster & Co., of this city, bought the 'drag.' For some time it stood in front of their warerooms, then at Fifth-ave. and Fourteenth st., where idlers gazed at it with nothing expressed upon their faces but the merest curiosity. Finally, it proved to be a fertile seed and from it has sprung the New-York Coaching Club. Col. William Jay and Thomas Newbold in a stroll along Fifth-ave., chanced to see it and induced Frederic Bronson and S. Nicholson Kane to join them in buying it. The quartette can be truly called the forefathers of coaching in New-York." There were many celebrated "whips" who went "tooling over the drives"—and far away on long runs—for the sheer joy of it, or in the glorified subsidy of a means of private public transportation all through the gold leaf years of the final revival of a once strictly utilitarian means of motion: four members of the Belmont family (August Sr., August Jr., Perry, and Oliver H. P.); James Gordon Bennett; E. Victor Loew; T. Suffern Tailer; William K., Alfred G., and Reginald C. Vanderbilt; James Hazen Hyde; Reginald W. Rives (responsible for the copiously illustrated, authoritative account that was published in 1935: *The Coaching Club Its History, Records and Activities*) and a number of other devotees.

On April 27, 1895, E. S. Martin, in "This Busy World" (a feature of *Harper's Weekly*), took time out to meditate: "There is some doubt as to whether the fun of coaching lies in owning the coach and driving the horses, or in putting on one's best morning clothes and newest gloves and riding gloriously up the street and out of town on another man's conveyance. If you must drive, coaching is a dear sport, but if riding satisfies you, the men who like to drive four-in-hand make the more passive form . . . a pleasure that is easy of accomplishment. Every morning now in New York a coach leaves the Brunswick Hotel and goes to the Westchester Country Club, at a fixed hour and a fixed price for seats." This was the "Pioneer," splendid in the accompanying illustration by W. S. Vanderbilt Allen, a specialist in vehicular portraiture. "There is a benevolence," Martin continued, "about the dealings of the coaching-men with the public. . . . Nobody takes you yachting for hire, but the coaching-man does something that is pretty closely analogous to it, and does it out of devotion to sport."

The Illustrated American of June 20, 1891, called the pastime that so captivated these gentlemen coachmen "an exotic that only flourishes under the most favorable circumstances of wealth and leisure," but underscored its popular fascination: ". . . the only street rivals it has as 'drawing cards' are the circus and some big man's funeral. A parade of four-in-hands will always attract a crowd of all sorts and conditions of men. The great unwashed and the Fifth Avenue dandies; ladies of high degree and little girls with unkempt hair, dirty clothes, and dirtier faces; hostlers and stable-boys, and nearly every Englishman who happens to be in town, will be found at the meet. And if the horses be only well groomed and the harness

159

Charles F. Havemeyer's party arriving
at Claremont, May 25, 1895
Riverside Drive, nearly opposite 125th Street

has been properly burnished; if the driver knows how to handle the ribbons and there are a number of pretty women on the coaches, what more attractive sight can any city afford? Every man who has done much driving must feel his pulse quicken and a sense of enjoyment pervade his whole system when sitting behind four quick, well-put-together horses. . . . Add to this a pretty woman on the box-seat and a picturesque road, and the man who can sneer at this combination of attractions must be a surly dyspeptic or a snarling hypochondriac." The writer was critical of the "turnout" of several of the nine drags involved in the May 23, 1891 meet: "Some of the drivers . . . [chivalrously spared humiliating identification] do not know how to handle the ribbons. . . . Some of the horses are screws—in one case, evidently not 'the private property of a gentleman' who drives them; there is often an exhibition of harness-room carelessness and a lack of smartness in the action of the grooms. But, take it all in all, it is a very creditable parade, and fair women make up for what men, horses, coaches and harness lack." One four-in-hand escaping censure was that drawn by "the famous Havemeyer team of high-stepping bays." Charles F. Havemeyer and his party are here shown upon their arrival at Claremont following participation in the May 25, 1895, meet. The drag, according to his brother Henry, was owned by their father, Theodore A. Havemeyer (see page 96). The event is reported in the *Tribune* of Sunday the 26th: "The New-York Coaching Club had its annual parade yesterday, making the start about 11:45 o'clock in the road in Central Park leading from the Eighth-ave. entrance to the Mall. The beautiful weather had the effect of attracting many spectators ["Thousands," according to *The New-York Times* and "comparatively few people" because of "little advance trumpeting" if one followed *The World*], who early took possession of the [neighboring] benches. . . . Spectators on bicycles ["One feature not noted in the previous parades," commented the *Herald*] were numerous enough nearly to fill the road about the spot where the line was being formed." The ten participants, in their allotted order, were Colonel William Jay (President of the Club from 1875 to January 2, 1897) on his yellow and black Park Drag—a conversion of the "Dorking" Coach he had purchased in England in 1874—with red wheeling gear, behind brown wheelers and chestnut and brown leaders wearing clustered apple blossoms; Prescott Lawrence, in a turnout of primrose and pale rose; Perry Belmont, with a stag party atop his maroon and claret outfit; Dr. W. Seward Webb on a dark blue drag; the Philadelphian Nielsen Brown, who favored the same color and had an all male company; Colonel E. D. V. Morrell, also of the Quaker City; Charles F. Havemeyer; August Belmont, whose white-faced bays were harnessed to a maroon and claret coach; Reginald W. Rives, who drove a dark blue equipage, and had no fair companions on this bright day; and Frederick Bronson on the box of his black and red pride. All the various Sunday papers gave complete listing of the dramatis personae (Mrs. Jay cautioning the *Times* reporter: "You won't forget to mention the horses") as well as contradictory fashion notes. I will spare you all but the subject of this photograph: "Charles F. Havemeyer, on his black and blue coach," quoth the *New-York Daily Tribune* of May 26, "drawn by four bays, was accompanied by Mrs. Havemeyer ["looking prettier than ever since her illness," *The World* assured], wearing a gown of pearl-gray silk, combined with black satin, trimmed with white lace, and a small black hat; Mrs. Charles Morgan, who wore a costume of black and white silk and a small bonnet of roses; Mr. and Mrs. Eustis, the latter in a summer silk of pearl gray and a white hat, and Amos Tuck French." Northward along the West Drive the caval-

162

cade tooled to the Seventh Avenue and 110th Street Gate for the presidential review, known as "The Manœuvre"; down the East Drive to the original rendezvous for dismissal; then across Seventy-second Street and up Riverside Drive—festal with decorations for the Firemen's Parade—to Claremont. Here, according to *The World*, "An elaborate luncheon was served on the north aisle of the broad balcony . . . hung with heavy red cloth, with gold fringe on it, with various coaching emblems, such as whips and horns, by way of ornamentation. There was one long table and on this was a huge central, oblong mound of purple lilacs, bordered with pink and red roses. At each end were similar circular beds of these flowers, tipping off with mauve orchids." *The New-York Times* added: "Not only did the members and their friends partake of the good cheer, but covers were laid in an adjoining room for the twenty-four coachmen and grooms who looked after the horses." During the afternoon Lander's Band played, and the last homeward bound coach left Claremont at 4:30.

On the following and twentieth annual repetition of this gay traditional rite in 1896, *The Illustrated American* of May 16 commented: "One of the peculiar social features of life in New York is the parade of the Coaching Club [an event twenty-nine times honored in the thirty-five-year period terminating with the final 1910 Spring Meet]. And it is a brilliant sight to see the exquisitely-groomed horses 'cherry-picking' their way over the park's smooth, yellow roadway, the glittering coaches, and the beauty and chivalry atop. The women are attired in gay colors, and as the coaches rumble along in the sunlight one mentally likens them to giant baskets of flowers on wheels."

. . . . Take the day of a hunt

"AT LEAST a score of these [country] clubs, so enthusiastically kept up by fashion these days, have already been established on the outskirts of New York, and more are likely to follow, for not all the 'sets' have as yet been taken in, and new clubs are easy to found." E. Idell Zeisloft, editor of *The New Metropolis* (New York, 1899) devoted a long chapter to this phase of New York's social life. "Two hunting clubs have been in existence here [on Long Island] for many years—the Meadowbrook [incorporated on May 5, 1881] and the Rockaway Hunt. Both have elaborate and expensively run clubhouses, and from them hunting is carried on on a gorgeous scale. Of the two, the Meadowbrook Hunt has the greater name and fame. . . . Very little that is imposing or beautiful greets the eye at this famous Meadowbrook. The clubhouse [about a mile from Hempstead and three removed from Garden City] is a low, old fashioned two-story building, the stables and kennels plain and unpretentious. The colony of buildings looks simply like a well-kept stock farm. Yet within these stables are many of the finest horses money can buy, and the largest and the best pack of English foxhounds in America. There are actually two packs, for besides these English hounds a collection of Yankee hunters have been bred." Four of these "Famous Dogs of the Meadowbrook Hunt Club"—Yarrow, Boleno, Limerick and Garrick, "The Finest in the Pack"—were introduced to perusers of *The New York Herald* Colored Section on Sunday, September 25, 1898. *The New Metropolis* continued: "No other hunting club in America has such a list of members, in point of view of horsemanship, wealth, or social prominence. Those who belong to it are known in New York society as the 'hunting set,' or the 'Meadowbrook set,' and constitute a *coterie* almost by themselves. The Meadowbrook is the most costly of all the country clubs about New York to belong to, and the amount of money spent each year at this clubhouse is simply fabulous. . . . Take the day of a hunt—the early morning. The fresh wind blows sharply over the Hempstead Barrens. By courtesy this is a 'fox hunt' . . . but the aniseed bag replaces the lithe little animal," thus eliminating the cruelty of what Oscar Wilde described as "the unspeakable in pursuit of the uneatable." The trail, laid in advance by the drag boy, was often plotted "with diabolical ingenuity," *Leslie's Weekly* of November 25, 1897 tells, "and apparently with an intent to bring about as many croppers as possible." However, Meadow Brook did not always adhere to this adulteration of the English-imported sport, or the calculating pursuit of a released captive animal, for the *New-York Tribune Illustrated Supplement* of May 8, 1904 quoted Foxhall P. Keene (M.F.H., 1903–1904), as having said: "I maintain that the only way to have fox hunting is to hunt the wild fox. These Meadow Brook hounds . . . do not hunt a fox released from a bag. All last year there were only two occasions upon which bag foxes were hunted. . . ." But Mr. Zeisloft is becoming impatient: " 'Yoicks! Ho!' Men and women in the yard are mounting their . . . mettlesome hunters. The women are arrayed in perfect-fitting riding habits; the men are in 'pink coats' . . . [over the flashlight blue waistcoats of Meadow Brook], 'toppers' . . . or derbys [the M.F.H. and the Whips wearing hunting caps, of course], riding trousers of white, and high [black] top boots. The hounds held in leash, are wildly jumping here and there. . . . Near them, his sharp eye taking in every detail, is the master of the hounds. . . . Men and women who will not join in the hunt itself, but will ride along the road and watch its progress from certain points are having their traps brought up. . . ." At last the moment of the "throw in" comes. "A sharp crack of the master of the hounds' whip. The leashes are slipped. Behold, the dogs are on the run! Out of the yard, into the road, thence over hill and down dale. The pace is terrific. His long whip cracking, the master of the hounds is after them, and behind, at their best speed, all the others, it may be fifty or more. Across field and furrow, over fences, brooks, through woods and pastures, it matters not where, all these hunters are riding for dear life. Few can keep up the pace to the finish. Each mile after the first four or five sees one after another drop out. . . . This applies particularly to the women of this 'hunting set.' There is but one, in fact, who has the reputation of invariably being in at the finish; she is Mrs. J. Kernochan, perhaps the finest rider in America."

However, there was another "queen and huntress" of Meadow Brook, who held rival court. *The World* of December 9, 1900 described her: "Mrs. [Adolf] Ladenburg does not look the typical Diana, save in a pair of keen black eyes that look unfalteringly over a horse's head, no matter how desperate the mark in front. She is a pretty woman, with clear olive complexion, small regular features and a face of classic oval. Although light of weight and light of hand, her seat in the saddle is as firm as a rock and her control of her horse is absolute." On Thursday November 22, 1900, in a performance that "will live in hunting history," she wrested the supremacy from Mrs. "Jimmy" Kernochan. *The World* described the feat in admiring detail: "The day's run [of eleven miles] had been a long and hard one. . . . Two hundred yards ahead was the last jump . . . a tall fence" described as "5 feet 8 inches of timber." "Never for an instant did Ralph N. Ellis, Master of the Meadow

The Meadow Brook Hounds, 1899
Cubbing (training the young hounds)

Brook hounds . . . think that any one would attempt the jump. But he reckoned without a just regard for the courage of a black-eyed woman, whose bony sorrell hunter was carrying her straight for the high fence. It was Mrs. Ladenburg, her hunting crop lashing the sides of her thoroughbred at every jump. Within fifty feet of the great fence there was a cluster of carriages, their fashionable occupants eagerly watching the finish of the run. Mrs. Ladenburg sent her tired hunter straight at the fence. Women shrieked and others turned their faces away in terror. Ralph N. Ellis, close behind the daring huntress, rose in his stirrups and cried a warning. . . . Like a whirlwind the reckless woman took the jump. In her desperate eagerness she lifted her gallant horse ["Winchester," a borrowed mount] for the mighty effort. It looked like death for horse and rider. But the unexpected occurred. Under the dauntless woman's light, firm hand the tired horse rose with magnificent power, shot free of the top rail with a scant half inch to spare and landed safely in the road— quivering and spent. Game horse, unrivalled rider!"

The Meadow Brook Hounds, 1892
A Check (pause in the middle of the Hunt)

. . . . *Light may the Boat row*

"Oh! calmly may the waves flow,
And lightly may the Boat row,
And safe and swift the Boat go,
That my Lad's in.
He plys the oar, so tightly moves,
In the dance so sprightly,
So gracefully and lightly,
Oh! there are none like him."

Jonas B. Phillips, *Light may the Boat row*

DEDICATED TO the New York Boat Clubs by its composer, J. Watson (who copyrighted it in 1836), this "Duett Sung . . . by M^rs & M^iss Watson" met with "unprecedented applause, having been usually called for and repeated three times on each evening of its performance" at New York's Park Theatre and in the capitals of Europe. Its decorative cover (lithographed by A. E. Baker), showing a regatta off Castle Garden, graced at least eight editions in romantic tribute to our local oarsmen. Walt Whitman too celebrated them in early August, 1881, when engaged in "putting the last touches on the printer's copy of my new volume of 'Leaves of Grass'—the completed book at last." (The poet is referring to the Boston edition—to be banned from that city's Post Office—printed by Osgood and Company, 1881–1882.) "Work at it two or three hours, and then go down and loaf along the Harlem river; have just had a good spell of this recreation. The sun sufficiently veil'd, a soft south breeze, the river full of small or large shells (light taper boats) darting up and down, some singly, now and then long ones with six or eight young fellows practicing—very inspiriting sights. Two fine yachts lie anchor'd off the shore. I linger long, enjoying the sundown, the glow, the streak'd sky, the heights, distances, shadows." (*Specimen Days and Collect,* Philadelphia, 1882–1883.)

Not long before (on June 28, 1879) pictorial evidence of the popularity of this manly sport appeared in *Harper's Weekly* in the form of a wood engraving after a drawing by C. A. Keetels, titled "Saturday Afternoon On The Harlem River," and described as "a picture of the animated scene that may be witnessed every pleasant afternoon, during our long boating season, on the Harlem River just above the bridge. This part of the river forms the practice course of various rowing clubs of New York, and affords also opportunity for every one to row or sail who can command a shell or a sail-boat. . . . Boats of all descriptions crowd the river whenever the weather is pleasant, and a more lively and attractive scene can hardly be imagined."

In the waning summer of 1895, it was Byron's turn to seek Manhattan's upper margin and build his composition with its background of "Down Easters"—typical three-masted schooners, born around Wiscasset or Damariscotta-way to carry Maine logs and fragrant timber to the lumberyards fringing the Harlem River. In the foreground are two double shells of the

167

Scene on the Harlem River, Fall of 1895
South of the 149th Street Bridge

Nonpareil Rowing Club, the oarsmen wearing its orange and black colors. Organized (as was the Wyanoke) in 1874 and still in existence, this organization was junior to the Atalanta (founded in 1848), the Friendship (1862), the Dauntless (1863), the Nassau (1867), the New-York Athletic (1868), and the Union (1869). It held seniority over the First Bohemian Boat Club—recruited in 1881 from the ranks of the Turn Verein, according to the *New-York Tribune Illustrated Supplement* of May 30, 1897, which quoted the sally that its members "race with anything, from a log which floats past their house to a steamboat"—and the Harlem Rowing Club (1893), the youngest member of the Harlem Regatta Association. "These clubs all have boathouses on the Harlem River, some of which are handsomely furnished. . . . The members come from all walks in life, and men of leisure and mechanics frequently meet on Scullers' Row, where the best oarsman is the best man, no matter what his station in life may be," the feature article stated.

The year 1895 began badly for the lads who plied the oar. On the night of Washington's Birthday a fire originating in a watchman's shanty at 141st Street destroyed five of the boathouses, including that of the Nonpareil. Its Captain Canavan consummated a $4,500 bargain, reported in the *New-York Daily Tribune* of May 11th, in purchasing "the famous old Columbia College boathouse . . . no ordinary affair. It was built and given to the college by the father of one of the boys in the crew which Columbia sent to Henley, and which won the cup in 1876 [error for 1878]. It is a well-gotten-up, slate-roofed affair, costing originally $18,000." Dear to the Morningside Heights campus is the song by John Tempest Walker, Jr. ('84): "And if I had a daughter/ I'd dress her up in Blue,/ And send her to the Hudson,/ To coach the Freshman crew," the name of the waterway in the lyric changing back and forth with the location of the collegiate rowing headquarters. While the scholarly shells were transferred to the North River for a time, the press account relates that "The Nonpareils will tow their new purchase down to a position near their present headquarters in the Oliver boathouse, for it is to be anchored, or rather firmly and evenly placed on a new and carefully constructed bedding of piles, between the Wyanoke and Nassau Boat Club floats."

With the spring the Harlem fleet—which, according to *The New York Herald* of April 7, consisted of about four hundred boats—took to the water, and the twenty-ninth annual regatta held on Decoration Day was pronounced "a success in every way" by the *New-York Daily Tribune* of the next morning. "The day was all that the most enthusiastic of the oarsmen could desire, and at no Harlem regatta on record was a larger or more enthusiastic throng of spectators present. The banks of the stream from Macomb's Dam Bridge to the railroad bridge at Fourth-ave., were black with excited spectators . . . and all the clubhouses above the railway bridge were decorated with bunting and crowded with spectators, most of whom were of the fair sex." The champion challenge cup went to the Bohemian Boat Club, whose eight-oared shell passed the finish line "less than half a length" ahead of the New-York Athletic Club's straining crew in "as game and well-fought a race as has ever been seen on the Harlem."

"That up-to-date annihilator of distance, the bicycle, having conquered, or at least seriously affected, all means of travel on land, is now accused of seeking newer and damper fields," the *New-York Daily Tribune* of July 5, 1896, regretfully pointed out, "for the seductive influence of the wheel is drawing scores of oarsmen from the Harlem and other rivers in the vicinity of New-York to the smooth roads of Westchester, Long Island and New-Jersey. . . . Oarsmen, as a rule, are unwilling to admit that the bicycle is responsible for the decay of their favorite amusement [although many of their clubs had cycling divisions]. As is well known, racing on the water is expensive. . . . Then the overcrowding of the rivers by traffic, and the rapacity with which the shores have been gobbled up for business purposes, have tended to reduce the enthusiasm of the oarsmen below the point where a man will place his life in danger for the pleasure of aiding to win a banner or a cup that nobody can drink out of." On the current situation, the *Tribune* quoted a former champion who declared with bitterness: "It's well enough for some of the more enthusiastic amateur rowers to assert that the bicycle has not cut much of a figure in the decadence of the sport, but I'll tell you that it has. Why, don't you know, many boat clubs are kept up merely for society's sake. In fact, there are more dances in the clubhouses than there are crews in training, and receptions are doubly as numerous as regattas. The club regattas, which were formerly contested with almost as much vigor as the interclub regattas, are largely drifting matches between boatloads of beefy men."

> "Oh! calmly may the waves flow,
> And lightly may the Boat row. . . ."

"THE BATHING suit and the camera—these are the twin betrayers of our innate savagery." This penetrating anthropological statement is to be found in *The Illustrated American* of August 20, 1892. Further analysis of the twofold threat is conducted in the typical after-a-hummingbird-with-a-howitzer quasi-facetious manner so often employed by that weekly guardian of the mores of a generation: "The crude, inchoate device of flimsy flannel first pressed the button that rung up the curtain on our real carelessness: the kodak did the rest. Students of human nature have sought in vain for an explanation of the utter rout of supposedly ingrained sentiments and conventionalities that attends the donning of a bathing-suit." Then the blast veers again to the poor photographer, portrayed fully clothed with his lethal instrument upheld in one hand and a balancing black umbrella in the other, his only defense against the tropical sun and the hypertensive author: "Under the magic touch of the man with the gelatine film seemingly inherent manners turn out to be mere evanescent affectations." Back to human frailty: "The haughty dowager, the exquisite maid, the formal-minded matron, the pompous buck, the pretty dandy, don with their unconstricting garb of bath-flannels, a devil-may-care disregard for the modes and conventions of fashion that reminds one strongly of the wise man's comments on the close relation between womanly pudicity and its outer guard. Complexion [we are duly warned] isn't the only thing that the sea-water washes off. That delicate veneer, dainty and rare as the vernis Martin, the work, as one fancies, of at least three generations of complete gentility, the exclusive heritage of transmitted wealth and quintessential culture, the pride of the Knickerbocker, the despair of the pork-packer and his blooming brood—the softest surf snatches it in a moment from its proud possessor. . . ." And, after final beady fixation of blame—"What an unconscionable iconoclast that kodak is! How it shatters our idols of grace and beauty, our models of brawn and physique!"—we are led on to the ultimate imprecation: "Rot seize your kodak! A murrain on your films!"

Bathing at Coney Island, 1896

Bathing at Far Rockaway, 1897

Bathing at Far Rockaway, 1897

"(I WANT to protest in this place against the term 'crank' as applied to the baseball enthusiast. The word is too rough, it is an exaggerated imputation—a sentence out of all proportion to the offense. The word 'fan,' meaning fanatic probably, is clearly wrong. I have reason to believe that the so-called baseball 'crank' is fond of the national game because he studies its finer points, and sees beauties in the game, as played, that the average spectator does not realize. . . .)" This apologia appears in the pages of *Once A Week* for April 18, 1895.

While not otherwise lacking in patriotism, I confess a certain indifference to affairs of the diamond. Notwithstanding this hereditary taint (for I come from a long unbroken line of spectacularly disinterested obscurantists, as far as batting averages are concerned) I nevertheless found myself magnetized by the candor of the photograph (page 179), captioned " 'Well' 'Well' 'Well' Frank" on the Byron negative. Percy C. Byron remembered the forthright figure and the wild shout that gave him his soubriquet, but could not furnish more definite data. A six months' stand on the walls of the Museum of the City of New York as part of a "Play Ball" exhibition failed to bring identification from the thronging visitors; amateurs, columnists and professionals alike—while some recalled the character—disclaimed knowledge of his name. Finally, my letter of appeal, generously published by *Sports Illustrated* of September 27, 1954, elicited a single reply from "An Old West Side Fan" (see issue of October 25, 1954) now living in exile at "Isle of Hope," Savannah, Georgia, far from the Windy City bleachers:

"In the old days of the famous Tinker, Evers to Chance infield combination [1903–1912] on the Old West Side of Chicago, a lawyer—by the name of Frank Childs—sat in about the same place, just off first base, each day. Then the grandstand, on the right side, extended up to first base, and the Cubs had their dugout there. Whenever the Cubs made a misplay of any kind, he would howl in a foghorn voice: 'WELL, WELL, WELL, WHAT DO YOU THINK OF THAT!' Since this went on day in and day out, Childs became well known for this saying of his. It always brought great laughter from the fans. Charles W. Murphy, then Director of the Cubs [1906–1913], tried to ban that man from the ballpark, on the grounds that Childs was simply trying to publicize himself. I think the case went to, or was attempted to be taken to, Court. Whatever happened I never bothered to notice. . . ."

With the aid of the Chicago Historical Society, I located a likeness of Frank Hall Childs (1859–1954), a spare, dapper gentleman with considerable hirsute adornment and a slight squint, by no possible imaginative stretch in any way related to our subject, except by the binding tie of baseball and the use of a hallmarked (no pun intended) warwhoop.

And then one day my omniscient editor, A. L. Hart, Jr., of The Macmillan Company, pounced upon this photograph with joy: "Why, he must be the hero of the Zane Grey story, 'Old Well-Well'!" Marshall B. Davidson (author of *Life in America*—history *sans pareil*) too, had the same immediate reaction, and—knowing my two mentors could not err—I put in a call slip (purposively ignoring the puzzled glance of the young man on Sunday duty at The New York Public Library Desk) for *The Redheaded Outfield And Other Baseball Stories* (New York, 1920), for proud confirmation of faith. Their boyhood delight lay before me:

"He bought a ticket at the 25-cent window, and edging his huge bulk through the turnstile, laboriously followed the noisy crowd toward the bleachers. I could not have been mistaken. He was Old Well-Well, famous from Boston to Baltimore as the greatest baseball fan in the East. His singular yell had pealed into the ears of five hundred thousand worshippers of the national game and would never be forgotten." The aged aficionado, marked with the stigmata of fatal illness, had pulled himself together for the gratification of a sick-bed sigh: " 'If I could only see one more game!' " When Burt, his nephew and protégé, came to New York's Polo Grounds as a new player for the visiting Phillies, Old Well-Well made the supreme effort and it was on this day that the narrator sought a bench across the aisle from him in the bleachers. "No one accompanied him; no one seemed to recognize him. The majority of that merry crowd of boys and men would have jumped up wild with pleasure to hear his well-remembered yell. Not much longer than a year before, I had seen ten thousand fans rise as one man and roar a greeting to him that shook the stands. . . . Old Well-Well settled himself comfortably in his seat and gazed about him with animation. There had come a change to his massive features. The hard lines had softened; the patches of gray were no longer visible; his cheeks were ruddy; something akin to a smile shone on his face as he looked around, missing no detail of the familiar scene."

For a play-by-play description of the game (far beyond my fluttering comprehension) I refer you to the atmospheric story itself (first published in *Success Magazine*, July, 1910) and overtake you at the twelfth inning, toward the sad but satisfactory end of a baseball classic. Needless to say, for two fans at least, it was a one-man battle. Earlier in the afternoon, at a tense moment, "Old Well-Well [had] breathed hard. Again the wrestling of his body signified an inward strife. I began to feel sure that the man was in a mingled torment of joy and pain, that he fought the maddening desire to yell because he knew he had not the strength to stand it. Surely, in all the years of his long following of baseball he had never had the incentive to express himself in his peculiar way that rioted him now. Surely, before the game ended he would split the winds with his wonderful yell." At last in the third overtime inning, with the score at 4–3 in favor of the New York Giants, two Phillies on bases, and his nephew at bat, "the old fellow . . . was gazing toward the field with an expression on his face to which no human speech could render justice. He knew what was coming. It could not be denied him in that moment." After two fouls "Burt's lithe shoulders swung powerfully. The meeting of ball and bat fairly cracked." Victory was already won when the second of the men on base crossed the plate, but "the tension never laxed until Burt beat the ball home in as beautiful a run as ever thrilled an audience. In the bleak dead pause of amazed disappointment [on the part of rooters for the home team] Old Well-Well lifted his hulking figure and loomed, towered over the bleachers. His wide shoulders spread, his broad chest expanded, his breath whistled as he drew it in. One fleeting instant his transfigured face shone with a glorious light. Then, as he threw back his head and opened his lips, his face turned purple, the muscles of his cheeks and jaw rippled and strung, the veins on his forehead swelled into bulging ridges. Even the back of his neck grew red." And forth came what Zane Grey described toward the end of the tale as an "Ear-splitting stentorian blast! For a moment I was deafened. But I heard the echo ringing from the cliff [Coogan's Bluff], a pealing clarion call, beautiful and wonderful, winding away in hollow reverberation, then breaking out anew from building to building in clear concatenation. . . .

"'Well!— Well!— Well!!!'"

My story should end here; but museum workers are noted for their inquisitiveness—among other repugnant occupational idiosyncrasies—so I wrote to Mrs. Zane Grey and was rewarded by her confirmation: "That he was a living person, I am quite sure for I remember my husband speaking about him many years ago." I could not let poor Old Well-Well rest in anonymity, so—not having plagued the National Baseball Hall of Fame and Museum about this problem for a baker's dozen of months—I risked another letter to Ernest J. Lanigan, the Historian there, and he started to circularize the elect of his calling. Within no time at all he forwarded the solution, offered by Lee Allen (expert on affairs of the diamond and author of well-known books on the subject) in the form of an excerpt from *The Sporting News* of December 19, 1896: "Frank B. Wood, the 'Well, Well!' man of baseball fame, invaded Madison Square Garden during the recent six-days' cycling race and smuggled his delicate voice in with him. He walked along in front of the boxes and carried a huge rose in his buttonhole. Stopping in front of a box containing a number of chappies, 'Well, Well!' remarked, 'Gentlemen, I am not in society, but I enjoy these functions immensely. It pleases me to see that you enjoy yourselves. If I can contribute to your happiness by a few yells just to draw attention to this part of the garden, please command me.' He was about to open his face for an effort when the chappies yelled in unison for a policeman and 'Well, Well!' was hustled away with a bad case of lung congestion owing to suppressed vocal enthusiasm."

Having brought "Old Well-Well" out of the realm of fiction, Lee Allen pursued the matter further and furnished me with the approximate date of Frank B. Wood's passage into the realm where the home team always wins. Further delving on my part revealed that this legendary fan died at his residence, 259 Hudson Street, New York City, at 2 A.M. on December 9, 1914, a month short of his seventieth birthday. His end did not go unnoticed, for Heywood Broun devoted an article to him in the *New York Tribune* of December 11: "Old Giant Rooter Hushed By Death. . . . Fans of the modern Brush Stadium have forgotten him, but fifteen years ago every rooter knew Frank B. Wood. . . . They did not know him by that name, though, but as 'Old Well, Well!' . . . So regular was 'Well, Well!' in his attendance at the Polo Grounds that he was known to all the players on the circuit. Wood was a Giant rooter at a time when the fortunes of the team were at their lowest. Nothing could dampen his optimism. Often he would seek to root his team home against leads of anywhere from 8 to 10 runs. . . . By trade the faithful fan was an electrical engineer and something of an inventor, too, but he tossed away all his jobs in order to cheer for a tail end team. By and by the fortunes of the Giants rose, but those of Wood declined. With the coming of better teams came finicky fans. To them the loyal rooting of Wood seemed just so much tireless reiteration. . . . In fact, complaints were made and Wood was barred from the park for many years. One day last year Tom Foley, the Polo Grounds chief of police, saw a man hanging about the gate disconsolately. Every cheer from the field inside seemed to give him acute physical pain, and at length Foley passed him in. Mike Donlin stepped to the plate as

178

Wood reached his seat, and for the first time in seven years the Polo Grounders heard the 'Well, Well, Well!' slogan. It was not so loud now, but Mike heard and he remembered the call, for it had come to him tagged with abuse back in the days when he was a foe and played with the Reds. He waved his cap to the bleacherite, and then struck out. For the rest of the game Wood was silent. Not only his voice had weakened, but his optimism, too. He left in the seventh inning because the Giants were four runs behind. He did not come back all season, and no one heard his call again."

A Giant Rooter at the Polo Grounds, 1897
Eighth Avenue and 157th Street

. . . . *The dim, awful perception of a great mystery*

"To CENTRAL Park this afternoon," George Templeton Strong wrote in his diary before retiring on August 10, 1869, "to inspect the live critters assembled in and around the old Arsenal building—the nucleus of our future Zoological Garden. The collection is not large, and consists of donations sent in and received without any system: sundry bears, black bears and a grizzly bear, prairie dogs, foxes, beautiful ocelots, owls, eagles, two meek camels, pheasants, monkeys, macaws, etc. It amounts to little. But the critters look healthy and receive much attention from visitors." Four years later, on August 25, 1873, finding his Fulton Street law office overrun "by certain Philistines with ladders and paint pots," he "fled to Central Park and spent most of the clear, cool day there roaming about, lunching frugally at the Casino, visiting the 'Belvidere' and the dairy and inspecting the animals." Philosophizing, he went on: "No man can look at a menagerie without the dim, awful perception of a great mystery."

New Yorkers had ever evinced an interest in the animal kingdom. As far back as 1763, the subjects of the Crown had been entertained by exhibitions of wild beasts; in the early 1780's a popular form of diversion was afforded by traveling menageries; in 1788 Thomas Pool, an American equestrian, organized a zoological display; six years later, Gardiner Baker, the keeper of the Tammany Museum, started a similar enterprise—the most noteworthy of several such in town—on a vacant "corner of Pearl Street, fronting the Battery"; the *New-York Commercial Advertiser* of May 17, 1805, tells that as of May 4 "A menage of living Animals and Birds is forming in this city, for public exhibition . . . at the upper end of Broadway road." A melodramatic aquatint—"Magnanimity Of The Elephant Displayed In The Preservation Of His Keeper J. Martin, In The Bowery Menagerie In New York"—copyrighted in 1835 by the recognitory Mr. Martin, shows his rescue, in December of 1826, by "the friend of man," whose trunk lifted the petrified victim far beyond the reach of a tigress, while a cooperative lion seized the cat and roared his outraged indignation. In 1838 Edward W. Clay executed a drawing, lithographed and published by H. R. Robinson, evidently at the request of Messrs. Welch, Macomber and Weeks, showing "The Majestic And Graceful Giraffes, Or Cameleopards, With Some Rare Animals of the Gazelle Species . . . captured in the wilds of South Africa, by Mr. [John] Clayton, and recently imported, at an immense expenditure" for display at their beautiful pavilion, No. 509 Broadway, below Prince Street. On July 2, Philip Hone took his daughter Catharine to join the "great numbers of persons pay[ing] their respects to the distinguished Strangers." A little later, a wood engraving in the *Illustrated News,* August 6, 1853, commemorates the newsworthiness of the "Disembarcation Of The Two Giraffes, Colossus And Cleopatra, From The U. S. Steamship Washington New York," reiterated in *Gleason's Pictorial Drawing-Room Companion* on May 13, 1854, when these long-necked curiosities were to be seen at Barnum's American Museum. A Hippodrome such as Franconi's, or the four-footed captive creatures in the circuses of Van Amburgh or L. B. Lent always spelled bewitchment.

180

The Menagerie in Central Park, 1895

It is far from illogical, therefore, that the *Second Annual Report Of The Board Of Commissioners Of The Central Park*, issued in January, 1859, preconized that "Ground is reserved for . . . a Zoological garden." It was at first planned to use Manhattan Square—since 1877 the home of The American Museum of Natural History—but pending the resolution of drainage and other problems, the present location of the Zoo served for what was thought to be the temporary habitat of the "Living collection." By the close of 1866, this included 797 specimens (465 Mammalia, 311 Aves, and 21 Reptilia) presented by interested donors at home and abroad, with valuable contributions sent in by Army and Navy officers from their far-flung stations, to be supplemented later by winter loans from shows that took to the road in the warmer months. In 1870, before summer's end, the castellated "Arsenal Museum" in the Park near Sixty-fifth Street was surrounded by a "series of buildings . . . ornamental in design and convenient to the public . . . one for the carnivora; one for the birds and monkeys; open-air sheds for the bears, wolves, &c.; roomy and open-air cages for the eagles, domestic fowls, &c.; an inclosed building for elephants, camels, and various tropical animals, and (in process of erection at the west of the Museum buildings) a larger structure intended for carnivora, tropical cattle, &c. To these buildings and sheds . . . all the animals and birds in the Museum [already containing the recently uncrated exhibits of The American Museum of Natural History] were transferred, and the premises formerly used for them were adapted to use as offices of administration for the [Park] Department and its clerks." When the Board of Commissioners Of The Department of Public Parks took over the work of the original Board on April 20, 1870, the plans hitherto made for the *Tiergarten* were referred to as "immature," and in its 1872–1873 report the recently organized body gave an estimated average of not less than 7,000 daily visitors to the realm of the beasts. *The Annual Report of the Department of Parks* for 1899 rejoiced that "The Menagerie in the Central Park retains its great popularity despite the installation of the New York Zoological Garden in Bronx Park," dating from November 8 of that year.

Nine twelve-months later, Israel Zangwill wrote into his play, *The Melting-Pot*, " . . . New York is the great stone desert," and when the heroine's mother remonstrated, "But ze big beautiful Park vere ve drove true?" the response was: "No taste, Baroness, modern sculpture and menageries! . . ."

. . . . The Bois de Boulogne of New York

". . . WE CAN only think of the split shell of a Galapagos turtle," suspirated the *New-York Daily Tribune* on its editorial page on November 27, 1876, circling the rearward aspect of the statue of Daniel Webster, the latest addition to the Park's nascent Age of Bronze—the subject of Zangwill's later barb. The earliest arrival had been Johann Christoph Friedrich von Schiller, his bust with clavicle-length curls by C. L. Richter rising above the rocks in the Ramble, as the 1859 gift of the Germans of New York. Then appeared the head and shoulders of Alexander von Humboldt by Gustav Blaeser, placed near the Plaza entrance by his hyphenated compatriots in 1869. The much becloaked Sir Walter Scott with his adoring dog, by the Edinburgh sculptor, Sir John Steell, was presented by "Resident Scotsmen and Their Sons" in 1871, and in the same year Samuel Finley Breese Morse (the first American to be so dignified in the Park enclosure, as perpetrated by B. M. Pickett) with one hand on his most famous invention, the other uncomfortably protruding from the folds of his coat, was placed there by the telegraphers. The next permanent guest was J. Q. A. Ward's pensive Shakespeare (see page 427), who came to meditate on the Mall in 1872. These five were numerically overshadowed by thematic subjects (listed in the order of their advent): the pitiless *Eagles and Prey* by Christian Fratin (1863); the symbolism of Jules Fesquet's *Commerce* (1864); *Auld Lang Syne,* carved in "New Brunswick Stone" by Robert Thompson (1865); the maternal *Tigress and Cubs* by Auguste Cain (1867); Ward's *Indian Hunter* of the following year; the gracile figure of *The Falconer* by George Simonds (1872); *The Seventh Regiment Memorial,* again by Ward (1873); and the healing Angel of the *Bethesda Fountain,* the work of Emma Stebbins (1873). By the time Zangwill's spokesman registered his complaint, the galaxy had increased to a justificatory point.

Webster, then, came into a goodly if in some instances ill-interpreted company, when his colossal statue was unveiled on November 25, 1876 by the ten-year-old son of Gordon W. Burnham, its donor. The fourteen-foot bronze (cast by Muller in Munich) was the work of "Thomas Ball of Florence" (born in Charlestown, Massachusetts) who relates in his auto-

Summer in Central Park, 1895
The Statue of Daniel Webster and the West Drive
near Seventy-second Street

biography, *My Threescore Years And Ten* (Boston, 1892), that from boyhood he had wanted
to paint Webster's "godlike" head. In 1852, turned sculptor, and engaged in realizing this
ambition in clay, he left his improvised *trespolo* (with its converted ash-barrel base) to watch
his hero passing in procession along Tremont Street, Boston, on the way home to die. "This
bust, my first of life size, is the one I have used, without alteration," wrote Ball, "for my several
statues of the great man." It was his 30-inch statuette of the national figure—in Mr. Burnham's
library for twenty years—that brought him the magnification of the Central Park commission.
He returned to Italy a week before the impressive dedication ceremonies and so escaped
the *Tribune*'s blast: "The pose of the figure may, perhaps, be true to life, but it is not altogether agreeable in an artistic sense . . . it makes no difference to the world whether Webster
wore such baggy and impracticable 'dual garmenture' . . . as he here, unfortunately, must
wear for centuries. . . . The pedestal of gray granite (designed by Batterson, Canfield & Co.
of Hartford) is perhaps the finest possessed by any statue in our city." On this substantial
119-ton base, are carved in relief a younger Webster's clarion words (words that rang

183

out in the Senate on January 27, 1830, during the debate with Robert Y. Hayne of South Carolina on the blazing issue of State Sovereignty and Nullification): "Liberty *and* Union, Now and Forever, One and Inseparable."

The heroic statue (shown on page 183 under the protection of a patrolman of the gray-uniformed Department of Parks Police, known as the "Sparrow Cops," who became part of the regular force on January 1, 1898) stands on a green island in the Grand Drive, the first four miles of which were opened to the public on November 12, 1859. From the very beginning, the macadamized and gravelled roads (increased to 9½ miles by 1866 and—according to the *Guide to The Central Park* by T. Addison Richards, published by James Miller—"so admirable in . . . finish that slippered feet might almost tread them with ease and pleasure") were much traveled, for the *Fifth Annual Report of The Board of Commissioners Of The Central Park* (for 1861) claims their usage by 467,849 vehicles that year, with 23 arrests for "fast driving" (that is, in excess of 7 miles per hour). On March 21, 1865, George Templeton Strong diarized: "Fifth Avenue from Forty-ninth Street down was absolutely thronged with costly new equipages on their way to Central Park. . . . It was a broad torrent of vehicular gentility, wherein profits of shoddy and of petroleum were largely represented. Not a few of the ladies who were driving in the most sumptuous turn-outs, with liveried servants, looked as if they might have been cooks or chambermaids a very few years ago." The French *littérateur* Paul Bourget—evidently oblivious of the world of high fashion that patronized the Park circuit and the reaches beyond—followed the same path during his 1893–1894 visit (reported in his *Outre-Mer Impressions of America*, 1895): "By carriage up Fifth Avenue and through Central Park, which is the *Bois de Boulogne* of New York. . . . A whole people throng its paths this Sunday afternoon, a veritable nation of working folk at rest. I have not met two private victorias on these roads, swarming as they are with vehicles. They are all pleasure carriages, packed full with women and children, or tilburys driven by their owners. . . . The people who pass you by in these vehicles and on the sidewalks are substantially dressed and without elegance,—not a single workman's blouse, and on the other hand not a rag nor anything which would betray poverty. . . . The women are small . . . and without much beauty. In . . . [their] dress there is a visible abuse of high colors and of trimming. It is like an immense walking emporium of ready-made clothes."

*   *   *

During the long winters (which actually were more gelid then) sleighing was extremely popular. In the four white months of 1869, if we are to believe the Thirteenth Annual Report of the good Commissioners, 47,872 sets of runners passed over the snowy surface. The British Dean, S. Reynolds Hole of Rochester, in *A Little Tour in America* (London and New York, 1895), commenting on the variety of equipages seen in Central Park ("every kind . . . from the imposing drag with its 'four spanking tits,' to the wee conveyance . . . drawn by goats") gives a fine picture of hibernal traffic: ". . . there can hardly be a more inspiriting or amusing spectacle than that which is there exhibited, when the snow is deep enough for the sleigh, and, in the bright sunshine and keen fresh air, the Kentucky horses, with their smart harness and coloured plumes, and their cintures of merry bells, go swinging along with the grace and swiftness of a deer." *The Illustrated American* (January 13, 1894) furnishes a reportorial description of the Park under "niveous conditions": "Every possible contrivance that can speed on snow is to be seen scurrying along the three-arched highways of the beautiful clove.

Sleighing in Central Park, about 1897

Gorgeous Russian affairs, with horses, driver, and riders buried in furs, run cheek by jowl with nameless devices built apparently, on short notice, of potato bins and sections of cast-off railway tracks. Tandems, four-in-hands, omnibuses, trucks, baggage wagons, village carts, phaëtons, and drays, are put on runners and sent to swell the motley procession that flies up Fifth avenue, through the Park, out to Riverside—the finest driveway in the world—and thence back through the Boulevard [Broadway] to town again."

185

Coasting in Central Park, 1896

"Recent Vision of Jollity in Central Park," February, 1898

IN THE early morning hours of January 31, the first snow of the winter of 1897–1898 enveloped New York in temporary whiteness in a fall lasting twenty-four hours, followed after twelve-hour surcease by a second precipitation; but the full impact of the "winter hurricane" by-passed the city in favor of New England after newspaper morgues had been pillaged for facts and figures about the Blizzard of 1888.

Among those capitalizing on the comparison was Herbert Harding, who paraphrased a Danish juvenile folk saying, "The white bees are swarming," in the title of his piece in *The Illustrated American* of February 19, 1898: "There is a slang expression to the effect that in winter the poor are obliged to eat snowballs, and this is almost literally true of the poets, who are the only persons who profit by the beautiful phenomena, if the poor fellows who clean the streets and sidewalks are excepted. He is but a poor poet who cannot turn a blizzard into a sonnet." Mr. Harding might have added photographers to the list of weather profiteers, for his article was enhanced by several irresistible Byron photographs, including the upper one reproduced. After describing the devastating act of Nature, the author continued: "All was not suffering and disaster that was borne on the wings of the wintry gale. . . . The parks and squares of the Eastern cities have not yet ceased to ring with the happy laughter of happy childhood as it revelled in a carnival—a veritable saturnalia of snow." Having delivered himself of this lyricism, he could not resist a return to the stream of social consciousness so characteristic of his day: "Within sound of their merry voices was to be heard the crunch of the shovel of the proletariat as they cleared the way for carriages in which they or theirs are destined never to ride. Snow is for children and poets. For the proletariat—the shovel."

❊   ❊   ❊

How often one discovers in Byron's most felicitous compositions all the qualities—even the retained color image—of a well loved canvas that has become part of one's permanent aesthetic collection! In my mind the lower photograph is invariably and inevitably paired with *Central Park: Winter*, conceived about 1905 by William J. Glackens (one of "The Eight") and owned by The Metropolitan Museum of Art. The blue coldness of the snow, the warmth of the maternal sharing of childhood pleasure, the wintry trees, the constant rocks, the sounds of steel against ice and of the young voices—all are to be found and felt alike in the painting and the print.

As EARLY as August 15, 1785 *The New-York Packet* published a letter signed by "Veritas," saying in part that "It is a general complaint that there is not in this great city, nor in its environs any one proper spot where its numerous inhabitants [at that time an estimated 23,614] can enjoy, with convenience, the exercise that is necessary for health and amusement." "The Commissioners' Plan" of 1811, which marked the beginning of the modern city, made no provision for a great open space except "The Parade" (Third to Seventh avenues, Twenty-third to Thirty-fourth streets) although the gridironed streets were projected almost the full length and the entire breadth of Manhattan Island. Perhaps the first to actively champion a large public park were William Cullen Bryant, who began to editorialize on the subject in *The Evening Post* of July 3, 1844, and Andrew Jackson Downing, with his spearheading letters of 1849 and 1850 in *The Horticulturist.* By the mid-century mark, poets, planners, and politicians were advancing the scheme, and the controversy became one of geographic location, some favoring the pastoral Jones' Wood (along the East River between Sixty-sixth and Seventy-fifth streets) while others argued for a more pivotal site. On July 21, 1853, the legislature authorized the city to take the area bounded by Fifty-ninth and One Hundred and Sixth streets, Fifth and Eighth avenues, for public use. This was then a goat-infested terrain adorned with squatters' shanties and their inevitable components of misery, crime and under-privilege. In September, 1857, sponsored by the literati and other far-seeing citizens, Frederick Law Olmsted—a thirty-five-year-old landscape architect with faith in the democratic idea and prodigal imagination tempered with practicality—became the Superintendent of what had been christened "The Central Park." Before the year was out, Calvert Vaux invited him into partnership in the competition for the design of the Park; and their anonymously submitted collaboration, the "Greensward" Plan, triumphant over the work of thirty-nine other contestants, was awarded first prize on April 28, 1858. With Olmsted as architect-in-chief and Vaux as consultant, the work of laying out this intelligent scheme of beauty began about June 1. Olmsted, defying administrative difficulties, periods of political indifference and even hostility, carried through in the spirit of creative idealism the building of "the first real park made in this country," completed in its principal features by 1876.

Andrew H. Green—a key figure in the development of the American *Bois de Boulogne*—stated in the *Second Annual Report of the Board of Commissioners of the Central Park,* dated January, 1859: "A Lake of about twenty acres above Seventy-sixth street . . . has afforded healthful amusement and recreation for thousands in skating; the lower lake at Fifty-ninth street near the Fifth avenue is also well advanced." And the following year it was noted that "whenever the ice was in a condition for use" the skating pond was "in the daytime and evening a constant resort, presenting a scene of gaiety." The young Winslow Homer was among the artists who captured the hibernal rhythm and jollity, while Currier &

Ives, along with other lithographers, set it down on still favorite stones, and wood engravers made it their own in the days before the surroundingly skyline started to impinge on the *Rus in Urbe* of the original scheme, which anticipated a circumference of low buildings veiled by a parkside fringe of trees. In 1880, Edward Clark, one of the founders of the Singer Sewing Machine Company, called on Henry J. Hardenbergh to design the nine-story "Dakota" (the pioneer West Side "skyscraper" in the right background, at the northwest corner of Eighth Avenue and Seventy-second Street). At first known as "Clark's Folly," it became—and still remains—an aristocrat among apartment houses. South of it appears the less venerable, shorter-lived 600-room Hotel Majestic, here seen in its newly opened glory, fresh from the drawing board of Alfred Zucker, and standing, according to *The Illustrated American* of January 26, 1895, "like a massive fairy vision before the rambler through Central Park."

Skating in Central Park, 1895

"Moored at the eastern end of the Lake, the visitor will see the Venetian gondola, presented to the Park, in 1862"—on September 20th, to be exact—"by John A. C. Gray, Esq., formerly a commissioner. This is a real gondola and not a mere model, but it is not used, because Mr. Gray did not, at the same time, present the Commissioners with a Venetian gondolier to manage it! However, it looks sufficiently romantic, lying in all its low, black length upon this water hardly more ruffled than that of its native canals." So we read in *A Description Of The New York Central Park* by Clarence Chatham Cook (New York, 1869). It is comprehensible that Mr. Thomas S. Dick, licensed in 1861 by The Board of Commissioners of The Central Park to operate two classes of boats ("the passage or omnibus" variety at a ten-cent fare for the two-mile round trip, and "the call or private" genus) might have encountered surmountable difficulty in finding the talent requisite to stand on the *poppa* and man the long oar, as there were relatively few Italians in New York at this time. Despite this imaginative block, Dick did a thriving—if at that time unremunerative—business, for under his

The east end of The Lake, Central Park, 1895. (Another version of this subject—also by Byron—was reproduced as the cover of *The Illustrated American* For the Week ending September 7, 1895.)

admiralty (which came to include a non-contractual but speculative interest in the amatory status of his clientele) 25,298 of the 4,195,595 visitors who frequented the new park in 1862 availed themselves of his floating conveyances; and among other responsibilities (including the payment of a $100 seasonal fee for each of his eleven craft) it devolved upon him to see that his employees were "neat in appearance, civil, and attentive." During this war year, four additional landings were provided, according to the Park Department's Sixth Annual Report, each with "a tastefully constructed shelter, where persons may comfortably wait the arrival of the boat in its circuit, or sit to observe the boats as they pass, or the water-fowl in their playfulness."

By 1872–1873, work to the tune of $2,360.92 had progressed on the construction of a boat-house (seen at the extreme right of the photograph) "made necessary by the enlargement of the boating business and the insufficiency of the existing arrangements at the esplanade of the Terrace." This structure, based on an architectural elevation (lent by the Department of Parks to the Museum of the City of New York) bearing the stenciled names of Calvert Vaux and J. Wrey Mould, was replaced by a rustic wooden building in 1924, and, thirty years later, by the present red brick, white limestone-trimmed terminus, the $305,000 gift of the late Adeline and Carl M. Loeb.

Misfortunately, however, John A. C. Gray's imaginative munificence has not been replaced. That its romance carried over into the present century is proven by a photograph reproduced in *The Saturday Evening Mail* of June 15, 1907. It had its celebrants. Toward the end of the 1860's, for instance, Julian K. Larke, in *Davega's Hand Book of Central Park*, recommended inspection of the Venetian exile (with an ancestry dating back—in recorded literature at least—to the year 1094) "that floats lazily in the centre of the Eastern arm of the Lake." On July 29, 1893, we find it—or its successor—in duplicate, "drawn especially for *Once A Week* by Parker Newton." Nor did it escape the editorial eye of E. Idell Zeisloft, for in *The New Metropolis* (1899) the Lake is described as being "large enough to afford a pleasant tour in a skiff or gondola in summer time." Artists such as Asa Coolidge Warren; illustrators, among them C. Graham; photographers including J. H. Johnston and Byron; later designers of post cards—all were taken with the picturesque potentials of the gliding blackness singly or in multiplication, with passivity turned utilitarian. My own collection even shows it as the glass-imprisoned ornamentation on a paperweight.

This exotic craft also gave rise to a much bandied, oft told New York tale—in line with the gullible sale of the Brooklyn Bridge, the vocal salute of the Library Lions upon the passage of a virgin along Fifth Avenue, and other regional folklore—for a discussion of its popular appeal is said to have evoked a politician's suggestion that since one gondola proved such a patent attraction, it might be decidedly advantageous to have two and breed them.

. . . . *The hideous beauty*

" 'IN TH' manetime,' says I, ' 'tis ho! f'r th' Sthreets iv Cairo,' I says. 'An' I wint. An' so goes ivrybody.' " So Finley Peter Dunne's protagonistic Mr. Dooley, the humorously philosophical saloonkeeper of the "Windy City," told his friend, Mr. Hennessy, in one of those dialogues on current topics that leavened even bitter moments with laughter from the nineties into the new century. The shrewd sage of Archey Road was expatiating upon the exhibits at the World's Columbian Exposition—"The White City" that cast a Beaux-Arts spell on American taste for a generation—but in describing the delights of the Midway Plaisance he could have been talking of Coney Island's Bowery and Surf Avenue, which later aped many of the less edifying features of the widely imitated Chicago World's Fair of 1893.

Coney Island, 1896

On June 2, 1895, in an article on "Coney Island Wakes Again," *The New York Herald* announced "A New Enterprise," enlivened by "the clashing of cymbals and the howls of . . . Arab swordsmen": "It is called the streets of Cairo, and there George Sheriff has assembled camels, Egyptian donkeys, ponies of all degrees and a queer array of Arabs and Egyptians. They had a start on Decoration Day, but the management said that it wasn't for fair, so they'll do it all over again to-morrow." The *New-York Daily Tribune* of Sunday, May 31, 1896 described the coming of spring to New York's neighboring City of Pleasure by-the-Sea: "On every hand carpenters and painters are plying their vocations and new lumber is piled on every side. The Streets of Cairo, decorated with stranger emblems than the Valley of the Nile ever knew, is all but finished, a poor imitation of the Egyptian architecture of the New-York Tombs [transplanted to the southeast corner of Surf Avenue and West 10th Street]. Instead of dull grey the Streets of Cairo are bright yellow, decorated with blue hieroglyphics, birds and beetles. The sacred ibis is presumably there, but the sacred cat does not appear in the external decorations. . . . [The] Ferris Wheel is having its big buckets put in place. . . . The dens and dives are running in full blast." (It should be mentioned that the original Ferris Wheel, of which the one shown on page 193 is a humble version, had been introduced to fair-goers at Chicago, where it stood "up against the sky like a huge spider-web," inspiring Josiah Allen's Wife—Marietta Holley, the much traveled Samantha—with feelings "about half and half—half sublimity and orr" as she looked down on "the hull glory of the world." And,

"The Streets of Cairo," Coney Island, 1897

"The Algerian Theatre," Coney Island, 1896

furthermore, according to his company's brochure, it placed George Washington Gale Ferris "in the front rank of engineers of his time.") Fortunately, according to *The Illustrated American*, July 25, 1896, the "mass of the multitudes indicate their essential wholesomeness of mind" by a healthy preference for "the funny sights of the streets of Cairo" (with its talent imported from near-by Manhattan rather than from North Africa) to the "severely unpatronized" exhibition of the *danse du ventre*—shades of Chicago's "Little Egypt"—and other debasements extolled by "fakirs in human flesh." In a Fourth of July editorial that year, the *New-York Daily Tribune* urged vigilant policing of that portion of Coney Island known as "The Bowery," ". . . a portion of the crowded West End, which is given over to cheap shows and catch-penny devices of all kinds, . . . among them . . . some that are clearly indecent and immoral . . . [into which] people are drawn by the alluring announcements of professional 'barkers'" like the derby-decked tout drumming up trade for the "Algerian Theatre"—another Chicago derivative. "A ride on the camel . . . is another 'superb sensation' not to be despised," wrote A. T. Colley (in the *Metropolitan Magazine* of September, 1897) passing along the evidence "that for the munificent sum of two dollars one can taste to the utmost limits the dissipations of Coney Island." At this time, the way by water, aboard the Iron Steamboats, instead of the "more expensive but less airy cars," (some of them luxuriant with parlor chairs, under the supervision of a porter) provided the favored form of transportation, although many came by bicycle, some by carriage, and a limited few by yacht, before the subway started its catapultic spewing of the city's millions onto the once sparkling sands in 1920. The lunch basket—supplemented by "the mysterious edible dainties displayed in the booths"—has always been standard equipment.

The resort dates back to the 1820's. From the first, the ocean was the basal attraction (the Swedish authoress, Fredrika Bremer, in *The Homes of the New World,* described the strand as "solitary" and possessed of a "wild charm" when she picnicked there on the evening of August 26, 1850) but palace hotels (once equally celebrated for their epicurean delights and their band concerts under such famed conductors as Anton Seidl and John Philip Sousa); gambling and the lurid attractions of the vice-ridden "Gut"; horse-racing; prizefights; Pain's fireworks making night incandescent; the side shows; the freaks with their poor capital of deformity; the shattering, shrieking, screaming rides into controlled space and through amatory tunnels; the great amusement parks (Steeplechase, Dreamland, and Luna) with their endless spectacles and contrivances; the carrousels and the carnivals; the "Modern Venus" contests and the Incubator Babies; the beer and the pop, the red and yellow of the mustarded "hot dog," the dripping ice cream cone, the poisonously colored whorls of spun sugar; a hundred thousand sights and a hundred blended olefactions—all these conglomerate multichrome cacophonies have been part of the hideous beauty of Coney Island.

Of all those who have excoriated, execrated, mocked, celebrated and creatively loved this galvanic, irrepressible resort in song and verse, essay and novel, play and motion picture, photograph and painting, there was one who became above all others her Artist Laureate and (although he said in sadness, "There are no masters today") "The Master of Coney Island." Reginald Marsh, who told me in 1954, the last winter of his life, "Nature doesn't compose very well," wrote in a magnificent credo ("Let's Get Back to Painting," *Magazine of Art,* December, 1944): "It was in the early 1920's . . . that I took up the subject matter I still like to paint best. Frank Crowninshield sent me out to Coney Island one day to make a drawing, and I've been going out there every summer since, sometimes three or four days a week. . . . I like to go to Coney Island because of the sea, the open air, and the crowds—crowds of people in all directions, in all positions, without clothing, moving—like the great compositions of Michelangelo and Rubens."

"THE NIGHT BEFORE HER WEDDING."—so Charles Dana Gibson titled a drawing, in which his pen caressed nine laughing, lovely girls, toasting one of their number. Each of the ladies-in-waiting differs from all the others in the degree of her emotion. Affection, friendship, happiness, excitement, hope-filled visions of her own approaching election, a touch of envy, a twinge of jealousy, a tinge of regret, a glimpse of love and a look of longing—all these, the artist coaxed into the slope of a shoulder, the lift of an arm, the line of a neck, the twist of a lip. Every one completely apart from all the rest in her thoughts and in her loveliness. . . . And yet, fifty long years later and beautiful still, Mrs. Gibson told me how she had been her husband's model that day, for the entire court and its queen. The enchantment is preserved in the pages of *Life* (October 28, 1897) and the black and white in the collection of the Chicago Historical Society.

That drawing and Byron's photograph (pages 198–199) are in many ways affinitive. *The New York Herald* of Sunday April 23, 1905, describes the festive occasion here shown: "Mrs. Eben Wright gave a charming dinner party at her residence, No. 12 [10, if one favors accuracy] West Fifty-third Street, on Wednesday evening [April 19th] for Miss Julia Lorillard Edgar, . . . who is to be married to Mr. Richard H. Williams, Jr., on Tuesday. The table was decorated with spring flowers and ferns. Besides Miss Edgar the guests included her brides-maids and a few of her girl friends. . . . The bride's souvenirs to her attendants are emerald bracelets."

The hostess (née Miss Leta Pell and later to become the Marchesa Emilio del Sera-Fiaschi) was identified by her daughter, Mrs. Grafton H. Pyne (the former Leta C. Wright) as the second from the right. To her left, in svelte, encasing black, with a pompadour, is Miss Mary W. Soley, today the widow of Howard C. Dickinson; to her right is Miss May E. Sands, who in 1908 married into the Irish peerage, when she became the Hon. Mrs. Hugh Melville Howard. The sister of the bride and her Maid of Honor, Miss Caroline S. Edgar (who died as Mrs. Henry Sanford in 1935) chose to wear black that night. Beyond her are Miss Gertrude Pell (Mrs. Francis C. Bishop, who survived until 1953) and Miss Elizabeth A. Morton (soon to wed Sidney S. Breese; later Newell W. Tilton; and now living on Long Island as a divorcée). The bride-elect (seated), currently residing in Massachusetts, was destined for over-early widowhood, as Colonel Richard Henry Williams (who graduated from Harvard the year of his marriage; presently spent fifteen years in the coal firm of Williams & Peters, founded by his father; saw distinguished overseas duty in the purchasing division of the Federal Remount Service in the First World War, and was a leading figure in club and turf circles) died in his forty-eighth year.

But I have not told of the marriage ceremony, which took place on April 25, 1905 at the Church of the Incarnation, at the northeast corner of Madison Avenue and Thirty-fifth Street. *Town Topics*, the weekly scourge of society published by Colonel William D'Alton Mann, in its issue of the 27th could only refer to the occasion as "Tuesday's most fashionable wed-

The Bridesmaids' Dinner, April 19, 1905

ding"; and of the bride it could only say that she was "the second daughter of the Newbold Edgars [of 28 East Thirty-ninth Street] and prominently related." It noted that she and Mr. Williams had been much fêted, citing Mrs. Eben Wright as "one of those who entertained for her." The writer listed her attendants as "the Misses Caroline Le Roy Edgar, Edith Brevoort Kane, Gertrude Pell, Louisine Peters, May Sands and Agnes Edgar—the last as flower-girl," and lamented "The absence of pretty Miss Elizabeth Morton in the march to the altar was a disappointment," for "Being in mourning, she was obliged to withdraw." *The New York Herald* of April 26, describing the "Fashionable Nuptial Event," reported that the bride's gown was of "white satin, draped with old point lace, once worn by her mother and grandmother. . . . The veil, also of point lace, was a family heirloom. She also wore a collar of pearls and diamonds and a necklace of diamonds with pendant of sapphires [the gift of the groom]." According to the *New-York Daily Tribune*, the bouquet was "of white orchids and roses," while *The New York Times* saw it as being made up of "lilies of the valley," and noted that the bridesmaids (who varied astonishingly in nomenclature, identity, and attire, depending on which newspaper one favored) were clad in "trailing skirts of tucked white chiffon and lace coats, topped by large dark-green crinoline hats trimmed with ribbon and clusters of green ostrich tips. Their bouquets were white and green." The ushers, too, were subject to variations in reportage, but Ogden L. Mills (later prominent in New York State Republican affairs) was universally conceded to have been best man, and mentions (plus or minus) were made of Francis H. Potter, Kenneth P. Budd, W. O'Donnell Iselin, Joseph G. Wells, W. Earle Dodge, Edward H. Carle, Arthur S. Dixey, J. Searle Barclay, James Markoe Robertson, and Harry T. Peters, whose engagement to Miss Natalie Wells had been announced in February, and who became the leading authority on Currier & Ives and the world's foremost collector of "America on Stone."

. . . . *Nothing shall mar the dignity of the occasion*

THESE GAY blades were posted at the Yale Club recently—not for non-payment of dues, but in the hope that one of today's members might look upon them with a shout of hilarious recognition, identifying a moment of lost youth or the features of a grandfather, uncle or father. Unfortunately, anonymity has been preserved both here and at New Haven, where an indifferent Alma Mater—through forgetfulness, ingratitude or disdain—would not acknowledge the sonality of any one of them; prominent graduates of their vintage could not recall fraternal ivy-clad moments; debutantes of their year did not sigh over a remembered waltz; exposure on museum walls brought forth delighted cachinations, but nobody staked a claim to this riant young manhood. Even Mr. Byron—ever the court of first and last appeal—could not break the deadlock with a left-to-right listing of the line-up, but the occasion made lasting impress, for he wrote to me: "While I was under the cloth focusing the picture one of the boys threw a butter plate at me just missing the camera, I believe they were all drunk especially the pitcher." The use of such dairy-laden ammunition would not have been countenanced by Mrs. Frank Learned (Ellin Craven Learned) in whose *arbiter elegantiarum* of 1906—*The Etiquette of New York To-day*—we read that "A bridegroom gives a farewell

200

bachelor dinner for his best man and ushers a few evenings before the wedding, taking care that nothing shall occur to mar the dignity of the occasion." However, the cartoonist Otho Cushing (in *The New York Herald*, December 13, 1903) saw fit to incorporate similar misbehavior in No. 6 of his series, "Marriage À La Mode   A Century Or Two After Hogarth," in which he gives a comparative study of intoxication, with two ushers reduced to somnolence, a third seated, with a vague diabolized grin, a fourth with arm raised in meaningless salute, a fifth—more empathetic than his fellows—clasping the hand of the wavering bridegroom-to-be, while a cynical waiter is earning corkage for the management by opening a superfluous bottle of champagne.

Our successful suitor and the groomsmen, pledged to deliver him early at the altar, were not giving thought to the vanished threat of a measure maltreated at Albany in 1903, when

Bachelor Dinner at the Yale Club, 1904
30 West Forty-fourth Street

a legislator from New York's VIIIth Assembly District (known to its constituency as "de Ate") "introduced a bill taxing bachelors and spinsters." The *New-York Daily Tribune* of February 15 of that year reports with vindicable levity that "after a profound debate as to what committee it should be referred to, including those on Internal Affairs, Public Health, Federal Relations, Indian Affairs, Unfinished Business or State Prisons, [it] was finally sent to the Committee on General Laws, which amended the bill so that it will affect only the introducer."

Nor did the hero of the evening honor the lady of his choice as had a 1904 patron of "Del's" in commissioning the confectionery department of that establishment to celebrate her loveliness in spun sugar or some other tortured edible. *The New York Herald* of March 20 bears witness to his ardor: "At Delmonico's were exhibited several designs that required genius for execution. The centerpiece for a bachelor dinner consisted of a sculptured likeness of the host's bride elect. It was reproduced from a dashing photograph that lay on the designer's table, and the picture was copied even to the green plume on the hat."

. . . . A long, sticky, muddy pool

"MISS ANNA GOULD AGAIN." So the exasperated *New-York Daily Tribune* of February 8, 1895 headlined the rumored engagement of Marie Ernest Paul Boniface, Marquis de Castellane, to the fickle young heiress, whom in the later days of his disillusionment he was to designate as "my Light that Failed."

Since the bride declined to embrace Catholicism (because, as she candidly informed her favored suitor several breaths after consenting to become his wife, this would preclude a divorce) the nuptials were solemnized in her brother's Fifth Avenue mansion. On the morning of March 4 (according to the *Tribune* of the following day) a crowd forgathered there, and presently policemen and detectives to the number of 72 were compelled to use "actual force" to control the 4,000 uninvited "outside guests"—ranging from the "nursemaids, shopgirls, the hoodlums and loafers out of the park" who had established squatters' rights as early as nine o'clock, to the "large leaven of the richer and better-dressed classes" whose endowment of equal curiosity but lesser endurance brought them to the scene at a more fashionable hour. Under their collective feet the soft earth of the unpaved portion on the west side of the Avenue became "a long, sticky, muddy pool"; and, as the mob oozed over the cobblestoned roadway, stages and trucks had to detour eastward.

Within, the hothouse fragrance of a floral display, accounting for sixty-six lines of newsprint, and the music of a twenty-piece orchestra under the baton of Victor Herbert, contributed to the malaise of the prescient mother of the groom, described by her sympathetic and adoring son in his "Confessions" (published in 1924 under the title of *How I Discovered America*) as on that day resembling "an ancestral portrait purchased by a millionaire." Such indispensable niceties as gold Sherry-designed wedding-cake boxes with embossed coronets, enclosed in white-lined mauve satin cases topped by the penniless Count's crest—but omitting his family motto, "Honour above Honours"—made the union memorable, if evanescent.

During the eleven years before the divorce, Castellane admittedly spent over $12,000,000 of his wife's legally foolproofed fortune on what he empirically enumerated as "My general existence, my châteaux, my palaces, my bibelots, my racehorses, my yachts, my travelling expenses, my political career, my charities, my fêtes, my wife's jewels and loans to my friends. . . ."

Withal, in the effulgent light of his connoisseurship in the field of fine and decorative arts, he asseverated with becoming modesty: "I claim to represent the *best investment that the Goulds have ever made!*"

The Castellane-Gould Wedding, March 4, 1895
Scene in front of the home of Mr. and Mrs. George Jay Gould
857 Fifth Avenue, northeast corner of Sixty-seventh Street

ON OCTOBER 10, 1895, *Life* devoted its entire editorial page (tastefully if not tactfully adorned with vignettes of a monkey seated on a sack marked with a dollar sign, a monetary symbol reiterated in fleeting patterns of a girl, a heart as yet unbroken, and a sprinkling of butterflies) to the engagement of Consuelo, eldest daughter of William K. Vanderbilt. "LIFE presents its compliments to the young Duke of Marlborough and begs to congratulate him. . . . He is heir to a famous title and a famous, though somewhat impoverished estate. He has excellent facilities for spending money, and he needs the money to spend. . . . Of course Miss Vanderbilt's mother is pleased that her daughter is to marry a likely young duke." The acuminous editorial mind then turned to swift calculation of Mr. Vanderbilt's compounding wealth—"To say that he has money to throw at birds does not adequately describe his circumstances" and conservatively hazarded that ". . . if his fortune doesn't crush the life out of him prematurely, he will live to 'be worth' . . . perhaps two hundred

and fifty millions of dollars." The editorial evinced tolerant understanding of Mr. Vanderbilt's cheerfulness at the prospect of such "fiscal relief as may accrue to him from his daughter's marriage," and the penultimate paragraph theorized: "Of course there will be those who will sigh at this prospect of a new exportation of American gold and wish that Mr. Vanderbilt's plethora of funds might have been relieved at home . . . but it must be remembered that one of the considerations that deter our contemporary Croesi . . . from dumping money around . . . is the fear that it will do positive injury to the recipients . . . by depriving them of the incentive to work. In the case of an English duke no injury of this sort is to be feared. The Churchill [Marlborough] family . . . was so effectually pauperized in the reign of Queen Anne that it is safe to surmise that for the last two centuries no member of that family has depended on his own exertions." In a final burst of philosophical ratiocination, it was conceded that "One particularly redeeming feature is that some of the money may be spent on Blenheim, and good Americans who pass their vacations in England may have a chance to gaze on the results."

Returning to the fray on November 7, *Life* defined the wedding—at which the reluctant bride by her own subsequent admission was twenty minutes late because of final frantic efforts to repair the ravages of a torrent of untraditional tears—as "The great sporting and social event of the week" and, with studied naïveté, trusted that the groom would "stay married a long, long time, and live in peace and grow up to be a good man." Sympathy was all for the poor little bride (see *Life* of November 28), eclipsed on her day of days by such "supplementary fixtures" and "extraordinary outfit of attractions" as "a duke, a family quarrel, a symphony orchestra, the greatest flower show ever seen in a New York church, the governor of the state, the British ambassador, and a collection of the finest people in New York."

Harper's Weekly of November 16 was equally aggrieved but less acidulous: "And so passed off a very notable wedding, perhaps unequalled in magnificence by any . . . this country has seen, and surpassed by very few in the degree of popular interest." After the ceremony, the bridal party "drove away to Mrs. Vanderbilt's house on Seventy-second Street . . . where took place the wedding breakfast. . . . Mrs. Vanderbilt's cook outdid himself, a spirit of cheerfulness prevailed, and the bride and groom in due time slipped away. . . . Whether it is profitable to us Americans to have our countrywomen marry British dukes is a question about which a variety of opinions obtain; but as to this much there is agreement—that if they marry dukes at all, they do well to marry good ones, and marry them young, and grow up with them, that their spirits may be the more at peace, and their days longer and happier in the land of their adoption"—from which, it should be added in the interests of sociological documentation, many returned unencumbered and blissfully alone.

The Marlborough-Vanderbilt Wedding, November 6, 1895
Coachmen outside St. Thomas's Church
Northwest corner of Fifth Avenue and Fifty-third Street
(This edifice, consecrated in 1870 and almost wholly destroyed by fire in 1905, occupied the same site as the present church.)

. . . . The sacrifice of a flock of pelicans

OF A bright autumnal morning, six days after the Marlborough-Vanderbilt nuptials, the Gothic Revival glory of Richard Upjohn's swan song again awaited the coming of a *Burke's Peerage* (if not an *Almanach de Gotha*) bride: this time Pauline, elder daughter of William C. Whitney. She was to wed Almeric Hugh Paget, 6th son of the late Lord Alfred Henry Paget and grandson of the 1st Marquess of Anglesey, in another of the currently endemic international alliances that so aroused Charles Dana Gibson's black and white ire in the pages of *Life*. "The Anglo-American marriage epidemic does not seem to abate," declared *Munsey's Magazine* of February, 1896, in belated reference to this union. "Correspondents of the English papers are propounding all sorts of schemes to prevent the continued annexation of British titles by the conquering daughters of America. . . ." The grievance and the anxiety were somewhat misdirected in this instance, for primogeniture on his father's side and the multiparity of his mother had placed the groom far from the succession (although he was raised to the Peerage, becoming Lord Queensborough two years after his wife's death in 1916). Furthermore, he was the builder of his own fortune, having already amassed considerable wealth in the great American West.

Once again, within the Church, the horticulturist triumphed temporarily over the pioneering happy collaboration of architect, sculptor and artist, for a triple series of white chrysanthemum arches spanned the nave, while the tropical foliation at the chancel completely obliterated Saint-Gaudens' reredos and the murals of John LaFarge. Several thousand invitations had been sent out, and among the guests was President Cleveland, who came from Washington to do honor to his first-term Secretary of the Navy. Mme. Nordica and Edouard de Reszke sang of worship and love before the rainbow procession moved to the altar. The six bridesmaids, carrying tiny feathered muffs, were amazingly arrayed in prismatic poplins, trimmed with Russian sable, and small velvet hats copied from a Dutch master.

After the ceremony a breakfast reception, attended by a few hundred "intimate" friends of the young couple, was held at Mr. Whitney's home, 2 West Fifty-seventh Street. Not on display (according to the *New-York Daily Tribune* of November 13) was the "Long List Of Superb Presents" that ranged from two tiaras, an assortment of dazzling necklaces and other jewels quite eclipsing the gift of the groom (a diamond pin qualified with astonishing candor by the *Tribune* reporter as "small") to such esoteric offerings as Ruskin's *The Seven Lamps of Architecture* and a complete set of Parkman's works. Even ornithology was represented by an eiderdown rug or coverlet bespeaking the sacrifice of a flock of pelicans.

206

St. Thomas's Church decorated for the Paget-Whitney Wedding, November 12, 1895

. . . . Mated amid roses

"ONLY A FEW STATEN ISLANDERS WERE HONORED." This was the bank (newspaper terminology for a subheadline) appearing under the names of the principals in the Tiffany-Cameron wedding as reported in the umbrageous brevity of four paragraphs (one of which was consecrated to a partial listing of the favored localites) in *The Staten Islander* of June 5, 1895. The incredulity of pique marked the reprise of the opening sentence: "But few Staten Islanders were present. . . ." Contrariwise, *The New York Herald* of the 2nd—giving over almost two full Sunday columns, with a centered portrait of the bride—felt that the insular aristocracy had not been slighted: "The leading residents of Staten Island were well

A country wedding, June 1, 1895

represented in the gathering at the church, and their carriages, with the omnibuses [bearing the Manhattan contingent], completely filled the roads" leading to St. John's Protestant Episcopal Church at Clifton. The *New-York Daily Tribune*, too, saw no evidence of high-handedness: "The wedding was a gala occasion, all the prominent families of the island being represented."

A special steamer, the *Magenta*, brought about 150 metropolites from the foot of White-hall Street to the Quarantine dock, and Ex-Commodore Elbridge T. Gerry's steam yacht *Electra* landed there with a party to witness the noon wedding of Anne Fleming Cameron, daughter of Sir Roderick Cameron (chief owner of the American Pioneer Line of freighters) and Belmont Tiffany (son of George Tiffany and grandson of Commodore Perry). The bride, also celebrating her birthday, looked "extremely handsome in her . . . gown of white satin, the skirt, with a four-yard train, being made perfectly plain and the high corsage sparingly trimmed with point lace," one reads in the *Tribune* account. Her sister Catharine acted as maid of honor, and the eight bridesmaids wore "gowns of white silk," with "bodices of embroidered mousseline de soie" and "veils of white tulle fastened with white feather aigrettes." After the ceremony, carriages and stages conveyed the guests to "Clifton Berley," Sir Roderick's country home at Rosebank, on The Narrows, where, according to the *Herald*, "Everything was in readiness in the way of wedding cheer."

On the most torrid June 1st in a quarter of a century, the Byron Company carried massive equipment across the Bay, to make what today goes under the heading of a "candid camera" record of the occasion for the June 13 issue of *Once A Week*, which carried a half page of pictures. A set of prints in the Museum file preserves the romanticism (unfortunately obliterated by overzealous and disillusioning research) implicit in the *Herald*'s display line— "MATED AMID ROSES."

. . . . *The pride of the American belief*

SIXTY-THREE days out of Hamburg, in the year 1848, a young man of nineteen from the little town of Ermreuth in Bavaria stood on the deck of a sailing ship that had borne him, along with his mother, from the political turmoil of the German states into the port of New York, into the land of which he was fiercely anxious to become an integrated part. His apprentice-learned trade had enabled him to pay for their passage in some measure, as he cut and stitched and sewed clothes for the crew. Unlike so many of that influxive group of compatriotic immigrants, he refused family aid and asylum and found occupation with a New England tailor in Norwalk, Connecticut, where, in the determination of unhyphenated assimilitude, he mastered the language within the twelvemonth. Presently he returned to New York and here, originally as employee and soon as head of his own establishment, he lived out his characterful ninety-one years. In 1856 he joyfully took the blessed oath of allegiance and became a citizen of the country of his unequivocating choice.

Two years short of the half-century mark, too, "Hannchen" (affectionate diminutive of Hannah) Floersheim, from Heinlein in Hesse-Darmstadt, came to the United States, and on April 20, 1852, was married to Joseph B. Guttenberg. A young woman of great intelli-

Byron N.Y.

Golden Wedding, April 20, 1902

gence and high learning, a profound reader always, she bolstered her husband in his business, serving as cashier in busy seasons. She bore him ten children—six sons and four daughters; but five died of scarlet fever and diphtheria in the decimation of a single dark winter, and three alone survived their twenties. Family tradition has it that Mr. Guttenberg took part in the suppression of the Civil War Draft Riots in New York. A man of no eccentricities, he became a real estate owner, operating his own properties, and about 1893 found himself—by prideful dint of unafraid work—in a position to retire from tailoring.

One day in 1894–1895, he bought a new home, still standing at 118 West 120th Street between Lenox and Seventh avenues—a white house with a high brownstone stoop, in the security of what was then a quietly dignified middle class neighborhood. Here he was to live until shortly after his wife's death in 1917.

An article in *The New York Herald* was probably read with interest by Mr. Guttenberg on Sunday August 2, 1903, for it gave a record of gradually incipient transition: "It is a general but erroneous belief that that part of the city known as Harlem is entirely devoted to flat and apartment houses and to business structures, and that it is entirely devoid of private residences. This is indeed very far from the truth. . . . Harlem, of course, cannot be called a private residence section, but it does contain something besides the flats which furnish material for the joke writers. Believers in the section freely acknowledge that it is upon flats, apartments and business structures that the present prosperity of Harlem realty is based. . . . Still it is noteworthy that there are scores and even hundreds of private dwellings located in this populous part of New York which compare favorably with the homes of citizens living in the private residential sections farther down town. . . . When private homes of Harlem are spoken of, it is invariably the Mount Morris Park section which comes in for first comment. It is an attractive residential district still, but hardly what it used to be in the days when there inhabited it some of the leading lights of Tammany Hall, and when Mount Morris Park itself buzzed with political talk as the sachems gathered there on the benches in the cool evenings. Some prominent men still live there. . . . The houses bordering the park are mostly four story brown stone front dwellings, as sombre and respectable as anything that the Fifth avenue section can show. They never lack tenants, but not so large a percentage of them is occupied by owners as was the case ten years ago. . . . Just here it may be noted, in general, the keynote of Harlem's history in the past decade. Dwellings ten years ago were scarce, also rather high priced in the park section, and there was only a small demand for them. The situation now is that dwellings are more plentiful, cheaper and meet with a larger demand. To size up the situation in a few words, there is a large demand for Harlem residences in the sections which have acquired or retained a certain residential character. . . . Unquestionably the choicest section of private dwellings in Harlem is that in and to the west of Mount Morris Park, between 119th and 124th streets, over to Seventh avenue. Many of the houses here bring $1,800 a year. . . . In the Mount Morris Park section, even, where well to do families still hold sway, there have been built some apartment houses, of a high class, however."

The Guttenberg home was a comfortable dwelling place, elaboration concentered in the dining room, with its prized wrought-iron ornamentation and chandelier, all flower-concealed in solemn festivity on the 20th of April, 1902, when Mr. and Mrs. Guttenberg—fifty united years behind them, and fifteen more ahead—celebrated the Golden Anniversary of their

212

faraway wedding day. Next to Mrs. Guttenberg is her son-in-law, Herman Scheuer, and then his wife Theresa; their children—Jacob H. Scheuer (father of Mrs. Robert H. Kridel, who aided in the identification), Sadie Scheuer (who was to become Mrs. Alfred Stein in 1907) and Alwin Scheuer; beyond them, Mrs. Amy Rosenstein (youngest of the Guttenberg girls) and, next to his grandfather, her six-year-old son, his eyes—so he remembers being told—dulled by a fever of 104° and his cheeks bright with shared excitement. To him—the sole survivant—I am indebted for this touching saga of two members of the courageous generation that lived and loved and struggled and died in the pride of the American belief.

. . . . *The purple splendor of his ways*

THE NAMES of Miss Katy Cogan, eighteen, of 2544 Eighth Avenue, and Miss Sophia Peterson, fourteen, of 70 West 142nd Street—both decidedly blonde and blue-eyed—were omitted from the list of the 600 representatives of Society and Bohemia invited to commingle at the most climactic fancy-dress affair New York had seen since the Bradley Martin Ball of 1897. However, these "two young and pretty Harlem girls" were so dazzled by the Fourth Estate accounts of the festivities that they ran away from home, with no intention of returning until they had achieved a place in the aloof enchantment.

For the Byron Company, the night of Tuesday January 31, 1905 was one of profitable insomnia, as Percy C. Byron relates that between eight P.M. and six A.M. five operators (see page 216) made 189 11 × 14 negatives in an improvised studio next to the ballroom, in the horrendous and unflattering yellow-green glow of their new and indispensable Cooper-Hewitt lights (mercury-vapor lamps, first used professionally by Pirie MacDonald in 1903).

Madame Réjane, too, found that she was not indefatigable, for she was obliged to cancel her promised recitation at a benefit for St. Mary's Children's Hospital the next day, to allow for recuperation by curtain time that evening, when she "gave a sparkling and piquant performance" in *Ma Cousine*, the first of six farewell appearances at the Liberty Theatre. Her "bewitchment of pretty ways," "blandishments of demure grace," "wiles of tantalizing mischief," and "roguish significance of droll vocal inflections" (so described in the *New-York Daily Tribune*, February 2, 1905) transcended the "rattletrap settings" berated by *The Metropolitan Magazine* of June, 1905.

James Hazen Hyde (see page 214) provided a less niggardly backdrop at his eighteenth century costume fête. The twenty-eight-year-old pivotal figure of this Francophilic entertainment had compensated many times over for the hayseed awkwardness of his Harvard undergraduate days and bore his heritage (control of the Equitable Life Assurance Society of the United States, founded by his father, Henry Baldwin Hyde in 1859, and concomitant directorship in forty-six corporations) with a royal insouciance. The purple splendor of his ways reached its apogee on the night of January 31, 1905, when—in his New York Coaching Club "coat of bottle green . . . cut in customary evening fashion, with the revers of dove colored silk; black silk knee breeches; black silk stockings; low black slippers; white shirt; standing collar and white tie"—he greeted his guests in the Versailles setting contrived by the Beaux-Arts trained architect, Whitney Warren. While some came in conventional evening clothes,

The Countess de Rougemont (née Edith Devereux Clapp) and
James Hazen Hyde at his Ball, at Sherry's (Southwest
corner of Fifth Avenue and Forty-fourth Street),
January 31, 1905

others were spectacularly attired. Mrs. Clarence Mackay, for instance, we learn from J. C. Cartwright in *The Metropolitan Magazine* of June, 1905 (substantiated in the frequently reproduced portrait by John W. Alexander), "had conceived the idea of going to the ball as Adrienne Lecouvreur . . . in her great rôle of Phêdre. Her dress was of silver cloth studded with turquoises, with a silver tunic and skirt. From the shoulders there fell a long train . . . carried [throughout the evening] by two tiny negro boys in costumes of pink brocade. . . . [She] wore two large breast-plates of turquoise, silver sandals, and a tiara of turquoises and pearls" with a matching necklace. "Her hair . . . fell in two long braids, intertwined with turquoises, over her shoulders. She carried a scepter in her hand." The entertainment opened with a gavotte by the outstanding debutantes of the season, clad "à la Camargo," and some of the gilded young men about town (a feat promptly made to "look like thirty sous," *The World* of February 5 tells, by the "poetic ballet turn" executed by Mlle. Enrichetta Varasi, "premiere danseuse from the opera"). After these divertissements a comedy, *Entre Deux Portes*, cleverly woven about the party in progress and written especially for it by Dario Niccodémi,

214

allowed Madame Réjane (whose entrance was effected "in a sedan chair, supported by four court flunkeys") the seized "opportunity for some very clever acting." Then trumpets summoned the guests to supper on the floor below "transformed into . . . a beautiful Versailles garden." Several centuries out of context, myriad multicolored electric bulbs peeped through "the thousands of blooms," and over each of the sixty tables "a rose bush in full bloom reared itself." Even Sherry's waiters wore period livery. At this juncture, Harry Lehr extrovertially demanded hard-boiled eggs and a glass of milk. After the repast Madame Réjane, standing on a table, recited a poem by Robert de Flers and G. A. de Caillavet, entitled "Apropos," stressing Franco-American amity. The exertion of dancing in the ballroom necessitated resuscitation with a second supper beneath a tent supposedly on the palace lawn, while several orchestras—the one in the main ballroom that of the Metropolitan Opera House under the baton of Nahan Franko—made music until the seven o'clock breakfast was served to the gallant survivors.

All this innocent merriment ultimately resulted in the public airing of the intramural Equitable feud, which since December, 1903, had been making existence less redundant for

Madame Réjane at the James Hazen Hyde Ball

The Byron Photographic Staff at the Hyde Ball
Left to right: Joseph Byron, William Whiles, Percy C.
Byron, Louis Philip Byron. Seated on floor: Tom Lunt

Guests at the Hyde Ball. Seated: Sydney Smith, Mrs. Stuyvesant Fish. Standing, left to right:
Mrs. Sydney Smith, Philip A. Clark, Mrs. James A. Burden,
Stanford White, James Henry ("Silent") Smith, J. Norman de R. Whitehouse

James Hazen Hyde. On the Day of All Fools (so the vindictive editorial in *The World* of April 2, 1905 relates) he drove "jauntily downtown in his private hansom cab, a bunch of violets nodding at the side of the horse's head, another bunch nodding from the coachman's hat and a third bunch breathing incense from the buttonhole of the young man himself," and was forced to abdicate his patrimonial throne. Followed the close courtroom scrutiny of the affairs of fifteen life insurance companies by the Armstrong Insurance Investigation Committee of the New York Legislature through fifty-seven public hearings extending from September 6 to December 30, 1905; the emergence of Charles Evans Hughes as the conductor of the inquisition; many changes in high company officers and policy, and on December 28 the flight to France of the shorn "Caleb" (as Hyde's classmates called him)—the beginning of a voluntary exile that lasted until the Second World War compelled inconspicuous repatriation in 1941.

To revert to *The Metropolitan Magazine* of June, 1905: "Mr. James Hazen Hyde has for the last three months fairly shared the honors with President Roosevelt in being one of the most talked of men in the country. A facetious commentator remarks that the scheme of life is now, like Gaul, divided into three parts: The Simple Life as taught by Mr. Charles Wagner [the French pastor who had been expounding his Rousseauian theories on a visiting lecture tour], the Strenuous Life as exemplified by Mr. Roosevelt, and the Equitable Life as exploited by Mr. Hyde."

. . . . *In the service of five generations*

"THE STEVENS family was rowed across the Hudson river from Hoboken to attend services" at St. Paul's Chapel "in a barge lined with plum colored velvet, by servants in livery of the same hue." At least, so the oft repeated story goes.

It may be that one of Peter Lee's forbears manned an oar, for his grandparents, Peter and Nancy, had been given by James Alexander to his daughter Elizabeth, sister of Lord Stirling, on the occasion of her marriage to the Hon. John Stevens in 1748. In New York, the following year, a son was born—the third John of that name in America, engineer and inventor, with a genius for harnessing steam to the uses of transportation. In 1784 he bought at an auction conducted by the State of New Jersey all of what is now Hoboken, along with a part of Weehawken, and soon built Villa Stevens as his summer home on the Island hillside with the Indian name of Hopoghan Hackingh (Land of the Smoking Pipe)—first described by Robert Juet of the crew of the *Half Moon* as "a Cliffe, which looked of the colour of white greene, as though it were either Copper or Silver Myne." From this glorious vantage, he and his wife, Rachel Cox, intent on their growing brood of eleven, could look across the river at New York, where they wintered at No. 7 Broadway—an address abandoned about 1814 for the vast New Jersey acreage. Here, high on the west bank of the Hudson, in the year 1804, Peter Lee came into the world a slave; and here—with the exception of two days— he lived out his ninety-eight years in the service of five generations of his illustrious family. Where he went, or what he did during this brief voluntary exile after he received his freedom from the State of New Jersey, was never revealed and forever lost; but on the third dawn the household was aroused by a great upheaval and commotion, and the returned prodigal administered a sound thrashing to his innocent and bewildered replacement. He witnessed great steps in the development of steam transportation, for "Colonel Stevens of Hoboken" was engaged in building the 100-foot steamboat *Phoenix* the year before the *Clermont* made history on the Hudson; and in 1825 the quiet of the estate was broken by the chugging of the first American-built steam locomotive on its circular track. Many and far-flung were the inventions of John III and his sons, chiefly Robert Livingston and Edwin Augustus Stevens. Their mother, meanwhile, ruled over the almost feudal domain of Castle Point (a corruption of the "Point of Castile," the Colonel's earlier name for what he considered his "American Gibraltar"); and of all her numerous Negro retainers it was Peter Lee who sprang most often to her bidding.

Before 1850 Robert Livingston Stevens ordered the beginning of the forty-six-room manor house shown in the background of this photograph. Completed two years before his death in 1856, it was affectionately spoken of by the villagers as "Castle Stevens," and since 1911 has been part of the Stevens Institute of Technology (founded by the will of Edwin Augustus Stevens, who died in 1868). Martha Bayard Dod, daughter of the Rev. Albert Baldwin Dod, D.D., of Princeton and bride of Edwin Augustus I, became the "First Lady of the Castle," and Peter Lee was her major-domo. He kept the young sons of the family in line; protectively followed Mrs. Stevens through the streets of Hoboken; welcomed guests to the frequent, generous hospitality of Castle Point (twice yearly turned over to the house staff for balls); and even when the trembling hand of old age spilled the wine at the table, insisted on his prerogative of serving. His concepts and conceits were many and often endearing. Although professedly democratic, he took a domestic's delight in the reflected glory of his family and its aristocratic circle. His inability to count beyond his fingers led to a much vaunted bargain with a local jeweler, whereby he persuaded the salesman, after long argument, to accept $12 for a $10 watch. Convinced of the inefficacy of medication—a weakness to which he thought he had never succumbed—he had to be tricked into a sort of remote control therapy. Although he was persuaded to retire after the death of his mistress in 1899, he continued to wear the Stevens livery—not the earlier plum color, but the gray and blue chosen by Rachel Cox Stevens—until, his century almost rounded out, he died on January 29, 1902, and was laid to rest in the Stevens family's hillside burial plot in the Hoboken Cemetery at North Bergen, among many of those he had loved and served. In his memory a tablet was placed by members of the Stevens family in Hoboken's Church of the Holy Innocents (erected by Martha Bayard Stevens in 1872) where he had been conditionally baptized in 1889, so that all might read of his devotion and their gratitude. He died secure in the belief that he had been an eyewitness to Henry Hudson's arrival in 1609, and that the lordly river flowing by Castle Point to the sea existed simply and solely for the benefit of the Stevens family.

218

Some of the Stevens Family Retainers at Castle Point, Hoboken, 1895
Identified by descendants of Mrs. Edwin Augustus Stevens, "The First Lady of the Castle," as

(Top row, left to right): Dilly Shane, kitchen maid; Peter Lee; Fannie Niedbeck, lady's maid of Mrs. Edwin A. (Martha Bayard) Stevens; Selma and Annie Johnston; Christine Muller; James McFadden and Henry Tangerman

(Bottom row): Lizzie McKeon, laundry maid; Henry Ott, footman, and later butler-valet of Richard Stevens; Benjamin Coleman; and beyond *Zurich,* the dog, Nora Lacey, parlor maid; Polly French (?), lady's maid, who asked her mistress, Mrs. Archibald Alexander (Caroline Bayard Stevens), to choose between her and a second marriage, carrying out her threat to return to France when Mrs. Alexander became Mrs. Henry O. Wittpenn in 1915; and Mary McQuillen

. . . . Not that I care for moderation myself

SEVENTY LIGHT years and a world away from the little village of Florida, Missouri, where he was born on November 30, 1835, Samuel Langhorne Clemens—better known as Mark Twain —was fêted by over a hundred and fifty literati (labeled by the *New-York Daily Tribune* "Innocents at Home") who gathered in Manhattan at the behest of Colonel George Harvey (President of Harper & Brothers) to pay affectionate birthday tribute to one of their truly great masters and peers.

    Guests at each of the twenty chrysanthemum-decked units moved, table by table, into an antechamber, where in varying degrees of self-conscious posing, they faced the Byron cameras set up to record this aristocracy of the pen. Here, with the guest of honor, in the conventional clockwise order, are seated Kate Douglas Wiggin (Mrs. G. C. Riggs), pioneer kinder-

The Mark Twain Dinner, December 5, 1905
At Delmonico's,
Northeast corner of Fifth Avenue and Forty-fourth Street

garten worker, author of the brief classic *The Birds' Christmas Carol*, and immortalizer of *Rebecca of Sunnybrook Farm*, described by Thomas Bailey Aldrich as "the nicest child in American literature"; the Congregationalist minister and editor of *Some Old Puritan Love-Letters*, the Rev. Joseph Hopkins Twichell; Bliss Carman, Canada's most distinguished poet; the witty and vivacious Ruth McEnery Stuart, first to describe the post-bellum plantation Negro in his own social environment and past mistress of the southern "character" tale; the bearded Henry Mills Alden, editor of *Harper's Magazine* and one of the last representatives of the old New England tradition in American letters; Henry Huttleston Rogers—one of the handful of non-literary figures present—capitalist and long Mark Twain's business manager and counselor; and Mary E. Wilkins Freeman, subtle writer of the short story.

In response to a tribute and toast by William Dean Howells, the honored septuagenarian—a demi-decade still ahead of him—with characteristic humor gave out his formula for longevity in terms that would make a modern geriatrist toss aside his shingle: "I have achieved my seventy years in the usual way: by sticking strictly to a scheme of life which would kill anybody else. . . . In the matter of diet . . . I have been persistently strict in sticking to the things which didn't agree with me until one or the other of us got the best of it. . . . I have made it a rule never to smoke more than one cigar at a time. . . . As an example to others, and not that I care for moderation myself, it has always been my rule never to smoke when asleep, and never to refrain when awake. . . . When the others drink, I like to help; otherwise I remain dry. . . . I have never taken any exercise, except sleeping and resting. . . . I have lived a severely moral life. But it would be a mistake for other people to try that. . . ."

. . . . *Laurel wreaths in their hair*

"'And you—have you nothing to say?' asked the Fairy of the Talking-cricket.

'In my opinion the wisest thing a prudent doctor can do, when he does not know what he is talking about, is to be silent.'"

This colloquy took place during one of the most famous medical consultations in literature, when three physicians, "namely a Crow, an Owl, and a Talking-cricket," were called to Pinocchio's bedside to determine whether the injured puppet were alive or dead.

In the case of the photograph on pages 222 and 223, I must fall back on wisdom learned from the Italian classic of childhood by C. Collodi (Carlo Lorenzini), for I have been unable to discover anything about these sober gentlemen crowned with wreaths of laurel. Only one of the assemblage has been identified—Harrison Grey Fiske (see page 236), at the right of the elderly man with the white beard. So sharp was Byron's focus that the engraved letters M and C, intertwined, can be deciphered on the half-empty glasses. Armed with these clews, I have made a reasonably thorough investigation from various angles, ending nowhere. I have communicated with authorities on the host (or honored guest) and his actress wife; I have consulted men and women connected with the art and life of the young century. I have penetrated into gentlemen's clubs, talked with everyone from their presidents to their aged retainers; I have enlivened bulletin boards about town with copies of this print, and distributed them across the land. I have made comparison with whole galleries of portraits of people and of

banquet rooms here and there. I have conducted a vast correspondence on the subject. I have searched newspapers and periodicals, from *The New York Dramatic Mirror* (edited by Fiske) up and down, on microfilm and in tatters. I have missed the turn of the road, for somewhere the facts are plain. This photograph was among the first to be chosen for this

Dinner given by or for
Harrison Grey Fiske,
Winter of 1900–1901

book out of more than ten thousand possibilities, and, having lived with it for a full five years, in undiminished enjoyment and increasing frustration, I am loath to file it away in the Museum archives. It is too delicious a document to discard, because, as the great mountaineer George Mallory replied when asked why he wanted to climb Mt. Everest, "it is there."

. . . . *In the annals of a satiated society*

IN OPEN defiance of the thirty-six original situations of the eighteenth century Italian dramatist, Count Carlo Gozzi, and at a time when New York society was accustomed to finding
beautiful damoiselles in its "Jack Horner pies," accepting white mice as favors with a somewhat mitigated degree of squealing enthusiasm, attending banquets for dogs and dolls and
even in honor of a "Corsican Prince" who turned out to be a diminutive monkey attired in
white-tie splendor, the capitalist and "American Horse King" C. K. G. Billings reached
uncharted heights in planning for the discomfort of his thirty-six guests. On the eve of the
opening of his new $200,000 stable at 196th Street and Fort Washington Road (in the
present Fort Tryon Park), built to house ten times that valuation in "matinée" and Speedway horses, he gave a dinner to fellow Pegasus fanciers in the grand ballroom of Sherry's,
converted into a woodland scene by means of full-scale scenic backdrops, landscaped with

224

The Horseback Dinner, March 28, 1903
At Sherry's,
Southwest corner of Fifth Avenue
and Forty-fourth Street

slightly irrelevant potted palms and with acres of realistic floor covering for local color and the protection of the establishment's interests. Out of praiseworthy consideration for the high-strung, high-stepping stars of Billings' own harness brigade, somewhat less nervously aristocratic and better trained steeds, imported from local riding academies, were brought up to this rustic paradise in freight elevators, to serve as rather unsteady seats for the trotting enthusiasts, who degusted the various courses placed on miniature tables attached to the pommels of the saddles, served by waiters dressed as grooms at a hunting party. Toward the close of the banquet, elaborate oat-filled feeding troughs were set before the patient equine guests, who then dined with their riders. A vaudeville show covered the exit of the four-legged members of one of the strangest conclaves in the annals of a satiated society.

225

To MRS. Astor's picture hanger fell a task rivaling the intricacies of Ward McAllister's floor plan, with its arbitrary division of this crimson-and-gold room into "Four Hundred" fettered and equal parts; while the guests at her traditional annual ball held on January's third Monday stood abreast in serried ranks, the paintings soared ceilingward in a solid pattern sometimes six deep, frame to ornate frame in the fashionable proximity of the day. This canvas acreage, once appraised at twice the $276,000 investment it represented, brought a fractional $35,295 at the auction of April 21, 1926 (held prior to the demolition of the Astor château at Fifth Avenue and Sixty-fifth Street). On that vernal day, such once admired subjects as Émile van Marcke de Lummen's *Dans les Landes* (seen at the left of the photograph, covering 74½ × 106 inches of precious wall space), *The Connoisseurs* by Ferdinand Roybet,

French Artillery from the easel of Édouard Detaille (in the second tier, near the porcelain fireplace), and *On Guard* (*Dog Herding Sheep*), so typical of the mood of Constant Troyon, were knocked down to one of the great of the circus world, who bequeathed his collection to the State of Florida, as The John and Mable Ringling Museum of Art at Sarasota. Jules Breton's *Le Repos* brought $3,800—the culminant price of the sale—while *The Monte Pincio, Rome* by Corot fetched a paltry $900. Among the other popular nineteenth century French masters figuring largely in this "Astorperious" aggregation of over one hundred oils were Cabanel, Lefebvre, Berne-Bellecour and Bouguereau (represented by his *Young Girl Winding Wool*).

At the time that Byron was summoned to photograph the art gallery and ballroom in the four-story red brick boxlike mansion (first occupied by William Astor—grandson of John Jacob—and his bride of three years in 1856, and later to relinquish sovereignty in unreasonably rapid succession to the Astoria side of the hyphenated Waldorf and the Empire State Building) *the* Mrs. Astor (née Caroline Schermerhorn) had abstained from ballgiving since her 1892 widowhood and was not to entertain again on that highly personal scale until 1896. During this solemn interlude she dutifully limited her domestic parties to luncheons, and large, overpowering prefabricated sometimes weekly dinners (three-hour-long feats of endurance leavened by the use of the golden service or the silver-gilt dishes and a seemly four hundred *Gloire de Paris* roses) chiefly remarkable for a surpassing sterility in conversation and ideas. One "Mr. S." (described in *The Illustrated American* of January 9, 1892 as "a courtly old gentleman with a *fin de siècle* appetite and . . . generally regarded as the foreman of . . . [the] gastronomic jury") pointed out that "Mrs. William Astor, for instance, always orders her big dinners from outside. The dishes are generally prepared at the restaurant some time in advance [a practice not uncommon in the magnified social operations of the period], and the finishing touches done in the house. The result is that the dinner has a slightly faded, *passé* taste which, perhaps, only one person in ten would notice."

In a rare access of sensitivity and fine feeling, Mrs. Astor gave a highly selective farewell feast (before abandoning 350 Fifth Avenue to the demolition squad) on Saturday evening February 2, 1895, at a table decked with mauve and pink orchids, while the decomposing body of her discharged mentor and cavalier servente—Ward McAllister—lay in rigor mortis awaiting burial, a short two blocks away.

The Art Gallery and Ballroom in the home of Mrs. Astor, 1894
350 Fifth Avenue, at the southwest corner of Thirty-fourth
Street

Ward McAllister's funeral, February 4, 1895
Passing down Fifth Avenue
View looking north from Thirty-fourth Street

Ward McAllister's funeral, February 4, 1895
After the services at Grace Church,
Broadway and Tenth Street

. . . . *And secured the respect of my butcher*

ON JANUARY 31, 1895, the same blood that had made Charlotte Corday "the angel of the assassination" ceased to flow through the somewhat hardened arteries of seventy-eight-year-old Ward McAllister, who claimed kinship with Marat's murderess as part of his maternal heritage. On the snow-flurried morning of February 4, the funeral cortege left his residence, 16 West Thirty-sixth Street, and clattered lonesomely down Fifth Avenue (where, wrote Mrs. Burton Harrison, in her chapter on "Externals Of Modern New York" in *History Of The City Of New York* by Mrs. Martha J. Lamb and Mrs. Burton Harrison, New York, 1896, conversation was "not possible otherwise than at a strained and fatiguing pitch of the voice" because of "the incessant jar from the passage of vehicles over stones").

Past the marble pile once a monument to A. T. Stewart's dry goods millions and at this time occupied by the Manhattan Club, past the less pretentious red brick house where McAllister and his *grande dame*, Mrs. Astor, had tyrannized over the social life of a city, was borne the body of the great cotillion leader, on to Grace Church, where Lander's Orchestra played the "Dead March" from *Saul* in final salute to the man who had given the band employment on many a festive night. Women shoppers, deserting bargain counters to invade the sanctuary before the service, later swarmed past the departing mourners to pluck flowers from the altar and the banked pew of the deceased. To this came "The Aristocrat of the Drawing Rooms," whose youth had seen the gold fields of California in that mad mid-century rush, who had presided over logistically planned dinners in his villa at Pau as an apprenticeship for the studied rusticity of picnics in Newport and the larger arena of New York's ballroom world. In 1890 his septuagenarian reminiscences appeared between covers under the title of *Society As I Have Found It*—a combination cookbook, wine list and document in fatuity, studded with such endearing aphorisms as "If you want to be fashionable, be always in the company of fashionable people," "In planning a dinner the question is not to whom you owe dinners, but who is most desirable," and such pardonably prideful boasts as "For forty years I have always marketed myself and secured the respect of my butcher." Probably his most enduring monument is the reputed shaping of three digits into what has become a generic term—"the Four Hundred"—based on his quick calculation of the number of cubic feet in Mrs. Astor's ballroom and their potential content in terms of pedigreed humanity. This phrase (in figures) was canonized by the protecting arms of quotation marks in the *New-York Daily Tribune* as early as April 8, 1888. Some years later, O. Henry observed in a volume of his tales "But a wiser man has arisen—the census taker—and his larger estimate of human interest has been preferred in marking out the field of these little stories of the 'Four Million.' "

"THE STAGE is my studio"—this was a Joseph Byron trademark, instituted about 1891. How he and his followers achieved success in the specialized field of theatre photography is the subject of a Sunday feature—"Taking Scene Pictures. The Difficult Art of Getting Them by Flashlight"—in the *New-York Tribune Illustrated Supplement* of October 25, 1903. The account is here excerpted.

"The art of taking theatrical flashlights of scenes from new plays is difficult to master. Until a few months ago there was only one firm in the United States [undoubtedly the Byron Company] able to produce the best results. In the last year several competitors have appeared, and now there are at least three concerns in New-York, one in Boston and one in Chicago which bid for this lucrative and at the same time hazardous business, for there is an art in this kind of photography which, perhaps, is still in its infancy, in spite of the dexterity shown by the photographers who have made a specialty of this line of work.

"Scene pictures are the large reproductions of important scenes from new plays. You may see dozens of them in the lobbies of theatres. The illustrated magazines and the newspapers sometimes print them. No doubt it has puzzled people to understand how a newspaper published the morning after a new production is made at a theatre is able to print a flashlight scene of the play. No flashlights were taken while the audience was present, and as the programmes and the manager probably asserted that the play had never been done before, how was it possible to secure a photograph of the actual performance?

"Scene pictures are always taken at the dress rehearsal of a new play. . . ." (Here it should be interpolated that the enterprising Byron Company frequently—in fact almost half the time—covered the out-of-town tryouts. Percy C. Byron tells me that he and his assistants, Jack Ferris and Tom Lunt, traveled "hundreds of thousands" of miles to record over 1,000 shows in advance of the New York première.) "Most actors resent the necessity which compels them to pose for the scene pictures, but there is no alternative. Scene pictures are necessary for the advertising frames and for the magazines. . . .

"The photographer who takes the scene pictures arrives at the theatre with three or four assistants before the dress rehearsal begins. . . .

"The photographer carries with him a portable platform, which is erected in the centre of the house, on top of the orchestra chairs. This can be moved forward to enlarge the group of figures photographed, or backward if he wishes to take in the entire stage setting. His camera is one of the largest made, and one of the best.

"During the first act . . . the photographer sits out front and makes notes . . . so that he can get photographs of the strong climaxes. When the first act is over, and just when the women are about to go to their dressing rooms to change their costumes for the next act, the stage manager cries out:

" 'Everybody on the stage! Don't any one change costume without permission!'

"Then, when the players line up on the stage, the photographer orders a certain set of players to assume a pose which he had noticed early in the act. He has made his notes with cues. . . .

"'Steady, now—that's good. One moment!' cries the photographer from the front of the darkened auditorium. Then there is a tremendous flash of fire, a loud explosion and the players, almost blinded by the glare, stagger back in confusion.

"The flashlight explosions by the photographer vary in proportion to the size of the picture. If he takes a full scene of the entire stage he will use two or three charges of magnesium powder, all exploded simultaneously in different parts of the auditorium. If he is taking only a group from a close point of view, perhaps one charge . . . will be sufficient. But even one charge makes a tremendous flash, illuminating the entire theatre auditorium, and disconcerting players who are not used to having flashlights taken. It is as bad for the inexperienced actor as a soldier's first experience under fire . . . and it frequently makes feminine players who are new to the stage very nervous and timid.

"But before the flash has fully died away the photographer cries out again to the players:

"'Now give me the tableau at the end of the act—quick, before the smoke comes down!'

"And there is need for haste, since the smoke from the explosion is already rolling down in volumes upon the stage. At first it ascends to the roof a great gray mass of smoke, but finding no outlet there it gradually fills the auditorium. Unless haste is made it may mar subsequent pictures.

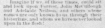

"But already the players have taken their positions for the final tableau, and the photographer is ready to explode another charge of powder. He may alter the pose of one of the actresses . . . or direct the villain to frown. Then he utters the warning signal . . . and a second blinding glare fills the theatre.

"Unless the smoke gets very bad, four or five flashlights can be taken. If the smoke interferes, it may be necessary to open all the doors and windows, and wait fifteen minutes until the atmosphere clears. This delays the players and annoys them excessively, since they always insist that taking flashlights is a hardship. . . ." (Here it seems appropriate to interject a statement made by Percy C. Byron in 1956, since the Company's *modus operandi* was a reversal of the procedure just outlined: "We started with the end of the last act & worked back to the first scene of the first act & left the stage ready for the next performance, never any other way.")

"Half a dozen flashlights of each act is about the average number taken of a new Broadway production. . . . The cost of twenty or twenty-five scene pictures ranges from $100 to $200, according to the number of prints ordered. . . .

"It is a dangerous thing to take these flashlights. Two or three assistants to work the powder explosions on specially contrived flashlight lamps are necessary, and in case of a premature explosion there is enough powder easily to blind a man or seriously cripple him."

Four-page circular describing "Charles MacGeachy's Presentation Of The Magnificent Novelty   Byron's Illuminated Stage Pictures," 1903 (As orginally presented at the Criterion Theatre, New York, on Monday afternoon, February 26, 1900)

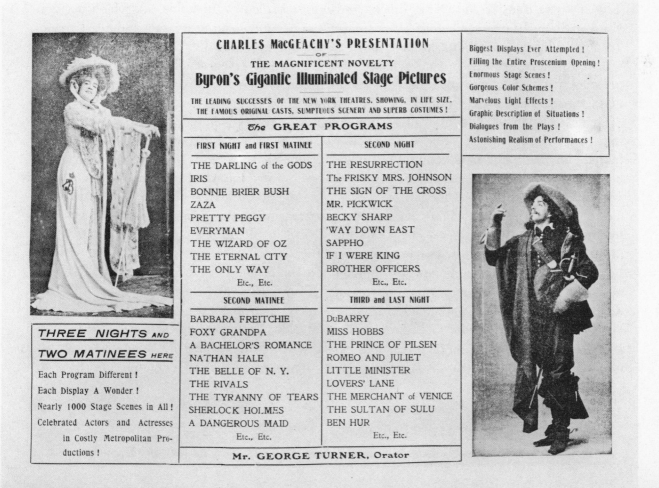

THREE NIGHTS AND TWO MATINEES HERE

Each Program Different !
Each Display A Wonder !
Nearly 1000 Stage Scenes in All !
Celebrated Actors and Actresses in Costly Metropolitan Productions !

CHARLES MacGEACHY'S PRESENTATION
OF
THE MAGNIFICENT NOVELTY
Byron's Gigantic Illuminated Stage Pictures
THE LEADING SUCCESSES OF THE NEW YORK THEATRES, SHOWING, IN LIFE SIZE, THE FAMOUS ORIGINAL CASTS, SUMPTUOUS SCENERY AND SUPERB COSTUMES !

The GREAT PROGRAMS

FIRST NIGHT and FIRST MATINEE	SECOND NIGHT
THE DARLING of the GODS	THE RESURRECTION
IRIS	The FRISKY MRS. JOHNSON
BONNIE BRIER BUSH	THE SIGN OF THE CROSS
ZAZA	MR. PICKWICK
PRETTY PEGGY	BECKY SHARP
EVERYMAN	'WAY DOWN EAST
THE WIZARD OF OZ	SAPPHO
THE ETERNAL CITY	IF I WERE KING
THE ONLY WAY	BROTHER OFFICERS
Etc., Etc.	Etc., Etc.

SECOND MATINEE	THIRD and LAST NIGHT
BARBARA FREITCHIE	DuBARRY
FOXY GRANDPA	MISS HOBBS
A BACHELOR'S ROMANCE	THE PRINCE OF PILSEN
NATHAN HALE	ROMEO AND JULIET
THE BELLE OF N. Y.	LITTLE MINISTER
THE RIVALS	LOVERS' LANE
THE TYRANNY OF TEARS	THE MERCHANT of VENICE
SHERLOCK HOLMES	THE SULTAN OF SULU
A DANGEROUS MAID	BEN HUR
Etc., Etc.	Etc., Etc.

Mr. GEORGE TURNER, Orator

Biggest Displays Ever Attempted !
Filling the Entire Proscenium Opening !
Enormous Stage Scenes !
Gorgeous Color Schemes !
Marvelous Light Effects !
Graphic Description of Situations !
Dialogues from the Plays !
Astonishing Realism of Performances !

"CATS ARE seldom public favorites, and yet there is probably no figure better known and more popular in New York's theatre world than is 'Monkey,' THE MIRROR cat. Every one knows 'Monkey,' and her acquaintance is one so comprehensive that it would be priceless to an advance man." The famous twenty-year-old weekly—self-styled "The Organ of the American Theatrical Profession"—devoted almost a half-page of its Anniversary-Christmas number in 1898 to the feline member of its staff. " 'Monkey' . . . receives her friends every day at THE MIRROR office, and greets with equal favor the sunny soubrette, the grim tragedian, the gentle ingenue, the well-dressed leading man, the stunning leading lady, the low comedian, the gay burlesquer, the heavy man, the comic opera queen, the genial pantomimist, the cheery chorus girl, the dashing emotional actress, the merry song and dance man—they all know 'Monkey,' and 'Monkey' knows them." The receptionist's pedigree cannot be traced in grimalkin genealogies: " 'Monkey' was a foundling. She walked into the Fifth Avenue Theatre one day, a little more than two years ago, surveyed the place carefully, and decided to stay. J. Charles Davis, then business-manager of the theatre, had a monkey. . . . The kitten learned to imitate the monkey's tricks, and was often seen hanging by the tail from the steam pipes and performing true simian feats of jumping and equilibrium. So it was that . . . [she] was called 'Monkey.' When the season of 1896–97 closed at the Fifth Avenue, 'Monkey' was transferred to THE MIRROR and duly installed as the office cat, which position of no small importance she has held ever since with uncommon authority, tact and intelligence. To all regular callers at THE MIRROR office the preferences and the prejudices of 'Monkey' are well known, and those who have had the temerity to bring small dogs into 'Monkey's' presence are especially acquainted with her chief abhorrence. . . . To her friends, she freely gives the glad paw, and exhibits a tender, sympathetic, regard."

One of the pair of silhouettes illustrating the article shows "Monkey" in attitude of greeting. Just why Byron the elder was not elected her official photographer cannot be determined, for the publishers thought so well of him that he was accorded two separate encomiums in this very special issue. On page 116, we are informed: "Joseph Byron, whose studios are in the Alpine, 1286 Broadway, . . . has established a unique reputation as a flash-light photographer, taking pictures on the stage with the delicacy, shading and lifelike appearance of the highest order of gallery work, and making a special feature of the promptness of finishing. Mr. Byron's renown in this line of art is international, as is testified by the following recent notice in the London *Sketch* [of October 19, 1898]: 'Joseph Byron, of New York, stands without a rival in this difficult art. How Mr. Byron manages to do this is not clear, and even London photographers stand amazed at the clearness of his work. Perhaps there is something in the atmosphere of New York, but the secret is mainly Mr. Byron's manipulation." For those readers who did not progress beyond page 114 (and so missed this amazed British chauvinism, with its biased reflection on climatic conditions in

234

"Bookkeeping and Exchange Department" of *The New York
Dramatic Mirror*, October, 1898
1432 Broadway (southeast corner of Fortieth Street)

Manhattan) there was this wholly native tribute to the man who had forsaken England in 1888: "Joseph Byron has become noted for his work as a photographer. Mr. Byron appears to get the best results, no matter what the conditions may be, his exterior views being noteworthy for clear definition and artistic perspectives. His flash-light work in interiors it would be difficult to improve upon. All the photographic views of local exteriors and interiors in this number, illustrating the various theatrical resorts and clubs and societies, as well as those illustrating THE MIRROR's quarters, are the work of Mr. Byron."

As the tattletale wall calendars attest, it was in the tenth month of 1898 that the last mentioned set of photographs, including this typical period-piece office portrait, was taken. Pausing in their fevered efforts to meet the weekly deadline and their frenzied concentration on the projected grandiosity of the double-barrelled December issue, could doubtless be recognized some of the faithful, duly accolded on page 113 of that gargantuan feat of summary and self-love: "The [business] staff is composed of Lyman Otis Fiske, business-manager; Joshua Henry, who has been associated with the paper almost from its beginning, general bookkeeper; Ed B. Bave, assistant bookkeeper; W. S. Wilkinson, advertising agent; J. H. Gerhardt and George Loomis, in the advertising department; Georgie Hart, Stenographer; Gabriel Phillips, mail clerk, and Daniel Hanlon, clerk."

Even further back than Mr. Henry's initial entry, the "dramatic newspaper" (to die in its 43rd year—1922—after going to press 2,249 times) sent out its first issue, under the masthead *The New York Mirror* on January 4, 1879, from 12 Union Square, "then the very center of the Rialto," which the organ logically followed north to Broadway and 40th Street in 1891, after an intermediate four-year pause at 145 Fifth Avenue. "It was an unpretentious sheet of eight pages, generously 'leaded,' . . . small in size, and its news and literary features were limited indeed and seem puerile when compared with those of THE MIRROR of to-day."

On July 17, 1880, the name of Harrison Grey Fiske (1861–1942) first appeared as editor, although he was not new to that responsibility. He became the sole proprietor in 1888, and two years later the husband of Minnie Maddern, forever to be remembered as one of the special shining virtues of the American stage. He served as his wife's manager, presenting her in the first production of Ibsen's controversial plays in the United States, stood behind such stellar figures as Otis Skinner, Bertha Kalich, and George Arliss, and also found time to become a playwright. Under his leadership, to terminate in 1911, THE MIRROR prospered, so that the story of its first two decades was the summation of our native theatre through those proud years. It numbered among its contributors A. C. Wheeler ("Nym Crinkle"), H. C. Bunner, Mrs. D. G. Croly ("Jennie June"), James L. Ford, Joaquin Miller, Sydney Rosenfeld, William Winter, Gus Philips ("Oofty Gooft"), William Archer, Brander Matthews, Paul Blouet ("Max O'Rell"), Henry Arthur Jones, Bronson Howard, and Clyde Fitch.

"During all these years," the editorial of October 1, 1898 stated without modesty, but with truth, "THE MIRROR has been the organ of the American theatrical profession. It has ever been the friend of the rank and file of that profession, as well as of its leaders. It has originated many movements and measures that have benefitted those who are the bone and sinew—the very body—of the native theatre, and it never has hesitated to champion any object that would make for the well-doing and well-being of the actor." (Its early editorials, for instance, led to the foundation of the Actors' Fund of America, that most touching evidence of the compassion of Thespian for Thespian.) "Reputable managers, too, the country over, recognize that THE MIRROR has always stood up for their honor and safeguarded their interests. . . . It has no rival in the esteem of the people who make up the theatre of this country, and for that matter there is no dramatic newspaper in the world that stands more persistently or more vigorously for the dignity and legitimate development of the stage . . . and whose position on the right side of every professional question of importance may, with confidence, be predicted in advance."

And in the holiday mood of the Anniversary issue there appears the following light-of-heart salutation:

> "Go forth, my winsome, merrie elf
> And Laugh, as I have laughed myself,
>   To Players' list'ning ears,
> And when they gaily jest with thee,
> Remember, pray, the sprightly glee,
>   Of twenty yester-years."

236

EVEN FLY posters had nightmares. This statement is substantiated by a comic entitled "The Bill-Posters Dream" (copyrighted in 1862 by B. Derby, the artist, and lithographed by Sarony, Major & Knapp), showing a despoiler of fences sprawled against a lamppost, fast asleep—one arm resting on a stack of advertisements, his pot of glue and brush alongside, and in the background a vast boarded expanse covered with overlapping cards to be read in sequence, such as "People's Candidate for Mayor" "The Hippopotamus at Barnum's Museum" and "Miss Cushman will" "Take Brandreth's Pills." And at the top, the classic prohibition, "Post No Bills." An 1866 piracy of the idea, issued by Chas. Hart, adds the consolation of a beauteous girl of the period, immodest in a display of exceedingly shapely limbs.

It was not until the eighties, as color lithography advanced, that the *affiche* began to take artistic shape. Then Jules Chéret proliferated his charming saccharinities up and down the adoring boulevards of Paris, his gay Pierrots and lovely Columbines and pretty girls inviting the purchase of every conceivable product from oil lamps to hours of entertainment. It remained for a knight of the ancient chivalry of France to give a swift new dimension to the art of the poster. Gustave Coquiot (in *Lautrec ou Quinze Ans de Mœurs Parisiennes 1885–1900*, published in 1921) recalls the trembling joy of his shocked emotion when *Moulin-Rouge* (*La Goulue*) first galvanized the French capital in 1891, and the name of an unknown passed from lip to lip in a crescendo that is still mounting.

In America, by 1895, *Harper's Weekly* (in its issue of February 9) was accenting a type of acquisitiveness then much in vogue: "Anyone who has ever suffered at any time from the mania for collecting, in any of its forms, must feel it in these days a constant tax on his powers of self-restraint to keep his hands off the current poster." And with particular emphasis on book and magazine window cards, the writer pointed up the criminality of neglecting the portfolio value of this awakening and direct art manifestation, less potently expressed here in its adaptation to the uses of the mimic world.

I venture to challenge the existence of another graphic record of a theatrical bill-poster's atelier at the century's turn. The document on page 238 was made to illustrate an article by Wells Hawks (in *The Theatre Magazine*, June, 1904) which pleads for quotation: "Every theatre has its advertising man. The term might suggest that he attends to the newspaper advertising, but he does not. His business is with paste and billboards. . . . In other words, he is a bill-poster. . . . It is his duty to see that every attraction is well represented along the streets, and in the windows by the means of large and small bills, frames of photographs, cards, pictures, and other devices that will arrest and perhaps hold public attention. . . . In New York, for instance, where there is a chain of houses under one management, there is a chief advertising man, who has under his control from ten to twenty men, who are constantly employed in posting bills. In this city there are about 300 bill-posters employed during the show season. They are an organized body with governing rules. . . . As soon as a play is placed

The bill-room of the Charles Frohman Theatres, 1903

in rehearsal, its manager orders the 'wall printing.' This is in various sizes, from the large stands (printed in sheets and put together by the posters) down to the smaller half sheets used on boxes and barrels and the narrow slips, or 'snipes,' that are pasted on fences or anything along a thoroughfare. All of this is sent to the bill-room of the theatre where the play is to be presented, and here the advertising man and his assistants 'lay it out.' This process consists in assorting the various sizes and arranging them for the different routes the posters will take [by wagon and afoot] in their task of 'billing the show.' Every city has some principal bill-posting corporation that controls the best locations. This work is done by contract, and a certain amount of paper, mostly 'stands' of 24 and 28 sheets, is sent to this company for its men to put out. The advertising agent keeps the smaller bills for himself and his assistants. The cost of this printing and the posting of it make an enormous item in the conduct of a large theatrical concern. . . . Some idea of this expense can be gained when one figures the cost of printing one of the large 28-sheet stands at a price ranging from $1.50 to $2.50, while the posting concern gets 84 cents for posting it. Then if it rains the next day and the wall is stripped, the same operation must be repeated. But it is the bill-poster

238

[salaried by the theatre] with the sack of small bills swung across his shoulder and with the bucket and brush who does the work often most conspicuous. No smooth surface that will hold a bill ever misses his eye. The sign, 'Post No Bills,' does not always terrorize him, for he has been known to post his bill over the warning. . . ."

Byron has caught the Frohman bill-posters in the act of plotting a campaign. On the wall at the left is a notice of John Drew, "the first gentleman of the stage," in *Captain Dieppe*, a comedy by Anthony Hope (of *The Prisoner of Zenda* fame) and Harrison Rhodes, produced by Charles Frohman at the Herald Square Theatre on September 14, 1903 for a disappointing sixty-six performances. Close by is a reminder of the Casino (then under Shubert management), home territory for a glittering succession of musical comedies; the portrait poster (long in fashion) shows Miss Eleanor Robson, stellar in Israel Zangwill's *Merely Mary Ann* that winter, seven years before marriage to August Belmont terminated her stage career. The immediate project under discussion is the publicizing of the Charles Frohman and George Edwardes production *The Girl from Kay's*, a musical play by Owen Hall (James B. Davis, see page 250) applauded by 205 audiences at the Herald Square Theatre, from November 2 on, with Sam Bernard as Mr. Hoggenheimer and Hattie Williams in the title role scoring a hit despite the tepidity of *The New York Herald's* drama critic, who on November 3rd pronounced "London's latest long skirt farce" a retarded vehicle in need of "more ginger." Its dashingly decorative poster is thought by old-timers in the prolific Strobridge Lithographing Company (which printed it) to be the work of Paul Jones, an artist connected with the firm in Cincinnati.

In this well composed photograph, so remote from the ordinary, the Byrons with their recording genius have preserved the reality behind "The Bill-Posters Dream."

. . . . *A world of wizardry in his eyes*

How to convey the magic of Martinka's? The very name is onomatopoeic, and one has but to mention it, as I did one morning, to that Prince of Thaumaturgy, John Mulholland, to see the whole world of wizardry in his eyes. He looked at Byron's photograph of "Martinka's Little Back Shop" (page 240)—to him and to his Compeers the magician's "Holy of Holies"— and told of its far-away origins. He pointed to the mustached man beside the stove, affectionately identifying Francis J. Martinka himself.

The brothers Martinka were born in Prague: Antonio in 1832, and Francis eleven years later. The elder became the mechanical genius behind Kratky-Baschik's theatre of magic in Vienna, while his polylingual junior had charge of the business end. Here Francis formed a partnership with the magician Louis Haselmayer which took them on a successful barnstorming tour of South Africa, from Capetown to the Kimberley diamond mines and back again by oxcart. In 1872 the Martinkas came to New York and, within the twelvemonth, established a magic supply house on Broadway near Duane Street, after thirteen years moving (with several intermediate stops) to the hallowed address which became the Magicians' Mecca. This long, narrow shop opposite Tenderloindom's celebrated resort, The Haymarket, was originally a rope walk, running lengthwise through the center of the Sixth Avenue frontage to the middle of the side-street block. Above the entrance, in letters of gold, were the

Martinka & Company's "Palace of Magic," 1906
493 Sixth Avenue (west side, between Twenty-ninth and
Thirtieth Streets)
Note: This print suffered damage in a previous reproduction.

evocative words "Palace of Magic." Having passed the tiny show-window display of the
appurtenances of the art, one penetrated into an infinitesimal gas-lit room with counter and
shelves holding the mysterious impedimenta behind illusion and sleight-of-hand. An aisle led
through a windowless chamber into the high-ceilinged "Little Back Shop" here shown, and
through the doorway was the famous "Théâtre Magique," with an appendage of construction ateliers where Antonio Martinka's inventive skill presided, and storage space in which
itinerant professionals were wont to deposit such unneeded properties as a living lion. But
the room of a thousand memories is the storied "Little Back Shop," where thirteen of the
great initiates—or "Saturday Nighters," as Mr. Mulholland calls them—on April 26, 1902,
moved to form The Society of American Magicians, the most venerable and revered organization of the fraternity in the world, of which the young John of the magic hands presently
became the first junior member and in which Milbourne Christopher (to whom I am also
indebted) now plays an important part. John Mulholland studied the photograph and called
my attention to the third member of the triumvirate, Pauline, wife of Francis, the beloved
little lady (wearing the white shirtwaist) whose clever fingers fashioned all the myriad handkerchiefs and flags and other props requiring her seamstress skill. On the work-table in the
foreground is the "Talking Skull"—a stock trick—and the craftsman is bent over an audience-
baffling Card Canister. Skied on the wall, at the west end of the room, are a poster and por-

240

traits of the Royal Family of Magic, the Herrmanns—Adelaide, Compars, Alexander, and Leon; and all about are hallowed relics, while the images of other great past "peddlers of wonders" look down on the living necromantics.

After Francis Martinka's retirement in 1917 the business passed through many hands, including Harry Houdini's; and now, amalgamated with about twenty magic-purveying companies, it is located at 304 West Thirty-fourth Street, under the aegis of Al Flosso, "The Coney Island Fakir," who welcomed me of a Saturday as he paused in a complicated negotiation with a neophyte.

And so I too, a stranger, have learned by transmutation the wonder epitomized in John W. Sargent's poem, a classic of magic, and feel with him and all the great ones that

"... there's no other place on the whole Earth's face
Like Martinka's little back shop."

A Workman at Martinka's, 1906
This artisan is putting final touches on the "Talking Skull"—
a stock trick; on the bench are a card sword and the trio of
vanishing Card Canisters (one of which the performer con-
ceals from his audience).

"A NOISY claque made it impossible to tell whether the first audience to witness 'The Christian' in New York [on October 10, 1898] really liked the piece or not." *Life's* critic (in the issue of October 20) very evidently left the Knickerbocker Theatre on the night of Miss Viola Allen's Broadway elevation to stardom feeling akin to the departing spectators he described as having "something of the same worn, drawn look to be seen on the face of a man who has been talked to death." However, Mr. Metcalfe rejoiced in this "partial endorse-

After the Clergymen's Matinée of *The Christian,*
November 3, 1898
Broadway, looking north from Thirty-eighth Street

ment" of his ". . . opinion previously expressed . . ." (in *Life* on October 6th) that the vehicle contained "a large amount of conversation for a given amount of play, and that the conversation is not of a very enlivening kind." He conceded that since "New York is now quite a wide-open town, and is devoting more of its time to booming Theodore [Roosevelt, on the eve of victory in the gubernatorial race] than to religion . . . [it was] perhaps . . . a good thing to have some large chunks of that latter rare commodity [even if of a "rather inferior grade"] hurled at it from the stage." He permitted himself the irresistibility of a parting thrust: "The claque had evidently been duly informed that Mr. Caine was part of the show, and at the right moment called for him with a promptness and unanimity which must have warmed the cockles of his Manx heart. He responded with a very pretty and carefully prepared little impromptu speech." For the charmful and beloved star, until now a triumphant member of the Empire Company, there were floral tributes—pronounced "old-fashioned" by *The New York Times* of October 11—including the trite symbolism of a "full-rigged sailboat" and somewhat tempered praise generally, despite which Glory Quayle became one of Miss Allen's most admired and oft-repeated roles. The novelist-dramatist and the critic William Winter were to fight a verbal duel in the *New-York Daily Tribune* of October 19.

Inasmuch as the redoubtable "W.W.," replying to an irate reader in the columns of the 17th, felt that while the piece had "many literary merits, and also . . . a few points which are dramatic . . . it contains [among other things not eminently desirable] far too many clergymen," it does not seem illogical that Mr. Caine should have invited ministers of various denominations, along with their families and friends, to be his guest audience at a special eleven-o'clock matinée on Thursday, November 3. At the third act's end he explained his motivation. "There was a great clapping of hands as Mr. Caine closed," wrote the reporter from *The New York Herald* (November 4), "But here and there I heard the subdued comments of clergymen who ventured to differ with the speaker. One who sat beside me turned to a companion and said:—'That is all very true, but it doesn't alter my opinion of the play.'"

And outside in the Broadway sunlight the Byrons waited with their cameras. What they recorded gives veracity to W. J. Lampton's verse in *Life* of October 20, 1898:

> "Now look at the wonderful things called hats,
>   With feathers of fishes, of birds and of bats;
>   Delirium trimmings of ribbons and lace
>   Leap-frogging, high-kicking, running a race.
>   Oh! what a wild wilderness over a face."

"Theatre hats" had been much in the nation-wide news throughout the period and the *Tribune* from 1893 to 1897 was peppered with articles relating to what one letter-writer called " 'gaff-topsail' bonnets" with fleeting reference to perambulant "roof-gardens." They were warred upon by both sexes; interdictory bills were introduced in the Legislature, one Assemblyman even proposing an amendment to include "puffed sleeves" in the act. On May 3, 1895, two sailors from the U.S.S. *Chicago*, seeking surcease from the monotony of the sea, found their enjoyment of *The Fatal Card* at the Academy of Music marred by millinery, and being men of action, "gently lifted the [offending] hats off the women's heads." Mrs.

Harriette Gross Cozzino, of 56 West Fifty-third Street, patented a contraption she christened "The Happy Thought"—"a round hook with a mirror in its face . . . fastened by screws on to the back of the theatre chair"—which she told an emissary from "The Only Woman's Page" of the *New-York Daily Tribune* (June 15, 1897) would simplify the storage problem of the "hat to be taken off, put away and re-adjusted; cloak, opera-glasses, bag and other accessories, such as handkerchief, fan or purse—if one goes in the afternoon." Moreover, the spring of 1896 found the "High Theatre Hat Nuisance Committee" of the "Women's Health Protective Association" of Brooklyn helpless, but determined to return to the fray in the fall, since several of the members spoke up in meeting, and, as reported in the *Tribune* of April 11, "in chorus declared [even in the face of sisterly ridicule] that they were frequently made subject to mental suffering by having their view of the stage impaired."

. . . . *No one shall pass*

"THE STAGE door! It leads to that mystic realm of light and tinsel, ever fascinating, never understood, intoxicatingly interesting, and always sought-after region by people who will never know 'behind the scenes.' To the uninitiated it is all mystery, to those initiated it is three dull brick walls, a mass of scenes, a tier of dressing rooms, a place of endless work." This from an article by Wells Hawks, with "Photos by Joseph Byron, N.Y.," in the May, 1904, number of *The Theatre Magazine* (so ably edited by Arthur Hornblow from October, 1900 through February, 1927). "The man who tends the stage door at a theatre may be old and decrepit, but he has lodged in every active faculty of his antiquated being one fixed understanding, and that is that no one shall pass the door he guards. . . . In the well-conducted theatre of to-day it is the rule that only those whose business brings them there shall be admitted. . . . It has come to be the custom that the stage doorkeeper is an old man. . . . He is either despondent over some melancholy fact that if the tide had turned another way he might have been a successful manager, or he is full of reminiscences of the old days. . . . Stage doorkeepers are quick to learn the faces of the members of a company. . . . The star is treated with the greatest courtesy. . . . It is a traditional perquisite for the stage doorkeeper to receive a generous gift from this exalted personage on the last night of the engagement. . . . Few players ever omit this gift to the man who guards the door. It is he who receives the mail and hands it to them . . . just as it is he who receives the flowers and sends them up to the dressing-room. . . . It is he, too, who keeps back that onslaught of youthful admirers who linger about the stage door for she who seems so beautiful in the limelight's glare. . . . A hundred cabs may line up before his door, and a great multitude of genus Johnny, crush hat and evening suit, adorn the pavement side, but he is as immovable as the hills. . . . If his theatre is playing some attraction where a large feature of the performance is a chorus [the "Casino girls"—for instance—were bywords of enchantment] . . . the stage doorkeeper's nights of guarding are a troubled sea. He is attacked and beset by every form of ingenuity to reach the inner portals by him who would take her to dine where lobsters are high-priced, where wine flows and bands play—that land of separation where fools and money part."

In the early years of the twentieth century, new-fashioned theatres started employing younger men to stand colder guard, kempt and uniformed; but not so the Casino, with a tradition dating back to October 21, 1882, when in still unfinished beauty it opened with the American première of Johann Strauss's *The Queen's Lace Handkerchief*. Montgomery Schuyler in *Harper's Weekly* of January 13, 1883, had only hallelujahs for the work of Kimball & Wisedell, the architects of Rudolph Aronson's novel house. The critic found the lavishly ornamented Moorish exterior "virtually a monochrome in red baked clay . . . uniformly well studied . . . [with] the masses so strong that the building nowhere seems overloaded," and declared that "it would not be easy to name an interior in New York which has been so thoroughly thought out in detail . . . and which has so much the appearance of having been 'designed all over.'" The curtain which rose on many fabled entertainments was described in the *New-York Daily Tribune* of December 29, 1882 as being "of different shades of blue and old gold silk plush, with fantastic Moorish designs worked in" and incrustation of "emeralds, rubies and sapphires so arranged that the light from the stage streaming through produces a beautiful effect." This Saracenic structure combined a theatre, a balcony terrace, a restaurant, and a summer garden (opened on July 7, 1883 as New York's first Roof, if one excepts Aronson's earlier Metropolitan Concert Hall promenade).

In 1893, Canary & Lederer took over the house which had held among its melodious memories the long delight of *Erminie* (opened on May 10, 1886, with Francis Wilson, Pauline Hall and Marie Jansen, later the star of *Nadjy*). I will let "Uncle Denny"—the stage door Cerberus from beginning to end of the second management—speak of his stewardship, through the intermediation of Lavinia Hart, who interviewed him for *The World* of December 9, 1900. "He's very old and very bow-legged and very moody," she wrote. "He's all that is left of the old Casino regime. . . . Through the halcyon days of the Casino . . . the time of [Lillian] Russell's first freshness; of Pauline Hall when . . . her smile was a danger signal, of 'Dainty Fanny Rice' . . . ; of Lulu Fuller, before she was 'La Loïe'; . . . of a hundred others before the fall [of the Lederers and the supersession of the Sires], Dennis stood guard. . . . 'Don't bother me. I'm sad,' he said wearily. . . . 'Oh, it isn't the management. . . . Sure I never seen the management. That's to the front, and Denny's to the back. It's just the times I'm complainin' against. There's no snap an' dash an' go in 'em. I might as well be doorkeep at the Raily [misprint for Rainy] Daisies. . . . Doorkeep at the Casino is a different job than it is anywhere else. . . . Isn't here where all the girls that can sing or dance or look a part come from? . . . But there ain't no Johnnies any more. The old ones have all died or settled down . . . and the new ones ain't grown up yet. . . . And there ain't no style about being a Casino doorkeep in a between-time. . . . Why, there was nothing but style. I can remember the time when I've snubbed on an average of twenty Willie boys a night. . . . Them was the days of Russell. . . . It's many a star we've had since then, but they wasn't stars clear through, like Russell was. . . . Russell had a way of one at a time, you know, but most of 'em have bunches. Pauline Hall, for instance. . . . And Nina Farrington! . . . Then there was that beautiful May Yohe. . . . And there was Theresa Vaughan. . . . There was the woman that's singing coon songs now at Weber & Fields's . . . Fay Templeton, I mean—but Dennis can remember her when she hadn't any voice, but just shape, and smiles, and eyes. . . . You see, we've had all kinds at the Casino. . . . But these is all old stars. . . . There's been new ones since, an' the best of the lot was Toby Claude, that played in "The Belle of New York" [in the 1900 revival, with Edna May still the Salvation Army lass]. Say, it seemed almost like the old times the rush that came to the stage door for the little Toby.'" Of *Florodora*—newly opened and perhaps the Casino's highest moment—he did not discourse; of such beloved actors as David Warfield he gave no reported opinion. A week after the interview, reading *The World* of December 16, one learns that Denny had been "deposed from his position of authority . . . [but] could not get out of the habit of coming down to stand at his old post. . . . 'Why hello, Denny! How are you?—Glad to see you,' and similar greetings smote his aged ear, as the fair ones tripped into the theatre. . . . 'I feel mighty bad' was the response."

They do not remember Denny; Denny has been forgotten by Peter Mason (the Frohman factotum at the near-by Empire) and the "old No. 1 Union men" he consulted about this photograph. Nor do they—who met so often in a favorite bar at Sixth Avenue and Thirty-eighth Street—recall Byron's subject by name, although they believe him to have been a German. The fine figure in the long overcoat—I am informed—is William Monroe, later President of Theatrical Protective Union No. 1, together with several of the brotherhood. Present, too, is a bill-poster with the bucket of his trade. Nor does Peter Mason recall William Reilly, although Thomas C. Leonard wrote in the *New York Herald Tribune* of

"The Casino, one of the most famous stage doors in
New York," 1904. Thirty-ninth Street, east of Broadway

February 16, 1930, that "From the very start, . . . [he] guarded the stage door and continued there through successive managements." Under my cross-examination, Mr. Mason testified: "One thing I can tell you, in those days we had two stage doormen. So both men mentioned [Denny—who had forgotten his own last name—and Reilly] could have worked at the Casino. They worked 12 hours a day seven days a week." In any event, it would seem that Reilly stood watch at the famous door of the home of comic opera until the final curtain fall on January 18, 1930. During his tenure the house saw twenty-eight years of Shubert direction (from May 21, 1902, on), and survived the fire of February 11, 1905, which—demolishing Jake Wolff's 39th Street corner café—brought about redecoration of the highly praised auditorium. Under this final regime well remembered actors (Eddie Foy, Jefferson De Angelis, Sam Bernard, Henry E. Dixey, De Wolf Hopper, and James T. Powers, to catalogue a few) bowed their thanks to laughing audiences; such lovely ladies as Fay Templeton, Jobyna Howland, Julia Sanderson, Blanche Ring, Fritzi Scheff, and Alice Brady passed through the stage door into delight. It was old Denny who in his impartiality spoke a tremendous truth: "Charms is charms, it don't matter who has them."

. . . . *Are there any more at home like you?*

> "Tell me, pretty maiden,
>   Are there any more at home like you?
>   There are a few, kind sir,
>   But simple girls, and proper too."

"ONE MOMENT, Mr. Stuart. How did you come to write 'Tell Me, Pretty Maiden'?" "Oh, I don't know; came to me suddenly, I suppose, I always had had a desire to write a concerted number for six men and six girls." "And why six?" "Because they would just comfortably reach across the stage. The difficulty was that I could not hit upon a suitable phrase to carry the song. One evening, about two weeks before the [London] opening of 'Florodora,' I was standing in front of the Lyric Theatre . . . [there], and for some unaccountable reason the phrase, 'I must love some one, it might as well be you,' occurred to me. I haven't the slightest idea what put it into my mind. It just struck me. . . . 'There,' said I to myself, 'there is the phrase for the sextet,' and I turned from the theatre and went home. Two hours later I had composed the music, thought out the business, and put it all on paper." This dialogue forms part of an interview published in *The New York Herald* on Sunday October 27, 1901. The reporter assigned to the pleasurable task found the newly arrived young Liverpudlian, who had "set four continents whistling one air and started a couple of hundred thousand street organs, more or less, grinding out the musical conundrum, 'Are there any more at home like you?' . . . to be a young man, not very tall, rather slight in build, smooth shaven, affable and—for the benefit of anxious inquirers—married."

At this point *Florodora*—which had seen its New York première at the Casino Theatre on November 10, 1900—was just two performances short of the 400 mark, and well along its way to the captivation of 547 metropolitan audiences. The initial notices had not been overwhelmingly rhapsodical, but a group of the "Sons of Eli," who had joined in the catchy chorus at the New Haven tryout, followed the show to town, and, by repetition of their

The Florodora Sextette, 1900

collegiate vocalism had started a cyclic success that was to make musical comedy history, and cause later commentators to invoke even Thorstein Veblen's *The Theory of the Leisure Class* in explanation of a theatrical phenomenon. Leslie Stuart who, with Owen Hall (a pseudonym reflecting the momentary impecuniosity of James B. Davis, librettist of *The Geisha, The Gaiety Girl* and *An Artist's Model*) was responsible for this delight of the local second generation *jeunesse dorée,* had his own rationale. The farsighted New York producers, John C. Fisher and Thos. W. Ryley, he said, "were urged to 'Americanize' it, but they didn't. They retained its English atmosphere, and this, I think, affords one of the reasons of its success." He found the Gotham sextette "streets ahead of the originals" but disapproved of the tempo—accelerated in spots. ". . . let me tell you," he said, "that the rapid and irresponsible style of the pieces now in vogue in New York [such as *The Liberty Belles, The Little Duchess* and *Hoity-Toity*] has reached its limit, and 'Florodora,' if I may say so, with its calm and pretty surroundings, and its lighter music, was conspicuous and met with popular approval. . . . Believe me, this method you call 'snap' and 'ginger' will recoil on the managers. I don't think your audiences demand blaring trumpets to every song and 'rag time' accompaniments to every melody. . . . All 'coon' songs [and he had previously been responsible for many] sound alike to me, and I suppose there is no musical piece in New York, except 'Florodora,' that is not fairly soaked with rag time melodies."

The name of this exception to all rules derived from a mythical island in the Philippine archipelago (then much publicized because of the Spanish-American conflict) and a perfume distilled from its fragrant flowers in a factory preempted by the villain of the piece. The defrauded native heroine, the inevitable hero, a Scotland Yard detective, and a young English noblewoman bent on second mating furnished a plot far overshadowed by the double sextette of frock-coated "Clerks" and "English Girls"—Gibsonesque visions dreamily clad in frilly pink topped by black picture hats with long gloves to match and twirling parasols. Four of the original half dozen were maids, one newly widowed, and one a wife. These basic patterns of the chorus girl concept were: Marie L. Wilson (to invade the *Social Register* as Mrs. Frederic Gebhard); Vaugn Texsmith (a simple Smith from the Lone Star State, who espoused I. J. Hall, a wealthy silk merchant); Agnes Wayburn (already the bride of Ned Wayburn, of dance fame, and following early divorce, to be transplanted to Johannesburg by marriage to a diamond fortune); Marjorie Relyea (whose first husband R. D. Holmes, a nephew of Andrew Carnegie, dropped dead four days before the opening night, leaving her to become Mrs. Albert Stokes at a date much later); Daisy Greene (destined to be a prima donna and to leave the world of the theatre as the wife of a Denver stockbroker); and Margaret Walker (subsequently Mrs. W. B. Crowell). During the engagement, it was found that there were many more at home like them: 130 pounds of small-waisted exquisitude spread over 5 feet, 4 inches, with encrowning glory of dark brown or red hair. All told, about seventy-six successive Pretty Maidens (including Evelyn Nesbit, Mabel Carrere, Nan Patterson, and Edna Goodrich) took six nightly encores to the consistent applause of such connoisseurship as Stanford White's and the athletic salvos of those who had taken advantage of the programme note, "Bicycles checked free in the Main Corridor." After curtain-fall all this incarnate loveliness was to be seen at the Waldorf and at Rector's, everywhere and here and there, with full press coverage and echoing advertisement, smilingly acquiescing to the universality of the invitation "Then take a little walk with me . . . ," but asking only of the footlit escorts

> "Tell me, gentle stranger
> Are there any more at home like you?"

to be reassured

> "There are a few, sweet maid
> And better boys you never knew."

.... *"I turn you out;*
For on the field of Wagram I'm at home!"

ON A December afternoon in 1950, a great lady arrived at the Museum of the City of New York unannounced. She carried the insignia of sovereignty carefully hidden in her knitting bag; but there was obvious royalty in her bearing, splendor all about her, a beauty in the far gaze of her blue-green eyes. May Davenport Seymour, Curator of the Theatre and Music Collections—herself in the glorious tradition of the American stage—called me across the corridor, from my office to hers, so that I might meet Miss Maude Adams, there to present the jeweled crown she had worn in *A Kiss for Cinderella*. A moment in the long ago welled Proustian in my mind, and I confessed to Peter Pan that when over the footlights came the appeal "Do you believe in fairies?" my childhood had betrayed Tinker Bell with an indignant "No!" while my young parents looked at one another in the full horror of the realization that they had begotten a monster. I told Miss Adams that if she were to give me the never given gift of second chance, then and there, my negation would be less absolute.

Another of my regrets eternal is that—despite the poor notices—I was not here to see her play the Little King of Rome. She opened on October 22, 1900, in Louis N. Parker's English adaptation of *L'Aiglon*, by Edmond Rostand, at the Knickerbocker Theatre, under Charles Frohman's banner, for a run of 73 performances. James Stetson Metcalfe, drama editor of *Life* from 1888–1920, told his following in the November 1 issue that the star "was as pathetic a picture in the play as Reichstadt is in history." *Munsey's Magazine* of January, 1901, was less implacable: "In the lighter scenes Maude Adams is admirable. She looks the part. She succeeds in imitating a masculine walk and carriage almost perfectly. She is really charming. In the strong scenes she is hopelessly inadequate; yet, such is the sympathy that she establishes between herself and the audience, her shortcomings are forgiven." The coup de grâce came from William Winter, for forty-four years the paradoxically sentimental and satirical dramatic critic of the *New-York Daily Tribune*, then past his apogean days as arbiter of the playwright's craft and theory, but ever the supreme analyst of the art of acting. He left the theatre on that opening night to scrawl his illegible review from the vertical stance he favored for composition, and, making comparison with the reports from France of the "passionate excitement" created by Sarah Bernhardt's playing of the mirror scene (in which the Eaglet shatters the looking-glass tauntingly used by Metternich to bring home to him his failure and futility as Napoleon's son) and her powerful acting on "the haunted battlefield" of Wagram, reflected cruelly: "Miss Maude Adams also, at these points, creates a tempest, —but it is a tempest in a teapot." When the French actress—for whom Rostand had conceived

251

Maude Adams in *L'Aiglon* by Edmond Rostand (1900), Act IV. Set designed by Ernest Gros
From left to right: J. H. Gilmour as Flambeau; Maude Adams as the Duke of Reichstadt;
William Crosby as Count Sedlinzky, Prefect of the Austrian Police; and other members of the Company

the role and written his stirring Alexandrines—brought the play to New York as part of her repertoire, Winter, on November 27, 1900, described her impersonation as "one of beautiful symmetry," and again fell back on a bitterness unseconded, among others, by *The Sun's* emissary, who favored the interpretation of the American star. "That the play is much more ably and effectively acted, in almost all of the parts, by Sarah Bernhardt and her associates," wrote W. W., "than it is by the English performers . . . is beyond question. . . . [She] may not be a dazzling prodigy . . . but, in contrast with such a vapid, flaccid and colorless performer as Miss Maude Adams, she is a leopard alongside of a kitten." To him, Maude Adams was "essentially a delicate, fragile actress, void of power and puny in style . . ." and "Possessed of a gentle personality . . . capable of a piquant behavior . . . a sprightly and bonnie lass in 'The Little Minister,'" which "doubtless . . . furnished the measure of her talent." The New York première of this James M. Barrie play, on September 30, 1897, "marked the inception"—so Lloyd Morris, master of words, tells us more than half a century later in *Curtain Time* (his own untimely farewell to American letters)—"of that amazing relation-

252

ship between the American public and the star which, beginning as a one-sided love affair, developed into a worship without precedent or subsequent parallel."

Maude Adams died on July 17, 1953, at the age of eighty, leaving the memory of her mellifluous voice, the never-to-be-forgotten toss of her head, and the elfin sound of the laughter she had learned to the cadence of a trotting horse, going faster and faster.

. . . . *A little lady of the finest theatrical stock*

A BIG red apple—for "speaking her piece good"—was the avuncular gift of John Drew when Ethel Barrymore opened in *Captain Jinks of the Horse Marines* at the Garrick on February 4, 1901. Thereafter this token became a symbolic first night interchange between the head of "The Royal Family" of the theatre and his relatives.

Reviewers were not impervious to the charm of the twenty-two-year-old star, but there were those unimpressed alike by her talent and her vehicle, "A Fantastic Comedy" proliferated by Clyde Fitch as one of four of his plays running concurrently that season (the others being *Lovers' Lane*, *The Climbers* and *Barbara Frietchie*). The *New-York Daily Tribune* of February 5 concentrated on the première of Henry Miller in *Richard Savage*, to which William Winter devoted a column and a quarter, tossing a mere two dozen lines in the direction of the "semi-farcical composition" presented by Charles Frohman, "with Miss Ethel Barrymore,—a juvenile performer, still in the experimental period. . . . The acting was chiefly done by Mr. Reeves Smith, a dry and quaint humorist, and by Mr. Edwin Stevens, long and justly esteemed as an exceptionally clever comedian. Miss Barrymore presented a pleasing appearance, and the proceedings in general were cheered by the friendly plaudits of a considerable audience." James Stetson Metcalfe (in *Life*, February 21), after somewhat damnatory praise ("She is successful because the most has been made of her personal attractiveness, and the strain is not too great for her immature powers") advanced a sound prediction: "She has a very dainty and sympathetic part and does what she has to do so prettily that her audience is with her, and we miss our guess if many stern parents do not have to drag their youthful sons away from the stage door . . . during the period of her engagement." Followers of Alan Dale read in the *New York Journal*: "A girl who seems to have plighted her troth to half the population of this rock-bound isle, and who with Miss Cissie Loftus may lay claim to the title of the Betrothed Phenomenon, is certainly interesting, but not necessarily to the stage." *The New York Herald* branded the plot as "a conventional one," but underscored the "taste and spirit" of the "refreshingly pretty" actress's interpretation. One critic (writing for *The Sun* of February 10), more prescient than the rest of the pack, found it "hardly worth while to separate Miss Barrymore's personality from her skill in estimating her practical success. It may be said fairly, however, that if she adds really great proficiency to her natural outfit she may stand ahead of all living comediennes." *The World* was filled with fervency: "A little lady of the finest theatrical stock aimed at a shining mark last night—and hit the bullseye." About a month after the opening, Charles Frohman ordered the name of his new star emblazoned on the marquee, and on February 24 the *Tribune* relented to the extent of admitting "The performance seems to be growing in favor,

Ethel Barrymore in *Captain Jinks of the Horse Marines*,
1901
Act III. Madame Trentoni's Parlor in the Brevoort
House (Fifth Avenue and Eighth Street)

and all the houses thus far have been large." They continued to be so for the initial run of 168 repetitions as Miss Barrymore, commanding a weekly salary of $125, nightly carried a gardenia bouquet from "L'Inconnu." The scenes were gracefully set—by virtue of the designs of E. G. Unitt—in the New York of the early seventies and although according to the programme the costumes were "designed by Percy Anderson and from Godey's Lady's Book for 1872," Miss Barrymore in her *Memories* (New York, 1955) gives couturière credit to Mrs. Wilson, dressmaker and keeper of the West Thirty-sixth Street boarding house patronized by the leading lady.

The photograph here selected from the Byron coverage shows Miss Barrymore as Madame Trentoni—little Aurelia Johnson, European-trained native of the New Jersey capital—just after her triumphant operatic debut at the Academy of Music, about to be recaptured (after a modicum of misunderstanding) by Mr. H. Reeves Smith, in the title role identified with the oft undercurrently introduced 1868 popular song:

> "I'm Captain Jinks of the Horse Marines,
> I often live beyond my means,
> I sport young ladies in their teens,
> To cut a swell in the army."

Present, too, is John Hughes, as Peter, "the newsboy in the livery of a hotel servant," whose adoration and "first month's wages in advance" have been poured into the oversize horseshoe of red and white immortelles on the table.

To satisfy an equally devoted following, further enslaved by the star's performance in *A Country Mouse*, Gustav Kobbé reported on "The Girlishness of Ethel Barrymore" in the June, 1903 issue of *The Ladies' Home Journal*, recording a visit to her eight-room apartment on West Fifty-ninth Street, which could be identified by Central Park pedestrians glimpsing "the plaster cast of the 'Winged Victory' in one of the windows of the sitting-room . . . [standing] like a beacon to the homing-place of this girl." The article inventoried the music-loving young actress's predilections: in dress, simplicity in black and white; in literature, Balzac, George Eliot, Robert Louis Stevenson, Lewis Carroll and Henry James (who found her—she tells in her autobiography—"rather Gothic . . ." and reminiscent ". . . of a cornice on a Gothic building"); in art, Rembrandt and Whistler—a reproduction of whose maternal classic hung on her wall, along with *The Pearl Diver* (*Figure d'Etude*) from The Louvre, which she liked so well that she was utterly disinterested in the identity of its creator (Jean-Hippolyte Flandrin, 1809–1864, just for the record).

The following year (1904), Ethel Barrymore herself improvised her own thematic line, not to be found in the script of *Sunday,* a play by Thomas Raceward (the nom de plume cloaking a trio of actors—Thomas Wigney Percival, Grace Hodges and Edwin Irwin), in which she created the role of an orphaned girl—named after the Sabbath—who grew up under a quadrilateral protectorate of adoring miners. Transplanted to English elegance by a somewhat dilatory aunt, the second act finds her reading a letter from "the boys" to an audience of her new environmentals. Coming to a part she did not wish to share, she gave abrupt pause, and in answer to urging, was by playwright required to say "No—that's all." To a Barrymore, this savored of discourtesy, and during a rehearsal directed by Charles Frohman she made mitigating amend—"That's all there is. There isn't any more."

. . . . *Except to live, to love, and to die*

"That light we see is burning in my hall.
How far that little candle throws his beams!
So shines a good deed in a naughty world."
The Merchant of Venice, Act V. Scene I.

"IT WOULD cost David Belasco ten thousand dollars to stage these three lines," I once heard Clayton Hamilton say.

In the summer of 1899, when the perfectionate realist thought that the French poet Jean Richepin was going to create a play based on the career of Madame du Barry which would serve as a good vehicle for Mrs. Leslie Carter, so transported was he by the Gallic dramatist's enthusiasm that, according to his own story (quoted by William Winter in *The Life of David Belasco*) he immediately "bought yards and yards of old du Barry velvets, antique silks, and furniture of the period" as prelude to an undertaking that was to involve the expenditure of over $98,000. When the manuscript, even after patient revision, failed to please him, he jettisoned it and set about fashioning his own compelling—if historically inaccurate—version of the story of the little milliner who became the mistress of a king and died on the scaffold.

The creative throes of the dramatist are revealed by Vanderheyden Fyles in *The Metropolitan Magazine* of November, 1910, in which he harks back to his youthful eavesdropping days, over the months when his father (Franklyn Fyles) and David Belasco were laboriously fashioning *The Girl I Left Behind Me*, with which Charles Frohman's Empire Theatre began its star-filled career on January 25, 1893. "If . . . [this play] may be taken as typical, Mr. Belasco ruins one room for each drama written. . . . My father, pen in hand, sat at a large table in the center of . . . [his] library. Mr. Belasco never sat. He walked and walked and walked. His left hand he ran continually through his . . . hair; in his right he held a pen. I don't think I ever saw him write with it. But every time he passed the center table he dipped the pen in the ink bottle, and . . . splashed the black fluid nervously over rugs and chairs as he wandered, tangled in knotty thought. Another diversion was supplied by a handful of poker chips . . . and as the somewhat mysterious genius wandered and pondered . . . he distributed them in exact little piles on bookcases, mantel, tables. Then, retracing his course, he would collect the chips, presently redistributing them in new combinations. . . . [This] was the only aid to Belasco thought which did not leave ruin in its wake. . . . So much for floor, furniture and walls. . . . The writers were as one in their fondness for sarsaparilla, . . . And . . . they used to seem to take deliberate aim, opening the bottles with a pop that sent the corks spattering to the ceiling." It was also a Belasco custom, as

David Belasco in his study, 1909

257

Du Barry, Act V, 1901

cameras attest, to use walls and screens as a sort of visible file for memoranda relating to the play in progress. This *modus scribendi* worked, for by 1894 Belasco—apart from his reputation as "one of the ablest stage managers in America" (according to an article by "Triumvir" in *The Illustrated American* of April 7 that year)—had been connected with more than a hundred for the most part successful pieces of theatre, as playwright, dramatizer, or adapter (sometimes alone, sometimes in collaboration) and was "accounted the best paid dramatic writer" in the country.

Describing his solo battle with *Du Barry*, Belasco stated, as faithfully recorded by William Winter: "For the first time in my life I found myself in the hands of a really bad woman. . . . I felt a desire to rush to her defence. . . . But—I need not have troubled myself to defend the lady, for, good or bad, from the first night [a tryout in Washington prior to the New York première at the Criterion Theatre on December 25, 1901] until the close of the play three years later the public liked the French milliner and the houses were sold out. . . . When the curtain rose [on the five-act, eight-scened drama with its 147 interpreters] it afforded . . . an opportunity to see how a manager's hands were forced by the very prodigality of the subject he had chosen. My production was lavish because the play was laid in a lavish time. The mere 'suggestion' of luxury would not do,—or so I thought."

On December 29, 1901 *The New York Herald* sent the not altogether convinced Dorothy Adams to the Fifth Avenue Hotel apartments of Mrs. Carter for a joint interview with the star and her playwright entrepreneur, both prostrated by rehearsals often lasting twenty hours. "I am Mme. du Barry reincarnated," declared the actress. "I believe—I have always believed—that in a previous existence I was that unfortunate woman." Asked about his tamperings with history, Belasco replied: "In my delineation I have tried to draw a fair and just picture of the woman as I became acquainted with her through years of reflection [an intimacy dating from his boyhood] and diligent investigation of the gentler phases of her kaleidoscopic life—those phases which history has left almost inviolate. That is my Du Barry." The conference became a play about a play, of necessity telescoped here, with lines drawn from the reportorial account:

MRS. CARTER (drawing her long white fingers across her forehead): And that is my Du Barry.

MR. BELASCO (enthusiastically, beginning to pace the velvet carpeted floor): That is the real Du Barry.

MRS. CARTER [beginning with a sigh and working up to a trickle of tears]: Poor girl! Poor, misguided, unfortunate girl! It is too bad she did not stay in the country lanes and in the shady forests of Fontainebleau. . . . Poor thing, she loved the modest, quiet, sweet little violets, but she plucked great red roses instead, and she scratched her little white hands. . . . Du Barry's was a game of destiny—the toss of a coin. Heads lost. She was the doll of the world—a pretty plaything for kings and princes and Ministers of state. . . . Men could not help loving her, and she—well, what is there for a woman to do, anyway?—a woman of her nature especially—except to live, to love and to die?

DOROTHY ADAMS: And where did you study your part of the drama?

MRS. CARTER: Over in Paris I read all the books I could find upon the subject of the French Revolution. . . . I haunted the milliner shops of Paris. . . . I spent weeks and weeks in the country, in the neighborhood where Du Barry was born.

DOROTHY ADAMS: What did you do there? Pick violets?

MRS. CARTER: Yes, I picked violets every day, just like poor Jeannette, just like my former self once did. . . .

DOROTHY ADAMS: And is it true that you lived in Du Barry's palace at Luciennes, and that you slept in her bed and ate off her gold dishes?

MRS. CARTER: Dear me, no. I visited it very often, . . . but as to the furniture and gold dishes, there are few of them left. We have $75,000 worth of her stuff in the production of the play—her superb drawing room set, tables, cabinets, tapestries, porcelains and plate.

DOROTHY ADAMS [turning the conversation to a bit of repeated stage business involving a powder puff]: Now, Mr. Belasco, don't you think you overdo the importance of that toilet accessory in your version of Du Barry's life?

MR. BELASCO [smiling]: Not a bit of it.

DOROTHY ADAMS: But, seriously . . . don't you think it inappropriate to make the poor creature stop to powder her face before going to the guillotine [the scene here depicted]? . . .

MRS. CARTER: No, I don't think so. . . . It was as much a part of herself as her king conquering eyes, her musical speech, the gestures of her marvellous hands. With it she expressed all great emotions—love, hatred, jealousy, joy, despair—and it more than anything else revealed her real nature when she, full of the love of life and light, went forth to walk in eternal shadow.

After the New Year's Eve performance, an affecting postlude took place. The cast presented Mr. Belasco with a silver loving cup, inscribed with one of the lines from the play: "Remember that we have loved you; we loved you through it all."

. . . . *What funny little pantalettes*

"When all the Muses meet together, they dance." Such was Degas' affirmation.

. . .

"IT'S DAMES fer de bally." So said a messenger boy with equal sagacity and conviction, as he passed the curious crowd pressing close to the stage entrance of the Metropolitan Opera House where, according to a Sunday feature writer for *The New York Herald* of September 16, 1900, "two lines of pushing, struggling feminity strained for a goal." Other inquisitive passers-by had hazarded less accurate guesses. "Race riots," shouted a "newsie." "Hen convention—looks like," volunteered a substantially built citizen. "On the trail of a new tenor," was the guess of a boulevardier. "Maybe a beauty show," doubted some Thomas. "Go on! it's a mothers' meeting," quipped a bystander. The reporter edged his way into the building, to find Luigi Albertieri (the Ballet Master since 1895–1896) sorting replies to an advertisement he had placed in the *Herald*, it goes without saying. The illiteracy rate was high. One applicant wrote with assurance that she had scored a triumph in "livin' pitchers." A second felt that her feet—because of their tinyness—"could pick up dancing very quick." A third boasted that she was "an experienced toe dancer, kicking as well with both feet, and generally work for the interest of the co. It all depends." Still another felt that the fact that she was "a grand waltzer" and a blonde by nature—"no dye"—made for valid qualification. The doors opened, and a candidate rushed up to Signor Albertieri to report a loss of "three pounds since last Saturday," and, assuring him that will power would continue triumphant, begged "Let me balance the front row." "She would balance the building," said the Maestro in muffled aside.

The familiars gathered on the stage for the trial. "Some twirled about on their toes, danced a little pas seul or kicked swiftly in seeming delight at the prospect of being again in harness. The amateurs clustered by themselves, gazing with awe at this careless proficiency. . . . The novices had almost to a unit donned bicycle skirts and were surprised to see the professionals garbed in long, sweeping garments. They all bloomed as to millinery, the poultry yard, the flower bed and the grape arbor appearing to have been robbed. . . . It was curious to note that many of the old timers were liberal in their use of 'make up,' unlike the average chorus girl, who customarily presents a washed out appearance at the morning rehearsal. Alberteri [The *Herald* was consistent in misspelling his name] called the roll. Then divided them into two lines, the larger ones to be employed as the boys in the ballet, the smaller ones for the girls. The two lines were in the main composed of professionals. . . . Room was made for . . . [the maître de ballet] in the middle of the first line. They all clasped hands and at his command kicked their way with him toward the footlights in an intricate step. Taking

Ballet rehearsal at the Metropolitan Opera House,
September, 1900
West side of Broadway, Thirty-ninth to Fortieth Streets

a position in the centre he faced them, ordering them to repeat the step. . . . 'You stand on one side,' he requested of the awkward ones. 'Now, again, if you please. All right, you are excused. Tomorrow at ten.'" He spared the amateurs—"girls . . . nervous with their feet" he called them—the added misery of a mocking audience, and put them through simple paces. Among them one saw an aspiring cloak model, making hopeful use of her lunch hour, and eager to introduce her manicurist "chum"; a traveling salesman's bored grass widow in search of "fun," but soon deterred by the prospect of the daily eleven-to-two practice grind; a gigglesome girl who would "rather dance than eat" (she was hired); "a well-known acrobatic dancer," tired of playing second fiddle to "a trained pig on the bill," who felt that her introduction of "a cakewalk in 'Aida'" would add "a new wrinkle" to "gran'op'ra."

The great lyric temple was about to embark on its seventeenth season—a season that marked the end of the sovereignty of Jean de Reszke, for the crimson curtain was to fall on his New York farewell at a gala performance on April 29, 1901; a season that saw the Metropolitan beginnings of Louise Homer, Fritzi Scheff, Marcel Journet and Charles Gilibert; a season during which the red-and-gold auditorium with its Diamond Horseshoe stirred to the accustomed sound of such poetry-filled voices as those of Lillian Nordica, Nellie Melba, Ernestine Schumann-Heink, Johanna Gadski, and Antonio Scotti.

As the preparations for the 1900–1901 season accelerated at soul-break pace, *The New York Herald* reporter was again sent behind the scenes to gather material for a Byron-illustrated article that appeared in the Sunday edition of October 7. During his tour he "reached the old Opera Club room, where the brisk Alberteri was rehearsing his sylphs and fairies for the ballet." The journalist expressed a melting disillusionment: "However, the sylphs and fairies were not quite as sylphlike or fairylike as when seen in the softening rays of colored lights or in their gay and glittering costumes. Dear me, what funny little pantalettes they had on, and what stockings! Instead of the shapely tricot of uniform tint, they seemed to have on their everyday wear—black stockings, blue stockings, red stockings, tan stockings and what not. As for their bodies, they had on shirt waists, or any other old thing that they didn't mind spoiling, and the only thing that suggested the ballet were the little gauze skirts, which stuck out in the most amusing way from the prosaic garments of everyday wear. . . . It was evidently a moment's rest for the ballet [here camera-caught, with the Ballet Master standing by the piano]. Some were sitting down taking rapid stitches in garments that had been made . . . the worse for wear by the morning's rehearsal. Others were munching pieces of cake; two of the girls were feeding each other with bananas. One had a foot placed on the seat of a chair and was giving a tightening pull at her stocking. Three or four 'ponies' were grouped near the window like cigales warming themselves in the sunlight. 'Tannhausaire!' shouted Alberteri at that moment, and a long distance pianist . . . in his shirt sleeves . . . half munching, half smoking a stogie, clawed at the ivories and started up the Venus Berg scene. Eight of the ballet girls came forward. . . . Alberteri rapped on a chair . . . as a signal to begin. Then he got in between the girls, clapped his hands and led them forward, backward and this way and that, showing them all kinds of graceful arm movements, beckoning, motioning away and holding up the arms during a long interlude until every gesture, every vibration of the body, every step seemed wedded to music, and every girl began to express herself . . . with hands, arms, legs, feet and body. In the meanwhile you heard Alberteri's voice shouting 'Chassez a droit! Repetez a gauche! Avancez ensemble!'"

Tableau Vivant, 1897

. . . . For charity forsooth!

"Cousin Henry, who writes editorials for a country paper, and rarely comes to New York, feels it his duty to his constituents when he does get to town to see some of its shows. He was here a fortnight since . . . and saw Cissy Loftus and 'the living pictures.'" So *Harper's Weekly*—his coz-germane in journalism—patronized in the issue of February 23, 1895. Despite the fact that the rural newspaperman sat in a state of hopeful respiratory suspension for a good quarter of an hour, he could not find "the least violence done to propriety" in the stellar performance. "As for the 'living pictures,' Henry was impressed with the great beauty of some of them, but the expositions of the nude in art disappointed him, and made him realize, he said, better than ever before the reasonableness of the interest of womankind in clothes. It is a fact . . . that the nude 'living pictures' are not quite indecent enough to be scandalous, not nearly decent enough to be nice, not well constructed enough to be satisfactory as art, and not much good at all except as curiosities. They do, however, help to reconcile the observer to clothes, and that is a rather useful office."

Only Cousin Henry's place in the time cycle had saved him from an earlier contact with artistic nakedness, for in the late 1840's this type of entertainment was all the rage. It began on the night before a September morn—the evening of the 23rd, to be exact—in 1847, when Dr. Collyer presented a mixed troupe at the Apollo Rooms. A celebrative lithograph published by James Baillie the following year reveals "The Three Graces, As exhibited by the MODEL ARTISTS of New-York" in all their classic and shockful splendor. In 1894 Kilanyi's "Living Pictures"—an entertainment form popular in London music halls—reactivated the Gotham vogue that evoked the country cousinly yearning for furbelowed frills. Austin Brereton, writing of "Plays and Players" in *The Illustrated American* of that April 7th, vouched that "these pretty pictures . . . which include statues as well as paintings" could not "offend the most fastidious," and held that "the unnecessary draping of some of the figures" was due to "prudishness on the part of some one connected with the management, or else an ill-founded fear of Dr. Parkhurst and his myrmidons." He commented that "The old device of presenting the pictures in a massive gilt frame, situated in the centre, but at the back of the stage, led up to and surrounded by claret-colored cloth hangings, is resorted to with good effect." In his opinion Kilanyi's ensemble at the Garden Theatre was a counterirritant to such exhibitions as that of the Society of American Artists, for he felt that our local painters, when treating the nude, were perversely inspired "to indulge in unnatural figures, in coarse types, and in coloring which never had any existence save in their own imagination." By June 30th, the same magazine—since "its pages were meant for polite eyes"—found it impossible to put down the fitting epithets for these multiplying "unseemly spectacles" which a few years before, "Had they been attempted in the most disreputable resorts of the vicious, the remote fens and sumps of the town . . . would have called forth angry protests . . . and invoked the interference of the constabulary." However, since such iniquities were cloaked

A Living Picture, 1901

under the name of "Living Pictures," "Those clothed with the authority, and possibly with the inclination, to protest against the infamous appeal to the baser phases of humanity are intimidated by the semblance of respectability thrown about the glaring indecency of the device, and the evil has rapidly grown into proportions of terrible suggestiveness. In the beginning there was some pretense at modesty and seemliness," but now "in their stead there is a brazen pandering to all that is . . . depraved."

For a window display variant of these alleged obscenities, *The Illustrated American* was all laudation. Mary Bacon Ford wrote in the November 3, 1894 issue: "There are two or three artists on Broadway who are doing a new thing. They are giving living pictures in flowers for nothing to anyone who happens to walk by. The so-called living pictures about town are not pictures at all. . . . Some of our florists [among them Fleischman] . . . have left the stiff and the beribboned and got to color and form, and the result puts Broadway ahead of any Boulevard in any foreign town. The dripping, drooping, maidenhair ferns in Thorley's are finer than all the feathers on all the fine birds unshot."

At year's end *The Standard* devoted the better part of its December 22nd issue to the epidemic, in the form of "A true story published especially" for its readers, taking them back stage to share in "An Evening In The Life Of A Living Picture." In a series of five dressing room flashlights, the heroine was shown in various narcissistic attitudes, lost in admiration of her hands—a process involving considerable exposure of limbs shapely and remote—and culminating in "The realization," a vision uncomfortably recumbent on a rock against the background of an unlikely coast line. Revisited, the model was shown commencing "as before to prepare herself for the sacrifice" only to hear from the intimidated management that her wholly innocent "turn" must be omitted because of the presence of "Lady Henry Somerset's watchers." Later the Temperance peeress was described as "an estimable person . . . afflicted with . . . the 'not knowing what you are talking about' bacillus," which malady had brought her all the way from London "to tell us how to do." In the next sequence, we behold the object of the titled indignation confiding to a friend that "Lady Henry must have 'wheels in her head' " and settling down to enjoy "an extra rest with the prospect of gratuitous advertising." Contrapuntally, photographs of "Society Women And How They Dress, Showing The Difference Of Gradations Of Modesty" were set before the literate public, with an account of the crusade of Mrs. Elizabeth B. Grannis, a former school-teacher—"middle-aged . . . of excellent preservation" and withal "a charming woman"—"against the shockingly low-cut bodices worn by the fashionable dames and demoiselles at the Opera House." The good matron felt herself much maligned, since it was not her habit, as had been alleged, to apply "the word 'protuberances' when speaking of a woman's breast." Mrs. Frank Leslie (see page 98) championed other views, maintaining that Mrs. Grannis was "opposed to the display of beautiful shoulders because she hasn't any," and admitting to a pardonable pride in that part of her own anatomy. A photograph of Mrs. Leslie in décolleté is submitted in juxtaposition to Mrs. Grannis's modest neckline, and the captive reader is given permission to "decide for him or herself."

Cleveland Moffett, rhetorically pursuing urban turpitude in a series of articles entitled "Is New York Degenerate?" gloated in the June 22, 1895 number of *The Illustrated American*: "And what is this craze for living pictures in all our theaters and music halls but a sign of degeneracy? What is a living picture anyway but an opportunity for exhibiting before . . .

perversely disposed people a series of women who are practically nude, and in some instances are really so but for a thin covering of bronze paint. New York has had the honor of leading the world in this new departure of shamelessness, for until we set the example not even Paris would have dared such effrontery, except in certain places severely under the censorship of the police. And now we have our society young women, under august leadership, doing these same living pictures, for charity forsooth!"

Another sequela of the extraordinary popularity of this theatrical divagation was the flight of the model from the artist, who could not compete with managerial offers of fifteen to twenty dollars a week for a few brief moments of nightly exposure. Lillian Baynes, in *The Illustrated American* of October 19, 1895, lamented that "within two months from the time Living Pictures came into vogue, more than half the best models were to be found before the footlights," and proceeded to exonerate du Maurier (see page 385) from the obloquy that had fallen on Trilby's profession to the extent that "To-day, love nor money cannot find respectable lodgings for a model, if her business is known."

By midsummer, 1896, *The Illustrated American* (of July 11) felt some slight sanguinity, for Henry Tyrrell was able to report that "The beautiful moving pictures"—produced by Edison's Vitascope and "the various other 'scopic' adaptations of instantaneous photography" —"have completely eclipsed and turned to the wall the fleshly and not always artistically suggestive 'living pictures' of last season." However, as the century started to turn, the evil lingered, for on June 18, 1899 *The World* related that Mlle. Lotty (the daughter of the French aeronaut, Anatole Brissonet, famous for her "poses plastiques") "Clad in silk fleshlings, which fit her like a glove . . . robes and disrobes in view of the audience at the Aerial Magnolia Grove on The New York Theatre Roof each evening. . . . [Her] beautiful creations are only gowns of light. . . . Mlle. Lotty is projected against a background of dull black. The theatre is darkened. Suddenly she shines forth, the rays of the stereopticon outlining her figure brilliantly." This "Modern Venus" was again seen during the latter part of July, 1901, and through that August, at the Cherry Blossom Grove (the New York Roof having changed its arboricultural name at the beginning of the 1900 season). "None of her almost countless imitators has equalled Mlle. Lotty's original work in this splendid act," applauded *The New York Dramatic Mirror* of July 27th. Vaudeville competition was indeed fierce. There were "Living Art Studies," "Art Studies & Bas Reliefs," "Reproductions of Famous Statuary," and so on, all about. "In the work of moulding the artistic tendencies of the people," Dean Howell had stated in the *Metropolitan Magazine* of April, 1895, "the living-picture shows are supplementing the museums."

. . . . *Lord Byron will take me in my rooms*

THE KISS lingered in his memory a full fifty years and more.

On an afternoon in February, 1896, during the fourth of her nine American tours (a recurrent series of "Farewell Appearances") the "Divine Sarah" saluted the young photographer (then sixteen) in her dressing room at Abbey's Theatre on Broadway at Thirty-eighth Street. In 1949 Percy C. Byron told of how his father had managed to secure Mme. Bernhardt's permission to photograph her in *Izeÿl*, allowing him an impatient quarter of an hour, and of how in seven revolutions of the second hand the Byrons had recorded eight scenes. When they submitted the prints for pre-release approval at the matinée the following day, Byron *fils* recounts, "She was so pleased she kissed me and said my father was a prince and that we must photograph all her plays, which we did."

And so, later in the season, it came to pass that when a writer from *Munsey's Magazine*—granted a full day's audience—waited on the supreme actress in her Hoffman House suite, the "*voix d'or*" called from another room: "*Attendez, attendez,* you are in time for the photographs!" Then, "Like a happy go lucky boy she ran through the great doors, pulled aside the curtains. . . . 'Such happy hours we shall have now. Lord Byron'—for so she insisted on calling the photographer—'will take me in my rooms. I want my pictures to catch me just as I am in my own apartments. They are for *nos intimes* and for my family.'" A somewhat elastic group if one includes the 700,000 purchasers of the June, 1896, issue of *Munsey's*, in which this photograph, along with three others taken that day, appeared in illustration of the marathonic interview here quoted! "The lithe figure moved with a rapid grace, and her laugh rang out with a silver note as she called to 'Suzanne' [Mlle. Seylor, an actress in the company and her companion] to 'come and sing for me while I play. . . . This is the way we often spend a half hour, I accompanying Suzanne; so let us be photographed this way, *n'est ce pas, ma cherie?*' With great interest Mme. Bernhardt inspected the camera and the flashlight apparatus. Finally all was ready, and with a 'Steady!' from the photographer the light flashed through the room, followed by a stream of smoke. Madame laughed as she puffed out her cheeks to blow the vapor away, and seemed more than ever like a roguish gamin [at 52]. Open went the windows, and though it was a cold day in early spring she stood there driving the smoke out. 'Now, come, another pose!' . . . So she was photographed again.

Sarah Bernhardt in her suite at the Hoffman House, 1896
West side of Broadway, Twenty-fourth to Twenty-fifth Streets

271

. . . She fell into each pose easily, never changing a line of her gown or allowing the photographer to make a suggestion. Everything must be perfectly natural, just as she was, without any studying out of effects."

On this occasion, the captive journalist tells us, "La Grande Sarah" wore "a trailing skirt of velvet with a short coat of the same material—the style of gown most affected by madame when off the stage. The full, lace ruffled bodice peeped out when she moved, and great folds of the lace fell over the jeweled hand. The only ornaments on the coat were exquisite buttons of rare workmanship. Several chains were around her neck, all suggesting bizarre oriental art. With her hands in the pocket of her short jacket she paced the room, touching and smelling this flower, or asking who had sent the other vase of roses."

So moved the eternal actress, who held and dominated the stages of the world for fifty-three of her seventy-eight years. New York audiences applauded her American debut in the role of Adrienne Lecouvreur at Booth's Theatre on the evening of November 8, 1880 and bade her a final farewell on January 14, 1918, when, undaunted by the amputation of a leg, seated or recumbent, she played scenes from her great successes with all the proud magnificence of her motto—"QUAND MEME."

. . . . Come Down Ma Evenin' Star

"LADIES AND gentlemen, I give you a vision of loveliness and a voice of gold—Miss Lillian Russell!" So, on the evening of November 22, 1880, Tony Pastor, in a moment of rare understatement, introduced "the beautiful English Ballad Singer" (Helen Louise Leonard, born in Clinton, Iowa in 1861, currently the wife of Harry Braham, the music conductor, and already a mother).

A quarter of a century later, *The New York Herald* of Sunday October 1, 1905, told its readers: "There is quite a flutter of excitement among the patrons of Proctor's Twenty-third Street Theatre, and with reason. For, though Mr. Proctor provides a very good vaudeville bill there, he now proposes to give his clientele something out of the ordinary in what is practically the vaudeville début of Miss Lillian Russell, for it is so long since she was a feature of Pastor's Theatre that it is as good as forgotten. . . . Miss Russell has an engagement for ten weeks [at $3,000 a week] . . . and will sing three songs, exclusive of encores, at each performance, including Sundays [when so-called "concerts" were held]. But that is not all. She is to be radiant in new and magnificent toilets—she has twenty gowns . . . not only of the present fashion, but ahead of it. And as for the value of them, according to the press agent . . . the bill would even make a life insurance director think it was a pretty steep total." For an explanation of this anti-actuary innuendo, I refer you to the account of the James Hazen Hyde Ball (page 213).

In the magazine section of *The World* of Sunday, October 22, 1905, Lillian Russell herself described "The Costliest Gown of the Present Theatrical Season" in which she is shown (page 274) in all its resplendence. Her remarks are prefaced by editorial comment on the fact that "make-believe in stage effects is passing," that food and drink *en scène* must be both edible and potable, jewels real or expensively facsimilous, and footlight fashion the standard of society, rather than a tawdry aping of the *haute couture* of the day. "I do not as a rule buy my gowns abroad," declared "Airy, fairy Lillian," as her father was the first to call her, adding a consonant to the name of Alfred, Lord Tennyson's "innocent-arch . . . cunning-simple" epitome of babyhood, in the days before the diva had added avoirdupois to pulchritude. "I frequently get materials and the designs there and have them made in New York, for I believe that our home dressmaking is fully equal to the highest European standards, if not superior to them. This gown was made for Wilhelmina, Queen of Holland, and the lace on it cost me $1,500. The entire gown cost me about $2,000. The body is made of baby Irish crochet, with poppies and daisies of large Irish crochet. It is of gold cloth, foot trimmings consisting of ruffles of gold, edged with blue and gold lace; the sleeve trimmings are the same. The gown is cut princess. The hat is of Irish lace, with gold ribbon and blue aigrette [plumage according to an 1892 English music sheet, the "Society Craze," and to come under legal ban in New York State in 1910] running through a diamond buckle, with a tulle rosette on the side. The muff is composed of all-shaded blue ostrich tips and a large blue aigrette. I wear my two pearl necklaces and a torquoise [sic] brooch with it."

Thus attired in the rejected panoply of young royalty, with the additive glamour of a drop curtain proclaiming her magic name in 12-inch electric orthography, against "a set of scenery [especially painted for her, so the *New-York Daily Tribune* of October 1st announced] representing the interior of a palace, in cream and silver" the still pink and white and gold "Queen of Beauty," become the "Empress of Vaudeville," nervously made her initial Monday matinée appearance to the accompaniment of an orchestra "augmented by the installation of a harpist and several strings and woodwinds." According to the *Tribune's* report of October 3, "When she does not force her voice, Miss Russell still has command of her middle register, extracting therefrom sweetness of tone. But the rest is a memory. Clad in a beautiful lace gown and bearing a bunch of orchids in her hand, she sang yesterday 'L'Amouresque' by Bergère (in Russellized French), Edwards's 'Napoli' and one or two lesser songs. The house gave her almost as much applause as it did to Josephine Cohan's dancing, and ticket speculators thronged the sidewalk. . . ." On the following Sunday, October 8, the *Tribune* published a statement received from "the Proctor passionate press agent," proclaiming that the sovereign songstress's "loyal subjects from the captured provinces of 5th-ave. and Riverside Drive were there to do her homage, and their equipages made 23d-st. [for the first time in several years] look like Broadway and 40th-st. on a grand opera night." *The World* of October 3 allowed that this "small army" came "armed with flowers, which were first massed in the foyer and later tossed over the footlights," and that "the result of a long summer of strenuous training was shown in a better figure than Miss Russell has possessed since her Lady Teazle days. While not exactly sylph-like, it was not robust."

Myriad lives in loveliness lay behind the storied beauty that was an active legend and became an epochal emblem. Oft repeated rumors and trite distortions were compounded about such themes as her friendship with "Diamond Jim" Brady (a purely platonic interchange, according to her daughter, lasting from 1902 until his death in 1916). Counterfeit tales still circulate about the famous gem-studded wheel (in actuality a gold-plated affair presented to her by the Columbia Bicycle Company).

Against this backlog, multiple lives, too, lay ahead: as actress; as syndicated columnist; as bride for the fourth time, when in 1912 she became the wife of Alexander P. Moore (Pittsburgh newspaperman, to carry an Ambassador's portfolio to Spain in 1923); as political

campaigner; as lecturer; as propagandist; as cosmetician; as consecrated worker in World War I, active in recruiting and the sale of war bonds; as a Special Investigator of Immigration abroad under President Harding. It was in this service that she died on June 6, 1922 and to her was accorded the military funeral of a full colonel, buglers of the Army, Navy, and Marine Corps sounding taps over her flag-draped silver coffin.

One song she sang sings for her always—Robert Smith's lyric set to music composed in dedication by John ("Honey") Stromberg, conductor of Weber and Fields' Music Hall, to which she imparted some of her splendor. Found on his suicide's body in 1902 (so Parker Morell tells in *Lillian Russell   The Era of Plush*, New York, 1940), was the Paris-green-stained, newly written score of "Come Down Ma Evenin' Star," with its remembered refrain:

> "I wonder who you are,
> Set up so high like a diamond in de sky.
> No matter what I do,
> I can't go up to you.
> So come down from dar, ma evenin' star.
> Come down! Come down!
> Come down from dar, ma evenin' star."

Lillian Russell at Proctor's 23rd Street Theatre, 1905

Mr. and Mrs. John Drew and Miss Louise Drew on the porch
of "Kyalami," East Hampton, Long Island, 1902

"THE MATINÉE girl is legion, hydra-headed. . . . She is a powerful theatre patron worth cultivation. Her opinion is a golden one. . . . Three actors, now appearing in New York in very successful plays hold the matinée girl in leading strings," wrote Kate Jordan, hurrying to meet the deadline of the November 7, 1895 issue of *Leslie's Weekly.* The members of this trio were E. H. Sothern, then the pallid hero of high romance in Anthony Hope's *The Prisoner of Zenda,* Joseph Holland, playing *A Social Highwayman,* and "John Drew, who wears a bandage around his head in 'Christopher, Jr.,' which she 'comes miles to see.' . . . John Drew has been a favorite with her since the early Daly days . . . and as *Petruchio* [in which role he tamed the Shrew for the first time on January 18, 1877] he leaped into a place in her regard from which he has never been dethroned. In the matter of clothes he . . . can't be outrivaled by the most exquisite example of the tailor's art to be found sauntering at noon along the sunny side of Fifth Avenue. . . . Never was hair more geometrically parted in the middle than his, nor boutonnières more nicely selected. . . . The characteristic points of his style are, an affectation of helplessness in trying positions, a quiet, forceful, half-impertinent manner; more than all, what might be called 'the Drew stare,' a wide, inquiring gaze at his audience, in which he seems to appeal to every mother's daughter there to help him win the heroine. He wouldn't seem John Drew if in a dilemma he did not plunge his hands in his pockets, banish all expression from his ruminative eyes, bite his under lip, and say 'H'm!' "

The master of the monosyllable—who has been called "The hero of a thousand dress suit plays"—was then just short of his forty-second birthday. On the night of March 22, 1873, he had been introduced to an audience at the Arch Street Theatre in Philadelphia by Mrs. John Drew, its manager and his mother: "What a dreadful young man! I wonder what he will be like when he grows up," she interpolated as he made his entrance in *Cool as a Cucumber.* From 1875 until 1892 he had been a member of the Augustin Daly Company—that constellation without "stars," in which he so often played brilliant opposite to Ada Rehan—and on October 3rd of the Columbian year he first appeared under the management of Charles Frohman, in Clyde Fitch's adaptation of *The Masked Ball,* with Maude Adams. Then came the successive triumphs of Empire Theatre seasons, which he metronomically began on or close to Labor Day for a run of eight or ten weeks prior to going on tour, sometimes to return for a spring engagement.

This domestic document was taken in the summer of 1902, prior to the September 4th opening of *The Mummy and the Humming Bird,* a four-act play by Isaac Henderson, which the *New-York Daily Tribune* of the 5th lambasted: "John Drew played through the part of Mr. Drew, alias Lord Lumley [a dedicated scientist with a frivolous wife to save from a figuratively feathered Italian author], alias the mummy, with ease and mastery of the stage situations. It must be said in justice that it was a thankless, often impossible, part, as written, to make a vital character of, and that John Drew is quite as pleasant a person to watch performing as a live mummy." It ran for 85 performances and returned for a two-week reprise on April 20, 1903, to be hailed by William Winter in the *Tribune* of the next morning as "a play that was received with much favor last fall. . . . The part and the actor are exceptionally harmonious, and the performance, in its authority, sincerity, and neat executive facility, is not less captivating to sympathy than pleasing to the sense of art." In the supporting cast from the first was Lionel Barrymore, making his initial hit in the role of an Italian organ-grinder. It was after this season's end that *The Ladies' Home Journal* of July, 1903, chose to use a series of informal Byron photographs (including this one) to illustrate an article by Gustav Kobbé on "John Drew and His Daughter," known as "Bee" (later to become Mrs. Jack Devereaux) and already a well-received member of the paternal company. His wife, the former Miss Josephine Baker, had retired from the stage following their marriage in 1880. Of "Kyalami," a Kaffir word, signifying "the place where we live," Kobbé wrote: "Three years ago the Drews spent a summer at Easthampton . . . and liked the place and its environs so much that they decided to build a cottage . . . an artistic but unpretentious shingle summer house. It is enough out of the world for . . . total relaxation . . . and yet sufficiently close to the more fashionable and society-loving colony at Southampton . . . to be of that world when the desire comes." The journalist maintained that the man's mundanity served the Thespian well. *The New York Herald* of September 11, 1904, gives a configurative glimpse: "As the Duke of Killicrankie Mr. Drew is one person . . . blithe, debonair, talkative and enthusiastic. . . . As plain Mr. John Drew . . . he is quite another person . . . serious, sedate and almost sad. More than that, if left to his own devices . . . he is as quiet as South Brooklyn at midnight. . . . He never smiles except when he is acting, and he is as serious as a new policeman and quite as uncommunicative as his own valet. . . . But at the same time he is never ungracious. . . . He is ever a gentleman, but he is taciturn. That is the John Drew of East Hampton and the Hotel Algonquin . . . self-contained, polished and silent. The John Drew of the Empire Theatre stage is a rattling, smiling, breezy sort of a man in a thoroughly correct way."

In every phase of the elegancy of his living, on scene and off, as actor and family man, as clubman and athlete—dividing his leisure (Kobbé tells) between "the saddle, the tennis court and the surf"—John Drew was the aristocrat always. Of him, his close friend Otis Skinner was to say at the time of his death on July 1, 1927, while on the road in a Milky Way revivification of *Trelawny of The Wells* that he had been born "with a dramatic silver spoon in his mouth and his life has always been tinged somewhat with a spirit of dramatic noblesse oblige." And Booth Tarkington wrote in the Foreword to the actor's autobiography: "John Drew would play Simon Legree into a misunderstood gentleman, I believe."

. . . . Several cycles under the sky

". . . THE PATIENCE of the public in the open air is amazing," James Huneker wrote of the renaissance of the roof garden, in *The Metropolitan Magazine* of September, 1906. ". . . the demand for summer foolery, for a new accent in the silly season," had first been answered in 1880, in a quiet, orchestral way, by "Aronson, then the debonair Rudolph," at the Metropolitan Concert Hall; but it was not until three years later that this impresario's potted palminess atop the Casino Theatre (see page 245) drew nationwide attention to New York's latest entertainment form.

In 1892 the *New-York Daily Tribune* shot an editorial arrow into the air, musing on April 17 that "Some of these days roof gardens [topping residences] will be the fashion" and lamenting the paucity of restaurants aloft—lacunae that would be filled before the end of the decade by the widespread use of privately staked-out starlight and hotel dining rooms raised to the clouds.

Three months later *The Illustrated American* of July 30, acclaiming "The City's Lotus Land," rejoiced sardonically in the comfort the "breezy aerial resorts" of entertainment brought the "round paunched, peony cheeked broker . . . [the] careworn merchant . . . the array of bookmakers . . . the sleek and smug-faced actor" far from the pastoral pleasures of resort verandahs, taking the measure of surcease afforded by the tables "tinkling and jingling with goblet, carafe, and decanter, scintillant with varied hues of claret, cordials, pousse-cafés, above which loom the painted faces of gorgeous Jezebels." The journalist shuddered at the thought of the "dangers and temptations" to which the estival bachelor would be exposed "but for these good-instilling fairy dells" and perorated with the usual sociological lament for the obverse side of the seam.

By 1893 the underprivileged upper classes (at this time the subject of considerable serio-comic concern, one organization in 1895 even going to the extent of proposing the establishment of kindergartens for the hapless children of millionaires) could choose from a variety of aerial diversions—in evening competition with excursions to Brighton and Manhattan Beaches, trips on the horse-drawn Eighth Avenue summer cars and other more or less innocent solstitial recreations—for the Madison Square Garden, too, had its roof, and on June 19 the very latest adjunct to New York's Thespian world, the American Theatre, opened its stratospheric promontory. It offered "By far the best of all the open air entertainments," according to *The Illustrated American* of July 15, which described it as a "somewhat small . . . nevertheless a comfortable and well-organized place of amusement," despite the overstating glare of the electric lights. The following summer (a depressed time from a "chrematic" standpoint, when the trend was away from risqué continental importations) this Roof was singled out by the police, with restrictive measures especially applicable to its Sunday night performances: a discriminatory policy possibly not unrelated in this local election year to a number in which John Ransome, in obvious caricature of Richard Croker, sang a political

American Theatre Roof Garden, 1898
Southeast corner of Eighth Avenue and Forty-second Street

ditty entitled "I'm the Boss of New York." On June 2, 1895, at the beginning of its third season in the moonlight, the *New-York Daily Tribune* reported, "There has seldom been a denser crowd at any resort of the kind since roof gardens were invented," listing the "attractions of the vaudeville bill" as a tenor, a soubrette, buck dancers, a sister act, and the new Gotham City Quartet. As Julian Jerrold wrote in *The Illustrated American*, July 25, 1896: "Everything goes, up there in the empyrean," with half a dozen such resorts from which to choose, Hammerstein's "Olympia" taking precedence and the American being "the West Side garden *par excellence*." Harry B. Smith, in a fall retrospective for *Harper's Weekly* of September 26, 1896, noted that while these paradisical refuges were a boon to the "several people in New York who do not ride their bicycles every evening from May to November"—poor prisoners of the city!—a falling off in patronage was reported in some instances. He pointed opprobriously at the wretched elevator service, the archaic variety shows, the lack of "vaunted coolness," and the high priced inferior quality of the ambrosial fare dispensed by extortionate waiters.

In 1897 Oscar Hammerstein again led the field, with noisy, ineffectual competition from the Tyrolean singers and brass bands of more apathetic promoters. Vance Thompson, reviewing the 1899 season in the September *Cosmopolitan* (in which this photograph was reproduced) set the town's nightly sky-borne visitants at 10,000, commented on the respectability these resorts had maintained since 1895, and thus described the clientele and climate of the American Theatre Roof Garden: "They come from what Mr. Hamlin Garland would call the 'middle-west' of New York. There are certain adventurers from Broadway, who have discovered that through the yellow arches . . . there is to be had a wonderful view—the cliffs and crags of the iron city—the North river with its fleets, and the thin lights of the Jersey shore—but in the main the audience is made up of those who speak of Eighth avenue as 'The Av'noo.' They are distinctly—defiantly—'Noo Yorkers.' The program humors their prejudices and cultivates their animosities. It is here, for instance, that you will hear the latest topical song. The actuality is shot as it flies. . . . [The American] lives up to its name. It is conducted on the Aristophanic principle that 'No country's mirth is better than our own.' It is to this roof-garden that the inquiring foreigner should give his nights."

By July, 1900, *The Metropolitan Magazine* was rounding out this first of several cycles under the sky with an obituary entitled "The Passing of the Roof Garden."

. . . . Dream of the field and the grove

"THE STELLAR debut of Miss Alice Nielsen, which was accomplished in Toronto last week, seems from all accounts to have been a decided success. The newly made star appeared in the new comic opera written for her by Harry B. Smith and Victor Herbert, 'The Fortune Teller,' and Toronto gave both star and opera a great send-off. This week the company are in Buffalo giving the finishing touches to the performance, and then they come here, to ask what New York has to say about them, opening at Wallack's to-morrow week." This jotting appeared in *The New York Herald* on Sunday September 18, 1898.

The Byrons were summoned to the railway depot to take publicity photographs of The Alice Nielsen Opera Company (presented by Frank L. Perley) about to go on the road for

282

the Canadian tryout. I have been unable to find a newspaper or magazine account of the departure, but have consulted several railroadians about the series, which includes shots of the train shed. Of all collectors, these "high iron" experts are the most meticulous and the maddest. I once visited the home of such a devotee, to find the locomotive motif a thousand times repeated in every corner and household accessory, while a parrot invited extinction by shouting "All Aboard!" into my offended ear at two-minute intervals of agony. All this dedicated knowledge would only hazard conjecture regarding the point from whence Miss Nielsen started on her journey. It is known that the New York Central & Hudson River Railroad was the only one in the metropolitan area to use this type of sleeping and parlor car,

Alice Nielsen, Toronto-bound, in a Wagner Palace Car,
Early September, 1898

and, since the station shown on shots not included here bears no resemblance to the earlier Grand Central Terminal (on the site of the present one) the conclusion is that the troupe set forth from Weehawken, New Jersey, where the West Shore division of the N.Y.C. & H.R.R.R. may have had a special train ready to leave for Buffalo and thence on to Toronto. Another possibility would have been the old 31st Street station on the west side, where the freight yard was located.

Miss Nielsen is seated in a Wagner Palace Car, a point positive since the letters "Wagn[..]" over the vestibule lintel caught Mr. Walter A. Lucas' knowledgeful eye as he studied another print in the set. Judging from the interior alone, even the Pullman Company—that moulder and perverter of the taste of an era (if one follows Edward Bok's diatribes in *The Ladies' Home Journal*)—could not differentiate between its own product and the Wagner variety, although one venerable employee held to the later proven Wagnerian concept. The two rival outfits were to merge in the fall of 1899. In any event, "Travelling palaces" were these, as *The Illustrated American* of April 18, 1891, tells. "But they are something more than mere palaces. They supply more than the more cheerless luxuries. They give you the highly prized comforts of your own fireside." While this article (after generalizations about the rival manufacturers) goes on to deal with a crack Pennsylvania special en route from New York to Chicago, the description fits the splendor of Miss Nielsen's wheeled home: "It is a flying hotel in which you find yourself. . . . The drawing and state-room sleeping-car is a spacious apartment. It is handsomely furnished, the upholstery and finishing being rich and tasteful. Pay particular attention to the hard-wood finish. Note how handsomely it is carved. See how cunningly the exposed surface of the upper berths is inlaid with delicate tracery, or covered with appropriately tinted embossed velvet. Perhaps you will appreciate all this best at night, when the several chandeliers, their glistening clusters lit by electricity, shed mellow radiance over the exquisite workmanship which they illumine."

Other leading ladies traveled in even greater panoply. Arthur Brooks wrote in the *Metropolitan Magazine* of June, 1898: "The modern luxury of railway travel is no more clearly exemplified than in the private palace car of the 'star' actress of the present day. Mlle. Anna Held is the proud and happy owner of the car owned at one time by Mrs. Langtry. . . . Instead of undergoing the discomforts of 'one-night stands' in the conventional railway hostelry, the fortunate possessor of a palace car may summon comfort and repose in an environment suggestive of the luxury of the Waldorf-Astoria." Miss Held's combination parlor-boudoir-dining-smoking-and-observation room "cost in the neighborhood of twenty-two thousand dollars, and will go to Europe with the actress. . . . Few of our multi-millionaires boast of private palace cars, but, with true democratic spirit, share with others the ordinary comforts of the Pullman and Wagner service."

Alice Nielsen had spent part of the summer of 1898 in Japan and was an inured traveler. *The New York Herald,* after reporting on September 25 that she was "well received in her brief preliminary road tour," commented two days later: "Miss Nielsen, who plays the dual rôle of Irma and Musette, besides masquerading as Fedor [a dashing Hussar and her convenient twin brother in the convoluted plot] acted and sang with delightful freedom throughout. If she was in the least nervous over her New York stellar début she didn't show it. She entered right into the spirit of the opera—and the music is snappy, and the action full of fun—and went through her rôle with lots of dash, and now and then a smile at the audience,

284

as if to let them know how much she was enjoying herself." The supporting cast (which included Eugene Cowles, Joseph Cawthorne, Marguerite Sylva and—according to advertisement—"100-Voices-100" all told) as well as Paul Steindorff, the conductor, was highly commended. *The World* was less whole-hearted, describing the star as "pretty, a little crude and unrestrained in her speaking lines," with a "fresh, sweet small voice, [which] if lost in the concerted numbers, is heard with delight in her many well-sung soli." According to this report, the triumph was to the composer: "Victor Herbert . . . had his apotheosis . . . last night. . . . The score is a remarkable one. . . . His music wooes, it jeers, it jests, it elucidates. . . . It is really a rare score, written by a brilliant, daring, optimistic musician. If the music is the real success of this new production, the librettist, Mr. Harry B. Smith, deserves his share of the credit." Their second-act "Gypsy Love Song" lingers:

> "Slumber on, my little gypsy sweetheart,
> Dream of the field and the grove;
> Can you hear me, hear me in that dreamland
> Where your fancies rove?
> Slumber on, my little gypsy sweetheart,
> Wild little woodland dove!
> Can you hear the song that tells you
> All my heart's true love?"

. . . . *Out of the primitive life of this mining camp*

> "Foul Tenderloin! Least wholesome spot in town,
> Where vice and greed full many a man brought down,
> Where smiling spring a visit never paid,
> And parting summer's ling'ring glooms delayed.
>
> . . . .
>
> Sunk are your hovels, but in wholesome ruin,
> Freed from the stigma of much 'shady doin'.'
> The iron horse has sent your dives to join
> The other nightmares of the Tenderloin"

IN THIS strain, "With abject apologies to the gentle shade of Oliver Goldsmith," Fritz Steele (in the Literary Section of *The New York Herald* of Sunday, May 10, 1903) metrified the story of "The Deserted Village" as told by one of the paper's less prosodic writers: "With the advent of the Pennsylvania's big station and tunnel in the heart of the old Tenderloin, that famous landmark of vice and blackmail passes into history. 'Killed by a railroad' should be its epitaph. . . . Dives disappear before derrick and stone masons. Politicians and boodlers vanish before the headlight of the railroad. . . . In March, 1900, the directors of the Pennsylvania road authorized an increase of $100,000,000 of stock. . . . No hint of the company's real purpose was then disclosed—to acquire the Long Island Railroad, to tunnel under the two rivers and the big city and to erect a monumental station near Herald square. In December of the following year the Pennsylvania purchased several parcels of property in

Thirty-third street between Seventh and Eighth avenues. That was the beginning of the mad rush for property in the neighborhood. Next came the final struggle for all the real estate left, which ended early this spring in the complete acquisition by the company of the valuable territory betwen [*sic*] Seventh and Eighth avenues, Thirty-first and Thirty-third streets. . . . When the purchases were announced, how the rats began to scatter!"

"A prominent politician," resident in the district for forty-four years, described its mutations to a *Tribune* reporter (*vide* the issue of June 15, 1902): "I have lived here long enough to see the complexion of the place change many times. At first it was a straight American crowd, later came a combination of Germans and Irish, and up to within a few years [ago] no negro dared set foot east of Ninth-ave. or west of Seventh-ave. . . . but then they entered, and now we have some sixteen hundred of them." *The New Metropolis,* edited by E. Idell Zeisloft (New York, 1899), contains this statement: "From Twenty-third to Thirty-fourth Streets, on the east side of the way [Seventh Avenue], is the negro promenade, the 'African Broadway.' On the west side are blocks of old clo' and old furniture shops, a Jew colony,

"A Saw Sharpener," 1904
In the Negro district (scene on Seventh Avenue, about Thirtieth Street)

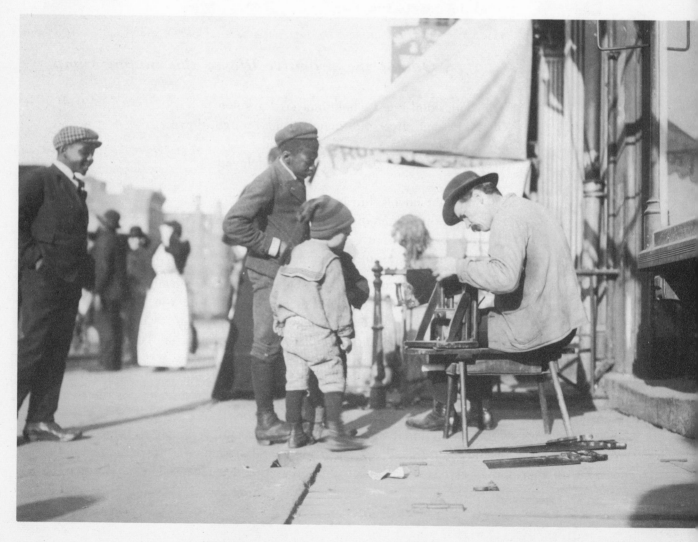

266 Seventh Avenue, about 1903
Between Twenty-fifth and Twenty-sixth Streets

where much trading is done." R. W. Riley, "an old resident, and for nine years postman from Sub-station E to the condemned locality," was interviewed by the same newspaperman: "We have had lots of trouble in getting the mail adjusted . . . but the entire bulk of the mail is not large, the people being the tenement crowd. . . . The heaviest days for the carriers were what we called the steamer days, which brought letters from Italy, France, Germany and Ireland. I can remember the time when in Thirty-second-st., between Eighth and Ninth aves., there were nine Italian restaurants. The business of the lodgers in these blocks was mainly hotel and restaurant waiting and hack driving. The vandalism has been an interesting feature of the migration. There is a gang of young hoodlums, which hangs out in front of the West Side Boys' Home [201 West Thirty-second Street]. . . . Then it is an interesting accompaniment of the movement to see the sympathetic evacuation of the neighboring blocks. . . . The condemnation proceedings have been a great blow to business in all directions for a radius of five blocks from the doomed district. . . . One grocer tells me that his business has been affected to the extent of $300 a month."

Then came "The Great Quarry in the Heart of New York City," which Byron's documentary eye recorded (see page 288), while George Bellows made it the striking subject of two 34 × 44 canvases: *Pennsylvania Excavations* (achieved in February 1907) and *Excavations at Night* (dating from 1908). *The New York Herald* noted on October 29, 1905: "The appearance of the busiest sections of the Panama Canal [the only comparable and largest engineering feat of the period] is reproduced . . . within a block of Broadway. The immense tract . . . today is a

The excavation for the Pennsylvania Station, 1906
Looking north from West Thirty-first Street, between Seventh
and Eighth Avenues

very anthill for activity. As quickly as the [500] buildings disappeared from this once closely populated district an immense amount of excavating machinery was installed. Railroad tracks were laid in every direction and the ground soon lost all semblance of its former civilization. Today the resemblance to the canal zone is complete. The land . . . has been ridged and furrowed until its original topography is but a memory. Long, uneven alleys stretch east and west upward of half a mile in length, through which noisy trains pass on a very busy schedule. The depth of these valleys at many points completely hides the trains from the surrounding country. . . . There are several miles of . . . tracks in constant use, with switches and crossings—a complete railroad system. One of the most picturesque features of this district are the temporary buildings . . . erected as . . . outposts along these lines. They lend to the general effect much of the appearance of a railroad enterprise on some extreme Western frontier."

At about the time this photograph was taken, Marshall Merton described the "great $25,-000,000 hole" in *The Metropolitan Magazine*, April, 1906: "The excavations, originally started at many points . . . by the closing of Thirty-second street, have been united into one gaping cavern, crossed by a narrow bridge, which is Eighth avenue. Here the street is supported on a trestle-work from which passersby can look down at either side into a yawning abyss thirty to fifty feet below. This great hole, stretching for two blocks on both sides of the avenue . . . is now a mass of rock and débris, over which tram roads have been laid, and through which hundreds of workmen are digging, drilling and blasting their way down to the depth required for the foundations of the subterranean station. This will be at a distance level with the bottom of the two tunnels that have been bored under the Hudson River from the New Jersey to the New York shore, and through which the trains of the Pennsylvania road will enter the station."

Out of the "primitive life" of this mining camp and from the fecund genius of Charles F. McKim and William S. Richardson sprang the inspired vastness of a McKim, Mead & White *coup de maître*, its interior reflorescent of the Baths of Caracalla.

Early on the morning of September 8, 1910 (four years and a little more than three months after the commencement of the foundation work on June 1, 1906) "Rapid transit between points on Long Island and Herald square, the Hub of the Universe, the thing which residents on the other side of the East River have dreamed of for a generation, became a reality . . . when the Long Island Railroad Company started its fast service through the tunnels under the river from the Pennsylvania Railroad Company's new terminal," jubilated *The New York Herald* of September 8. November 27 marked the operation of the first Pennsylvania train. On Sunday, September 4, the fortunately situated newspaper had panegyrized: "All barriers to direct rapid transit between the mainland of the United States and Long Island have been swept away by the successful completion of the greatest subaqueous tunnels in the world and by the partial completion of the world's furthest-reaching electrified railroad system. Far beneath the conquered waters of the North and East rivers and the thronged streets of Manhattan, New Jersey and Long Island have been brought within a few minutes' reach of one another by the construction of the Pennsylvania-Long Island Railroad tunnels." Pages were devoted to the social and economic influences of this "Undertaking Without Precedent" and "Everlasting Monument to the Mastery of Science Over the Greatest Physical Barriers of Nature."

"New-York has to put up with the horsecars because it is against the law to operate overhead trolleys. If that statute was not written in the law books, it would not be three months before every horsecar in the city was broken up for junk. Electric cars, with brilliant lights and buzzing trolleys, would be running over the crosstown and belt lines," said an official of the Metropolitan Street Railway Company, quoted in the *New-York Daily Tribune* of July 28, 1901. The picturesque obsolescence—so superbly preserved in one of Alfred Stieglitz's most famous photographs, *The Terminal*, 1897—owed its anachronistic survival to the fact that while conversion to an overhead electric line would cost a mere $25,000 a mile, the installation of an underground or conduit system could only be achieved at an expenditure of $125,000 for every twenty blocks. The *Tribune* reviewed the demoded situation: "This city has more miles of horsecar lines than all of the other cities of the United States put together, and almost as many as the total horsecar mileage of the cities of the world. . . . There are 132 miles of single track in the city over which nothing but horsecars ever run. The lines cover about seventy-five miles of streets. It takes 1,200 cars and 6,200 horses to carry the horsecar traffic, which, in 1900, amounted to 60,000,000 cash passengers and 10,000,000 who used transfers. The total distance covered by horsecars last year was 15,000,000 miles. There are sixteen different lines all of which are operated by the Metropolitan Street Railway Company. With the exception of four lines, the horsecar mileage is restricted to that part of Manhattan Island which lies below Twenty-third-st. The lines which lie outside of this district or extend from it are the First-ave., Ninth-ave., Twenty-eighth-st. and Twenty-ninth-st. The magnitude of these figures will be realized by those who know that there are but four miles of horsecar line in the State of New-York outside of this city. . . . The Metropolitan company perhaps uses more horses than any other company in the world," with the possible exception of the London Omnibus Company. The captious feature story belies the nostalgic sentimentality that has made the horsecar iconological with the emetic "ye goode olde" concept of today's patronizing backward glance. " 'Why do all your horsecars look so dilapidated?' is a question often put to Metropolitan officials [at least, so the *Tribune* tells]. 'The cars are not dilapidated,' was the answer. 'You think so because of the contrast with the brilliantly lighted, highly polished electric cars which run in other parts of the city. . . . The public would call a brand new car a "rattletrap affair" if they saw horses drawing it. They are not as fine as the electric cars, and you can't make people believe that you are giving them brand new rolling stock. They don't expect it in horsecars.' " Then a word about the human equation: "There was a time when the drivers . . . considered themselves members of a profession. Young men were ambitious to become drivers of cars and worked hard until they learned how to do it. . . . That day is gone. No one is training to became [*sic*] a horsecar driver now. The men who drive are either relics of the old days . . . or they are men who have failed to get work in other lines and drive as a makeshift. There is a certain

290

knack . . . that cannot be acquired in a day or a year. . . . Much of the skill lies in handling the brake. Some drivers are much easier on horses than the others. Under some the horses grow fat and seem to enjoy their work. Other drivers will almost kill any team given them."

This photograph is one of a series taken by the Byron Company during the aftermath of the Blizzard of 1899, which had genteel beginnings on Saturday evening February 11, continued with polite intermittence throughout Lincoln's Birthday, and at dawn on the 13th attempted to eclipse the revered tradition of eleven years before. The *New-York Daily Tribune* of St. Valentine's Day reported that the snow, flying "horizontally across the city on the wings of a full-fledged gale . . . stuck to everything like a coat of lead" in the close-to-zero temperature, and piled up 14½ inches, compound interest on the 8½ inch deposit of the 9th and 10th, making a total of 23 inches as against the mere 20.9 achieved by the 1888 classic. New York was indeed a "White Captive," for "it was practically impossible to get into or out of the city, and to travel within the limits of Manhattan was possible only with much delay and inconvenience." However, "The Broadway cable-cars covered themselves with glory. . . . The elevated trains in this borough . . . were running . . . up to a late hour last night

A horse car at the time of the Blizzard of 1899
On Madison Square

at infrequent intervals. Not a ship entered or left this harbor yesterday. . . . While as a whole travel on all lines was more or less crippled . . . lines operated by horse power suffered the most. . . . The most noticeable thing was that the passengers on all the lines complained in the most caustic language of the frigidity of the cars, a great number having left their seats and preferred walking to travelling on wheeled ice-boxes. It was noticeable that all of the horse cars had two drivers. One was supposed to take the place of the other should he collapse from the cold. As it was, one devoted his time to the operation of the brake while the other held the lines and directed the half-frozen horses, whose number had been increased from two to four and from one to two. The surface car lines, with the exception of the Broadway and Third-ave. cable lines, were practically stopped by night. The underground trolley lines, which ran with great difficulty all day, stopped entirely early in the evening. . . . The Tenth-ave., Boulevard and Forty-second-st. crosstown horsecars ran at irregular intervals. . . . The Avenue B, Avenue C and First-ave. horsecars stopped in the afternoon. The Fulton-st., Delancey and Spring-st., Grand-st., Canal and Desbrosses-st., Fourteenth-st., Seventeenth-st., Eighteenth-st., Twenty-eighth-st., Twenty-ninth-st., and all of the downtown horsecar lines not mentioned stopped running last evening. The Thirty-fourth-st. line had a few cars running. A few cars were also running on the Eighty-sixth-st. line." Superintendent C. H. Hankinson, of the Society for the Prevention of Cruelty to Animals (founded in 1875 by Henry Bergh) is quoted as having said: "We have insisted that all horsecars must have four horses while this weather continues. We have to-day sent about fifty horses back to their stables, leaving the vehicles where they were. We have shot four horses that had entirely collapsed."

The *Tribune* article of July 28, 1901, introduced at the beginning of this piece, perorated: "The work of conversion is progressing slowly, but none the less surely. The Forty-second-st. crosstown line was the last to change [hoof power having been abandoned on June 18, 1899]. The Seventh-ave. line is now being reconstructed [while modernization of the Twenty-third-st. one had sent this photograph into history soon after it was taken]. It would take a prophet with more skill than is possessed by any of the weather jugglers under Chief Moore, however, to tell when the last horsecar will make its last trip."

It also takes the time of the better part of the staff of the Museum of the City of New York (I cannot speak for sister institutions, but I sympathize with their overworked retinues) to settle bets on the subject. It is our considered conviction that this question arises as part of the digestive process whenever two New Yorkers (or even as many commuters) sit down long enough to assuage their ulcers or raise a cocktail glass to their parched lips. In the interest of economy and the cause of patience, it might be well to have a tape recording made by some highly paid voice, so that the inevitable telephone call could be answered by a dramatic rendition of the valediction in *The New York Times* of July 27, 1917. "New York Loses Its Last Horse Car Bleecker St. and Fulton Ferry Line Abandons Franchise and Will Tear Up Tracks," the headlines read. "Passing through many changes [since its initiation in 1864], the line kept its honored place in the municipal railroad world until yesterday morning, when the last of the dirty old cars, with their faithful horses and husky drivers, were withdrawn, never again to reappear. What glory, therefore, that came to this giant and progressive city for maintaining the last horse-drawn car disappeared forever. We are now no more notable in transportation than Chicago or Philadelphia." The reason given for the abandonment was "the sordid one of lost money and lack of public necessity." The one car used in the months preceding, to hold the franchise, "was a sight. . . . One day, July 17 last, it earned 10 cents on the single trip it made. During 1916 the line carried only 3,567 passengers . . . and the total of receipts was $178.80. . . . But the upkeep cost the company $4,000 a year. . . . Two cars were waiting at Bleecker Street and Broadway, but . . . [all the notables] got into the first car, which was in charge of James Cusack, driver, who has held the same job for forty years, and Conductor Thomas O'Brien, who has been on the job more than thirty years. Those inside gazed with awe at the rusty old stove. But the stove was all right. A lot of paper was thrust into it and set afire, and the car trundled away with smoke pouring out of its battered pipe, to the wonder of the populace."

. . . . The next man who tears up Broadway should be lynched

"NEW YORK is not a Puritanical city," volunteered Harry P. Mawson in *Harper's Weekly* of September 26, 1891, "but it is perfectly safe to assert that since the Broadway Cable Road began tearing up the main thoroughfare of the town there has [*sic*] been more 'cuss words' uttered than have ever been heard before on Manhattan Island. 'The next man who tears up Broadway . . . should be lynched,' said an angry man, who dodged a loaded beer wagon lumbering over one of the 'rustic' bridges that span each crossing. . . . The Broadway people, in their petition to the Mayor and Aldermen for permission to lay the cable, declared it would revolutionize the roadway. . . . Broadway has been revolutionized beyond recognition; for four months and more it has been a yawning abyss, surrounded by extemporized fences, pasted all over with theatrical 'snipes,' mud from curb to curb, or raising a stifling dust." He granted, however, that, "in spite of the enormous discomfort . . . caused the public, the cable will benefit the street, simplify the traffic, and in the end really revolutionize Broadway. The work of laying the cable is the A B C of engineering; the difficulties to be overcome are connected with the labyrinth of gas and water mains, sewer, telegraph, electric light, and telephone wires in their underground conduits. . . . The width of the 'ditch' with which Broadway has been ornamented since June last is 15 feet; depth at yokes, 3 feet; and at man-holes, 4 feet."

Happier phases of this gargantuan laparotomy (with Thomas D. Crimmins as the contractor and Major G. W. McNulty of Brooklyn Bridge fame as the engineer-in-chief for the Broadway and Seventh-Avenue Railroad Company) were to be fresh pavement and the introduction of "an entire new outfit of rolling stock" that would be "an ornament to Broadway." Cars "29 feet over all" were being constructed by the J. G. Brill Company of Philadelphia and in the East Twenty-seventh Street assembly-lined shops of The John Stephenson Company, from whence issued most of New York's public conveyances—and indeed common carriers for all parts of the world—between 1831 and 1897 (in which year the firm moved to Elizabeth, New Jersey, there to build one hundred of Manhattan's first subway cars in 1904).

Three years after the first of Stephenson's omnibuses appeared on the city streets, the *New-York Gazette & General Advertiser* of August 5, 1834, reprinting a Charlestonian's views, informed the populace that these conveyances "exceeding a hundred in number, roll inces-

Laying the cable car tracks in Union Square, September,
1891, at the danger point later known as "Dead Man's
Curve"
A page from Joseph Byron's album

santly over the paved streets, administering equally to the purposes of business and pleasure, adding to noise and bustle, and forming an object of such prominent attraction" (with their scene-decorated sides), "as to cause New York, not inaptly to be termed 'The City of Omnibuses.'" They did not constitute the only form of public transit, for as the *Rail-Road Journal* (I:737) reported: "We were highly gratified on Wednesday last [November 14, 1832] as we were passing up the Bowery, with a view of the beautiful [Stephenson-built] Cars of the Harlaem Railroad Company. . . . They are spacious and convenient . . . the whole drawn by two fine horses abreast, at a rate of ten or twelve miles an hour." However, the omnibuses and their flavorful drivers ("a strange, natural, quick-eyed and wondrous race," celebrated by Walt Whitman) ruled Broadway and, by the end of the Civil War, were coursing up and down that strangling thoroughfare a mere fifteen seconds apart. In 1885, when New York's first cable cars appeared on the 125th Street and the Amsterdam Avenue lines of the Third Ave. R. R. Co., the omnibuses gave way to horsecars on Broadway from Bowling Green to Union Square—brief supremacy terminated in July, 1893, soon after the *New-York Daily Tribune* of June 12 headlined a day of experiment in a short inside page paragraph "No Horses On The Broadway Road Yesterday." The issue of May 17 had announced: "The cable road . . . is at last completed. The second trial trip [the first having taken place on May 10th] . . . over the entire road was successfully made yesterday. . . . In about two weeks the 180 new cable cars will be running over the road." On May 25, "The whole length of Broadway was lined with people who looked upon the large, handsomely-built brilliantly lighted and easy-going cars as though they made up the eighth wonder of the world," while the passengers "enjoyed themselves to their heart's content by 'guying' those who were in the street or in horse cars." The line extended from South Ferry by way of Broadway as far as Forty-fifth Street and then along Seventh Avenue to Central Park. Third Avenue, from Sixth Street to 130th, followed suit that December, and in 1899 pioneered in the electrification which was to spread to the Broadway, Columbus, and Lexington Avenue lines of the Metropolitan Street Railway Co. in 1901, the last of the laboriously installed cables being removed on May 25.

As usual, each change created the image and actuality of its own perils. An editorial in the *New-York Daily Tribune* on September 28, 1890, mocked the experienceful warning from Chicago (for following the successful introduction of this transit form in San Francisco in 1873, it had spread cross-country) that "The cable car is a Juggernaut, a murderer on wheels, a maimer of men and a destroyer of women and children." However, only a week later, in the contagion of hysteria, it stated: "Even in One-hundred-and-twenty-fifth-st. the swift approach of a cable car with its ringing bell, its rattle and its bang, is enough to startle a nervous horse. What confusion, terror and dire consequence such cars may cause when they come dashing down upon a tangle of trucks, business wagons and private carriages in a thickly jammed part of Broadway, must stir the most sluggish imagination." Frequent accidents (particularly at the perilful Fourteenth Street, Twenty-third, and Fifty-third Street curves) caused this journal to declare on November 26, 1893: "It is an indisputable fact that the Broadway cable road is making a shocking record. . . . We venture to say that there is an almost continual undercurrent of apprehension for himself and those dear to him in the thoughts of every citizen familiar with the conditions . . . on Broadway. It must be that thousands of persons are more or less vividly conscious of a new anxiety in lives already quite full enough of worry."

"THE SEA-PUSS track," the *New-York Daily Tribune* called the destination of these devotees of the kingly diversion, using other terms of endearment, such as "the plague-spot" or "Dismal Swamp of the American turf." The newspaper's sports writer took evident delight in lambasting the newly reconstructed Coney Island race course throughout the saturated season that opened on July 12, 1897, to the music of Lander's Band, which on the 13th vied with "the constant booming of the waves, that could be plainly heard in the grandstand and on the lawn," as they "sounded the warning that the days of the Brighton Beach racetrack . . . [were] numbered." The blast of August 14th was devastating: "The racing . . . yesterday was so thoroughly unsatisfactory in so many things that a great deal of space would be required to set forth all the faults. Brighton has been trying to break into the sanctuary of club life with a jimmy. It is all a mistake. The effort is certain to be a failure. Brighton will always be scorned by wealth and fashion . . . and beef and beans and sinkers and beer will always be the suitable bill of fare at this track. For Brighton to aspire to terrapin and Château Margaux is the wildest folly. Brighton can never soar above its swamps and its sand dunes. . . . Brighton is still trying to break into society with a jimmy. But until the Brighton officials and the Brighton management succeed in some way in making the racing there look less like the wrigglings of zoophytes and of the phytoid forms of life, the jimmy will be manipulated in vain." On Friday, August 20, he found some comfort: "The Brighton nightmare will end on Monday." And on the 21st he counseled and coaxed: "The wisest course for Brighton to pursue next year is to put away vain ambitions. Brighton was born a mud-hen. This year Brighton has borrowed a peacock's tail, and has put on airs. Brighton's true place on the turf is that of a modest, lowly, unassuming one-dollar-a-ticket stamping ground for the impecunious masses. When Brighton seeks to spurn the multitude of the people of small means, and aims to secure the favor of the people who take a complete bath every morning of their lives . . . Brighton is out of its element. The Fates made Brighton a mud-hen. Why, then, should Brighton bedeck itself with borrowed peacock's plumes? . . . Come down from your perch, Brighton. Shed your peacock's tail, and scuttle through the sedges as of yore. Peacocks are not bred in swamps or on sand dunes."

Bound for this "quagmire"—as the *Tribune* man in an affectionate moment called the dishonest home of "bad starts," "bad riders," and "bad races," where even the official timer had "an eccentric watch"—these heavily burdened open cars formed part of the rolling stock of the second oldest electric line on Long Island, in service from April 19, 1890 to November 30, 1955. An editorial in the *Tribune* of July 22, 1901 would seem applicable to the plight of the athletic guardian of company finance:

"The sympathetic observer on the Coney Island trolley cars is filled with compassion when he notes the desperate and painful struggles of the conductors to do their duty in the collection of fares. Upon many of these cars going to and returning from the shore every inch that can be stood upon or clung to is in the possession of some squeezed and harried passenger. All along the outer edges men and boys are hanging as thickly clustered as hives of bees in swarming time. The unfortunate conductors are compelled to perform arduous feats in gymnastics as they climb over and around the thickly packed masses bulging out from both sides and both ends of the cars. These poor fellows are often fit subjects for hospital treatment when their long hours of strain and worry and the hardest of hard work are over for the day or for the night.

"When conductors on the trolley lines are subjected to conditions so trying and so severe, is it surprising that they sometimes lose their tempers and are found lacking in patience and politeness? What saints they would be were they not now and then inclined to be peevish and irritable in the hottest days and nights of July and August, when the crowds of pleasure seekers are so great that their work is rendered doubly difficult and harassing? The passengers are making trips for recreation and enjoyment, but they are travelling in such multitudes that they overwhelm the hapless conductors with toil and worry and trouble. The motorman has no light task, it is true, but he has this advantage over the conductor—that he is always on the front platform and gets the benefit of the currents of air which the swift movements of the cars set in motion. He is often squeezed somewhat, but even the most stupid and unreasonable passengers know that they must get out of the way of the sweeping handle which controls the motive power. The motorman may have his troubles, but he is far better off than the overheated and much abused conductor.

"The people who travel on these trolley lines to and from the beaches should not be harsh or impatient toward the conductors, whose evident sufferings are frequently pitiable while the rush in each direction is at its worst. They are human beings, anyway. But they are often treated as if they were no better than the beasts which perish."

Going to the Brighton Beach Racetrack, about 1897
via the Smith Street–Coney Island Avenue Line of the
Coney Island to Brooklyn Railroad

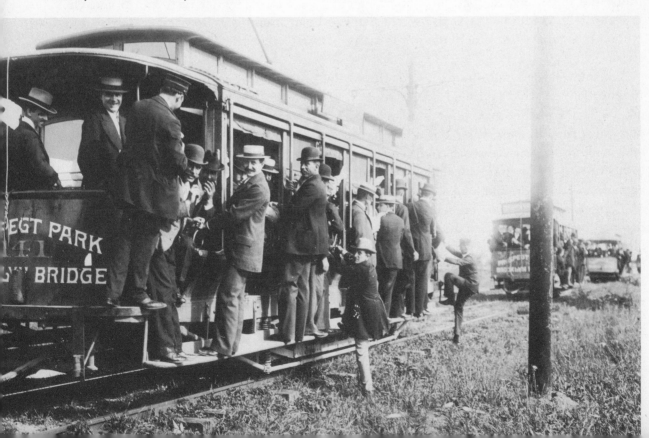

NEW YORK's first commuter was the intrepid Jacques Cortelyou, who emigrated from Utrecht in 1652 and became Surveyor General of the Province of New Netherland. He was wont to travel all the weary way from New Utrecht (West Brooklyn) or Nyack (near Fort Hamilton in the Narrows) to his New Amsterdam office in the Marckvelt (now Whitehall Street), where in the summer of 1660 he doubtless drew his lost original of the so-called "Castello Plan" of the little new-world city of about three hundred houses. At one point this suburban escapist may have lessened the repetitive monotony of the passage back and forth across the water by leafing through the *Pensées* of Pascal, for Jasper Danckaerts relates that in the autumn of 1679 he and his fellow Labadist missionary, Peter Sluyter, left with their Long Island host (Cortelyou) a copy of "this little book which we had lent to him and which he said he had found much pleasure in reading." It should be mentioned, *en passant*, that the cordial and sincere Jacques—while subconsciously he may have felt himself a martyr—was blissfully unaware of being a "commuter," for the opprobrious term (derived from the railway "commutation ticket") did not become a part of American English until about 1865.

Close to three centuries after Cortelyou first explored the redundancy of the round trip, E. B. White (in his blessed essay *Here Is New York*) sighs over the peculiar astigmatism of the devouring "locusts" who give Manhattan what he terms "its tidal restlessness." The Sage of Forty-third Street concedes: "The commuter is the queerest bird of all. . . . Except in rare cases, the man who lives in Mamaroneck or Little Neck or Teaneck, and works in New York, discovers nothing much about the city except the time of arrival and departure of trains and buses, and the path to a quick lunch. . . . The commuter dies with tremendous mileage to his credit, but he is no rover. . . . The Long Island Rail Road alone carried forty million commuters last year [1947]; but many of them were the same fellow retracing his steps."

The squirrel-cage pattern applies equally to the premises of one Richard Barry, set forth in an article on what he called the "hordes of Uitlanders" (see *Harper's Weekly*, February 26, 1898): "Probably over three hundred and fifty thousand brain-workers, manual toilers and wage-earners daily enter the artery center of . . . New York . . . which might now well include the busy district from Thirty-fourth Street south to the Battery." According to his turn-of-the-century calculations, in the neighborhood of 100,000 "workaday pilgrims" came from Brooklyn; about 13,000 of the "most long-suffering and . . . patient of men" out of Long Island; 105,000 "criminally good-natured individuals" through the area eternally damned by a Currier & Ives inscription as the "Jarsey Flats, opposit de United States," and other benighted and forlorn regions west of the Hudson; another 118,000 "butts in stock" of the comic papers via the Grand Central Station, leaving a mere handful of 7,000 to emerge from Staten Island and the south by way of the soulful, historic ferry trail from Stapleton to the Battery. Byron's preoccupied matutinal captives—a noteworthy number of women among them—have made use of this service, inaugurated in 1712, first established on a regular schedule by the sixteen-year-old future "Commodore" Vanderbilt in 1810 and municipalized since 1890.

More charitable than E. B. White, Mr. Barry of *Harper's* granted a certain protective coloring of urbanity to these strange components of New York's floating population, and insisted that "they are nevertheless men of the city."

The "Commuter Army" arriving in New York, 1901
Scene at the Staten Island Ferry, Whitehall Street

"BEE POWER" was a unit of measurement in the Eighth National Automobile Show, held at Madison Square Garden, November 2–9, 1907, under the direction of the Association of Licensed Automobile Manufacturers. *The New York Herald* of November 7 explains this curious departure: "In the galleries [is] an exhibit of 26,000 live honey bees . . . in their glass house. . . . [They] are supposed to typify the energy contained within the Witherbee batteries." According to the new A.L.A.M. rating ("the first standard system to be adopted in this country") the fifty-three different makes of cars—all of domestic manufacture—ranged in horsepower from 42 to 70.

In the neighborhood of 300 participating firms displayed 31 brands of gasoline engines, 8 varieties of electrics, 13 types of commercial vehicles, a solitary steamer, 15 assorted motorcycles, and 211 exhibits of accessories to the admiring gaze of about 10,000 aficionados on the rain-swept opening night, indicating to *The New York Herald* "that the flood tide of automobile enthusiasm is still running." The total audience for the week reached about ten times that figure.

Reporters for the dailies—in addition to being "wise to car"—had the added responsibility of listing the attending socially elite cognoscenti, their preferences and their purchases, and were also required to be critics of interior decoration. The *Tribune* man (November 3) felt that the salon "was worth a visit from a strictly spectacular point of view . . . a triumph over all former attempts at harmonious staging of the exhibits. Excepting for the big piece of stage scenery at the Fourth avenue end"—an oversize painting of an Italian villa—"there is nothing to hurt the eye." The gray and red harmony, offset by "pure white lamp pillars and staff work statues," was thought to be "more restful and satisfying" than the "confusion of color" of the previous year, and "The most novel feature of all . . . the telharmonic music pouring from huge white horns . . . mystified the crowd for a while."

Visitors saw "'the car beautiful' whichever way they looked," *The New York Herald* of November 5 assures. "They saw it in all sizes, all powers, all types and all prices," from the $850 Buick runabout to the Great Arrow limousine at $7,000; from the Franklin bucket-seated roadster at $1,750 to the $4,600 French gray Stearns "toy tonneau," "about which almost every visitor raves," and which divided honors with the Pope-Toledo of the yellow and black English mail-coach body as perhaps the "clou" of the show. There was a difference of opinion about the Packard "honeymoon" runabout—"heliotrope and white with gold leaf striping" and white patent leather upholstery—to be had for $4,500. "The most luxurious car" was perhaps a "40" Great Arrow, a vision in blue and red and deep russet, upholstered in embossed Cordovan leather and buffalo hide, enriched—above the line of its nine windows shaded by brown silk Pullman curtains—"with dainty accents of colored lacquer and gold leaf, reaching its climax in the ceiling, where the decoration radiates in the dome lamp, dividing the space into four panels" decorated with blue flowers. The interior metal trimmings are of oxidized copper, while the exterior trimmings are of antique brass. . . . Its price is $7,000." Other popular contenders were "a Royal Tourist limousine upholstered in goat skin; new town cars on Thomas and Franklin chasses [*sic*]; a Matheson country car in polished maple wood with demi-limousine top . . . ; a Walter landaulet . . . immediately convertible to a touring car; 'fire engine' runabouts on Pope-Hartford and Apperson chasses, to say nothing of the eleven different models of six-cylinder cars." Only three cars (all touring) were in the under $1,000 class—the Waltham at $600, and the Cadillac and Buick at $850. A self-starting device was a new Winton feature.

The *Herald* of November 7 asserted that "any woman with nerve and intelligence" could safely handle every model in the show, but tactfully suggested that "electric carriages" were "particularly adaptable to use" by more timorous ladies.

Contrary to expectations in a depression year, by the end of the November 8th session

The Eighth National Automobile Show
at Madison Square Garden, November 2–9, 1907

retail sales (exclusive of contracts with agents) amounted to $1,500,000, the Oldsmobile leading the field with a total of $131,850 for forty-four cars. "Practically every maker who came to the Garden with models of his 1908 product has disposed of the output," vouchsafed the *Herald* of the 9th, also commenting: "One peculiar feature, due to the present money stringency, is that upon some orders small deposits by check have been made, with the arrangements that the cars be held until delivery be ordered."

Among the "catchy" side lines of this very successful show was a head lamp inspired by a gorgiferous girl—the heroine of a weekly feature in the Sunday *Herald,* also cherished between covers over D. Appleton and Company's colophon (the drawings by Wallace Morgan pointed up in verses by Carolyn Wells enumerative of the occupational hazards confronting this newly poor, pulchritudinous damosel, whose gallant efforts to hold down an endless succession of jobs were forever being thwarted by the incredible universality of her attractions for the opposite sex); for whose title less floriously endowed maidens vied in sectional beauty contests; in whose image a doll was created; about whom a "Musical Mélange" (by John J. McNally, with several Jerome Kern songs), starring Hattie Williams, was to be brought to Broadway by Charles Frohman in 1908—who but the toast of the town, "Fluffy Ruffles"!

. . . . *Auto intoxication*

"P.S. As USUAL in the best of company—Panhard, Mercedes, Renault, S & M Simplex" cunningly concluded the advertised invitation extended in 1905 by Smith & Mabley Inc., "To the *Owner* of a Motor Car," urging attendance at the opening of their new building (see page 304): " 'The Finest Motoring Shop in the World.' If you don't believe it Stop in Oct. 17ᵗʰ 1 to 10 P.M." It was one of the "Four great new garages . . . under construction within a radius of three blocks in the upper Broadway automobile district," according to *The New York Herald* of August 6. The other members of this quaternity—"among the largest and best equipped in the world," designed "to house more than twelve hundred machines"—were the Decauville garage on the opposite corner of Broadway and Fifty-sixth Street, "the handsome building of the Automobile Club of America" on Fifty-fourth Street, west of Broadway, "to cost half a million dollars," and, "most ornate, as well as the largest" of all, that of the Auto Import Company, the market place for the Rochet-Schneider.

The new expansion of Proctor A. Smith and his brother-in-law, Carlton R. Mabley (formerly of 513–19 Seventh Avenue) was, according to *The New York Herald* of October 18, the "First of the great Broadway garages to be completed . . . one of the largest and most complete automobile salesrooms and storehouses in the world. It will accommodate 450 machines [of the 14,000 in the city, fractional of the 100,000 in the United States]. It has a turntable elevator [19 feet square] and . . . club rooms for chauffeurs. Several hundred automobilists, most of them owners of high priced foreign cars, attended the opening yesterday. There was music, there were refreshments and there were new models of the Mercedes, Panhard, Renault and Smith & Mabley Simplex automobiles. The [120 H.P.] Mercedes racer [unsuccessfully] driven by John B. Warden [of the German team] in the Vanderbilt Cup contest [the second repetition of this classic, which had taken place on October 15] was there, and also a handsomely fitted motor boat equipped with a thirty horse power S. & M. Simplex engine. The building . . . has four large storage floors and a repair department, comprising 76,000 square feet of floor space. Each floor is a complete garage in itself, being fitted with individual washstands, gasolene and compressed air supply, telephones and telautographs. The salesroom is on Broadway and the garage entrance on Fifty-sixth street. On the Broadway frontage on the second floor is an attractive club room for chauffeurs, with lockers, shuffleboard, bagatelle and provision for other games. . . . The . . . concern is one of the largest automobile selling houses in this country . . . sales . . . this year . . . amount[ing] almost to $2,000,000 and with the new contract for the Mercedes agency in 1906 it is expected that next year's business will be much greater." Among the guests at this motorized vernissage, *The New York Times* résumé stated, were "Hundreds of women and automobile enthusiasts," including William K. Vanderbilt, Jr., donor of the trophy, Robert Graves, and Commodore Morton F. Plant.

The firm—a member of the Association of Licensed Automobile Manufacturers—had entered the young field in 1902, four years after the historic March 24, 1898 first sale of an American-made car (a one-cylinder Winton) had been impetal in the development of the automobile industry in this country. In 1900, when Proctor A. Smith returned from abroad with an 8 horsepower Panhard, he found many people eager to pay a premium for the privilege of sitting behind its steering wheel in ownership. Fate-fingeringly, the family collaboration began, and resultantly in *The New York Herald* of January 11, 1903 one reads: "Negotiations have just been concluded whereby Panhard automobiles will be built in this country. They will be [monopolistically] manufactured by Smith & Mabley. . . . They will be exact reproductions of the product of the well known Panhard & Levassor Company's factory in France and will bear this company's name plate. . . . The parts of the Panhard chassis are all to be imported. The bodies will be built by J. M. Quinby & Co. of Newark, N. J., already well known as rebuilders of the tonneaux and decorators of the bodies of many of the imported French machines. . . . Smith & Mabley will continue as sole American distributors of the product of the Charron, Girardot & Voigt Company of Paris, and their Renault, Mercedes and Mors agencies will still be continued. 'The demand for French machines,' said Mr. Mabley, 'continues. We sold nine of them this week.'"

That the meteoric business of which the concern was a thriving part had its oscillations is borne out by an article in the *Herald*, surveying the field as of August 4, 1907. It is stated that between 1901 (the first year in which a systematic check of producers was undertaken) and 1907, of 308 aspirants 151 vanished with the yesteryearly snows. All these manufacturers shared a common culpability, for according to President Woodrow Wilson of Princeton University (as annunciated in an address given before the North Carolina Society on March 1, 1906) "nothing has spread socialistic feelings in this country more than the use of the automobile," which represented "to the countryman . . . a picture of arrogance of wealth, with all its independence and carelessness." So much for the soul and society; an internist had already spoken for the insult to the flesh on a page of "The Sunday Magazine" of the *New-York Daily Tribune* of December 11, 1904, at a time when New York State laws prohibited driving over ten miles an hour in congested areas, fifteen in less densely populated districts, and twenty on the open road. Dr. William Sohier Bryant bombilated on "High-Speed Diseases": "There is

The opening of Smith & Mabley's automobile salesroom and garage, October 17, 1905
1765 Broadway (west side, between Fifty-sixth and Fifty-seventh Streets)
Among the automobiles shown are: #9 Mercedes race car driven in the Vanderbilt Cup Race by Warden; left, 1905 Panhard; center, 1905 Mercedes; right, S & M Simplex, 1905

nothing newer or more fascinating to-day than the automobile. It combines excitement, speed, comfort, motion, fresh air, scenery and mechanical art and luxury. But behind all these lurks a grim specter . . . ready to seize and crush us to the earth if we violate too far the laws by which we exist." Warning the "operators" of damage to the nervous system "consequent from the high speed over an uncertain road," of eyestrain and of cerebral fatigue, he turned his clinical attention to the passengers, living in "fear of a sudden jar or accident," and subject to all the above trauma with additional, horror-fraught hazards. "Their muscles are fixed involuntarily, the hands are clenched and the jaws are set; the muscles of the neck are tense." This taut state gave rise to "an entirely new series of diseases"—not baffling to the diagnostician, but calling for a fresh therapeutic approach. Involved were such conditions as "auto-eyes" (ocular stress even being entailed in efforts to dodge the "iron posts of the elevated railway," whereas "flying over an unknown country road at speed approaching a mile a minute" imposed a degree of orbital concentration beyond Nature's provisions), " 'auto-leg,' various eye irritations from dust and wind, hysterics and sciatica," and the ravageous "nervous prostration." A patient of the clinician, "a lawyer, is debarred from automobiling for a long period . . . perhaps forever," by a "ciliary affection" which had "destroyed his confidence completely" following "a four-days' run." The physician found the motorized young married women of his practice were particularly prone to "attacks of hysterics." Often these painful sequelae were not immediately manifest, but would insidiously "declare themselves a day

304

afterward. . . . Time, nutrition and rest alone" could bring about restitution, "and there is nothing for the patient to do except be a patient patient." Lady motorists, too, of "more timid natures" than the alternate sex, were especially subject to "wry-neck" and susceptible to hysterics and melancholia—sometimes with such "eccentric results" as deafness and "paralysis of the legs"—because of the underlying "tax laid upon them by social and family duties," and the biological failure to "provide them so well as their brothers and husbands against wind and rain, or fit them so well for the outdoor strenuous life." On the other hand male gasoline addicts, with their residue of overwork, worry and too strenuous indulgence in sports, could more commonly look forward to the "worst of all . . . nervous prostration . . . due to the general overstrain . . . perhaps increased by not keeping the body protected with impervious wraps." The physician then proceeded to give the pathetic case history of a successful New York businessman who, two years prior to his collapse, had practically retired to immerse himself in an orgy of literal auto intoxication, with the result that he became a "complete nervous wreck" due to the punitive effects of acceleration, and whose ultimate recovery was still problematic.

"The only moral to be drawn," perorated Dr. Bryant (who recommended periodic check-ups for multiple-miles-per-hour motorists), "is that the human body is not fitted for high-speed automobiling."

. . . . About the sternest test of men and machines

"THE BRAVE and hardy men who set out from Times Square yesterday to make their way by automobile across this continent and through Alaska, Siberia, Russia, Germany and Belgium to Paris, had before their eyes the best possible evidence that their undertaking makes a deep and moving appeal to human interest." So *The New York Times* of February 13, 1908, waved editorial farewell to the six cars in the 20,000-mile race it was co-sponsoring with the Paris sheet, *Le Matin*. "Their departure was witnessed by a crowd of more than 150,000 persons, who packed Times Square and the nearby side streets and lined the route . . . northward out of the city, and they were attended by an escort of two hundred automobiles filled with men and women eager to participate in the beginning, but scarcely prepared to see the end of the venture." For the passage through often pathless snowbound regions "where nature has pretty conspicuously planted the sign, No thoroughfare," the self-propelled vehicles "presented, in truth, an unusual aspect—some [the American contender, for instance] having canvas covers like the old prairie schooners, all of strange build, and carrying an equipment of spare parts, ropes, jacks, picks, shovels, and firearms," as protection against hostile man and wild beast in preparation for "about the sternest test of the endurance of men and machines that has ever been undertaken."

On that Lincoln's Birthday, New York was a carnival city: "Automobile Row"—a geographic stretch, according to the *Times*, extending up Broadway from the early Forties to Seventy-second Street, but with boundaries of the spirit suddenly international and global in circumference—was the Midway; school children and classes at Columbia and Barnard were turned loose from learning to witness the narrowing of the hemispheres, and contrapuntally 5,000 visitors passed through the turnstiles of The Metropolitan Museum of Art.

The start of the New York to Paris Automobile Race, February 12, 1908
Scene in Times Square
Cars departing in order: Zust (Italian);
Sizaire-Naudin (French); De Dion-Bouton
(French); Protos (German first to reach Paris,
but disqualified as winner). Not seen on
photograph: Thomas (American and the victor) and
Moto-Bloc (French)

At the center of all this there were the six. The three French entries were a specially constructed De Dion-Bouton (30 horsepower, 4 cylinder, shaft drive) with provision for a mast to which could be attached a sail for facilitating travel over the frozen tundra of Siberia; a Moto-Bloc (24–30 horsepower, 4 cylinder, chain drive); and the lilliputian Sizaire-Naudin (15 horsepower, 1 cylinder, shaft drive). Italy was represented by a Zust (28–40 horsepower, 4 cylinder, chain drive), and Germany by a Protos (40 horsepower, 4 cylinder, shaft drive). The American contender was a simple 60-horsepower, 4-cylinder Thomas stock car (a 1907 Model D Roadster of French gray with red leather upholstery, four bucket seats, topless and without a windshield) manufactured by the short-lived E. R. Thomas Motor Company (1902–1913), and now on exhibition in Henry Austin Clark Jr.'s Long Island Automotive Museum at Southampton. This "Flyer"—whose hard-fought fortunes alone we can follow but sketchily—had been selected only six days before the race. With Montague Roberts at the wheel, accompanied by George Schuster as the hastily recruited mechanic, and T. Walter ("Skipper") Williams (*The New York Times* reporter who accompanied the party as far as Cedar Rapids, Iowa), it assumed an almost immediate leadership, sometimes disputed by the Protos, its closest competitor in the final tabulation. At Omaha, Captain Hans Hansen (an engineer and navigator with Arctic experience, who had forsaken the De Dion at Chicago because of differences with Bourcier de St. Chaffray, its driver and commissioner general in charge of the contest arrangements in behalf of *Le Matin*) joined the Americans as guide and interpreter. Roberts, relieved by Schuster, after a brilliant performance as far as the Wyoming capital, was succeeded by Linn Mathewson, who piloted the Thomas into Ogden; there Harold Brinker of Denver took over. With the arrival at San Francisco on March 24, Schuster, as captain and driver, assumed command, with George Miller (who had been recruited at Buffalo) as his mechanic and relief at the wheel during the final brutal day-and-night runs. The trip was by water to Seattle and Valdez, Alaska, where deep snows forced a change of route and return to the city on Puget Sound; thence shipment to Kobe and the fantastic drive across Japan to Tsuruga, to board the S.S. *Mongolia* for Vladivostok; over the ties of the Trans-Siberian Railroad to Harbin; across Russia to Berlin and by way of Belgium to Paris.

On the evening of July 30—170 stress-filled days (of which 105 had been spent in actual driving) and an estimated 13,341 road miles out of Times Square—it was Schuster who drove triumphant, with a twenty-six-day lead, through cheering crowds to the offices of *Le Matin* and, after an informal reception there, along the thronged, sparkling, café-bordered boulevards of the French capital into the Place de l'Opéra, to be arrested by a *gendarme* for failure to show the lights which had been broken en route. A passing cyclist offered his lantern, and by the grace of its monocular gleam, shining proudly from the front seat to which the two-wheeler had been hoisted to the place of honor between the begrimed, nervously exhausted, khaki-clad Schuster and Miller, the car flying the American flag was permitted to proceed to the garage at the end of the gasoline trail, with the ingenious rescuer riding in state in the back, alongside Hansen and George MacAdam (staff correspondent of the sponsoring New York newspaper, who had joined the crew at Seattle).

Editorially, the *Times* of August 1, 1908, drew the following conclusions: "The self-moving car is to play a very prominent part in our future history. It is to be used for freight as well as passenger traffic, to supplant the trucks and vans drawn by horses, to be applied to farm machinery, to be of service in war, if, as we hope, the wars of the world have not all been fought."

. . . . *On his left foot with his right leg extended*

THE FIRST man to look down on New York in a literal sense (for many before and after him have done so figuratively) was Monsieur Guille, who made an "Ærostatic Ascension" from Vauxhall Garden (on the Bowery, near Third Avenue) on August 2, 1819.

The sky over the city was not unfamiliar with such floating denizens when in 1893 a thirty-year-old captain in the Balloon Corps of the French Army, Emile Carton (the son of an air-borne father and himself the veteran of a hundred flights—including the safe transportation of 120 passengers and a round trip across the English Channel) prepared somewhat anxiously for his initial adventure with American aerial currents. He and his wife had constructed the *General Lafayette*, reputedly one of the largest balloons in the world, weighing about 500 pounds, approximately sixty feet in height and capable of carrying three or four men with their impedimenta. Starting at eight o'clock on the morning of July 12, while forty-two sacks of gravel kept the ship earthbound, the 30,000 cubic feet of gas were gradually poured into the globular bag; but according to the account in *The Illustrated American* of July 29 (which features on its cover the Byron photograph on page 310) the daring Frenchman was to learn that the Harlem variety was not very buoyant. At five o'clock that afternoon, the plucky Parisian and a friend readied themselves to float—they hoped—Hartford-ward, but the balloon refused to rise until—in true Gallic rotation—first the *copian*, then the hamper of sandwiches and champagne, and finally the sandbag ballast had been jettisoned. Having yielded to Madame Carton's entreaties to retain the anchor on board, the Captain felt privileged to refuse the thermometer she pressed on him with final wifely solicitude. As the *General Lafayette* lazily rose toward the estimated altitude of 1,500 to 2,000 feet, three thousand pairs of hands clapped their applause, distant cheers came from the crowd on the 155th Street viaduct and along the rocky slope of Edgecombe Avenue, and the elevated railroad engines tooted in parting salute.

We are indebted to the *New-York Daily Tribune* of July 13 for preserving the following acrobatic miracle: "As soon as the balloon was well clear of the ground Captain Carton climbed to the edge of the basket, and grasping the ropes in his left hand stood on his left foot, with his right leg extended in the air. Removing his cap, he waved it energetically, while an American flag floated from the balloon."

That Carton managed to extricate himself from this untenable stance is borne out by the fact that he figures in the subsequent literature of his profession, which also records the exploits of his helpmate (who, after sixteen years of shared experience in the air, in 1905 achieved the distinction of being the first Frenchwoman to make a solo ascension) and their little daughter Valentine, an aerial débutante at the age of seven. Emile Carton's prowess aloft at home and abroad, and his ingenuity in the construction end—including collaboration with Henri Lachambre and hence participation in the building of Santos-Dumont's first dirigibles —brought him the signal honor of the "Palms of the Academy," awarded at the banquet celebrating Louis Blériot's historic Channel crossing in 1909.

According to *L'Aerophile* of November, 1901, luck was always with Carton—even in New York, where in the course of eighteen ascensions made in 1895 he came down in the ocean on no less than four occasions. One of these forced marine landings was in the charming company of a fair young French teacher, with whom he was obliged to spend a long night afloat, before break-of-day rescue by the crew of the lifesaving station at "Far-Knockaway."

Captain Emile Carton's Balloon Ascension, July 12, 1893
Scene at Manhattan Field, 155th Street and Eighth Avenue

ELIAS B. DUNN denied guilt by association, long after the fact. In a 1932 letter to the Blizzard Men of '88 (a tightening little band of the survivors of New York's classic of the elements) he abnegated all blame for the "fair and warmer" prediction made for March 12, stating as an alibi that he had been off duty the day before the onslaught of the white havoc. Evidently the fraternity had forgiven the subversive belittlement of his 1895 utterance, when the *New-York Daily Tribune* of February 9 of that year, gloating in headlinear splendor over "Arctic Blasts Let Loose" the previous day, quoted the " 'author' of all this riot and uproar" (who "gloried" in his handiwork) as claiming that the storm surpassed the epic blizzard and ranked as "the most stupendous piece of weather let loose on his unfortunate constituency during his whole administration."

"Farmer" Dunn (whose nickname grew out of the transfer of the Meteorological Service from the Army Signal Corps to the U.S. Department of Agriculture, with the formation of the present Weather Bureau in 1891) was "a famous newspaper character," according to the *Metropolitan Magazine* of August, 1895; and he rather enjoyed press comments—including threats of bodily harm—on his personal responsibility for the vagaries of the local climate. He must have jubilated over the following denatured lampoon, which appeared in *Life* on April 16, 1896: "Farmer Underdunn's weather report for week ending April 23d, 1896. . . . For New York and surrounding districts, Thursday, Friday and Saturday there will be a dead silence, followed on Sunday by eighteen miles of solid crime with illustrations to fit, and deep wrinkles will form on the statue of Horace Greely [*sic*] in Park Row. Monday, live patients will be seen through the windows of Bellevue Hospital, and green grass will sprout in the reading room of the Metropolitan Club. Tuesday will open light and pleasant, with snow, hail and rain later in the afternoon, followed by loud claps of thunder, almost waking up the seven sleepers in the 'Evening Post' building. . . . Wednesday the sun will shine, raised letters being easily read by the deaf, dumb and blind passengers on the elevated roads, followed in the afternoon by high winds in Brooklyn, the City Hall being plainly visible above the prairie grass."

Born in Brooklyn in 1855, Dunn qualified for a Civil Service appointment as a Government printer. According to the Federal Records Center, he started to do something about the weather on February 17, 1874, and resigned from the Bureau on July 12, 1898. At the point of separation, he was "Local Forecast Official" of the New York station (where he had spent his last fifteen years of prognostication) at a salary of $1,800 per annum. A one-time member of the staff of the New York *Sun,* he became a free-lance writer, contributing articles to newspapers and magazines on subjects meteorological and giving occasional vent to corrosive criticism of his former department. He became President of the New York Press Club, and in 1920 his isolationist platform—"Americanism; local option; no entangling alliances"— brought about his defeat as Republican Congressional candidate in New Jersey. The Coral

311

The New York Station of the United States Weather Bureau,
1895
66 Broadway

Gables Chamber of Commerce must derive a vindicatory satisfaction from the fact that this pioneer weather expert elected to spend the final fourteen years of his life in the famed Floridian sunshine, dying at his son's home on June 4, 1943, at the age of 88.

Sergeant Dunn was described in *Once A Week* of April 1, 1890, as a man who "does not aspire above the medium height, . . . is broad of beam, cultivates a brief, dark moustache . . . is a good fellow although he resides in Brooklyn, and the genus reporter swear by him." He is here atmospherically portrayed in his ocean-liner-like office at the summit of the Manhattan Life Building, to which the Bureau removed from the Equitable Building in 1895, when the soaring confluence of the neighboring skyscrapers rendered the famous 120 Broadway address unsuitable for the sensitive tools of prophetic analysis. A corps of nine assistants manned the four upper floors of the new tower quarters, equipped with all manner of the delicate antennae of the mysterious science they interpreted. Elias B. Dunn, ever ready to admit the fallibility of his calling, would "tell you," according to the *Metropolitan Magazine*'s reporter, "that the corn on the farmer's toe is as powerful an indicator, in its way, of coming rain as a long reading in meteorology."

"A MODERATE dish of tea, without too many costly additions, where the more wholesome diet of milk is not plenty, is very acceptable, and is the common supper of the citizens." This interesting observation is to be found in *The Cries Of New-York,* ("Printed And Sold By S. Wood, At The Juvenile Book-Store, No. 362, Pearl-Street. 1808."), which warns: "But strong teas are hurtful, and a great deal of money is wasted about the tea-table, its furniture, and luxuries attendant; and too often is encircled with the unguarded, whose chat, as well as that of those over the bowl, tends to injure the characters of the absent, and wound their own consciences."

For forty-nine of his eighty-four years, Colonel William P. Roome, shown on page 314 seated in his place of business at 71 Watts Street, aided and abetted the citizens in the enjoyment, extravagance and Grundyism of this aromatic beverage, originally imported by the burghers of New Amsterdam in the mid-seventeenth century. First listed in the city directory of 1860–61 as a clerk, our hero marched away to defend the Union as a second lieutenant in the Sixty-fifth New York Infantry, rising to the rank of captain and assistant adjutant general. He sustained a grievous wound on October 19, 1864, and was brevetted major "for gallant and meritorious conduct at the battles of Opequan, Fisher's Hill and Cedar Creek, Va." In addition to this honorable scar, he brought back tales of having held an improvised umbrella, in the shape of a cracker-box, over the lofty head of Abraham Lincoln during a pluvial review of troops in a Washington railroad station, and of having been close by when a spent bullet struck the President while he was inspecting fortifications near the Capital. Back in New York, the veteran engaged in the grocery business until 1876, when with Thomas L. Vickers he founded the firm of William P. Roome & Company, tea importers, at 96 Water Street, in the heart of the district devoted to that romantic trade. Ten years later, coffee was added to the stock, and, according to William H. Ukers (in *All About Coffee,* New York, 1935) the colonel was "a Chesterfieldian figure" among the New York roasters. In 1903 he disposed of his business to the Westin Coffee Co., Inc., and for the next twenty years headed the tea and coffee department of Acker, Merrall & Condit Company. At eighty-three, he again set out for himself, in the packaging and distribution of tea balls, which he continued until two months before his death on December 13, 1925. The Society of War Veterans of the 7th Regiment, N.Y.N.G., the Companions of the Military Order of the Loyal Legion, New York Commandery, and members of the New York Bridge Whist Club (of which he was a founder and the treasurer) were invited to attend the funeral services at the 114 West Eighty-sixth Street residence which had been his home since 1890.

An article in *The New York Herald* of December 2, 1900 on Colonel Roome's vocation of tea taster asserted: "Few occupations are better paid. . . . There are in this city about twenty in the calling. The highest salary is $10,000 a year, while $5,000 is not considered to be more than ordinary compensation. Some of the tea merchants and importers save the

Tea Tasting, 1904

salary of an expert by themselves passing upon the quality of all teas which they handle.
. . ." The labors of the initiate—a figure of integrity and abstinence—are outlined: "American judges of tea grow up in the business . . . and work for at least five years before their judgments are accepted as final. . . . The tea taster is gradually evolved from the apprentice. The master has no time to calmly and deliberately give instructions, so the student sits at the teacups of Gamaliel and learns a little day by day. . . . In the large importing houses the most conspicuous feature is the table where the teas are tested. It is about four feet in diameter. The top is poised on a pivot. . . . On it is placed a second slab of wood about three feet in diameter, . . . raised an inch from the surface of the first layer. On the higher portion are placed the scales, the cans of tea, and the spoons. On the lower layer are ranged the cups from which the subtle brew is to be tasted. The liquid made from a sample is always placed exactly opposite the can from which the tea . . . was taken. The judge, sitting in his chair, by turning the table top, may bring any sample . . . within his reach." Follows a description of the tactile and olfactory "examination of the dry leaf." Then the "expert takes an amount of tea equivalent to the weight of a five cent piece. The herb is then placed in a cup of the finest Limoges ware . . . devoid of decoration, and . . . handle. The cups are the only articles in the dingy storerooms of the tea importers which suggest luxury. Upon the herb is poured boiling water from a brass or copper tea kettle, which is always standing on the gas stove. The tea taster permits the leaves to steep until they are opened out by

314

the action of the hot water ["the agony of the leaves" in technical parlance]. The size, form and color of the leaves play an important part in forming an opinion. . . . The tea taster carefully inspects the liquid. . . . The aroma as it ascends from the cup reveals a story to the examiner as to where and when that tea was prepared. Sight and smell have done their part, and it is now for the sense of taste to confirm the judgment. . . . Very little of the tea which the examiner takes into his mouth is swallowed. The tea taster expels all that he can of it [into the specially constructed overgrown spittoon seen at the left] as soon as his sense has reached a verdict."

. . . . *A Life-Saver's Bravery Recognized*

TWO MAYORS of New York officiated in this ceremony (see page 316) for Philip Hone—who held the City's highest office from January 16, 1826, to January 2, 1827—looked down from the wall at "Young Confield" as he received "A Gold Medal From The Hands Of Mayor Strong," the harried incumbent of 1895–1897.

The moment of a morning, here recorded by Byron's camera, would have been documented with equal vigor by Philip Hone in his own elegant idiom. One can almost see him reaching for the diary with which he kept delicious faith from not long after he left City Hall until within five days of his death on May 5, 1851; one can almost read his closely written account of the dignity of an hour. Born in a little wooden house on Dutch Street in 1780, of German and French ancestry—with the methodical stolidity of the one strain and the volatility of the other—he began his mercantile career as a clerk of sixteen in his brother John's auction and commission business and within three years became a partner. At the age of forty, securely happy as husband and father, and for the time being possessed of a large fortune, he retired from business to further his education and pursue a cultural leisure. Following a turn as Assistant Alderman in 1824, he brought to his intelligent, public-spirited, hospitable mayoralty the innate patrician elegance and worldly qualities that the hypersensitive, irascible John Vanderlyn (1775–1852) succeeded in conveying to canvas. The grandson of an artist, son of a house and sign painter, and renowned pupil of Archibald Robertson and Gilbert Stuart was recompensed by the Common Council with the sum of $150 on July 30, 1827 for this portrait of an American aristocrat high in the counsel of the Whig Party. "A fine copy, by Vanderlyn, of the Female Figure in the fore-ground of Raphael's Transfiguration" was included on his cultivated subject's walls, where, as Philip Hone informed William Dunlap in 1834, the works of "artists now living" predominated. "I do not know of a finer collection of modern pictures," he boasted, and as he installed them—along with a Teniers, three Ostades, a Ruysdael, and a Canaletto—in his new Broadway and Great Jones Street home in 1837, according to a carefully thought-out manuscript plan still a family pride, he allowed himself a luxurious pun—"Hang the pictures!"

The year of Philip Hone's departure from City Hall, William Lafayette Strong—his successor-to-be thirty-seven administrations removed—was born in Richland County, Ohio. He came to New York in 1853, with storybook determination to achieve great wealth, and died here a millionaire in 1900. At forty-two he established the immediately successful dry goods house of W. L. Strong & Company. Emphatically a Republican, member in good standing of the

Scene in City Hall, October 8, 1896

Union League, and a leader in the Business Men's Republican Association, he was swept into City Hall in the election of 1894 as the nonpartisan candidate of the Committee of Seventy, in the name of civic reform following the revelatory probings of the Lexow Committee. His political naïveté and inviolable integrity made his single term one long self-harassment, but gave New York the novelty of good government for the first time in many a year, along with the twin appointments of Theodore Roosevelt as President of the New York Police Board (see page 470) and George E. Waring (see page 473) as wielder of the clean-sweeping broom.

This meeting of these two Mayors and a hero—thin, unlikely moment in recorded time—was very probably covered for the *New-York Daily Tribune* of October 9, 1896, by one of the busy reporters at the left, all oblivious of Philip Hone's omnipresence and incapable of what would have been the diarist's more colorful evaluation: "Rudolph Confield, twenty-one years old, the life-saver, received a handsome gold medal at the City Hall yesterday. . . . The recipient has saved nine lives at Manhattan Beach, four of them this season. The medal is the gift of the Volunteer Life Saving Association. . . . [It] was presented more particularly because of Confield's daring on August 19 last in saving a man and a boy from watery graves off Manhattan Beach. The rescues were made at the risk of the saver's life, both of the rescued

316

being in the throes of death when taken ashore. In presenting the medal to Confield, Mayor Strong dwelt particularly on the noble work the volunteers had done in the last year, and he showed that on an appropriation of only $500 fifty-seven lives had been saved. . . . Mr. Confield's medal is a huge affair, with four bars and a pendant. The pendant is representative of a life-preserver, and across it are placed two oars."

. . . . Ink all over his flippers

"Pearlies on my shirt-front,
Pearlies on my coat,
Little bitta dicer stuck up on my nut,
If you don't think I'm de real t'ing,
Why, tut! tut! tut!"

So CHUCK CONNORS delineated himself. He was an American costermonger, a Bowery Aristide Bruant, a local legend. He lived too far from Montmartre to serve as a model for Toulouse-Lautrec; he was born too soon to become part of Reginald Marsh's "subcutaneous New York" (a great photographer's phrase for the painterly penetration). He was a man of many professions: newsboy, pugilist, song and dance man, fireman on an "El" locomotive, actor of sorts. He was the illiterate philosopher, the "lobbygow" or tourists' guide through a Chinatown partly of his own promotion. He provided copy for Roy L. McCardell of *The World* and Frank Ward O'Malley of *The Sun*, in way of reciprocal interchange of wit. He was Edward W. Townsend's "Chimmie Fadden." Contingents from the Four Hundred and delegations from under the "railroad on stilts" met on equal ground at Tammany Hall on the annual occasion of the ball of the Chuck Connors Association, at which functions his favorite dancing partners were known in true *Moulin Rouge* style as "The Rummager" (a six-foot lass tipping the scales at 200 pounds), "The Truck," and "Chinatown Nellie."

His ephemeral wisdom has been preserved in a booklet—*Bowery Life* By Chuck Connors Mayor of Chinatown—issued by the Richard K. Fox Publishing Company in 1904. The foreword tells of his belated introduction to the higher learning: " 'It was a pipe,' he says, 'to get next to doin' de act wid a pen an' ink, an' as fur de readin' gag, oh, good night. I wuz Johnny on de spot wid dat. But wot got me goin' was telling de time. On de level, it took me t'ree months before I got next. Wot twisted me up wuz the little hand always sneakin' by de big hand. Say, it was like a race between a thoroughbred an' a piker. But I'm on now, all right.' " There is a photograph to prove it, with Chuck in his customary modification of Cockney attire—"A blue flannel shirt, a short coat with white pearl buttons, a white tie and a very small hat"—toasting his new accomplishment: "Here's to me new graft. I'm one of dose guys now wot gits ink all over his flippers and looks wise. Say, it's a cinch, and I've got some of dem blokes wot writes books skinned a mile."

His *argot* and his arguments made him a favorite with the tourists and celebrities he conducted up and down "de lane," as he called his street, The Bowery, and in and out of maze-like manufactured opium dens and contrived Joss houses, serving a clientele that included Sir Henry Irving, Ellen Terry, Hall Caine, Israel Zangwill, Sir Thomas Lipton, Anna Held and Yvette Guilbert.

His views on matters monetary and eleemosynary bear quotation: "I wuz out wid a bloke, showin' him de sites uv de Reservation, an' he asks me wot I'd do if I had a million bones. It nearly took me bre'th away t'inkin' uv it, an' I ain't got over it yet. . . . But I guess blokes like Carnegie and Rockerfeller hez got more dan a million—I t'ink dey must hev two millions ennyhow. But if I had dere cush I wouldn't be buildin' no readin' rooms, en libraries, en t'ings like dat. Nixey, dey ain't no good. A guy wot's hungry can't eat de cover off a book. . . . An' besides, wot's de use uv holdin' on ter de coin. Yer can't only spend it wunce, an' w'en yer die, yer can't take it wid yer, kin yer? Dey ain't invented doze kind uv Mother Hubbards wid pockets in 'em yet. . . . Dere's nuttin' ter it. . . . De furst t'ing I'd do if I had a million would be ter go ter de Waldorf-Astoria an' hire er sweet uv rooms. . . . Den I'd give er dinner ter all de mob, wot u'd cost er hundred bucks er plate, an' after I'd got dem all paralyzed wid real wine, I'd send dem home in autermobiles. . . . I'd hire de parks every Sunday, wid . . . bands ter play 'Every Day'll be Sunday By an' By.' . . . Dancin? Sure. All de workin' fellers could hev der steadies an' twist ter a knockout, an' if a bundle got freckles in her t'roat—you know, got dry, see—I'd hev . . . waiters ter bring her a couple uv tubs uv milk so she could drown de freckles out. De fellers could hev everyt'ing on de bill uv fare, 'cept cigarettes—I wouldn't stand fer dem. I notice dere ain't no statues on de

Chuck Connors, "The Pride of the Bowery," in his "office,"
probably in Barney Flynn's "Old Tree House,"
at the corner of the Bowery and Pell Street, about 1899

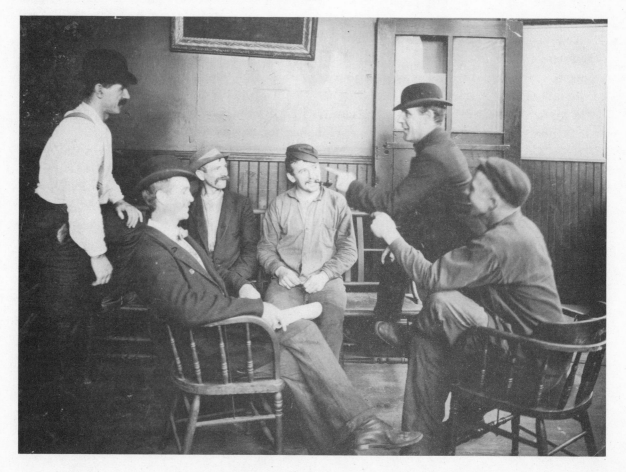

Bowery. Well, dere ought ter be, an' I'd hev statues of Carrie Nation, Dowie an' Dr. Parkhurst put up, an' I'd hev 'em decorated wid crape. An' I wouldn't hev nobody carryin' de banner, 'cause I'd hev free sleepin' cribs on every block. W'y should a bloke wot's poor hev ter pay fer sleepin' ennyhow? Me headqua'ters would be de Waldorf, but I would hev a telephone station in Chinatown, so I could git a hot chop suey w'en I wanted it quick. Ev'ry mornin' at 10 o'clock . . . I'd call up me Chat'am Square agent an' tell him ter give cologne ter der gals an' segars an' free lunch ter der gorillas. . . . I'd give out coupons ter all der mob ter go an' get a bath, a shave, a shine, a hair cut, an' a shampoo, so dey would be all polished up like a door knob, waitin' fer yours truly in his autermobile. . . . An' dis gag erbout art galleries. W'y, dat gives me stagnation uv me liver an' I'll pass it up. Dere'd be no art galleries in mine. I'd hev two or t'ree tons uv corn beef an' cabbage an' a hundred blokes wid pitchforks ter shovel it out. . . . A bloke w'ot's hungry ain't stuck on listenin' to a long talk by a feller w'ot's just filled in wid everyt'ing . . . an' a ham sandwi'ch is better to him dan a t'ree t'ousan' dollar c'romo. . . . I'd have de Board uv Health go round ter every joint an' see dat all de reg'lars is gittin' de right stuff from de guy behin' de fence. I'd cut out de horse show, 'cause de horses git show enuff. I'd give de people a show fer a change, and I guess by de time all dis would be done I wouldn't have enny more uv me million, an' I'd spend me life in bein' happy. . . ."

. . . . *"How can New York be made The City Beautiful?"*

"A REAL CONVERSATION EXTENDING
FROM WASHINGTON SQUARE
TO ONE HUNDRED AND NINETY EIGHTH ST.

Stenographically Reported On A Four In Hand."

[A Byron-illustrated article in *The New York Herald,* Sunday, April 29, 1900]

MANY PROJECTS have been advanced from time to time for the improvement and beautification of New York. In the real conversation published to-day the NEW YORK HERALD presents a discussion of the subject by men who have made a careful study of it. In order to treat the matter intelligently and at first hand these gentlemen were taken on the HERALD's four-in-hand drag from Washington Square up Fifth avenue through Central Park, with a detour to the new East River Park [Carl Schurz Park], up Morningside avenue and the Fort Washington road to One Hundred and Ninety-eighth street and back by way of Riverside Drive and Eighth avenue through Hell's Kitchen [where the photograph on page 321 was taken on Tenth Avenue] and to the Waldorf-Astoria [at Fifth Avenue and Thirty-fourth Street]. The route therefore included the finest and also some of the poorest quarters in the city. . . .

Driving Under Washington Arch.

Tell us what we can do to beautify Fifth avenue? What will be the style of architecture of the avenue in future years?

Mr. [Charles R.] Lamb [Artist and Decorator]—That will be governed by future legislation. If there is no restrictive legislation Fifth avenue will be filled with tall buildings, because with the enormous valuation of land . . . and our modern methods of steel construction it is easier and less expensive to go up than it is to develop laterally.

Fifth Avenue Between Tenth and Twenty-Third Streets.

Mr. [John] De Wolf [Landscape Architect to the Park Board]—The presence of tall buildings does not necessarily destroy the beauty of the street. For example, notice those trees in front of the Old First Presbyterian Church there. Don't they give a beautiful appearance to the street, despite the tall buildings all about?

    Why have trees not been planted?

Mr. De Wolf—The Park Department has encouraged it in every possible way. The trouble has been that the tree planting resulted in failure, and only a small part of the trees planted lived, because of the gases in the earth and the depredations of horses and other animals. . . . The expense . . . has been the chief obstacle to tree planting by individual citizens. . . .

Up Fifth Avenue to Fifty-Ninth Street.

    We have decided that it would add to the beauty of Fifth avenue to plant trees. . . . What else ought we to do?

Mr. De Wolf—For one thing we might build fountains at certain spots. Both ornamental fountains and drinking fountains for horses are desirable.

. . .

    How about restricting trade on Fifth avenue?

Mr. De Wolf—Well, that could be done.

    Do you consider it advisable?

Mr. [George C.] Clausen [President of the Board of Park Commissioners]—I certainly do. Of course, people living here have the right of communication with their houses. . . . There is not a city in the world that has not some restricted street or avenue.

    How about the rules of the road?

Mr. Clausen—They certainly should be enforced, but our streets are not policed with a view to that. . . . Incompetent persons should not be allowed to drive. I mean boys particularly, such as are often seen driving butchers' and grocers' wagons. . . .

Mr. [Fred B.] Pitney [of the *New-York Daily Tribune*]— . . . In my opinion every driver ought to be licensed. I think also that cable and electric cars should be compelled to stop just before they reach a street crossing. Such a rule would avert many collisions.

. . .

    We have been talking about the beautification of Fifth avenue and the restriction of traffic upon it, chiefly because we regard it as a great street for pleasure driving—is not that the reason?

Mr. Clausen—It is the only street we have for driving.

Mr. De Wolf—Of course it is a sort of show place, a place for pleasure seeking.

    Well, then, looking at it from a purely commercial point of view, would it not be more effective in its influence upon the people to beautify some other avenue rather than this?

Mr. Clausen—I think that this avenue is used more than any other. It is a great promenade, as well as a great driveway.

Mr. [Niels] Grön [Danish traveller and sociological expert]—Is it not a mistake to build magnificent avenues in a city? Wherever one finds magnificent avenues he is likely

The New York Herald's four-in-hand drag, 1900
Pausing in "Hell's Kitchen" during the course of a City Planning Tour
Scene on Tenth Avenue, between Fifty-fourth and Fifty-fifth Streets

also to find great slums.

But you do not find them in the same place.

Mr. Grön—It tends to classify, to develop one part of the city at the expense of the rest, and to make the city vain of certain parts.

Is it possible that you would say that because there are slums about Essex street traffic on Fifth avenue should not be restricted?

Mr. Lamb—The answer to that should be that each part of a great city must be treated with reference to its requirements. . . .

Mr. Clausen—Fifth avenue is almost as much used by the masses as by the classes. . . .

Mr. Lamb—If you get your masses to go to Fifth avenue and feel a personal interest in its beauty you help to eliminate your classes.

If you get your masses to walk on Fifth avenue you do not; but if you get them to live on Fifth avenue perhaps you do.

Mr. De Wolf—Don't you think the poor people take as much pride in this street as the people who live on it?

Mr. Clausen—I am certain that they do. You should see them flock along here on a Sunday afternoon.

Mr. Lamb—If a good example is set by a thoroughgoing attempt to improve and beautify one street, you will find that the improvement will extend to other streets and that in time it will have an effect upon the whole city.

Mr. Grön—Before I came to this country, and in all the time I have been here, it never has occurred to me to think of New York as being beautiful. Therefore all this talk of beautifying New York seems strange to me. . . . We expect of her power and magnificence, but not beauty. If a European came over here and found that New York was beautiful in the same way as the European cities he knew, he would be very much disappointed. I do not see how you can make New York beautiful in that way, with the laws and the democratic spirit that you have here. . . . The beauty of all the cities except New York owes its development to despotism in some form or other—to the sacrifice of the liberties of one class or another.

Mr. De Wolf—Do you not think it possible for us to be original here? We do not want to copy the systems of foreign cities, but to develop our peculiar natural advantages.

. . .

Along the East Drive in Central Park.

Mr. De Wolf—One thing to be borne in mind in regard to the parks is that they are for the people. . . .

Do you remember the investigations of the Tenement House Commission in the matter of small parks? . . .

Mr. Clausen— . . . we have a very limited number of small parks, considering our population.

Mr. De Wolf—Yes; there is a great need of new small parks.

Where is the greatest need?

Mr. Clausen— . . . in the tenement districts down town. . . .

The movement for improving Greater New York, however, exists principally in Manhattan, does it not?

Mr. Clausen—Oh, no. It is universal.

. . .

At East River Park.

How near has New York come to realizing the possibilities of her water front?

Mr. Lamb—I should say not more than one per cent of the possibilities has been realized. . . . This section of the city is going to have a tremendous development in the immediate future. . . . The East River has possibilities artistically second to those of no river of any great capital of the world. . . . One of the most desirable steps that the city could take . . . would be to convert the islands in the East River into public parks. . . .

In Upper Central Park.

Mr. Clausen—It has always been my aim to have some connecting link between Central Park, Riverside Drive and the Speedway, in order to make one continuous drive. . . .

Along Morningside Park.

How about a continuous drive from downtown—say the Battery?

Mr. Clausen—I have not thought of that. It seems to me, however, that it would be rather difficult to construct such a drive. . . .

How about restricting those ugly things—the bill boards?

Mr. Clausen—It could be done. They are kept out of the park, you know.

. . .

What is your opinion of the future of Washington Heights?

Mr. De Wolf—I think it is one of the best spots in the city for a residential section. People are beginning to see its advantages, especially that of its pure air.

During Luncheon at the Abbey.

[A popular roadhouse on Fort Washington Avenue near West 198th Street]

Mr. Lamb—After all, one of the greatest natural advantages in the way of beauty that New York possesses is to be found across the river there—the Palisades. . . . They are a part of the Greater New York. . . .

How about the movement to preserve the Palisades?

Mr. Lamb—That movement is practically assured of success. . . . What was said to be absolutely impossible has been accomplished by the force of public opinion, aroused chiefly . . . by the press. Except for the newspapers the Palisades would have been lost to the city of New York.

. . .

Mr. Lamb—A splendid idea for the improvement of the city is that suggested by President Clausen—to connect our park systems from one end of the city to the other by what we should call park roadways. . . .

. . .

Mr. Grön—The idea of beautifying New York is closely connected with creating the best possible comforts for the people?

Mr. Lamb—It is a question of providing the greatest good for the greatest number.

Mr. Grön— . . . . In Copenhagen we have a place called the Tivoli. . . . I know of no other institution in the world that does so much for the masses. . . . There is a high class restaurant like Delmonico's, and cheap restaurants as well. . . . The royal family and the nobility as well as the common people are to be found there. . . .

Mr. De Wolf—It certainly would be a good thing for the rich and the poor to mingle in their pleasures, but whether that scheme could be practically carried out here is a question.

. . .

Mr. De Wolf—Of course, all improvement should be utilitarian, and if properly carried out it is so. A city need not be enormously wealthy to enable it to become beautiful. . . . There is no doubt that beauty of surroundings has a higher commercial value now that [*sic*] it ever had before.

Mr. Lamb—Any improvements that may be taken up in the city of New York should be taken up first from the economic side, secondly, from the hygienic or sanitary side, and lastly, from the artistic side.

. . .

. . . . *Christmas lost its charms*

"LITTLE CHILDREN who had arisen early to examine the contents of stockings were only given time enough to gather up their little toys before they were borne out by the policemen. Men and women begged to be allowed to gather up some of their effects, but there was no time to be lost, and in some cases it became necessary to use force to drag them from their homes. Christmas lost its charms for them as they gathered in groups on the sidewalk and watched the destruction of their homes. Many of them were left almost penniless and dependent upon the charity of friends and relatives," reported *The New York Times* of December 26, 1896, describing "One of the most destructive conflagrations of the year." The six-story "flathouse" at 209 East Thirty-third Street, with its twenty-four families, and similar No. 207 were only two of the buildings involved in this grim holiday bonfire—almost an acre of hell. At about 7:15 A.M. a weary night watchman, thankfully completing his last monotonous round of the factories at Nos. 211–229 noticed a stove burning briskly in the Adolph Pinner snuff plant on the second floor. Moments later smoke cascaded through the windows. Policeman Will Young, at his Third Avenue post, turned in the first of four alarms, which brought "twenty engines, three water towers, and a number of hook and ladder trucks to the scene" at the wild climax of an unusual number of Christmas Eve blazes throughout the frozen city. The antiquated quarters of the Kaldenberg Mfg. Co., producers of pipes, canes, and ivory goods, and the lumber-filled premises of the Sebastian Sommer and Gibson piano companies were swiftly cremated and their falling walls spread destruction to Nos. 231 and 233 of the doomed block. Guests of the East River Hotel, a converted double tenement-house operated by William Schuller as one of the many similar evils that mushroomed out of the Raines Law, were assisted from their threatened retreat by the firefighters, whose efforts were hampered all along the line by icebound hydrants and equipment. A nurse, looking from a rear window of the Polyclinic Hospital, at 214–216 East Thirty-fourth Street, hastened to her superiors, and fifty-six patients, many of them postoperatives, were miraculously evacuated to the temporary shelter of the Delaware Hotel on Third Avenue, before the flames started to lick the institution's mansard roof at eight o'clock. The fire was subdued

Fire on East Thirty-third Street, December 25, 1896
North side, between Lexington and Third Avenues

after burning out the two upper floors and attacking the adjacent buildings. The sick (who had made displaced persons of the inn's grumbling, holiday-saturated clientele) were later allocated to various hospitals throughout the city.

All through the day, and into the next, according to the *New-York Daily Tribune* of the 27th, "Firemen were still at work at the ruins . . . playing streams of water on the smouldering embers" of the $500,000 fire of undetermined, many-theoried origin. However, not a single life was lost in this macabre Christmas celebration.

. . . . Pawed and patted and powdered

THE TONSORIAL art has had elegant practitioners in this city. In 1852 Phalon's Hair Dressing Establishment, at the St. Nicholas Hotel, on Broadway between Broome and Spring Streets, proclaimed itself in somewhat confused simile "as great a lion in its way as the palace of St. Mark in Venice," and "the most splendid establishment of its kind in . . . New-York— in the Union—probably in the world." The customer, as he reclined in one of its fifteen "magnificent shaving chairs" (representing an outlay of $100 each) could turn his eyes ceilingward to the "Fresco work" by De Lamano—"a brilliant triumph of a brilliant Art"—or gaze on his own reflection in the $5,000 wall of mirrors. The sum of $1,500 had been invested in the marble floor; and a like amount in the washstand with its statuary adornment, while "the silver toilet services" accounted for another $2,500 of the $16,000 total: "a larger sum than was ever before expended" upon any institution of a similar nature "since time began." A lithograph of the "St. Nicholas-Hotel," published by W. Stephenson & Co. in 1855, reveals that Edward Phalon (who was also a perfumer) advertised his "Paphian Lotion for the Com-

The barbershop of the Hotel Algonquin, 1906
59 West Forty-fourth Street

plexion" on the sides of a Gothic Revival sandwich wagon drawn by four pairs of plumed, prancing steeds. At least one British traveler—though, like so many of his compatriots, bearing the ancient grudge—was obliged to admit that in a single respect the former Colonials surpassed the Mother Country: *The Graphic* of London sent A. Boyd Houghton to make a series of sketches here, and the text accompanying his caricature of a "Barber's Saloon," in the issue of April 16, 1870, sighs over the sybaritic ritualism practiced in these adjuncts of the large hotels. Price Collier, writing anonymously and posing as a Gallic visitor of 1896 (in *America and the Americans from a French Point of View*, New York, 1897), was less impressed by the "horribly dirty, and painfully disagreeable" native custom followed by "correct and well-dressed young men" who permitted their faces to be professionally "pawed and patted and powdered" and then "without any further ablutions on their part" left the barbershop, and its "rows of small porcelain cups with the names of their owners"—in some incriminating instances actually known to him—"in gilt letters upon them . . . to make love, or to kiss their wives or their children," for all he knew.

With such antecedents, the wisteria bower that was the Algonquin's barbershop did not therefore merit mention in the literature of a hotel celebrated for many other attributes since its opening on November 22, 1902, and until his death in 1946 presided over by Frank Case, first as versatile employee, then as manager-lessee, and from 1927 on as owner. Here, from the very beginning, Thespians and writers forgathered; here in 1919 the fabled "Round Table," with its complement of wit, became a sprightly successor to the earlier literary tradition of Pfaff's Broadway cellar, carrying on its prandial effervescence into the thirties; here, *The New Yorker*—its first date line February 21, 1925—went through its blessed incipience. Mr. Byron, when I questioned him about the unsung department of "The Wayward Inn," replied: "Well! . . . while I do not just remember what the picture was made for, I know that [here] many an actor had his face shaved and his hair cut just to his liking."

. . . . *And lo! Madame is ready*

MR. BYRON has the gift of almost total recall. When I queried him about his father's extraordinary penetration into the confines of a Turkish Bath for Women, he replied: "This was a free lance job and it took a lot of selling; it was a little raw for those days, but the N. Y. *Herald* eventually bought and published the photographs." *Mirabile dictu*, after nine backbreaking hours, I came upon the full-page, copiously illustrated article in that venturesome newspaper, under date of Sunday November 6, 1904, aptly subheaded "An Arduous And Costly Pursuit." And I give excerpts from the feature writer's unsigned story (with an occasional bracketed aside in the interest of brevity).

"I stumbled across the latest thing in swelldom and cleanliness—the Turkish Bath Club. . . . There are already three such institutions, with the possibility of many more. There is one club, composed exclusively of actresses. . . . No woman weighing less than 150 pounds is eligible. . . . According to the programme, first comes half an hour in the hot room; then the same period in the steam room. The scrub and the 'pound' come next. The 'pound' treatment consists merely of turning on a large, heavy hose, capable of high pressure. . . . When the water is turned upon the back and hips . . . it reduces measurements more rapidly and

327

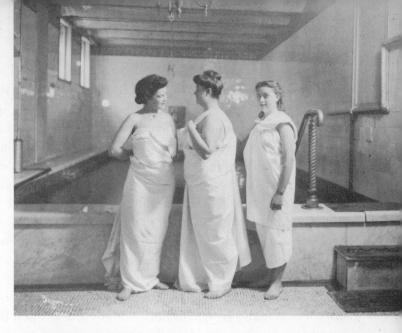

Scenes in a Turkish Bath Club, 1904

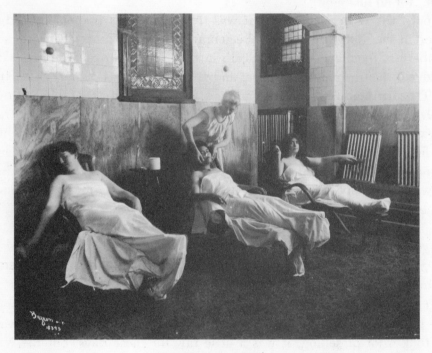

with less discomfort than any massage. Then comes the real work. . . . From the time they enter the pool until they leave it [a half hour later] they swim constantly . . . then the bathers retire to their dressing rooms for an alcohol massage. . . . Then comes rest [from fifteen minutes up]. . . . The bather . . . well seasoned to the programme . . . can get out in the remarkably brief period of two hours . . . several pounds lighter. . . . Ten dollars is about the minimum cost . . . with substantial additions if . . . [the negating victim] be lavish in tips and likes a pretentious luncheon with wine . . . served on dainty tabourets. . . . Good nature and good fellowship prevail at the sessions of the club. Strict formality and the elegance of wealth hedge around the meetings of another Turkish bath club, the members of which are figures in the society that begins with a capital S. They meet at a certain bath house not many steps from Fifth avenue [here depicted—in the East Seventies, Mr. Byron believes, near Lexington]. . . . It is here that the women who dazzle Newport, Narragansett and Saratoga gather during the New York season and spend the entire day. . . ." This voluntary weekly surrender involved submission to the ministrations of the facial masseuse, the hair masseuse, the rubbers; taking the modified exercise befitting exalted rank; allegedly sleeping for an hour usually devoted to the more vocal pursuit of gossip; undergoing manicure and pedicure before a substantial feast gracefully ingested in a reclining position in the best Roman-matron tradition, followed by a five-to-six-gallon hour-long shampoo; enduring the artifices of the coiffeur, the combing and clipping of fractious eyebrows and errant lashes, a final facial massage and the application of powder. ". . . and lo! Madame is ready for her maid and her drive home. . . . The Turkish Bath Club, which has its membership among the young business women of the city, is not [*ça va sans dire*] such an elaborate organization. . . . Its sessions are held in the bathrooms of a spacious old house on Twenty-third street in the vicinity of the shopping district."

. . . . *Only one other sex to try*

INTO THE primaveral evening, a cornet soloist sent forth the sweet strains of "The Last Rose of Summer," and his music—stealing across the incomplete faerie tracery of the East River span—was heard three miles away in a corner parlor on the second floor of the St. Denis Hotel, at Broadway and Eleventh Street. Here, on the night of May 11, 1877, Alexander Graham Bell of Boston was giving the first New York demonstration of his "speaking telephone" at the invitation of a distinguished gathering, which included Frederick Augustus Porter Barnard, President of Columbia College; the geologist John Strong Newberry; the physicist Ogden Rood; Isaac L. Peet, Principal of the New York Institution for the Instruction of the Deaf and Dumb; T. N. Gibbes, M.P., President of the Dominion Telegraph Company of Canada; Thomas Thompson Eckert, President of the Atlantic & Pacific Telegraph Company; and the artist Eastman Johnson. The uneven sounds emerged from an apparatus that, according to *The New York Herald* of May 12, "might have been taken by a casual observer for the cover of an ordinary sewing machine, except that at one end there was a mouth piece like that which is attached to speaking tubes. A couple of wires ran from the other through the room across the Brooklyn Bridge and into one of the offices of the Atlantic and Pacific Telegraph Company at 340 Fulton Street in that city." To and fro across the river sound floated, as the lecturer urged Mr. Gower, in the City of Churches, to "sing a song," to which the latter replied that he was "not much of a singist," but obligingly rendered Pleyel's hymn, "Children of the Heavenly King," and "Hold the Fort" (by P. P. Bliss). Following conversation back and forth, audience participation was invited, "and in nearly every instance the responses are distinct. The effect is wierd [sic] and almost supernatural. One imagines that he is a second Signor Blitz [magician and gastriloquist] talking ventriloquially to the imaginary body in the box." Despite the back page position accorded the story, the *Herald* expressed the belief that the thirty-year-old scientist's exhibition "of the wonderful power which he has achieved . . . must have satisfied the most sceptical person present that we are upon the eve of strange developments in the philosophy of life." So man spoke to man across space and "Professor Bell, in concluding, took occasion to say that it was as easy to talk 100 miles as two miles, and that he expected to be able to demonstrate in a short time that conversation could be carried on between England and America through the Atlantic cable [successfully laid in 1866] with even greater satisfaction than through land lines."

Earlier, throughout the week of March 19–24, less scientific audiences at the Theatre Comique had witnessed the topicality of Harrigan and Hart's new skit (written by the former) "on the sensation of the day," *The Telephone.*

During the early fall of the following year (1878) there was issued a long, narrow broadside (30 × 9 inches)—the first "List Of Subscribers To The Central Office System Of The Bell Telephone Company Of New York." The names of 45 "Banks, Bankers And Brokers" led all the rest; 26 firms devoted to "Diamonds, Watches, Jewelry, Plated Ware, etc." could be contacted immediately in case of need; 23 "Produce, Cotton, Oil, and Commission Merchants" were party to the project; 21 "Importers" were at the beck and call of the trade; 19 establishments engaged in the manufacture, distribution and sale of "Drugs, Chemicals, and Essential Oils" recognized the importance of instantaneous verbal exchange with their customers; 10 of New York's hostelries (the Albemarle, the Brevoort, French's, the Gilsey House, the Grand Central, the Metropolitan, the Park, the St. Cloud, the St. Nicholas, and the Windsor) could boast of their advanced ideas of communication; only one publisher— D. Appleton & Co.—allowed the privacy of the editorial ear to be sacrificed to the urgency of its authors; it was possible to reach a solitary weigher, a lone clothier, a single distiller, a unique hatter; lawyers, doctors, divines and undertakers practiced their callings in professional isolation, and a man's home was still encastellated. In all, there were 271 listings and the peace of 242 companies and services could be disturbed by name, since numbers were not used. The first telephone exchange in New York City was opened about October, 1878, at 518 Broadway, where the switchboard was makeshift and also used as a burglar alarm system.

Eighteen years later, Mrs. Burton Harrison (in her chapter on "Externals of Modern New York" in *History Of The City Of New York* by Mrs. Martha J. Lamb and Mrs. Burton Harrison, New York, 1896) could brag that "The telephone system of New York is the largest and most complete of its kind. In the first quarter of this year 1896 it consists of 15,000 subscribers' stations; 12 central offices . . . ; 38,000 miles of underground wires in the streets; and about 3,500 miles of overhead wires in the regions not yet closely built up."

A detailed description of the workings of this complex organism appeared in *Leslie's Weekly,* March 29, 1894, which gave over three pages to an illustrated article by A. Franklin Matthews on "What A Metropolitan Telephone System Is." A description of the office here shown is included: "Turning . . . to the front of the board one sees that it is divided into sections, and that three girls, seated on chairs on a slightly elevated platform, are allotted to a section. In the Cortlandt Street exchange there are forty-three sections. . . . Each girl . . . has about forty-five subscribers to look after, but the wires of every subscriber . . . run behind her section of the board, and each wire is tapped to a peg-hole in her section. Thus in that exchange there are forty-three places where Smith's wire may be tapped should . . . any other subscriber wish to talk to him. By this plan, when one of a certain girl's forty-five subscribers wishes to talk to another subscriber not of her forty-five, she does not have to run a long tube or cord to the one place, perhaps clear across the room, in the section where the other man's wire ends primarily, because each subscriber's wire actually ends in forty-three different places in that room."

Herbert Laws Webb of the Metropolitan Telephone Company, in *The Illustrated American* of May 9, 1896, furnishes some interesting statistics about "the most complete and efficiently equipped telephone system in the world": "The switchboard of the Cortlandt street exchange alone is longer than the west façade of the Madison Square Garden . . . and the separate pieces contained in it are counted by millions." The over-all picture is an imposing multiplication, as "there are at present some 15,000 telephone stations in New York . . . connected by special underground cables to twelve central offices or exchanges, distributed approximately a mile apart, from Broad street to Tremont. The [more than 500] cables contain fifty to one hundred pairs of wires or circuits . . . and the total length of wire would furnish a telegraph line clear round the world at the equator and another from pole to pole. The subway ducts under the street, if laid end to end, would reach from New York to Cleveland, with enough duct to spare to form a subway system for a small town. The switchboards of the various exchanges joined in line would make a fence, worth $1,000 a foot, around two sides of Madison Square. . . . In the operation of the plant some 1,100 persons are employed. About half of these are engaged in handling the traffic, and the rest are divided between construction and maintenance and inspection. The executive and managerial offices, including the engineering, contract, superintendent, auditor and treasurer's departments, employ some 200 more." In the "Woman's Special Supplement" of the *New-York Daily Tribune*, October 2, 1898, this spokesman for the company calculated that about one young American woman in every fifteen hundred was a telephone operator; it had been discovered early in the new communication era that masculine "Young America" lacked the essential attributes of civility and accuracy, leaving "only one other sex to try." He pointed out that the "comfort" of this fortune-favored segment was "well looked after." Day hours of duty were from eight o'clock to six, with a half hour for lunch and twenty-minute breaks morning and afternoon; and the night force worked from seven o'clock to seven, with three hours' relief. "At every exchange commodious quarters are provided for the operators."

The *Leslie's Weekly* article previously quoted includes a précis of the activities of one of these handmaidens of communication, "commonly—but very erroneously—supposed to be a pert young woman of much leisure." On the contrary, Mr. Matthews assures: "She is the busiest person, I believe, in New York. Her hands are constantly in motion . . . her eyes are always on the watch, and her ears are trained to catch the slightest noise through the machine. . . . Her body is swaying constantly, and every few minutes she is required to make some entry on a pad that lies in front of her. . . . Busy must be her brain, also, for often she has a dozen persons to care for at once and a dozen things to think of. Moreover, she must be abso-

The West Wing of the Cortlandt Street Board of the New York Telephone Company, 1894
18 Cortlandt Street

lutely faithful, besides being intelligent and quick." Supervisors, monitors, managers, men "making tests about town indiscriminately . . . to determine the efficiency of the service," and carping subscribers made it "practically impossible for a girl to neglect her duty without detection. . . . Test men . . . found that the answers to the calls averaged only nine seconds. . . . A telephone girl's work is really skilled labor. It takes nearly a year before she becomes proficient. . . . Most of the girls in the Cortlandt Street exchange have been with the company five years." These paragons "get paid about twice as much as the average shop-girl, and are not subject to that undesirable personal contact with Tom, Dick, and Harry that shop-girls encounter." In short, a maiden so employed "is a very superior person in the great army of working women."

The Byron-illustrated article in the *Metropolitan Magazine* for March, 1902, gave a more intimate—though disillusionizing—glimpse: "Prettiness is not an essential attribute of the 'hello girl,' and the bewitching face conjured up in the mind of the man at the 'phone by a pleasing voice might give way, were seeing as possible as hearing, to something much plainer." Nor did the writer tempt even the physiognomically ill favored to enter this vocally seductive field: "It may seem, to one visiting the operating room of a telephone exchange, that the girls appear uncomfortably like prisoners. The galley-slave of old, bound to his oar by chains, was not held closer to his work than these, with their curious headgear of steel bands and black auricles [dictating occupational coiffures], and the short stretch of insulated wire which holds them, literally by the head, at their places in front of the switchboard." After the standardized curiosity of "What number?" (to give way to the more ingratiating "Number, please?") and the silent manual plug insertions, there remained for the unpulchritudinous captive only the sadistic "Eight-one-o-six doesn't answer," or the deeper satisfaction of the ever incredulously received "Two-o-four-nine is busy."

Lessons in the womanly art of self-defense, 1906

. . . . Prudence whispers "Beware of him"

" 'WHAT SHALL we do in case we are attacked by some thief or ruffian?' is the question women have asked in every part of the country. . . . Few women possess the nerve necessary to use a pistol with effect when attacked. . . . What, then, can be provided for her that will be formidable to a foe, yet absolutely safe, as far as she is concerned, and ever ready at hand, whether wanted for use or not?" The *New-York Tribune Illustrated Supplement* of February 7, 1904, had a ready solution: "The answer . . . has been provided by those who make women's hatpins. A hatpin has been designed that is intended primarily for use as a weapon of defence. It is in reality a stiletto, masquerading as an innocent hatpin. It is made of fine steel that will bend but will not break, as sharp as a needle, and hardened at the end so that it can be used with deadly effect as a dagger, and with a handle that enables a woman to grasp it for use as a weapon and hold it so that it cannot easily be pulled from her hand. . . . The method of using it to the best advantage when attacked is to aim at the face of the highwayman. A woman armed with one of these stilettos is able to do more damage in a few seconds than a man unarmed. The wicked little blade . . . [is] so keen . . . that, thrust home by a woman frenzied by fear, it is likely to pierce through any ordinary clothing into a vital part of a highwayman's anatomy. There are times in most women's lives when a suspicious looking character comes into the offing and prudence whispers 'Beware of him.' While most women would shrink under these circumstances from pulling out a revolver, it is an innocent act to put the hand to the hat and draw out one of her stiletto-like hatpins. With this in her hand the nervous woman is ready for the stranger, whatever his intentions."

335

There were other methods as well. In 1904 President Roosevelt found time to master the art of *jiujitsu*. A two-page spread in *Leslie's Weekly*, January 12, 1905, extolled "The Marvelous Japanese Art of Defense, A Society Craze Among Women In London And Washington." H. Irving Hancock, author of several books on Nipponese physical training and "combat tricks," described the science that "upsets all of our preconceived notions about the art of self-defense." According to him, "Titled [English] women . . . became the pupils of the Japanese . . . [about three years in advance of our retarded civilization]. Last winter the *jiu-jitsu* thrill became powerfully felt in Washington. . . . Many . . . society women, with Miss [Alice] Roosevelt at the head of the list, are reputed to be experts. And now the craze has reached New York, where it bids fair to reach its American zenith in the number of women experts that next season will see."

Another well recommended technique emanated from the Mother Country, too, for the *New-York Tribune Illustrated Supplement* of August 30, 1903 (reproducing photographs from the August 1 issue of *The Illustrated Sporting and Dramatic News* of London) reasoned: "When a man is called on to face a ruffian, he needs no better weapon than a hickory walking stick. A revolver is likely to harm him more than to help. As soon as a man reaches for his weapon, his adversary has the right to shoot, and the accomplished criminal is almost sure to have his weapon ready first. The stick is the better weapon, because it is quicker. It is in one's hand already. It is always 'loaded'. . . . Should a New-Yorker combine both the tactics of the London stick man and the United States naval wrestler, it would be safe to say that the police of this city would have far fewer holdups and burglaries to record than at the present time." The "scepter'd isle" series (showing the use of cane and bumbershoot) bears a marked resemblance to this Byron set, loosely labelled by the photographer as "Dr. Latson's Method Of Self-Defense." Because of the pupil's sex, a furled umbrella alone is the lethal substitute for the walking stick, and when cunningly manipulated lands neatly on the attacker's proboscis with a force guaranteed to result in violent epistaxis and permanent impairment of the profile. In fair weather, the versatile Latson disciple depended on the weaponless skill of the *jiujitsu* adept. The worthy doctor has artfully dodged my vigilance.

On January 27, 1907, *The New York Herald* Magazine Section captioned an illustrated demonstration of sturdy masculinity in ten defensive poses, "Lessons By Marcellus T. Hayes, LL.B, Former Supervisor Public Playgrounds, New York City." This Bachelor of Laws was an advocate of barehanded resistance against the gradually vanishing race of "Animals known as 'street bullies.'"

.... *Harnessed and ready, day and night*

"ONE OF Warden Brennan's ambulances was on exhibition yesterday in the down-town streets. It attracted a great deal of attention." This statement appears in the *New-York Daily Tribune* of July 24, 1869, under the heading "The City.", and is amplified by a paragraph further down in the same column: "One of the four ambulances recently constructed for the Department of Charities and Correction made its appearance in the streets yesterday. It is well adapted to its intended use—the conveyance of bruised or wounded men to the hospital in the most easy as well as the most expeditious manner. The bottom slides out and in on rollers, and is fitted with a soft spring mattress. Medicines and surgical instruments are also carried, and there is a seat for the surgeon as well as the driver. Two of these ambulances will be kept in constant readiness for use." On July 27, it is reasserted that "The ambulances for removing persons who may be injured by accidents, or become sick in the streets, are kept harnessed and ready, day and night, at Bellevue Hospital."

Until that summer of 1869, the hospitals of New York—and of most cities throughout the world—waited for the sick and maimed to knock at their doors seeking admission; not until then did our citadels of mercy reach out an auxiliary arm to the suffering. One of the signal victories of the Civil War had been the initiation of the modern ambulance system, the first wagons for the wounded having been sent to the battlefront by the Committee of Union Defence of the City of New York. Here our local priority ceased, for it is a matter of record that civilian hospital ambulance service was instigated by the Commercial (now the General) Hospital of Cincinnati, Ohio, about 1865, with James A. Jackson as "driver of ambulance" on the payroll for the year ending February 28, 1866, at an annual wage of $360.

On May Day of 1869 the New York Commissioners of Public Charities and Correction logically requested Dr. Edward B. Dalton, Sanitary Superintendent of the Metropolitan Board of Health since its organization three years earlier, to outline a plan for a downtown reception hospital, incorporating his ideas for an ambulance corps. A graduate of the College of Physicians and Surgeons and of the Bellevue House Staff, following a Residency at St. Luke's he had achieved great distinction in the organizational and directorial end of military hospitals during the War of the Secession. Upon his return to New York, he had meditated on the possibility of a peacetime application of the merciful ambulance principle he had furthered so efficiently as chief medical officer of the Depot Field Hospital of the Army of the Potomac. He responded with such brilliance to the Commissioners' challenging request that his scheme became the basis of the present-day transportation of the sick. On June 30, 1869, Bellevue's Medical Board held an examination for ambulance surgeons and before long New York's pioneer civilian ambulances, designed by the Abbot-Downing Company, set forth on their alleviating errands. Other institutions slowly followed suit: the New York Hospital and the Roosevelt Hospital in 1877; St. Vincent's in 1879, and Presbyterian in 1880. By 1892 nine Bellevue ambulances were answering 4,858 calls received over telephone and

A Bellevue ambulance, 1896
Ready to leave the hospital yard by the Twenty-sixth Street gate

telegraph from the Police and Fire departments. According to *An Account of Bellevue Hospital*, edited by Robert J. Carlisle, M.D. (New York, 1893), it took "from thirty seconds to two and a half minutes" for the "drop" or "snap" harness to be adjusted on one of the eight horses maintained in the stables located just north of the Twenty-eighth Street wing, and for the surgeon to spring on board the vehicle, which, under the guidance of a well-versed driver traveled "a mile in from five to eight minutes in the business district, and from three and a half to six minutes in the less crowded parts of the city."

In addition to the Bellevue fleet, two ambulances at Gouverneur, two at Harlem and one at Fordham Hospital operated under the direction of the Department of Charities and Correction at this period.

Commenting on the plans of the Board of Health for a new combined "Vaccine Virus Laboratory" and station for ambulances to transport patients suffering from contagious diseases, the *New-York Daily Tribune* of November 22, 1896 speculated: "It is not outside of the bounds of probability that an automobile vehicle or two may be tried for this purpose."

338

"WHAT GRANDER or more beautiful spot can be found than Harlem and its little velvety islands and silvery rivers, in a golden sunset—sublimely picturesque in vernal bloom—the gorgeous landscape, which charms every visitor, and fills the mind and soul with rapture." This was doubtless one of the points at which the large audience crowding the Harlem Music Hall, at Third Avenue and 130th Street, on a winter evening in 1882, applausefully interrupted Colonel A. B. Caldwell's "Lecture On Harlem" (published in pamphlet form that July), the best received of a course of about fifty talks by prominent speakers under the sponsorship of the Y.M.H.A. of Harlem. "But a few years ago," he continued, "Harlem was nearly a barren waste. . . . Everybody was giving it the 'shake,' because it was giving the 'shakes' to everybody! Down-town people would scarcely come near us, except by the river, because to cross the Pontine Marshes, or 'Harlem Flats,' by land, would squelch the nose of a rhinocerus, and knock the breath out of a mule! . . . I am told that aquatic excursionists found it safer to burn brimstone as they came up through Hell-gate! . . . At the commencement of the Rebellion . . . Harlem began to grow, and few parts of our city have grown faster and been more beautified by new buildings, than this. New settlers are constantly arriving, trade is spreading on every street and avenue, and everybody says they are happy and making money, excepting the Elevated Railroad!"

Two years after this panegyric, the *New-York Daily Tribune*'s editorial page (March 27, 1884) informed that the Board of Estimate had made an appropriation of $12,000 for a hospital in Harlem, where "There is said to be great need for such an institution," as evidenced by the 1,200 ambulance calls received the previous year by the East 126th Street Station House. Perris & Browne's Insurance Map of 1886 shows a "Reception Hospital for Accident cases" at No. 533 East 120th Street, on property acquired by Henry Collins and Silas Downing in 1881. The house, with its formal garden, appeared on the 1851 Dripps Map, with Mich. Burke as the owner. In the 1867 Atlas the street was marked "Pagoda Place," presumably deriving its appellation from the fanciful structure erected in this little Eden during the intervening years. It was on April 17, 1887 that the name Harlem Hospital was applied to the former homestead—a comfortable three-story wooden dwelling with mansarded roof, colonnaded porch and grounds stretching toward the East River—converted into a twenty-bed institution for patients awaiting transfer to Ward's and Randall's Islands, boasting an ambulance service, and designated as an emergency branch of Bellevue Hospital. The Randall's Island ferry—first at 122nd Street—had moved two blocks south by 1886.

On April 10, 1892 (the day before the opening of Fordham Hospital and the inaugural week of Manhattan Hospital's new annex) the *Tribune* found that "Harlem hospitals have not kept stride with the rapid advance in building for some years, and there has hardly been a time in the history of upper New-York when the facilities for the removing and care of the sick in that section have been adequate to the wants. . . . Six years ago the Harlem Hospital in East One-hundred-and-twentieth-st., was opened. The small institution in East

A scene in the Harlem Hospital Dispensary, 1896
120th Street and the East River

Ninety-ninth-st. known as the first Harlem Hospital, was found to be of little use, and three years ago its doors were closed." According to the *Tribune* of April 24, 1895, when the Harlem Hospital had forty-one beds, it "was the subject of investigation on the part of the new Commissioner of Charities and Correction, Robert J. Wright . . . and a story of what was supposedly his opinion of the institution's shortcomings was published yesterday. . . . President H. H. Porter, who was in charge, said: 'We have known for some time that the Harlem Hospital will, or would, soon be too small for the demands made on it.' He added, however, that the report of Mr. Wright's talk on the subject of the hospital conveyed a wrong impression. 'There is but one operating table,' said Mr. Porter, 'but it does not often happen that several patients are taken to the hospital who are in need of immediate attention and compelled to lie and groan in agony until the patient ahead of them is operated upon. Mr. Wright must have been incorrectly reported in the matter of such serious overcrowding, inasmuch as at the present time we have twelve empty beds.'" However, the *New-York Daily Tribune* of December 12, 1899, reported the appearance of Dr. Dudley, of the institution's house staff at the monthly meeting of the Harlem Board of Commerce to reiterate his impassioned plea of a year before: "Since then conditions . . . have grown steadily worse. . . . The hospital is as crowded at times as the lowest tenement. . . . It is not unusual for us to have from two to six patients sleeping on canvas stretchers on the floor. . . . We are compelled to treat fifty thousand or more patients annually in the miserable outhouse on the pier. I have seen hysterical women awaiting care there while great ugly wharf rats played in and out of holes and crevices." Following this, "Dr. D. D. Clark presented a resolution expressing the Board's opinion that the Legislature ought to authorize the issue of $500,000 or more of bonds for the immediate construction of a new hospital."

The First Annual Report of Bellevue and Allied Hospitals, covering January 1 to December 31, 1902, described Harlem Hospital as "an old three-story wooden dwelling house . . . [in] a very dilapidated condition. Upon our first inspection in February the roofs of the main building, the dispensary and the stable were found to be leaking badly. The ceilings in the isolated ward, the male dormitory and the laundry were out of repair, portions of the plaster having fallen from time to time. . . . There were but two bath-tubs." The one for thirty-nine patients "was located in the middle of the diet kitchen of one of the wards. The water-closet for the use of the female medical patients was in the diet kitchen attached to their ward. The water-closet of the isolated ward was in the open ward with the beds, in plain view of the patients and with no ventilation whatever except into the ward." The Board of Trustees, which took over Bellevue, Fordham, Harlem, Gouverneur and the "Emergency Hospital in East Twenty-sixth Street" (until February 1, 1902, under the jurisdiction of the department of public charities of the City of New York), immediately instituted remedial measures and "at the same time work has been pushed on the plans of the new Harlem Hospital . . . which should meet the wants of the population for many years to come." In 1903 the present Harlem Hospital on Lenox Avenue between 136th Street and 137th was still in the planning stage. It opened its doors as a 150-bed institution on April 30, 1907, to grow into the present center in the heart of what James Weldon Johnson in *Black Manhattan* (New York, 1930) called "the recognized Negro capital" of America. According to Roi Ottley, in '*New World A-Coming*' *Inside Black America* (Boston, 1943), "Actually Harlem did not begin to take shape and character as a Negro community until 1910."

It was eleven years before, in the little plant by the East River, however, that there occurred an incident showing the far-flung influence of the clean-shaven Gibson Man. Full coverage was given in the *New-York Daily Tribune* on Monday, January 9, 1899: "Whenever any of the four other physicians in the Harlem Hospital have wished to have a little fun at the expense of Dr. [William Maxwell] Campbell, the acting house surgeon, reference has been made to the doctor's luxuriant black mustache. Ordinarily the doctor only laughed. But on Saturday morning the five healers were at the breakfast table, and someone sprang the old gibe of Dr. Campbell's hirsute ornament. He realized that it was in his way, and said so. . . . It was unanimously agreed that the mustaches [of the entire quintette] had to go and that the man who appeared at breakfast on Sunday morning without having applied a razor to his upper lip was to pay for a wine supper. . . . All the . . . physicians appeared at the table with hairless faces save Dr. [Samuel] Barshell. He is the youngest of the lot, and having to pay a particular social call in the evening, he begged for an extension of time. Portia before the Duke of Venice was not more eloquent than the young doctor, but Shylock was not more inexorable than the four physicians. To make sure of their man, they finally carried Dr. Barshell bodily to his room and there clipped his mustache. The nurses and attendants . . . did not know what to make of the reform, and all sorts of wild rumors were about the institution yesterday. Dr. Campbell had one patient, an old woman, who positively declined at first to permit him to approach her. He had some trouble in establishing his identity. Other equally ludicrous incidents were reported. The physicians declare that Dr. Barshell must pay for the supper. He laughingly threatens to have all indicted for 'mayhem,' as he says they cut off as much of his upper lip as they did of his mustache. And all four say with a wink, 'That's not unlikely, doctor.'"

. . . . *A composite picture of exquisite orderliness*

"DOCTOR, WHEN do you expect your hospital to be built?" a parishioner asked the Rev. William Augustus Muhlenberg, after his sermon on St. Luke's Day (October 18), 1846. "Never! unless I begin," replied the Rector of the Church of the Holy Communion (at Sixth Avenue and Twentieth Street). He had just addressed his congregation on an ideal institution he proposed to name after the Evangelist known as "the beloved physician," and he set aside half of the offertory for the establishment of a general hospital for the sick poor, regardless of race or religious affiliation. Thus, with the sum of $15, was founded this first effort on the part of the Episcopalians of New York to provide for the indigent ill. Mrs. Lindley Hoffman's contribution of $1,000, supplemented by the concrete support of other worshipers and answers to an "Appeal for a Church Hospital" circularized by various parishes, resulted in the incorporation of St. Luke's in 1850. Bishop Wainwright laid the cornerstone on May 6, 1854, at the Fifth Avenue and Fifty-fourth Street site chosen for the active realization of the divine's vision. Meanwhile, during the previous year the Sisters of the Holy Communion had started caring for the suffering in a rear building adjacent to the church and presently an infirmary was established adjoining their home. Here they ministered to over two hundred ailing persons while construction on the present location of The

342

Stairwell in the Vanderbilt Pavilion, St. Luke's Hospital, 1899
West 114th Street, between Morningside Drive and Amsterdam Avenue

University Club, the Gotham Hotel and environs was in progress, under the supervision of the architect, W. P. Esterbrook. On Ascension Day, 1857, the first services were held in the new hospital chapel, and on May 11, 1858, three of these dedicated women and nine patients moved into the tree-surrounded haven of refuge, where the Rev. Dr. Muhlenberg, as Pastor and Superintendent, lived from 1859 until his death on April 8, 1877. He gave his Hospital its motto—"Corpus Sanare. Animum Salvare." (To cure the body. To save the soul) —and its guiding code. He was succeeded by the Rev. George S. Baker in the administration of this church institution, which by St. Luke's Day, 1892, had treated 36,050 patients and graduated about eighty doctors from its house staff. July 1, 1888 saw the establishment of a Training School for Nurses.

The Hospital soon grew far beyond the Fifth Avenue landmark and on February 19, 1892, purchased the block bounded by Morningside Drive, Amsterdam Avenue, 113th and 114th Streets. Ernest Flagg, winner of the competition, was commissioned to erect his group of semidetached, passage-way connected buildings around the cornerstone laid on May 6, 1893.

"Despite the inclemency of the weather yesterday," reported the *New-York Daily Tribune* of January 25, 1896, "the arrangements made for the transfer of the [39] patients . . . from the old building . . . to the [Vanderbilt Pavilion of the] new hospital . . . were fully carried out. . . . The moving began at 9 o'clock in the morning, one ambulance being used and several stages and coaches." Other relays followed, and "By 4 o'clock the old hospital . . . was, save for a few of the officers, deserted and lonely." Its demolition was swiftly accomplished, while on Morningside Heights the earliest buildings—described by their architect as being "in the renaissance style of the modern French school"—were rushed to completion. They embodied the most up-to-date improvements inside their gray brick and stone walls. The annual report for the year ending October 19, 1896, was quoted by the *New-York Daily Tribune* of the 20th as stating that "Of the 1,439 patients treated . . . [1,161 of whom were non-paying] 554 were cured, 455 were improved, 98 were unimproved, 10 were transferred, 121 died and 201 are still in the hospital."

The Byron Company photographed the great plant in all its newness, and this fine composition has been selected as representative of their skill and of the "Model Hospital" described by Katherine Hoffman in the January, 1900, issue of *Munsey's Magazine*. She found the Nurses' Home in the Vanderbilt Pavilion "altogether a charming place. . . . The parlor is an enormous, sunny room where desks, bookcases, couches with many pillows, easy chairs, and a tea table invite the nurses to many agreeable forms of rest or diversion. . . . Their working day lasts for eleven hours, including nine . . . of actual work. . . . They have an afternoon off every other week. . . . Their bedrooms are charmingly arranged around the four sides of their pavilion, on the floors above the first." Of the seventy-one students in training she wrote: "Their appearance is all that the most inveterate reader of sentimental war stories could desire. They wear the neatest and prettiest uniform of blue and white striped gingham. Their bibbed white aprons, their neckbands of stiff linen, their crisply erect and airily poised little caps of sheer white mull, make altogether a composite picture of exquisite orderliness which must at once inspire hopeful convictions in the hearts of their patients."

344

IN 1889 a famous surgeon earned added immortality as the protagonist of one of the finest achievements of Thomas Eakins' career—*The Agnew Clinic,* a logical sequel to the artist's earlier but equally successful composition, *The Gross Clinic* of 1875. Another great surgeon—ambidextrous like D. Hayes Agnew, and master of the steel of sword, knife, and pen—received equally sensitive treatment in Byron's photographic study (page 346), which bears a fortuitous but immediate resemblance to its canvas predecessor.

John Allan Wyeth—a man instinct with humanity and of ineffable grace—was born at Missionary Station, Marshall County, Alabama, in 1845 and lived "more lives than one" in his seventy-seven years, as a few telescopic sentences from his autobiography (*With Sabre and Scalpel,* published by Harper & Brothers in 1914) attest. "I had been farmer and woodsman," he writes, "soldier . . . superintendent of a large cotton plantation, cattle-buyer, medical student for two years, and pilot . . . on a steamboat in the White River country of Arkansas, contracted for and built public buildings . . . in that state, speculated in lands, ran a telegraph office as operator, etc." He tells of leaving the Medical Department of the University of Louisville "The possessor of a pair of doctor's saddle-bags . . . diminutive apothecary scales . . . two forceps for extracting teeth, and a small minor surgical operating set of instruments, and last, but not least, a tin sign" which he affixed "to 'the outer wall'" of his first home-town office "after dark one night in March, 1869," only to take it down two months later following a death watch over his fourth patient. Humbly convinced of the inadequacy of his "didactic" but impractical training, he spent the three colorful Arkansas years lightly etched in above, accumulating money for further medical education—only to find, upon his arrival in New York in 1872, that postgraduate instruction was non-existent. After a year and a half in Bellevue Hospital Medical School, attending lectures, working in the surgical clinics and dissecting, he relates that in 1874 "I tacked my sign to the door of 226 Fifth Avenue, as a surgeon of the metropolis." As early as 1877 he undertook to organize a school where theoretical education could be supplemented by actual bedside, operating room, and laboratory experience. Lack of endowment obliged him to abandon the undergraduate phase of the programme, but he could later set down that his "founding of the New York Polyclinic Medical School and Hospital in 1881, which marked the introduction of systematic postgraduate medical instruction in America, was, if not the chief, at least an important factor in the great movement which . . . has revolutionized . . . the teaching and practice of medicine and surgery in the United States."

During the four decades he served his center (which he forged into a "skyscraper hospital" at 345 West Fiftieth Street) as President and Professor of Surgery, he made revolutionary contributions in surgical procedures and literature, with successful incursions into belles-lettres, and held the highest honors in his profession. After his death on May 28, 1922, his colleague Dr. John S. Enos of Providence wrote to the Editor of *The New York Times* that John Allan Wyeth was "idolized as a congenial and Christian gentleman and as, perhaps, the most remarkable surgeon in history. . . he was truly a maker of men. To know him was an education."

Dr. John Allan Wyeth performing an operation at the New York Polyclinic Medical School and Hospital, 1902 214 East Thirty-fourth Street

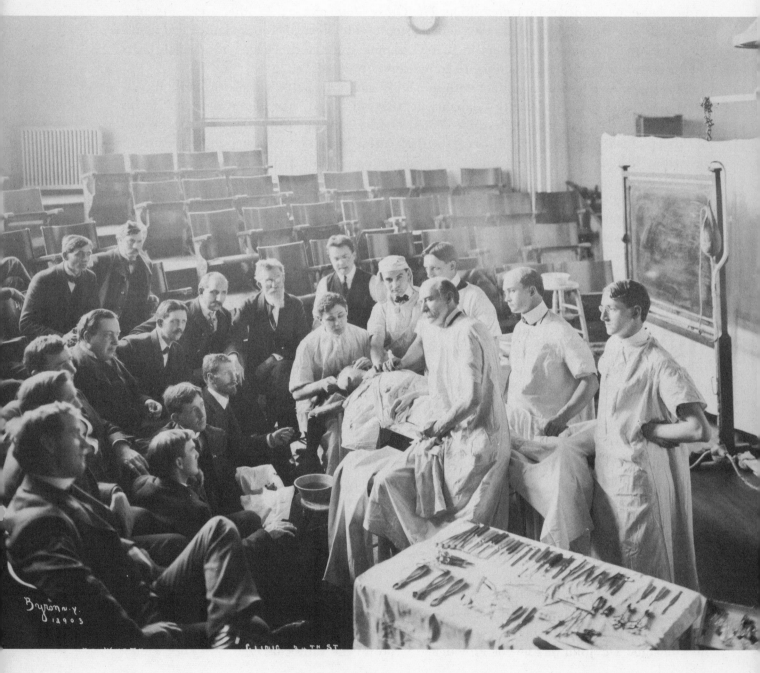

. . . . A limited number of patients free

"FAMED BONESETTER Here To Cure Our Rich Professor Atkinson, of London, After American Patients and Dollars." In this cavalier fashion, the *New York Journal* of September 14, 1897, heralded the arrival on the 10th of the self-styled "mechanic in joints," an early advocate of the present-day practice of prompt postoperative ambulation. "I coax and manipulate the muscles," said the forty-three-year-old graduate of the Royal Veterinary College, who had studied "human anatomy under the best masters" in Paris. "I feel and know the exact amount of force which must be exerted to attain a certain end. I cannot further explain what is an instinctive feeling."

The celebrated manipulator's dedication had begun in his eighth year, when he watched Hutton, a famous bonesetter, bring relief to an injured gamekeeper on the parental estate at Milnthorpe in Westmorland. Not long after, he was himself a patient of this unauthorized healer, who gave him his first lesson in skeletology. Single-mindedness brought success: wealthy and titled sufferers as well as famous athletes found freedom from pain in Atkinson's Hamilton House Clinic on Park Lane, while he treated two- and four-footed cripples for moderate fees or gratis at St. Paul's House—otherwise known as "The Animals' Institute"—in South Kensington. "Now," the *Journal* of September 19 said reiteratively, he "has come to New York . . . prepared to make our lame millionaires [among them, by rumor, the self-made mercantile princeling, Charles Broadway Rouss] hop, skip and jump about the town"; and ventured the prophecy "that probably his arrival . . . will be the forerunner of a different style of footgear for the fair members of the Four Hundred," who wished their tortured "trilbies" restored to human semblance and maintained in serviceable loveliness. Reproduced are drawings of the Professor's powerful hands (his only "tools," as he termed them, for he used neither surgical instruments nor anesthetics), described as being "abnormally large and well developed . . . short and thick, the fingers stumpy at the ends, . . . [while] the muscles on the under side . . . stick out in great bumps." Some thought he bore a physical resemblance to A. Conan Doyle.

"Now Prof. Atkinson I recall very well," Mr. Byron wrote to me in 1955. "Who sent him to our studio I never knew but think it was W. R. Hearst for shortly after Hearst rented the Grand Opera House . . . for morning lectures and [a] sort of clinic where Prof. Atkinson had people come up on the stage and raised their arms above their heads though they . . . had not been able to do such for quite sometime, often years. We made eleven by fourteen photographs showing the doctor and the audience, but those prints are gone" (the "Photo-Drawing," signed by L. L. Roush, on the cover of *Leslie's Weekly*, October 14, 1897, would seem to be a secondhand survival). "When I first saw him in my father's office [then on the top floor of the Alpine Studios, 1286 Broadway], he was working on a little girl . . . who had a terribly swollen knee, she sat in my father's desk chair. Prof. Atkinson was a very big man way over six feet, quite heavy with muscle not fat . . . with the kindest of faces. He

347

rolled up his sleeves, got down on his knees and talked to that child till she felt here is a good friend . . . and in a few minutes he had that leg straightened out and she but a few days from complete recovery. Our studio was next to Marshall P. Wilder, humorist, his father was a doctor, they both stood by our door while Prof. Atkinson was attending another doctor that had been thrown from a horse twelve years before and had never been able to raise his arm . . . since. In little more time than it takes me to write this poor scribble of mine that job was done to the astonishment of the patient, the humorist and his doctor father."

Byron's plate and mind so often seem to have been equally sensitized, and the pages of the *New York Journal* confirm the complete synchronization of camera and memory. By September 22, this newspaper had done a complete volte-face, for at its behest "Wizard Atkinson" had consented to treat little Esther Novak's fractured ankle (which had defied more orthodox care) in his office at 16 West Thirty-third Street, and by the 25th his philanthropies were front page news. His letter to the Editor appears in two-column facsimile: "I shall be pleased to treat a limited number of patients free for the Journal, & to demonstrate my system to the Medical Profession on Saturday afternoon Sep 25ᵗʰ 1897." The seance was held at the Gramercy Lyceum, on Twenty-third Street, west of Sixth Avenue,

Professor John Atkinson, the English bonesetter, Fall of 1897

hired by the sponsoring sheet. A Lourdes-like procession—"such a gathering as has never been seen in this city before, pathetic beyond description," wrote Edward W. Townsend in the *Journal* of the 26th—passed across the stage at this and subsequent sessions held here, and later on, in October, at the Grand Opera House. Crutches were dramatically discarded; rigid limbs made pliable once more; shortened extremities lengthened, and signed statements of gratitude duly published in the exploiting gazette. While some doctors were inveigled as spectators and even as patients, others inveighed against unorthodoxy.

One of these clinics was described on the 28th: "Long before the hour set . . . the maimed and the halt began to congregate. . . . Some limped and hobbled; some leaned on canes and crutches; some were supported by friends; some were carried; there were feet and arms and hands grotesquely twisted. And in the eyes of every sufferer shone a pitiful light of eager hope. When Professor Atkinson arrived at the hall he first walked up and down the aisles to examine briefly the various cases. . . . Twenty of the most deserving patients were selected, and ranged in a semi-circular row on the platform, and when Professor Atkinson, in his shirt sleeves, stepped in front of them there was a hush of anticipation." Ignoring his own discomfort, for he had sustained an injury to his eye, the bonesetter labored for two and a half hours. "Stiff knees and ankles, twisted fingers and dislocated hips, came before him in a sad procession. In some of the cases there seemed to be a positive improvement of greater or less degree; some the Professor said at once were hopeless; some, he said could only be benefited by a long course of treatment. When . . . the Professor said that he could treat no more, the people who had not reached their turn were in despair. . . . 'Just me, just me!' wailed an old woman, dolorously. 'Just me!' cried a poor old man, hobbling on worn-out crutches. 'Just me!' wailed a little girl."

. . . . *Pre-eminently parexcellent*

"I AM POSITIVELY IT IN PAINLESS DENTISTRY." No exclamation point was necessary to heighten the effect of this 20-by-110 foot sign or William Beebe's other promotional phrases stressing the absence of agony that was his client's merciful gift to humanity in its inevitable passage from dentition to edentulousness. "THE WONDERFUL WIZARD OF PAINLESS DENTISTRY" had even been known to exhibit supposedly extracted false mastication aids to an open-mouthed patient, in persuasive endeavor to disprove the existence of anguish under his ministrations. Beebe—a graduate of circus press agentry, who undertook to promote Dr. Edgar Rudolph Randolph Parker—was the master of consonantal alliteration, with emphasis on the sixteenth letter of the alphabet: "PAINLESS PARKER, PRE-EMINENTLY PAR-EXCELLENT IN POSITIVELY PAINLESS PERFECTION OF PRACTICE" and "PECU-LIARLY PLEASING PARTICULAR PATIENTS AND PHILANTHROPICALLY PREDIS-POSED TO POPULAR PRICES" read two of his mural legends. It is hoped that none of the fastidious phalanx that frequented the parlors were prone to faltering patterns of pronunciation.

The apotheosis of this dental villain was colorfully undertaken during his earthly course by the team of Richard Donovan and Dwight Whitney in a tripartite profile published in *Collier's*, January 5, 12, and 19, 1952, under the title of "Painless Parker   Last of America's

Tooth-Plumbers." In 1948 Bob Hope, starring in *The Paleface* as "Painless Peter Potter," a borderland D.D.S., brought him to the screen in thin disguise. Such national magazines as *Life* and *Newsweek* reported his octogenarian end (which took place on November 8, 1952), while in pure *Time*-ese (issue of November 17) he was pigeonholed as "U. S. chain-store dentist."

It all began quite simply in the little town of Tynemouth Creek, New Brunswick, Canada, in 1872. After two abortive attempts at becoming a Doctor of Divinity, spaced on either side of a roving experience as a ship's cook, he worked his extracting way through the New York College of Dentistry and the Philadelphia Dental College, and during a summer's practice as an adjunct to a barber shop grossed 75¢ for professional services rendered to his home townsmen. With the corner druggist's aid, a local palliative he christened "hydrocain" was brought to the salvation of that overpoweringly large part of humanity ignorant of the epochal initial use (in 1844) of nitrous oxide in dental surgery, undergone at his own behest by Dr. Horace Wells, a Hartford dentist, and of that historic date—September 30, 1846—when William T. G. Morton, D.D.S., of Boston, first employed the vapor of ether as an anesthetic in tooth extraction and so revolutionized the conquest of pain. To his analgesia, the youthful Parker added vitriol, in the form of menacing sermons to music, on the subject of dental neglect and its tragic consequences. He carried his campaign through Maine towns and Canadian cities, even into the wilderness, and as far as Alaska and down to San Francisco, pursued by the hounds of professional orthodoxy and his own schizophrenic conscience, which almost to the end was torn between the desire to be an "ethical" and the tempting costumed melodrama of his own more lucrative methodology, carried on with the aid of a road show. So fascinated was he by the histrionic that what he earned by the forceps he lost by the buskin, appearing personally in a dramatic production entitled *The Lunatic Asylum*. When the end of its successful tour found him financially denuded by off-stage extravagances, he followed his family to Brooklyn and in 1895 started a reformed conventional practice in a one-room office, where his lonesome meditation was intercepted by the rent collector in the person of the aforementioned Beebe, who lured him Mephistophelesically into dental bypaths, billboarded and blatant. It was Beebe who persuaded him to drop his collection of given names in favor of the forthrightness of "Painless Parker," which adjectival handle became legally his in 1915. From the moment of the meeting of this uninhibited pair, practice—begun in the back of a horse-drawn "office" to the accompaniment of a performing troupe—while continuing al fresco, also turned indoors, and at the end of ten months required fourteen assistants, manning three chairs each, behind the façade here shown, with a mounting intake that reached $5,000 a day and led to the opening of five branch offices in Brooklyn, the appearance of the Parkerian signs on a five-borough basis and the upstate invasion of Albany and Troy. His ten years on the far side of the East River, punctuated by adverse publicity, malpractice suits, and audible antagonism on the part of his banded "ethical" colleagues, netted him almost a million dollars. A breakdown in 1905 caused him to migrate to California, where his beginning forties found him the proprietor of the largest dental chain-store business in the country, with a promotional circus as a feed line for the multiplying branches.

The quality of Dr. Parker's mercy extended to performing tigers and walruses, publicly relieved of their dental difficulties by his magic drill; and his artistic nature fought for

350

The establishment of "Painless Parker," about 1895
124 Flatbush Avenue, Brooklyn

expression in the application of richly engraved, smile-enhancing gold caps, and the insertion of diamonds in such resolute maws as that of "Fighting Bob" Fitzsimmons.

Forty-six years later, in 1951, licensed to practice in one-sixth of the States of the Union, with 78 dentists and 240 employees staffing his twenty-eight offices, the veteran "tooth tinker" who had done so much to educate the masses in the care and preservation of their molars was still brandishing the implements of his painlessness.

There were a pair of souvenirs of which this maverick among dentists was more than ordinarily proud: one, a damaged prop—the bullet-torn high hat perforated by an Alberta farmer's fury, made increasingly draughty by the swift passage of two Alaskan leads, and again an appropriate target in Medicine Hat; the other, a unique necklace composed of the 357 incisors, canines, bicuspids, and molars (in varying stages of cariousness and discoloration) he had extracted in the record course of his best day's work. As one of his signs told a credulous world, "THERE ARE PARKERS AND PARKERS But Only One PAINLESS PARKER."

351

Kings County Almshouse, 1900
Clarkson Street, in the Flatbush section of Brooklyn

"THE AMERICAN Atget!" I have heard photographers say, as they studied these Byron master-pieces, smiling their enthusiastic wonderment as the Frenchman's name—today, due to the efforts of Berenice Abbott, conjuresome in the history of Photography—came forth with the affectionate spontaneity that is part of true respect.

By 1900—when Atget, all unknown, was beginning his documentation of the people and of the city of Paris that he loved with his heart and caressed with his camera more than ten thousand times between 1898 and 1927—the Byrons had already taken an equal number of photographs of New York over a ten-year period: some by way of speculation; many on com-mission; almost all *con amore*. The Kings County Almshouse series has a mood apart in quiet pathos.

The Thirty-Second Annual Report of The State Board of Charities For the Year 1898 placed the "estimated weekly expense" per inmate at $2.71, while the inspection of February, 1900 (found in the 1899 summary) told what this pittance provided and the conditions masked by these tender Byron documents. A sixty-five-acre tract—with six acres under culti-vation, including a truck garden—was shared by the separate and distinct Kings County Hos-pital, the Long Island Hospital for the Insane, and the Almshouse. The female section of this refuge dated from 1850; the male accommodations, from 1869. The shabbily immaculate, cheerless dining halls—erratically heated, with their seven serried ranks of twenty-four-inch plank tables—made two sittings necessary. The inelastic dormitories were hopelessly over-crowded: "The consumptive, paralytic, blind, feeble-minded, ulcerous and other diseased inmates," herded with the "simply aged and infirm, and in some cases . . . able bodied," so that a hundred of the seven hundred men had to sleep on benches in the day room. On the date of the inspectors' visit a merciless downpour had driven all the denizens indoors, and this pathetic recreation area "was packed to its utmost capacity. Every bench was filled, and beside the seated men about 150 others were compelled to stand or move around the room, having no place to sit down. The men moved in a constant circle around and around, remind-ing one very much of the milling of cattle after a stampede." During the kinder months, the physically less unfit were set to work on the rock pile, breaking stones, while others (as here shown) enjoyed the dubious result of the landscaping so roseately described in the Annual Report of the Department of Charities and Corrections of Kings County, N. Y. For The Year ending July 31, 1897: "The entire grounds about the buildings have been beautifully laid out, and ample walks built and shrubbery of various kinds planted. A large number of settees have been provided, and the old women of the Almshouse are permitted to roam about in the park or rest themselves as they choose."

"DOROTHY, DOES YOUR MOTHER BELONG TO THE DAUGHTERS OF THE REVOLUTION?"

The little girl lost in the large wing chair looked up from the big book and answered the lady with the lorgnette: "NO; I THINK SHE BELONGS TO THE CONTINENTAL DAMS."

A James Montgomery Flagg cartoon so captioned appeared in *Life* on November 24, 1904, but the social situation it mirrored was not neoteric. In 1896 Mrs. Burton Harrison, in her chapter on "Externals of Modern New York" (in *History Of The City Of New York*, By Mrs. Martha J. Lamb and Mrs. Burton Harrison, New York, 1896) explained the trend that mayflowered into Grant-Woodeness: "Significant features of the life of to-day are the marked expression of the taste for genealogical research, the study by New Yorkers of Americana and of their own forebears, and their desire to perpetuate the memory of the deeds and virtues of the founders of the Republic, which have given birth to many patriotic societies. The Sons of the Society of the Cincinnati are first by right of historical distinction; after them the Sons of the Revolution, the Sons of the American Revolution, the Holland Society, Ohio Society, Mayflower Descendants, Daughters and Sons of 1812, New England Society, Southern Society, Society of Colonial Wars, the Colonial Dames of New York, the Colonial Dames of America, and the Daughters of the Revolution fall into line."

Somehow, Mrs. Harrison omitted mention of the Daughters of the American Revolution, here shown in determined but undocumented meeting. This photograph has been scrutinized by many present day "Daughters of the Annual Rumpus," as they call themselves in moments of affectionate self-examination, but after transported identification of pinship all recognition fades—no cousins or sisters or aunts or grandmothers or great-grandmothers these. That they are indigenous to Manhattan's subsoil Mr. Byron guarantees, and their 1899 appearance in *The New Metropolis* (though with the erroneous caption "Daughters of the Revolution") places them directly in our midst.

The New York City Chapter, D. A. R.—known as the "Mother of Chapters" because of its local primacy in the National Society—received official sanction on October 11, 1890 (the birth date of the parent organization) and was formally organized on April 19, 1891. Its first Regent, Mrs. Roger A. Pryor, was succeeded by Mrs. Donald McLean in 1895, and her incumbency, interrupted only by the call to the President Generalcy (1905–1909), continued until her death in 1916.

We shall attend one meeting only—that of January 5, 1901, by courtesy of the *New-York Daily Tribune* of the 7th: " 'Duchess of the D. A. R.-lings' is the new title which has been bestowed by a prominent Southern jurist on Mrs. Donald McLean, regent of the New-York City Chapter of the Daughters of the American Revolution. Mrs. McLean made the announcement of the new honor at the celebration of the anniversary of Washington's wedding day, held at Sherry's on Saturday afternoon. She stated that to her it is the proudest of titles, because the society of the Daughters is the purest, truest, finest organization of women in existence."

354

THE FOLLOWING identifications (from left to right, omitting the first at the left) were made by Miss Rose Schneiderman, in a letter of January 18, 1956: "2 Violet Pike a graduate from Vassar College in 1909 and volunteered her services when the Strike began. Violet was a lovely young woman and came from a very nice family—not rich but comfortable. She served on the publicity com. 3 Miss Helen Marot Secretary of the League and a very able one at that. She was a believer in Trade Unionism and worked very hard throughout the Strike. 4 is Allis Bean a young English girl who was a stenographer. I do not recognize #5. Number 6 is myself. Part time organizer and vice president for the League but during the duration of the strike I gave all my time on part time pay. Seven and 8 I do not recollect. There were so many volunteers at the time. . . . 9 [standing behind desk] is Elisabeth Dutcher also a Vassar grad came from a very Conservative family and who had taken up Social work but quit her job and gave all her time to the strike as Chairman of the publicity com. 10 Leonora O'Reilly who was a shirtmaker in her youth had joined the Knights of Labor and was a devoted trade unionist. Was one of the founders of Manhattan Trade School for girls and taught power machine operating. She was a founder of the New York League. She was the greatest woman Orator of her time. Next to advancing Trade union organization of working women she was also very active in the suffrage movement. . . . 11 . . . is a young volunteer by name of Gladys La Fetra."

"Ha, ha, ha! that's a joke. By Jove, it is. I'm a striker." Dated November 23, 1909, this is the opening entry in *The Diary of a Shirtwaist Striker* by Theresa Serber Malkiel (1873–1949). Mrs. Malkiel and her husband, an eminent lawyer, were among the founders of the *New York Daily Call;* she was a member of the Socialist Party, an ardent advocate of women's suffrage, and later an authority on naturalization and adult education. In this all but forgotten cry of the cause (a ninety-six page book, published in 1910) Mrs. Malkiel injected herself into the inmost reaches of her heroine—Mary, just past twenty during the tormented days of the "Uprising of the 20,000"—and by projection told the story of this first of a series of strikes in the garment industry. The factualized fiction (following the newspaper reportage with almost complete fidelity) was based on the author's experience as one of the volunteers working side by side with the underpaid, overworked girls in their struggle for amelioration. The Mary of the Diary continued: "I must say I really don't know why I became . . . [a striker]—I went down just because everybody else in the workroom did. They did try to explain it all to us girls, but all I could make out from the woman's speech was when she raised her eyes to the ceiling and exclaimed, like they do on the stage: 'Sisters, mine, we are all with you!'—the lot of good it'll do us. Oh, pshaw, if one was to believe all they tell you down there! The idea of their telling us that us girls are nothin' but slaves. Perhaps they are, but not I. I'm a free-born American, I am. Some of them speakers look too silly for anything, especially that one with the long bushy hair. An' the way he screamed at the top of his voice, one would think that the house is on fire. I wonder if it hurts him—this strike does? I guess Jim [with whom she is keeping company] wouldn't mind my being a striker if he knew what fun I'm getting out of it. . . . I can just hear him call me an anarchist. And yet, it's a good thing, this strike is; it makes you feel like a real grown-up person. . . . I simply can't get over the way little Ray Goldovsky jumped on a chair and suddenly, without a minute's notice, stopped the electricity. I must say, it's nothing but her bravery that took us all. Why, we were simply stunned. And Mr. Hayman, [the employer] too, was taken off his feet. Before you could say Jack Robinson we all rose, slipped on our duds and marched down the stairs, shouting, yelling and giggling about our walkout, as they called it. . . . What in the world do I want with a union [the Ladies' Shirt Waist

Headquarters of the Women's Trade Union League of New
York, January, 1910
43 East Twenty-second Street
During the Shirt Waist Strike (November 22, 1909–February
15, 1910)

Makers' Union of New York City]? . . . The only thing that keeps me with them is that it may help those poor devils who have to work for three and four dollars a week. It's but very few of the girls that make such wages as I do.

"November 24.—Well, well, I think this strike is a more serious business than I thought, otherwise the papers wouldn't make so much of it. . . . It really feels good to be somebody. . . . Why, the Vanderbilts themselves ain't in it any more—the people are too busy with us. . . .

"November 26.—How some people do contradict themselves. Here's Mr. Hayman furious because the girls have made up their minds to form a union. And what does he do but go to work and organize one himself [a reference to the Associated Waist and Dress Manufacturers]. . . . I think I'll try my hand at picketing tomorrow. It ain't only our girls that are out doing that job, there is a lot of college women, members of the Woman's Trade Union League, who spend their days watching our factories. And a fine lot of women they are at that." (The League was founded in 1903—along the lines of its thirty-year-old English prototype—". . . to assist in the organization of women wage workers into trade unions." Included in the gallant band were Mary E. Dreier, President of the New York League; Mrs. Henry Morgenthau; Lillian D. Wald, forever of Henry Street; Carola Woerishoffer, Treasurer; Bertha Poole Weyl; Ida M. Tarbell, "muckraker" par excellence; Mrs. Mary K. Simkhovitch of Greenwich House fame; Helen Marot; and a host of others, together with such workers as Leonora O'Reilly, Rose Schneiderman, and Ida Rauh.) "I've come to know quite a number of them. What sets me a thinking is the fact that these women could go on living to their heart's content. They needn't come downtown among us if they don't want to, and why should they do it? It can't be for the sake of what's in it, for there ain't much fun in standing around the bleak, cold corners, being arrested by the cops and taken to the station house and police court. . . . I must admit the league women are the goodest of the good. And the Woman's Trade Union League in general is a mighty good thing for us girls. . . .

"November 30.—This morning I had to go and see the Mayor [McClellan]. . . . True enough, he was as sweet as pie to us. But I'm sure that's where it will all end. . . . What galls me most is this constant cry—that girls shouldn't be striking. . . .

"December 3.—. . . we've had one of the finest parades I ever saw [organized by the League workers]. We went to the Mayor's office, but—to tell the truth—it wasn't so much for what the Mayor may do for us as to let the people see for themselves of whom this strike is made up—mostly children more fit for the school room than the shop. . . . About half-past 1 there were ten thousand girls in line ready to tell the boss of the City Hall . . . that they're willing to work, provided they are paid enough to make an honest living. . . . Of course, it was just as I thought it would be—the Mayor accepted our committee, listened to its tale of woe, shook his head and promised to look into the matter. I guess he is as bad as the cops. . . .

"December 4.—. . . Stopped on the square this afternoon and listened to them that talks votes for women [at this time Mrs. Rose Pastor Stokes was arguing at various strikers' meetings that the question of women's suffrage was ". . . of greater importance . . ." than winning the strike, while other prominent suffragettes too injected this issue]. It's all very true. I also say that a woman is every bit as good as a man and should have the same rights with him. But us girls have something else to think of just now. We must see to it that we win the strike for bread and then we can start one for the ballot. . . .

"December 5.—Lord! I never saw anything like it in my life—that Hippodrome meeting [financed by Mrs. O. H. P. Belmont]. . . . It is really a wonderful feeling that comes over one when a body finds itself surrounded by thousands of people all assembled for the same purpose . . . it's like an immense giant born for the purpose of doing justice to all. . . .

"December 6.—Lord! My nerves are all on edge, but I'm glad that I read the law to her. The scab on the body, as a rule, comes from hunger and privation, but with Mame [a former intimate] it is nothing but a case of sheer cussedness. She's just a mean, vile, paltry scab from scabby land! . . .

"December 7.—. . . And now I'm a real striker—felt the grip of a policeman's hand, had a free ride in a patrol wagon, spent a few hours at the police station and was arraigned in court. . . . Now I always thought that a court house was a magnificent place. . . . But what a sad disappointment—the place they brought us to wasn't much better than the station house. The judge looked as though he had been out on a spree. The lawyers—a lot of cheap guys that you see hanging around the corner saloons. And the audience—well, they beat it all!

"December 17.—[The Women's Trade Union League brought Mary to the fashionable Colony Club, at the invitation of Mrs. Egerton Winthrop, Miss Elisabeth Marbury, and Miss Anne Morgan] to hear about our misery. To tell the truth, I've no appetite to tell it to them, for I've almost come to the conclusion that the gulf between us girls and these rich ladies is too deep to be smoothed over by a few paltry dollars. . . . The women gave us a thousand dollars [the *New-York Daily Tribune* reported that $1,300 poured into the baskets passed by Mrs. Philip Lydig and Miss Elsie de Wolfe], but what does this amount to? Not even a quarter apiece for each striker. . . . Can't the working people realize that we are at the complete mercy of selfishness and greed? I did to-day when I was brought face to face with all those riches; if they'd know what's good for them they wouldn't bring us in their midst, for, if anything will, this is sure to arouse the spirit of rebellion. I know it did in me. I felt sore for the rest of the day. . . .

"December 20.—Lord! I do wish they'd stop to muddle us girls with their attempts of settlement. . . .

"December 31.—A human sandwich! Yes, that's precisely what I was today. . . . It seems to me that everybody ought to be willing to do what's right and that's just why I pinned on my chest and back those two large posters [an idea emanating from the Women's Trade Union League, whose members joined in this demonstration], picked up a bundle of Calls . . . and promenaded up and down Twenty-third street for more than two hours. . . . 'How vulgar,' murmured a lady coming out from one of the stores. She was dressed to kill and under her arm she carried a little puppy. . . . I think it's more than vulgar, in fact, criminal, to pay thousands for little puppies . . . and surround them with all sorts of comforts, while thousands of little children are dying for want of proper care. . . . There wasn't a person . . . but stopped long enough to read the poster and that's just what I wanted. . . .

"January 23 [1910]—. . . All hail to us girls—we got what we wanted—Mr. Hayman had to sign the agreement after all. . . . Well, well, he made me think of the animals at the circus—jumped and kicked and gnawed his teeth to the very last moment—but us girls had the strong whip over him—he must send out his orders and pride must go. Ours went long ago—we needed bread to keep up our life."

Omitted from the Diary is mention of a cherished contribution to the cause—an epigram by George Bernard Shaw. Elisabeth Dutcher (of the Women's Trade Union League of New York and appearing on this photograph) had sent him the cabled account of a police court colloquy between Magistrate Olmstead and a striker testifying against a scab:

The Magistrate: Are you at work?

Striker: Not now; we're on strike.

The Magistrate: I know you are, you are on strike against God and Nature, whose prime law it is that man shall earn his bread in the sweat of his brow. You are on strike against God.

Back across the ocean ricochetted the retort Shavian: "Delightful. Medieval America always in the intimate personal confidence of the Almighty."

. . . . *So sober, so thorough, and so far-reaching*

"I AM a firm believer in the usefulness of women's clubs." This was the tenet of Randolph Guggenheimer, civic-minded lawyer, President of the Municipal Assembly and several times acting mayor of New York during the Van Wyck administration of 1898–1901. His championing article was featured in *The New York Herald*'s two-page spread of October 22, 1900, "Busy Days Are These For The Club Women of America," who—after summer surcease —were preparing for the nation-wide November "Conventions, Councils, And Assemblies" at which "Delegations Representing Over A Million Women Will Discuss Questions Of Interest To Their Sex." Mr. Guggenheimer needed no introduction to the ladies, for he had been "a great lion among the clubs last year," and was "one man among the many who can see good in women's clubs." There were those who based their objections on the fact that "women do not go into club life as men do—for pleasure—but make such a task of it that it is enervating instead of being restful." Mr. Guggenheimer saw virtue in the stimulus: "The limited knowledge which I possess of women's clubs . . . leads me to believe that there is a higher ideal among the members of such clubs [than in the masculine fellowships] and that the primary object of such associations is mental development. No other result can flow from the discussions and from the preparation of essays on literature, science and art, which are, in all women's clubs, the object and reason of their existence. They are provocative of study, and tend to destroy the spirit of isolation and of insularity which has, in the past, made women a mere aggregation of separate and mutually antagonistic units. Women's clubs serve to unite women upon a common platform of protest against all social wrongs and inequalities. They will not reach the proper level of club usefulness unless they stand for the protection of their sex and its eligibility, I shall not say for the political arena, but for all business and professional opportunities."

A young organization in the very center of the proscribed palaestra had received a special salute in the *Herald*'s over-all picture: "The League for Political Education is perhaps one of the most interesting and instructive clubs in the city." To become The Town Hall, Inc., in 1937, this vital influence grew out of a question posed and an answer given on November

16, 1894, at 433 Fifth Avenue, the home of Mrs. Henry M. Sanders. Six ladies had met there to discuss the reason for the previous spring defeat of a proposed New York State constitu-

A meeting of The League for Political Education, 1899
Thought to be in the Berkeley Lyceum, 23 West Forty-fourth
Street

tional amendment designed to give women the ballot. The half dozen were unanimous in diagnosing the causative factor as political ignorance, and they forthwith organized The League for Political Education, drafting their hostess—forceful spouse of a leading clergyman—as reluctant President. The other members of the resolute coterie were brilliantly distinguished on varied planes of endeavor. The first vice president, Catherine A. P. Abbe, wife of the prominent surgeon Robert Abbe, was the founder of the City History Club; the second vice president, Lucia Gilbert (Mrs. Cornelius A.) Runkle, pioneer among women editorial writers, serving the *New-York Daily Tribune*, was rated "one of the most cultivated [of her sex] in America"; Adele M. Fielde, the recording secretary, had seen ten years of missionary service in China (1865–1875) and upon her return espoused the feminist movement; Dr. Mary Putnam Jacobi, corresponding secretary, gained high distinction in the joint practice of medicine with her husband, Dr. Abraham Jacobi; and Lee Wood Haggin, the treasurer, was the mother of the artist and scene designer Ben Ali Haggin.

In January, 1895, the first of a thousand and one lectures—"Some Duties of the Citizen"—was given by Professor Franklin H. Giddings of Columbia in Mrs. Sanders's drawing room, and early in that year, too, the League found its first permanent headquarters, a general office and a lecture room with a seating capacity of about 75, in the Berkeley Lyceum Building at 23 West Forty-fourth Street—space presently augmented by the rental of various auditoriums

March 3, 1895 was a prideful day. *The New-York Times*, under the headline "A Remarkable Organization," spoke of growing activity: "The League for Political Education is one of the most noteworthy embodiments of the remarkable interest which intelligent women are now manifesting in the study of our national, State, and municipal institutions. Although it has existed but a few weeks [error for months], it has already a membership of between 100 and 200, and the list is rapidly increasing. The membership fee is $2, and the members pledge themselves to devote whatever time and thought they are able to give to an understanding of politics, using the word in its broadest sense, as comprehending the art and science of government, as well as the specific workings of political methods. The organization is planned somewhat after the famous Sunday School Association pattern. In every Assembly district of the city, and by degrees in every Assembly district throughout the State, it is hoped to establish one or more 'Circles' for study, Fisk's Manual of Civil Government [*Civil Government in the United States*, 1891] being the text-book employed. Each 'Circle' is to be led by some woman . . . willing to qualify herself for this work by special preparation. Once a month each 'Circle' is to report its progressive methods at a general meeting of the league." After mentioning Professor Giddings's address, the *Times* went on to describe the dynamic programme: "At another [general meeting] Dean Smith of Barnard College spoke on the stimulation of thought which political activity aroused in the early Greek democracies. These general meetings are intended to kindle interest in all phases of politics. Other subjects to be considered are 'Individualism and Socialism,' 'The Single Tax' [the theory promulgated by Henry George], 'Proportional Representation,' 'A Municipal Party,' and others. Classes for study are also held at the league rooms, under the leadership of competent instructors. On Fridays, Miss Fielde has a large and hard-working class in the study of municipal affairs. On Thursdays, Miss Virginia Dangerfield, a recent graduate from the New-York Law School, gives a course of lectures on 'Married Women's Property Rights,' the 'Rights of Minors,' and similar subjects. Probably the most successful of these morning classes, however, has been Mrs. Runkle's, in civil government. . . . Her talks deal with principles as well as with methods, and are so enriched with illustrations from history and literature as to be as entertaining as they are valuable. She has been asked to repeat the course. . . . Like Lord Bacon, this energetic League . . . 'takes all knowledge to be its province.' . . . So many applications for tickets [to a Saturday series by Austin Abbott, Dean of the Faculty of the New-York University Law School, on "Sociology and Law," "Marriage," "Husband and Wife" and "Wealth and the Family"] have already been made that the league, finding its own rooms too small, has secured the hall of the Academy of Medicine [17 West Forty-third Street]."

In the winter of 1895, and for the three seasons following, a brilliant course by John Graham Brooks of Cambridge brought the League to the fore. At his instigation in 1899 (the year of the earnest rainy day conclave here depicted by Byron) Robert Erskine Ely—co-founder with Professor Francis G. Peabody of the Prospect Union, Harvard's unofficial university extension school, which he headed for ten years—was invited to give a series of lectures. He became part time executive officer of the League and, in 1901, its executive director, a post he was to occupy until April, 1937. Under his guidance the prediction made at the end of *The New-York Times* article already quoted came to be an ever-living reality: "Work of the kind which these women of the league are doing, so sober, so thorough, and so far-reaching, is not only entitled to the sincere respect of the community, but it as well lays an obligation of gratitude upon it. It is making an intelligent, conscientious public opinion, which will show itself an operative force in the politics of the near future."

. . . . Too innocent to know, too troubled to care

"UP TO a comparatively recent time it has been a justified boast that pure womanhood was its own sufficient protection anywhere in the United States." This statement appeared in the Second Annual Report of the Travelers' aid Society . . . For the Year Ending May 1, 1907. It went on to review the social mutations which were the *raison d'être* of the organization Grace Hoadley Dodge founded and fostered: "The belief is still held by many who do not realize how rapidly American conditions have changed in the last twenty-five years. The enormous influx from countries where freedom of women is unknown except as license, the changes in economic conditions that have brought millions of girls from the shelter of home into the dangerous independence of the factory, the shop, or the office, and the general relaxation of standards accompanying a growing cosmopolitanism, have worked together to make it unhappily true that a girl's innocence, instead of being her safeguard, may prove to be her worst enemy. Besides this problem of the native-born, there is another of the foreign girls who come here by the hundred-thousand . . . largely ignorant of the language, always ignorant of conditions under which they will live, too ignorant even to know of the existence of institutions that if appealed to in time might save them from the final depth. They form the natural prey of the procuress and the cadet, as well as of the army of minor parasites who live by one sort or another of extortion from the weak and the unwary. Whatever the operating causes may be, the number of women and even of children who 'drop out,' is constantly increasing. . . . In New York City especially, there is a leakage of human careers, if not of human life, steadily going on." This analysis anticipated a slender book published in 1911, *The Girl That Disappears The Real Facts About The White Slave Traffic,* by General Theodore A. Bingham, New York's Police Commissioner from 1906 to 1909, during the period when the agitation against the *Traite des Blanches* was rising to a crescendo of moral indignation, sometimes righteous and well intentioned, sometimes as prurient as the evil involved. One therapeutic measure was the Mann Act, passed on June 25, 1910. Grace Dodge and her associates faced the issue full-armed and four-squarely: "One of the great objects of organized charity is to stop this leak, and the formation of a Travelers' Aid Society shows that it has realized that stations and docks offer very exceptional opportunities for doing it. With many girls, a great [railway] station is their first point of contact with a larger world. . . . [In the terminal] a hundred things happen that dispose a girl to accept and profit by help or advice that she would otherwise be apt to reject. And what makes it imperative that we should not let this chance slip, is the fact that if we do, others will seize it. . . . This is one of the cases where it is necessary to go into the arena with the enemies of society, and defeat them upon their own ground."

Office of the Travelers' Aid Society, 1909
238 East Forty-eighth Street

Efforts in this direction had been made as early as the fall of 1888, when the "Flower and Fruit Mission to the New York Hospital" initiated a counselling service on the docks, which about a decade later became the province of the "Female Auxiliary Bible Society." For years Miss Dodge had bandied the question of protecting the itinerant stranger, and in 1905 she marshaled a sympathetic group of women to study the problem, with the happy result that the Travelers' Aid Committee of New York City was founded on May 1, 1905, and incorporated under the laws of the State of New York as the Travelers' Aid Society on January 25, 1907. "I can see almost unlimited possibilities," she said in about 1912 or 1913, "once you get your brain properly filled with what Travelers' Aid ought to do and to be." During the first half century of its existence, more than 16,000,000 bewildered people of both sexes and all ages were defended by the growing charity she envisioned.

Active work began in July, 1905. In the ensuing ten months 799 women and children were guided from the Grand Central and Pennsylvania depots "to some definite destination," while more than twice that number received aid within the stations. Before long the "Female Auxiliary Bible Society" transferred its dockside duties to the new nonsectarian organization, at first staffed by volunteers, whose efforts were supplemented by three paid workers in the spring of 1906. This gradually augmenting professional force—at least bilingual —was obliged to unravel the ragged sleeve of the traveler's care, make referrals to cooperating agencies, and maintain a complete set of reports and cross-referenced records, concluding with the entry of the homing follow-up postal pressed into the hand of each succored client. From the first, the Society integrated its work with that of similar organizations on a country-wide and international basis. The figures for the year ending May 1, 1907 (when receipts totaled $13,095.33 and disbursements stood at $8,635.93) tell an impressive story of assistance to 1,557 persons in the two major terminals, while the three dock agents aided 1,540 arrivals on 542 incoming ships. In 1908 there were fifteen workers on the pay roll, with a case load of 6,726. Touching evidence of the warm nature of the service lies in the fact that the station porters often refused tips for transporting baggage.

From 1907 to 1914, the Society occupied a high-stooped brownstone at 238 East Forty-eighth Street, and here the Byron Company came to take a set of photographs (of which this is one) to illustrate the Fourth Annual Report, for the year ending with the close of 1909. The busy house (where one double room was set aside for emergency occupancy by "stranded, but not of necessity, destitute women and girls") partook of the nature of a settlement, for most of the agents were resident. Wearing what remained the official badge until 1923—"a white enamel shield bearing the name of the Society and a representation of the Travelers' Palm which grows in the desert and gives shade and water to weary travelers"—these early workers pioneered in the always present task of giving aid to way-farers "too innocent to know, and . . . too troubled to care."

. . . . That young lady will make a scholar

"IN THIS metropolis a woman could obtain the gratification of every want, wish or whim save one—she could not get an education." This observation, made by Dr. Arthur Brooks, Rector of the Church of the Incarnation, at the time Frederick Augustus Porter Barnard became the tenth President of Columbia College in 1864, held pertinency until Barnard College opened the door of its four-story brownstone beginning at 343 Madison Avenue on Monday October 7, 1889. Prior to this emancipatory date, only the Normal College (founded in 1870 as an affiliate of the free City College, and known as Hunter College since 1914) offered training to women as teachers, without benefit of a degree, and even the private schools for girls were not on a parity with those that prepared boys for the advanced learning locally denied their sisters. Dr. Barnard had championed "equal opportunity in higher education for both sexes" from the outset of his pedagogical career, and long after the subject was first formally brought before the Trustees of Columbia in 1879, he had to combat such primitive superstitions as the inability of the frail feminine organism and the delicately constituted female encephalon to withstand the rigors of academic life. On June 8, 1883 the Board finally capitulated to the extent of endorsing a "Collegiate Course for Women" under such terms that one of the students, Annie Nathan, upon becoming the wife of Dr. Alfred Meyer, abandoned her scholastic pursuits to battle for the creation of a real college. The victory came in 1888, when the Trustees were prevailed upon to establish a separate annex, and a year later, following the death of Dr. Barnard, the State of New York granted a charter to the institution bearing his name. In June, 1893, degrees were awarded to the eight candidates of the first graduating class, and the little college had already outgrown its birthplace. A desperate fund-raising campaign was instituted to make possible the move to Morningside Heights, in which direction Columbia—to assume the dignity of a university in 1896—was already headed.

One of the later features of this long continued, intensified drive was a "garden party, flower sale and concert" held on May 13, 1896 under the sponsorship of the fifteen members of the Alumnae Association in the 100-foot square gardens maintained at Nos. 3 to 9 East Thirty-seventh Street by Mrs. L. P. Avery, Mrs. A. A. Anderson (née Elizabeth Milbank— one of Barnard's great benefactresses), and Mrs. Jacob Wendell, whose Thirty-eighth Street houses backed on this hidden park, with its fountains and statuary. Six or seven booths for the sale of a profusion of spring blossoms and nosegays and refreshments were decked with the blue and white of Barnard and Columbia, heightened by the more vivid hue of Yale, whose Glee and Banjo Clubs gave afternoon and evening performances from a central pagoda festooned with myriads of colored lights. The red-coated Hungarian Band played beneath the branches of a great tree, and ropes of Japanese lanterns made bright the festivities that added several thousand dollars to the coffers, providing for the decoration and equipment of the Ella Weed Library in Milbank Hall.

366

Preparations for a Garden Party to benefit Barnard College,
May 13, 1896
Held in an enclosure on East Thirty-seventh Street, just off
Fifth Avenue

Among the undergraduate attendants in charge of the floral booths was a Freshman, destined—as Dean of Barnard College from 1911 until 1947—to bear out the solid prognostication of Jimmy, the colored boy presiding over the front door of 343 Madison Avenue. "I think that young lady will make a scholar," he said, as he turned an approbative eye on the bulletin board resplendent with an unblemished row of midyear A's following the name of Virginia C. Gildersleeve.

COOKING CAME under the category of ammunition in Jacob A. Riis' war, *The Battle with the Slum* (New York, 1902)—"the only kind of temperance preaching that counts for anything in a school course," he declared it.

The skillet as a factor in the fight had long since figured in the thinking of a group of "wealthy and large-hearted women, residents of New York," who had—so *The Illustrated American* of January 10, 1891, tells in four-page laudation—"Very keenly . . . observed the unfortunate condition of domestic affairs in the tenement districts," and concluded that "a larger share of the discontent and general uncomfortableness of life prevailing in these big families of limited means arose, first, from the disorderliness of the home, and . . . from the uninviting arrangement and preparation of that most important family feast, the daily dinner. . . . How could a wife be taught," they pondered, that "the most potent weapon . . . by which she might guard against the temptations toward vices that are ever open to her hard-working helpmeet lay in the careful direction of his household, and the economical, wholesome, yet dainty arrangement of the table to which, three times a day, he sat opposite her to fare—well or ill?" And so, in 1878, the New York Cooking School was organized in rented quarters at 35 East Seventeenth Street for the free instruction of girls from twelve to seventeen, eager "to perfect . . . [themselves] in a household art 'tis not beneath the dignity of any woman to understand and practise." After a fluctuating early course, and temporary suspension in 1885, the project was reactivated in a "solid, brown-faced old pile" at 28 Lafayette Place, where "at four o'clock of any Wednesday or Friday afternoon" classes were conducted in two "cheery kitchens" on the second floor, for "Little girls from every section of the city . . . from Harlem and from Mulberry Street—usually the attendants of the public schools, and therefore by no means ignoramuses, plainly but always neatly dressed, politely mannered, and deeply interested in the contents of their pots and pans." Here they were indoctrinated in "Marketing and the purchasing of groceries, dish-washing, sweeping, paint-scrubbing, pot-cleaning, fire-building, and stove-polishing . . . along with the mere cooking." More advanced instruction for "Girls in their teens" consisted of orientation in "the innumerable kitchen phenomena of which few even accomplished *cuisinières* can give an explanation." Evening sessions were held "for young women busy all day in shops and factories," in preparation for the time "when they will be installed mistress of some cosey apartment home"; and married wage-earners, too, were brought in by hard-working husbands, for courses at fees in proportion to their purses. A nine-months' internship was arranged for "four or six young girls," who "In rustling seersucker gowns, white aprons and caps . . . step about the house, learning to perform faithfully and well all the manifold duties required of accomplished maids in private houses." Lectures and demonstrations were given to "circles of ladies" and girls from finishing schools desirous of understanding, as one "wise mother" explained, "the duties some day their own servants

The New York Cooking School, 1903; in the United Charities Building,
105 East Twenty-second Street

must perform, that they may direct with discretion the *ménages* confided to their care."
Professional cooks, too, received "special instruction," and nurses (many of whom later
became dietitians) from Bellevue, Mount Sinai, and other hospitals, were taught "the
decoction of wholesome, delicate sick-dinners" by the competent faculty of "soft-voiced
gentlewomen . . . models of all sweet virtues worthy of emulating." In addition, extramural
missionary work was carried on. In 1890, "over nine hundred women profited by the advantages offered" at a modest fee; and "from the public, that gains incalculable benefits by
the noble charity carried so bravely on from year to year, a mead of heartfelt thanks is
due to the school's able, benevolent president, Mrs. Theodore Bronson, and her assistant
officers, who count no effort lost or unworthy when benefit accrues to the great working
world and its humbler members."

From 1892 until 1916 the school was housed in the United Charities Building, 105 East
Twenty-second Street, from whence it moved to 158 East Sixty-first Street, disappearing
with a concluding flourish of the pan after the publication of the 1925 city directory.

To borrow a period-piece phrase coined and classicized but disclaimed by the controversial
one-time Chief of Police William S. Devery, "touchin' on an' appertainin' to" this culinary

369

college at the time it is here shown, *The New York Herald* of April 12, 1903 obliges with a Byron-illustrated article stressing an innovation, "The Favored to Carry Gospel": "The cooking school intends to ask the fashionable young women of New York to snatch an hour between teas to learn how to cook a poor man's dinner. They will be expected to miss a ten course luncheon or a dinner party . . . in order to explain to some uninstructed young working women who are about to marry the comparative nutritive value of sweet and round potatoes. They who have always considered marketing . . . an occupation within the province of the cook or the housekeeper, will now be requested to lay out to the best advantage the meagre sum which suffices for a tenement house meal. . . . During the winter months the cooking school [at this period under the superintendence of Miss Emily Huntington, long affiliated with local beneficent activities] is a great hive of industry, where children, mission workers, working girls, cooks, small boys, young men [embroiled in the "chafing dish craze"] and women of society alike devote themselves to the science of pots and pans. . . . The classes from which the school derives its greatest revenue, which enables it to offer instruction free or at nominal rates to persons of small means, are those to which fashionable young girls belong. These are made up by the young women themselves, who invite only personal friends to join them, in order that they may be congenial and may have much the same social engagements, so that they will be able to meet during the same hours."

. . . . *The last desperate sale of children*

In 1899–1901 one of the great famines in history lacerated India, with apocalyptic accompaniment of drought, earthquake and plague, the breaking-up of families and even the last desperate sale of children by starving parents, as jackals preyed on corpses everywhere. By January, 1900, it was estimated that about 22,000,000 people in the British territory and 27,000,000 in the Native States were catastrophically involved. Half-hidden accounts of horror were overshadowed by the more novel sensationalism of Boer War tidings, and the government-instituted work relief in the form of the building of roads and irrigation canals proved miserably inadequate.

The appeals of the *Christian Herald* of New York (a leading religious magazine first issued here in 1878 and in existence today) evoked a characteristic response, and by the spring of 1900 more than $130,000 had been cabled to India. Negotiations were completed with the British government empowering the United States to charter a vessel in behalf of the periodical, for the transportation of a record-breaking cargo of 200,000 bushels of corn and a quantity of seeds to the emergency area. On May 11, shortly after sundown, the *Quito* set sail from Pier 1, North River, loaded to the decks with life-giving, hope-bringing sustenance. The *New-York Daily Tribune* of the 16th of September told of her reception in Bombay, where this gesture "of pure philanthropy, by people living thousands of miles away, across three seas, . . . moved the hearts [of suffering Indians] . . . as a thousand sermons would not have done."

American Aid for India, 1900

"WE, WHO are privileged to live in the closing years of the nineteenth century, are for ever telling ourselves what a magnificent age it is; and we never weary of hearing and repeating the count of our numbers, our wealth, and our wisdom," reads an editorial in the *Scientific American* of May 23, 1896. "In the midst of this general advance, and in some measure as the result of it, the student of social economics can detect here and there the signs of a decided retrogression. . . . There was a time in this country when the entrance door into every trade was strictly guarded, and the boy who aspired to the dignity of being ranked as a journeyman carpenter, machinist, or builder could only hope to do so by becoming bound in an apprenticeship of greater or less duration. . . . But to-day as the French would say, 'we have changed all that.' Apprenticeship is no longer the invariable rule—it is the rare exception. . . . Under the present system . . . the boy helpers . . . are engaged to do menial labor, and it is only in rare cases of emergency that they get an opportunity to try their hand at a more important class of work. A 'green' hand in a machine shop is never regarded as a pupil. . . . But if the old system . . . is impracticable to-day, and the methods of to-day are so faulty, what . . . is to be the remedy? We think that it will be found in an arrangement which shall embody the best features of both systems . . . supplemented by that admirable institution known as the trade school. . . . If the American boy is to have any chance of holding his own against the incoming tide of skilled foreign labor, some radical change must be made in existing conditions."

An article in the *New-York Daily Tribune* of June 15, 1902, stated: "Almost the only manufactory about New-York which follows out old apprenticeship lines is the big one in Grand-st. which makes printing presses. The system [still in modified operation, and initiated about 1858 by "Colonel" Richard March Hoe, son of the English-born Robert, who with the Smith Brothers, founded the firm of R. Hoe & Co. in 1805] has been in vogue there for thirty-five or forty years, and with the growth of the factory the number of apprentices has increased until there are now three hundred of them. Even more striking is the apprentice school, in which the boys are taught the theoretical side of their work. Presided over by a headmaster and four assistants, this school does in two hours what other schools would need a full day to accomplish. . . . So great is the interest that more than half . . . [of the novices] are following regular courses. Boys who desire to become apprentices come to the factory with their parents, who are required to sign an 'apprentice engagement,' binding the boy to serve for five years. . . . The boy [who must be between 16 and 18 years of age, with at least four years' schooling behind him] agrees to perform his duties with fidelity . . . and to attend the night school. The company agrees to pay $2.50 a week for the first six months, and to increase the wages yearly until the apprentice receives $7 a week for his fifth year work . . . to give him every opportunity to learn his trade by moving him from shop to shop. . . . An effort is made to keep the boys [who sometimes become restless and

The R. Hoe & Co. Apprentice School, 1904
Scene outside one of the firm's former Grand Street factory
buildings

tempted to leave at the end of three years] for the full . . . term, and then to give them
employment in the factory at full wages [not less than $2.50 a day]. . . . The rules which
govern the apprentice are rather severe. . . . At 5 o'clock a large bell rings out the closing
hour. . . . The apprentices rush off to the washroom, and in five minutes are in line before
the storage building, where each evening [as is shown in this photograph] the company
provides a luncheon of milk and of meat sandwiches. . . . At 5:30 they go to their desks
. . . and for an hour and a half work over their books. There are seven classes, and the
average boy is expected to complete the work in each of them in four months. . . . A mark
of at least 65 per cent is required in all examinations. . . . [The subjects taught are] English,
mathematics, mechanics, free hand and mechanical drawing . . . and few . . . fail to pass.
The practical work which they do each day in the shops is of great help to them. The company keeps close watch of the apprentices, and has a man, an old mechanic, who visits their
homes when they are sick. . . . A couple of years ago the boys made trouble for some of
their masters. They threatened to 'chuck 'em out the window,' and for a night or two had
things their own way. Then a new headmaster appeared—a Columbia graduate. He is a
big man and an athlete of gridiron fame. It was necessary for him to stoop to get through
the schoolroom door, and he looked strong enough to knock apprentices' heads together at
will. There has been no trouble since."

The First Annual Advertising Show
Held at Madison Square Garden, May 3–9, 1906

"IF YOUR Business Isn't Worth Advertising, Advertise It For Sale," counseled the "Ad." men in the slogan of their first New York exposition, pointing up the inescapable nature of the hucksterial calling. Inspired by the success of an earlier Chicago show, nearly a hundred exhibitors took over the amphitheatre of the Madison Square Garden, "to tell the story" wrote *The New York Times* of May 4, 1906, "of what it is possible to do in the way of making the world buy." Into a country fair atmosphere, with "an energetic band" playing and a well intentioned but somewhat submerged soprano emitting occasional bursts of song, 100,000 visitors swarmed during the first three days, marveling at the looking glass upon which advertisements were thrown; watching a photo-engraving plant in operation; examining lithographic presses—"the kind that print posters and the like"; studying the original drawings for familiar advertisements; enjoying the novelty of watching automatons perform such skilled feats as blowing soap bubbles, smoking cigars, and slicing a cake. It had the elements of a machinery show in cheerful mélange with displays by publishers and agencies, calendar firms and sign manufacturers extolling the efficacy of defacing the great outdoors. One concern introduced a new development in blotters made of a composition stone, designed to serve as product-reminding paperweights. For ten cents, one could vote for a favorite actress: at first Maude Adams (then playing the seventh month of Peter Pan's shadow magic) was in the lead; but she was overtaken by Marie Dressler (concurrently cavorting in *Twiddle-Twaddle* and *The Squaw Man's Girl of the Golden West*) who, according to *The New York Herald* of May 5, was "at one time . . . several dollars more popular than her nearest competitor." A Chicago outfit, with breezy enterprise, had its headquarters in a roofless, tree-fronted Italian villa, which served as a background for its top promotional devices.

"Pretty nearly everything, from automobiles to complexions, has been on show in Madison Square Garden at some time or other," reflected *The New York Times* of May 4, "and now come the advertisers. Not content with advertising the things which they are paid to advertise, . . . [they] are now beginning to advertise their advertisements."

"The Shopper's Paradise," the *New-York Daily Tribune* of September 13, 1896 called "Lower Sixth-Ave. And Its Great Retail Establishments," pointing out that "The increase of trade in the Sixth-ave. shopping district . . . in recent years has been so remarkable as to upset the calculations of many merchants in other parts of the city, and to cause dismay to many small tradesmen. As a result of the flocking of thousands of shoppers to that region every day, there have sprung up great department stores." Constellated along the present Avenue of the Americas (the westerly boundary) between Thirteenth Street and Twenty-third were the dry goods houses of R. H. Macy & Co., B. Altman & Co., H. O'Neill & Co., Simpson, Crawford & Simpson, and the more specialized Knapp Sheppard & Co. (carpets and *meubles*), Baumann Brothers (furniture), Alfred J. Cammeyer (shoes), along with other lesser luminaries. The northern barrier, keeping pace with the theatrical and amusement area, was Forty-second Street. Some of the lower longitudinal stretches, especially Fourteenth and Twenty-third, westward from Fifth Avenue, were also involved.

On Saturday evening September 12, 1896, an estimated 150,000 people attempted to attend the opening of Siegel-Cooper's new dry goods palace—a titanic white edifice (still standing, along with many of its contemporaries) designed by De Lemos & Cordes in the then honorific tradition of the Chicago World's Fair style. Four extra elevated railroad guards had to man each platform of the Eighteenth Street Station to handle the mob, while a detail of 172 policemen controlled those who jostled their way victorious through the three arched entrances to the "veritable fairyland inside"—an heroic feat best appreciated "by magnifying a great many times the difficulties of getting through the usual elbowing crowd of women shoppers that descend upon big department stores on bargain days." At the ten o'clock closing time, Sixth Avenue "was still black with a crushing, pushing mass of humanity striving to get into the beautiful building." The following Monday, when "The Big Store" opened for business, people who in some exaggerated cases had stood in queued impatience since three A.M. broke one of the glass doors; during the stampede several women went into syncope; ambulances were called from New York Hospital, at 8 West Sixteenth Street, to transport the languishing and the maimed, while more than a hundred of "The Finest" were hard pressed to stem the human tidal wave.

The mirabilia of the fifteen-and-a-half-acre establishment's nine working floors (where everything conceivable was sold, with only an apologia for the fact that space in the Bird and Animal Department "does not admit of the exhibition of the larger wild creatures such as the lordly elephant or the monarch of the wilds—the lion") is hyperbolically described in *A Bird's-Eye View Of Greater New York And Its Most Magnificent Store*. This booklet, "Compiled Expressly For Siegel-Cooper Co. New York 1898," warns visiting provincials that unless they consecrated a minimal half day to "a systematic inspection" of the emporium, they "will have omitted to see one of the principal, and certainly THE most interesting

The Bargain Counter at "The Big Store," 1897
Siegel-Cooper Co.
East side of Sixth Avenue, Eighteenth to Nineteenth Streets

sight of the great metropolis," and reiterates that strollers devoid of serious acquisitorial interests are welcome to explore "this magnificent temple of commerce" without interference from its 3,100 employees. The "broad hospitality" underlying the much advertised slogan—"Meet Me at the Fountain"—immediately became a New York byword. This landmark, shown on page 378 in the lesser isolation of a later day, was "A deep marble basin . . . seventy feet in diameter," according to the advance report in the *New-York Daily Tribune* of August 16, 1896, which dwelt upon the central theme—Daniel Chester French's "famous female figure typifying the Republic. The statue . . . is a reduction of the colossal [65-foot] creation [which stood in the Court of Honor at the World's Columbian Exposition in Chicago], . . . yet the figure in this instance is of heroic proportions [measuring 18 feet from base to crown]. It is posed on a granite pedestal. The bust is done in pure white marble and the rest of the form is of highly polished brass, and so skilfully is the combination effected that the statue seems clothed in a richly falling robe of gold."

This "$15,000 reproduction" (as it is called in the pamphlet) remained a constant until

The Fountain at "The Big Store" (Siegel-Cooper Co.), 1908

the fixtures of "The Big Store" were sold at an auction beginning May 8, 1918. Sixteen years earlier, the J. B. Greenhut Company had bought out Henry Siegel, and in 1906, when B. Altman & Co. were preparing to desert the building across Sixth Avenue, Captain Joseph B. Greenhut and Henry Morgenthau (later United States Ambassador to Turkey) purchased that structure and reopened its doors under the name of Greenhut and Company. Early in 1911, the two organizations were consolidated under the name of the Greenhut-Siegel Cooper Company, which in May, 1914, became known as the J. B. Greenhut Company. After passing through a receivership the following year, it was finally announced on March 6, 1918 that, because of wartime business conditions and geographic shifts in the retail trade orbit, "The Big Store" would pay all its debts and close an honorable career. Gimbel Brothers then took over the stocks of merchandise on hand: and so passed from the Sixth Avenue scene the great mart once self-styled the "most stupendous achievement in the annals of Greater New York's commercial grandeur."

Later in 1918, when the Army converted the Siegel-Cooper building into a military hospital, Daniel Chester French came to the rescue of *The Republic*. For many years the symbolic figure stood lonely in the Marble Works of the famed Piccirilli Brothers, until in 1948 the

378

sculptor's daughter, Margaret French Cresson, sold it to Forest Lawn Memorial-Park ("The Happy Cemetery") in Glendale, California. In this mortician's Valhalla, where piped music and miracles of modern plumbing contribute to the comfort and everlasting peace of "The Loved One" (*vide* Evelyn Waugh's satirical chef-d'oeuvre and the glorified graveyard's consoling brochure in full color, entitled "Pictorial Forest Lawn," with "A First Step Up Toward Heaven" as Bruce Barton's testimonial foreword), a new "Court of Honor" (this time "The Court of Freedom") has been built to give added dignity to one of the most publicized statues in the world, and a fresher, deeper, more profound meaning to the imperative invitation—"Meet Me at the Fountain."

. . . . *Marble and mahogany*

"STEP ON—take a ride!" an attendant called to customers at Simpson, Crawford & Simpson's on the morning of October 19, 1900. To their amazement, shopgoers "found that it was as easy to get from the ground to the second floor as to stand still," the *New-York Daily Tribune* of the 20th related. "The new Otis escalator, or moving stairway, with which the store has been equipped was in operation for the first time. . . . Many took advantage of the mechanism who would otherwise have remained on a level with the street. . . . This escalator is the first of its kind to be operated in this city." The reporter's greenhornery or hebetude had caused him to succumb too whole-heartedly to the mesmerism of the inchoate, for, according to *The New York Herald* of May 14, 1899, eleven "inclined elevators" of Jesse W. Reno's invention were already in department store use at that time, following earlier successful operation at Coney Island and the Brooklyn Bridge. Moreover, on September 6, 1900, only six weeks before the *Tribune* man's fancied scoop, his own paper carried a story about the "reversed treadmill," as some called it, initiated on the downtown side of the Elevated Station at Third Avenue and 59th Street.

In any event, Simpson, Crawford & Simpson had many other wonderments to offer its easily uplifted clientele. Plans for this marvel of merchandising had been filed on August 7, 1899. It was to cover "considerably more than an acre," the *Tribune* of the 6th told in beforehanded glee. "The structure will be built in sections, and it is planned to finish the first section, in the rear of the plot, before removing any of the present store," founded twenty years before by William Crawford and Thomas and James Simpson. William H. Hume and Son were the architects of this $1,800,000 plant, slated to be "one of the handsomest establishments of the kind in the shopping district of any city in America." The dominant feature of the Sixth Avenue granite and limestone façade was to be a handsome entrance, flanked by "enormous show windows." Beyond the vestibule with its "handsomely paneled ceiling and a mosaic floor," spacious aisles and generous height were destined to furnish "abundant light and air; but in addition there has been provided a large court . . . rising through six stories to a rich glass dome . . . to be finished in the style of Francis I." Architect and decorator romped helter-skelter through French history, for the women's parlor on the second floor was to be Empire and the eighth-floor dining room—convertible into "an open air palm garden"—with a seating capacity of 1,200, harked back to Louis XVI.

With McKinley prosperity, Sixth Avenue between Eighteenth Street and Herald Square underwent "a transformation, entailing an expenditure of about $15,000,000, which in the course of a few weeks will stamp this thoroughfare as the leading shopping district of the world," euphorically related the *New-York Daily Tribune* of May 4, 1902, at the time of the opening of Adams & Company's new store, Ehrich's contemplated enlargement, the approaching completion of the Saks and Macy emporia at Thirty-fourth Street, and the modernity of Siegel-Cooper's, Altman's and O'Neill's below. A Simpson having been dropped from the company on January 16, 1902, and an annex having been added to the original plans, "The new store of Simpson-Crawford," still under piecemeal construction, was expected to attain completion by September 1st, progress having been "retarded somewhat because of the pains which have been taken in securing the best materials. . . . Marble and mahogany abound."

On Sunday March 6, 1904, it was front page news in the *Tribune* that the Henry Siegel Corporation was being organized by Henry Siegel, Frank E. Vogel, and associates, with a capitalization of $10,750,000 "to acquire the capital stock of Siegel, Cooper & Co., of Chi-

Shop window, 1905; Simpson Crawford Co.
West side of Sixth Avenue, Nineteenth to Twentieth Streets

Easter decorations at Simpson Crawford Co., 1904

cago, the Simpson-Crawford Company, of this city, and the new Fourteenth Street Store." About three weeks later the Simpson-Crawford Company doubled its capital stock, from $2,500,000 to $5,000,000. After the collapse of the Henry Siegel empire in 1914, the reorganized Simpson-Crawford Corporation lived on for a profitless year with the end result that on April 9, 1915, the news of its voluntary liquidation appeared in *The New York Times*. In a gleeful advertisement on July 3rd, Gimbel's announced that it would place the $680,000 stock of the defunct concern on sale on July 6th, its removal to Thirty-third Street having been a tremendous operation accomplished with the aid of "hundreds of enthusiastic workers, and more than a hundred . . . automobile trucks. . . . As an example, one truck load of furniture was dispatched every five minutes!"

But to hark back to happier days, I return you to Easter time of 1904, when a full-page advertisement in *The New York Times* of March 21 included a description of the miracle Byron has here recorded in the making: "Passing the portals of this great store to-day you'll change from the chill of lingering Winter of the outside world to an atmosphere freighted with the fragrance of palms, blossoming lilies, flowers, and the breath of Spring. . . . For the little ones—the boys and girls—there's a picture for them, too—one that's worth coming to see. Just at the end of the bank of flowers in the Rotunda is a broken egg—18 feet long and 10 feet high—that nestles in a bower of flowers. In the centre of the egg is a rabbit"— surrounded by over fifty smaller editions, all produced by the fertile genius of the Bronze & Papier Mache Co., of 345 West Broadway—"that sits up and turns its head." He could bow and wink, too, it seems. Intoxicated by the popularity of this Easter triumph, the copy-writers, gloating over the capture of "old Pappa Rabbit" himself, on March 26th extended an educational opportunity to the children of New York, inviting them to view this mechanical marvel, and posing the innocent rhetorical question: "Isn't it funny that the rabbits around Easter-time are held responsible for all the bright colored eggs which you enjoy so much on Easter morning?"

. . . . *Some particular dulcitude*

" 'SWEETS TO the sweet,' said Queen Gertrude when she cast flowers into the fair Ophelia's grave; but in this material age," according to the *New-York Daily Tribune* of December 22, 1865, "we often interpret the idea by giving candy and sweetmeats and bon-bons to those we believe blessed with some particular dulcitude. 'You love me no longer,' said an *enfante* [sic] *gatée* to her admirer, 'because you have ceased to bring me candy.' 'You want to get rid of me,' one might sometimes say, 'for you bring me stuff warranted to kill.' Candies are too often impure, if not absolutely poisonous. Some manufacturers adulterate their sweets with *terra alba*, which costing a trifle is a great saving when sugar is 18 to 22 cents a pound. But the fraud may be detected, if the confectionery is dissolved in water; the sugar melts, while the *terra alba*, or other foreign substance, is precipitated to the bottom of the vessel. But you need not try this experiment with anything you buy of:

Ridley & Co., No. 1 Hudson st., and No. 214 Fifth-ave.

Wm. Taylor, No. 55 Broadway.

Maillard, No. 621 Broadway."

The last of these confectioners so highly recommended to post bellum Christmas shoppers as part of the "Opulence of the Metropolis In Gifts," had been established at Montalimar, France, prior to 1840, with its local beginnings in 1848, when Henry Maillard, a thirty-two-year-old native of Normandy, brought his copper cooking utensils to New York and started his catering and confectionery business at 44 Walker Street. Two years later, he opened a retail shop at 619 Broadway, fronting his 158 Mercer Street factory, both overflowing into adjacent quarters as his products attained fame here and abroad. Tradition has it that Napoleon III was in the habit of presenting Maillard's candies to his exquisite Empress Eugénie, and according to the records of the firm similar delights were served at all of President Lincoln's White House entertainments.

The following article from *The Daily Graphic* of September 13, 1873, gives an idea of the magnitude of this saccharine empire: "Maillard's Bon-Bon Building. Since the fire which destroyed the chocolate and miscellaneous bon-bon factory on Mercer Street of M. Maillard, he has erected a new establishment at Nos. 116 and 118 East Twenty-fifth street, which is certainly one of the most curious buildings in the city. Each story is a special laboratory, having its own *personnel* and producing its own kind of goods. Three thousand pounds of chocolate come from this house daily, in all varieties of forms, and intended for a multiplicity of destinations. On the second and third floors, gums and bon-bons are manufactured in every variety. A steam-engine of one hundred horse-power drives all the intricate machinery used in the establishment. Although the quantity of confectionery turned out daily is enormous, there is no point of detail anywhere neglected, and not one object produced that is not of superior quality. M. Maillard has sent specimens of his work to Vienna, and has received a medal of merit. He deserves it, for his chocolate has a world-wide fame. His retail establishment is under the Fifth Avenue Hotel."

In 1876 came another award, given to Maillard in Philadelphia, where, according to the "Historical Register of the Centennial Exposition," he exhibited "a huge spire-shaped monument of white sugar, nearly fifteen feet in height, and ornamented with historical figures and groups in sugar and chocolate, illustrating incidents in the history of the United States," from the Landing of the Pilgrim Fathers on down; "side figures representing Sitting Bull and General Custer on horseback, etc. These figures are all made by hand. There are also two fine pieces of confectionery; the one a massive vase called the Medicis, of solid chocolate, weighing 200 pounds; the other a book of enormous size, containing 3,000 varieties of bon-bons and chocolate, made by Mr. Maillard, and appropriately entitled, 'Une [*sic*] Voyage dans L'Isle des Plaisirs.'"

White, Stokes, & Allen's Guide And Select Directory stated in 1885 that "Maillard's, under the Fifth Avenue Hotel, is noted for its delicious ice-cream, especially 'chocolate ice cream'"; and it was announced in *Frank Leslie's Illustrated Newspaper*, March 21, 1891, that lessons were given thrice weekly at "Maillard's New York Chocolate School." Annual exhibitions were held, the 1893 Yuletide one featuring "Bonbonnières Richly Decorated Porcelains, Fancy Baskets, Satin Bags, Christmas Tree Surprises Objets D'Arts . . . at the new Store, 1099 Broadway. . . . Also, 178 Broadway and 120 Broadway. . . . Eminent artists retained to execute special orders in decorating." The following year the great confiseur (who died in Paris on February 14, 1900, at eighty-four) turned the business over to his son, Henry, Jr. Always enterprising, in 1897 the firm joined Haig & Haig and Milwaukee Beer in sponsoring a pioneer outdoor advertising film on a special type of screen, which so

Henry Maillard's Retail Confectionery and Ladies' Lunch Establishment, Easter time, 1902
1099 Broadway, southwest corner of Twenty-fourth Street, under the Fifth Avenue Hotel

disrupted Herald Square traffic that a police order suspended the attraction after a three-day run.

Looking at this photograph, it seems tenable that Maillard's was one of the establishments described in the *New-York Daily Tribune* of March 20, 1902: "In addition to the 'flights' and flocks of winged and feathered favorites, and the ever present rabbit in every possible attitude, confectioners have graceful fawns, deer, dogs, cows, and even fish, mounted on bonbonnières, and a great variety of painted, satin mounted boxes, baskets and other fancy receptacles covered with masses of artificial violets, lilies-of-the-valley and rosebuds with knots of gay ribbons. A beautiful wreath of pink roses, so perfect that one scarcely believes it is a confection, is one of the most attractive 'sweets' of the confectioner's output."

It was during this same Lenten season that Byron photographed Mr. and Mrs. Maillard, their employees, the factory in all its departments, the popular ladies' lunchroom—so well remembered for its hot chocolate topped with whipped cream, and other succulencies—and the retail store in full Easter finery. The much admired ceiling decoration—an allegorical representation of "Fame"—was the work of Charles Mueller. 1908 saw the restaurant's removal to the southwest corner of Fifth Avenue and Thirty-fifth Street and 1923 to Madison Avenue at Forty-seventh Street—the last nectarious purlieu, which closed in 1941. The factory removed to Long Island City in 1925 and ten years later to Bethlehem, Pennsylvania. Today all the time-honored recipes and formulae are still used by The Maillard Corporation, but one celebrated package has been discontinued. "Miss Louise," who entered the firm's employ as a young girl in 1912, well remembers hearing about the turn-of-the-century day when Mr. Maillard made a winning wager with his rival and friend, Mr. Huyler, that he could sell a pound box of candy for $500. The catch was in the centerpiece—a diamond engagement ring; and this novel method of declaration became quite popular with shy swains, who bashfully presented the chocolate-surrounded solitaires to the ones they believed "blessed with some particular dulcitude."

. . . . *Sultar for Sore, Tired, Itching and Burning Feet*

PODODYNIA IS one of the most common ailments to which flesh is heir: Trilby alone among women never knew the pangs of podalgia. Her pedal extremities—each a symphonic composition of seven tarsal, five metatarsal and fourteen phalangeal bones, with glorious interplay of extrinsic and intrinsic muscles, concealed tracery of artery and vein, and glowing fleshly casing forever free of the universal clavus—were, so their ecstatic celebrant relates, "a true inspiration of shape and color, all made up of delicate lengths and subtly modulated curves and noble straightnesses and happy little dimpled arrangements in innocent young pink and white." In her role of artist's model, she posed for what she may have been the first to call "the altogether"—*l'ensemble*, you know—head, hands, and feet—everything—especially feet." And she undiffidently admitted that hers was "the handsomest foot in all Paris," with but a single rival in the entire city: her other foot. "Little Billee" was bewitched by these "angel's feet"; and from memory, "with the point of an old compass, he scratched in white on the dark red wall a three-quarter profile outline of Trilby's left foot, which was perhaps the more perfect poem of the two." And so it has come to pass that "The shape of those lovely slender feet . . . fac-similed in dusty, pale plaster of Paris, survives on the shelves and walls of many a studio throughout the world, and many a sculptor yet unborn has yet to marvel at their strange perfection." So George du Maurier, first in the music of his words and then in the miracle of his drawings (now enshrined in The Pierpont Morgan Library), declined a new noun. With the publication of the novel in London in 1894, its eight-part illustrated serialization in *Harper's New Monthly Magazine* (starting with the January issue of that same year) and its subsequent appearance between covers under the Harper aegis, everywhere "It was Trilby, Trilby, Trilby!" With the dramatization by Paul M. Potter (first acted in New York—following wild success in Boston and the hinterland—on April 15, 1895, at the Garden Theatre, with Virginia Harned in the title role, and later that year produced by Herbert Beerbohm Tree at London's Theatre Royal, Haymarket), two continents lost their heads and hearts to his heroine, "wistful and sweet." Throughout the rest of the nineties the feet of all women—however marked, marred, disfigured and deformed—became kindly know as "trilbies." There were of course a few dissenters from the pulpit and in literary clubs here and there. "This worship of Trilby," grumbled Cleveland Moffett—a local Savonarola who had not stooped to read the book—in his series on "The Seven Deadly Sins of America" (catalogued and excoriated in *The Illustrated American* from January 12 to March 9, 1895), "looks like a clear case of hypocrisy. Who was this Trilby any way, this peculiar person whom our mothers and sisters pretend to admire so vastly? . . . Now, every woman . . . who has either pure instincts or common sense . . . knows that when the glamour of surroundings and the charm of presentation is taken away, there remains an ugly, uncompromising fact. She knows that Trilby was a Latin quarter 'lady' with Latin quarter ideas. . . . She knows that should Trilby arrive in New York to-day, no woman who respects herself would invite her to her house or allow her daughters to associate with her. She knows that if Trilby took a seat in one of our fashionable churches . . . the other people in the pew would look at her askance and either leave their seats or have the usher ask her to leave. All this is perfectly well known by American women who hold up their hands in horror at 'Camille,' or 'Sapho,' or 'Manon Lescault' [*sic*], because in those really great books a spade is called a spade, but tolerate 'Trilby,'—yes, rave over it, because the unpleasant part is glossed over. . . . They feel no qualms of conscience in boldly proclaiming themselves worshippers of the Trilby cult; they enroll themselves eagerly in Trilby clubs; they give Trilby teas; they wear Trilby hats, and they carefully avoid all reference to Trilby virtue. If this is not hypocrisy, what is it?"

So manufacturers of all manner of articles—from scarf pins of silver and gold in the immortal cast of the human foot divine to articles of wearing apparel and smokers' delights —used the magic name. "The desire to share in the profits of *Trilby* seems almost as prevalent this spring as the bicycle habit," quoth E. S. Martin, in *Harper's Weekly* of May 18, 1895. "What sums Trilby has earned for charity no one will ever compute. There have been Trilby tableaux, Trilby burlesques, Trilby nights, and Trilby shows of every kind from one end of the land to the other." And still, everyone's feet hurt.

Possibly as a panacea, William Knight, proprietor of the Sultar Disinfectant Company (here portrayed by Byron amid the neat arrangement of his bacteria-destroying agent and foot balm) offered his output to suffering humanity. New York city directories from 1900 to 1915 (with a single oversight in 1902) list his place of business as 203 East Fifty-fourth Street. In the first year he resided at this address, but soon moved to nearby 212. My canvass of the oldest pharmacists and pharmaceutical manufacturers in town, not to mention several podiatrists, failed to yield any information about Mr. Knight or his "Registered Trade Name" product, so in long desperation I too have joined the worshipers of "la Grande Trilby."

The Sultar Disinfectant Company, 1901
203 East Fifty-fourth Street

"Some say the world will end in fire,
  Some say in ice."
      Robert Frost, "Fire and Ice"

THE *cor cordium* and intramural café of a microcosmic office palace found their end in flame and frozen water on the early morning of January 9, 1912, when the old Equitable Building "yielded up" what the *New-York Daily Tribune* of the 10th chose to call "its seared and worldly soul," in one of the city's best remembered blazes that left only a frosty shell standing on the east side of Broadway from Pine to Cedar streets. The reportorial adjectives were carefully culled in considered reference to the unforgotten furor of 1905 (see pages 215 and 217).

But long before it became a gale-fanned torch of auroral flame—which, according to the *Tribune's* story, "persuaded many a dweller on Brooklyn Heights . . . that the sun had risen in the west"—this temple of life insurance had been a many years' wonder. Designed by Gilman and Kendall, with George B. Post as consultant, it was the first office building in Manhattan to have elevators at the time of its opening on May 1, 1870. After a series of enlargements, Post remodeled it in 1886, stretching it several stories skyward. Of this incarnation the *Tribune* of April 12 wrote: "When the projected work is completed, instead of a somewhat rambling structure, there will be a thoroughly symmetrical and massive building. . . . It is the design of the . . . committee to make a 'bazaar of all nations' of the central court—a headquarters for lawyers, merchants, brokers—in fact, all downtown people, who will find there everything needed by a civilized man from baths and clothing stores to stock ticker and railroad offices." On January 10, 1887, the same newspaper reported that the expanded building, covering an acre, would be "one of the finished marvels of the city," "one of the sights of the world." This cynosuric wonder—"a mountainous pile of Quincy granite, solid and fireproof as a rock" (according to the eleventh edition of M. F. Sweetser & Simeon Ford's *How To Know New York City*, 1888) housed thirty-five hundred tenants engaged in "almost every kind of business capable of being transacted in offices." Gustav Kobbé told in *New York And Its Environs* (1891) that it had a daily traffic of more than thirty thousand people. With the novelty of a many-stored European arcade it had various autonomous features among which he mentions the United States Weather Bureau high in the clouds, The Lawyers' Club with its notable special library, and Café Savarin in the southwestern part of the basement, and the restaurant of the same name back of it across the hall—listed as "new" in the 1889 edition of *Appletons' Dictionary of New York And Its Vicinity*. E. Idell Zeisloft, editor of *The New Metropolis* (New York, 1899), proclaimed this meridian resort as nearby Delmonico's "first formidable rival . . . which equaled him in the altitude of the prices . . . and the quality of the cooking," but had the advantage of

Café Savarin, 1901
In the old Equitable Building,
120 Broadway

greater centrality. In an area which included such favored eating houses as Sutherland's at 64 Liberty Street, Cable's on Broadway near Pine and the Rathskeller in the Staats-Zeitung Building near Printing-House Square, these two led the field in their charges; but neither could match the popularity of the Astor House with its renowned Rotunda, "in whose lunch and dining rooms are to be found on any week day more representative business and professional men than can be seen elsewhere under any one roof in Manhattan." Nevertheless, a September 24, 1905 item in the *New-York Daily Tribune* read: "It is said that the café has been controlled by the Equitable for many years, . . . [the Assurance Company's] directors having been so-called 'overseers' of the place . . . which has paid over to the Equitable in the last year at least $150,000." It was in a back-stage part of the Café Savarin that the conflagration started in an unassuming way. So much for the culprit, and on to bravery in a lower level of the building's being.

The "great sub-basement of this towering block of granite" was extolled in the *Tribune*

The Pump Room of the old Equitable Building, 1902

of January 10, 1887: "The most striking features are the enormous steel boilers, nine in number, with a combined capacity of 900 horse power. There are also in the cellar three hydraulic [Worthington] pumping engines, probably the largest in use in any building in the world . . . [with] a capacity . . . sufficient to supply the water needs of an average city of 100,000 inhabitants. . . . There are other pumps in connection with great water tanks on the roof which make the Equitable . . . of public benefit to surrounding property in case of fire. The electric lights will receive their power from an engine of 400 horse power in the cellars. The building will be heated by a system of direct radiation, and fresh air may be introduced at will, the ventilation being one of the objects which received the care of the architect." From this underground maze, out of the "Subterranean Army" of the maintenance crew, came "a man who lived through perils which few men pass alive," the *New-York Daily Tribune* of January 10, 1912, reported. "Davis had charge of the boiler

390

rooms at night. He kept about his work . . . until the building was a mass of flames . . . and the boiler room was filled with smoke and water. Davis knew he was in great peril, but he knew, also, that if the fires were kept burning beneath the great boilers there would be terrific explosions, with attendant loss of life. He started to work, and drew the coals from the grates one by one. This required more than an hour. Then Davis tried to escape, only to find his way blocked. Again and again he tried to fight his way through smoke and flame and tons of water, some of it scalding and some of it freezing. It was not until noon that Davis made his way over the wreckage to the Pine street side of the building, battered and bruised, but content in knowing he had perhaps saved other lives." According to *The World* of January 10, "Davis wore his honors lightly, and said it was only what any self-respecting engineer would do under the circumstances."

The surrealistic picture that met his smarting eyes is best recounted by *The New York Times* lead writer, who had a whole day to fashion his description of the funeral pyre of a stone giant born of reconstruction and for some time headed toward ungrateful super-session. He wrote as one might of a strangely incandescent Alpine afterglow: "Ice seemed to form in the very air. . . . And it settled over the building in a gleaming sheath of white that made the fire a wonderful thing to see." The ruins became "a fantastic palace, with the rainbows arching at every turn as the sunlight filtered through the spray and smoke. . . . And of all the spectacles that kept crowds staring fascinated . . . the strangest was that of two despairing hands—a dead man's hands thrust through the bars from one of the basement vaults." Later darkness descended "on a structure marvellously sheathed in ice with the blaze of the timbers within still red" as "the shifting shafts from the searchlight of the Singer Building . . . took up their task of adding mystic glamor to the horror."

. . . . *Roast beef, coffee, pie and fixin's   35 cents*

"NEW YORK CITY is truly the home of the quick lunch caterers. Nowhere else in the world will you find a class of business people whose average time taken for their mid-day meal is but 15 minutes. From 9 A.M. until 5 P.M., the people in this bustling hive are on the jump. The day is not long enough, and everyone seems to act as if he was a little behind-hand and bound to catch up before the day was over. This hustling, hurry and rush has become a veritable mania with us. . . .

"But if you want to see the New York City business man in his most characteristic act, and one which depicts best his restlessness and commercial activity, just drop in one of Childs' Quick Lunch restaurants any day and see the people rushing in.

"Long before you have entered every one of the seats . . . have been filled, whilst standing up eagerly watching for a vacant chair, are others whose faces show that they are be-grudging the diners the time they seem to think the latter are evidently taking from them."

These are the opening paragraphs in an unsigned article—"Childs. The Quick Lunch Business In New York."—in *The Caterer Monthly* of February, 1898. While focalization is upon one link in the chain started by William and Samuel Childs on an August day in 1889 at 41 Cortlandt Street, the writer, in describing the 130 Broadway establishment, states: "The room in which you are standing is a good example of all of Child's [*sic*] dining rooms. The walls are of glass tiling and glass mosaic, the floors are of vitrified tiling. This style of fitting up [with its visible kitchen dining-car inspired and its façade and decor reputedly by the eminent architect of the World Building, George B. Post] was chosen for three reasons. First, on account of its general attractiveness; second, because of its ability to stand wear; and third, from the ease with which it is kept clean." This last was a suasive point at a time when augmentative public consciousness of germs was becoming almost phobic. "These dining rooms are always light and cheerful and impresses [*sic*] the diner with the fact, 'How can Childs afford to fit up his places so expensively?' There are no lunch counters before which one sits on a high legged stool in discomfort, but there is a place at a [polished mahogany] table, and an easy, comfortable chair for every diner, provided he waits long enough for it. . . . To give you some idea of the vastness of their business in their nine places, they feed an average of 15,000 to 20,000 people every day except Sunday. . . . A new system of serving has been introduced at 130 Broadway. . . . As you enter the restaurant you notice a large lunch counter at your left filled with piles of sandwiches and . . . pastry. Opposite the counter, and about four feet from it, is a metal, ornamental open partition three feet high extending the full length of the counter. Before stepping into the passageway you notice a big pile of empty trays from which each guest takes one. Now as you pass along the lunch counter you take off whatever you want, place it on your tray, not, however, forgetting to take a cup of tea or coffee from the big urns. At either end of the partition is a young lady who hands you a ticket punched 15c., 20c., or whatever sum represents the amount of food . . . on your tray. . . . The . . . check you of course pay to the cashier near the entrance door. The manager at No. 130 . . . [said that in the beginning] 'the guest did a good deal of complaining about becoming his own waiter. At first, he would forget his spoon, knife, fork or sugar; to-day, all have become educated to the plan, forgetting nothing. . . .' Though you are supposed to be taking a quick lunch . . . you forget your hurry; . . . the food you have selected is the best the proprietors can buy, the bread . . . is made by the best baker that can be found, Dahn & Son. . . . The butter is of the best quality and bought fresh the day before of Pettit & Reed. . . . Coffee is another one of their specialties. . . . For years they have been dealing with one house, Shapleigh, of Boston, who furnishes them the same coffee year in and year out. . . . Childs has always been complimented on the superior quality of their milk and cream. . . . The reason for this is plain, when we state that they have their own dairy farms. . . . The bill-of-fare is designed to please the average public. . . . In this Broadway place . . . Mr. Childs has introduced music [by a five-piece orchestra], and his verdict is that it pleases the majority of folks. . . . The ventilation of Childs' dining rooms is the most perfect that we ever saw. Forty-five Cortlandt street is the main office of Childs' restaurants. . . . Everything here is done with a system. For each place there is a manager who is governed by a list of rules. . . . By following the rules he cannot go wrong. He is but a part of the system, and the system permeates all their places alike. . . . These places are original, and that they have pursued the business on proper lines can be seen from the fact that starting only with $1,600 capital in the old Merchant's Hotel . . . they are able to have to-day nine places most expensively filled up, their last at 130 Broadway [with its three dining rooms], for example, having cost $100,000."

No mention is made of a typical feature of the Childs restaurants—a carry-over from the brothers' brief 1888 apprenticeship to A. W. Dennett, the pioneer in the first coast-to-coast chain of eating places, established in the face of the homemade box lunch and the saloon-made free lunch. As an attention-getting mechanism, Dennett had instituted the window display manufacture of wheatcakes. The cheerful Childs chef in his pristine linen uniform topped by a baker's cap, tossing the golden flapjacks behind the plate-glass front with the white enamel lettering of the young firm name [a facsimile of Samuel's careful script] became almost a functional trademark. Another innovation was the substitution of attractive waitresses for the often slovenly male servitors employed by most eating houses.

What with the Childs sanitary code and vegetarian emphasis, the growing chain had nothing to fear in 1906, when Upton Sinclair exposed meat packing malpractices in *The Jungle* and Theodore Roosevelt launched the investigation that led to the enactment of the Pure Food and Drugs Act (so valiantly championed by Dr. Harvey W. Wiley for two decades) in June of that year in the muckraking era.

A Childs Unique Dairy Lunch Room, 1900
Thought to be the one at 47 East Forty-second Street

In quest of the atmospheric, I noted the Childs sign in February, 1955, inviting passers-by to enjoy a "Real Old Fashioned Feast . . . 10 Course Dinner $1.99" with difficult choice of fried chicken or "Prime Sirloin Roast Beef." Leafing through the January 30, 1908, *Leslie's Weekly* I had impaled a reference in the initial installment of Louise E. Dew's four-part serial, "How I Saw New York For The First Time," in which the girlish protagonist, Lisbeth Dunn, a sedulous tourist, wrote: "Dear Home Folks: Well, here I am, safe and sound in the city of my dreams, way up on the twelfth floor of the woman's hotel in a snug little eyrie of a room, and wildly happy to think that I am really here. . . . Well, I've had dinner and gone over my accounts for the day. . . . Here is the itemized account, father:

"Subway fare, from Grand Central station, down town . . . . $.05
Table d'hote lunch at 'Fernery' [a popular tea room at 14 West
    Thirty-third Street] 30
Two car fares on surface line, up town 10
Dinner at a 'Childs' restaurant—roast beef, coffee, pie and fixin's   .35"

. . . . Shrine to saccharinity

"SODA-WATER is an American drink. It is as essentially American as porter, Rhine wine, and claret are distinctly English, German, and French." The apologue of the national beverage is propounded by Mary Gay Humphreys in an article on "The Evolution Of The Soda Fountain," which must have becharmed the readers of *Harper's Weekly* of November 21, 1891. According to this magazinist, a rare husbandry prevailed locally, for she states: "The chips of the marble cathedral [St. Patrick's] on Fifth Avenue alone supplied twenty-five million gallons of soda-water; thus economically we drink up unavailable bits of buildings (public and private), tombstones, and monuments." The dispensation of this "sparkling, bubbling, foam-crested liquor" (the principal ingredients of which—she tells—are the so-called "snowflake" dust and sulphuric acid) was once peril-fraught, for after these two impalatabilities "are cradled, and the gas generated . . . passed into steel fountains . . . two-thirds full of the water to be charged . . . [the] fountains . . . like huge bombs in size and almost as destructive, are carried in wagons through the streets to be stored under drug-store counters. . . . Formerly the actual process took place under the drug-store counter. . . . No one has yet estimated the decreased percentage in loss of life since the drug-store boy ceased playing with the vitriol, carbonates, and force-pump. . . . Explosions of soda fountains do now sometimes occur, but they have ceased to be a national feature." She then veers to the aesthetics involved: "There are hundreds of thousands of people to whom the soda-water fountain has given their first realizing sense of the beauties of art and the glories of architecture. There are thousands of arid little villages . . . to-day out of whose dull materialism it rises like the fountain in the desert to refresh the weary eye and soul. . . . Some of these old soda-water fountains are still found in odd, out-of-the-way places. In a west-side drug store now, there stands a temple of marble and silver. On top, under a crystal dome, a marble goddess in a continuous shower-bath is surrounded by four

394

nymphs. These are in turn guarded by four bronze knights in armor upholding gas jets. . . .
To heighten illusion in the national cry for ice in summer . . . the soda-water manufacturers forsook Greece and the goddesses, and the Eros, the Diana, the Helicon gave way [in retreat from the Classic Revival and as part of the democratic process, no doubt] to the Frost King, the Snow-drop, the Icicle, the Avalanche, the Aurora Borealis, the North Pole, created with frosted nickel-plate to simulate the jagged ice of the polar regions, over which scrambled polar-bears. . . . But once the imagination was enchained to give merely material satisfaction, the soda-water fountain became what it remains, simply an ice-box, but an ice-box costly and luxurious to an extent undreamed of in the Olympian period. . . . To the ideal succeeded architectural styles, worked out in magnificent marbles, inlaid with porcelain tiles, carnelian onyx, overlaid with plated ornament, and known . . . [oh, height of eclecticism!] as the Persia, the Ionic, the Doric, the Chalet, the Arabia, the Rialto, the France. The corruption of styles became more flagrant even than the native architecture, and the nomenclature bald and stupid." And with decadence, came palatal sophistries: "A half-dozen syrups . . . once satisfied those simple minds and tastes which looked upon the soda-water fountain only as a means of increasing human happiness. . . . The alliance of the fragrant fruit with the 'sylph-like draught' was as ideally perfect as moonlight, music, love, and flowers. . . . On the integrity of these syrups no one can cast a doubt. It is only in these last oleomargarinous days that we have learned of butyric ether, acetic ether; that in strawberry syrup we know cochineal, and malva flowers in raspberry; that here we discover aniline, and everywhere suspect that mysterious and sanguineous new compound 'ruddy gore,' widely advertised among the trade. All this was inevitable when the soda-water fountain took up with the drug store." Soon "soda-water fountains multiplied like saloons. . . . According to the confession of a drug clerk the effort to suborn the soda-water fountain in the interest of the drug store has been well considered and successful. . . . A few years ago a soda-water fountain that would give forth forty brews had reached its limit. There are soda-water fountains now in this city that number over three hundred combinations. To supply these the entire side of the wall is dedicated and made glorious with California onyx, rare marbles and plate-glass. Such [a] soda-water fountain . . . costs at least $40,000. . . . In the business parts of town the receipts from these splendidly equipped wells amount to several hundred dollars a day. . . . As a check to the influence of the drug store, a confectioner bethought him of ice-cream soda. . . . On a bright, exhilarating day, to achieve a cup of ice-cream soda, a place should be engaged some time in advance. Beauty and fashion surge about the counter. One of the sights of the town is the rows of bright faces, two and three deep, bent over their cups, and fishing within with long-handled spoons. . . . But the crowning merit of soda-water, and that which fits it to be the national drink, is its democracy. The millionaire may drink champagne while the poor man drinks beer, but they both drink soda-water. There is no quarter of this great town so poor that the soda-water fountain, cheaply but ostentatiously erected in marble and plate, does not adorn the street corners, and is not liberally patronized."

New York had long had its own vested interest in the soda fountain, for the name of one of Manhattan's adopted citizens—the English-born John Matthews (1808–1870)—early became synonymical with the beverage and its mechanical dispensers. Upon his arrival here in 1832, he established a machine shop. The following year he applied the experienceful knowledge gained at the Bramah plant in London, using the famous inventive engineer's technique of producing the sparkling drink, and constructing his own improved founts of cast-iron, tin-lined, out of which the bubbling aqua flowed. From peddling beginnings of product and equipment, Matthews lived to see more than five hundred retail outlets for his carbonated thirst quencher in New York alone, with a world-wide market emanating from the huge Twenty-sixth to Twenty-seventh Street and First Avenue manufactory he turned over to his sons upon his retirement in 1865. He lies buried in Green-Wood Cemetery. Further local affiliation with the industry is to be found in a mortuary monument described in the previously quoted *Harper's Weekly* article as being "made to resemble nothing so much as a marble soda-water fountain, up whose heights scaled polar-bears."

As Mary Gay Humphreys descanted on the national libation in the nascent nineties, so the writer Rupert Hughes made "The Distinctive American Drink" the subject of a summer Sunday piece in *The New York Herald* of June 17, 1906, the year Byron photographed this dazzling shrine to saccharinity. "In New York city there is a saloon to every 590 persons," the novelist affirms, and turns to counting spiggots: "It is surprising to find that the soda

Soda Fountain in a Hegeman Drug Store, 1907

fountain has grown to such popularity as to rival the saloon. There are 7,000 soda fountains in the city of New York . . . [one] to every 535 persons." This stable threat to the swinging door, he tells, "bunks in with a drug store or a candy business, often with a restaurant. . . . The expensiveness of the usual soda fountain is due to the lavish use of marbles. One manufacturer imports almost all his marbles and offers them in twenty varieties. They go in and out of fashion like women's fabrics. The old favorite Italian white has fallen into disuse, because it was easily stained with syrup and impossible to clean; the ideal marble, Belgian black, is also a bit antiquated. Marble itself is now yielding to onyx, which is more convenient and more ornate. . . . One catalogue lists seventy different flavoring extracts in common use. It is observed that in the business districts of New York, Chicago and other cities many shop girls, stenographers and others take an ice cream soda for lunch. The effect on their stomachs is doubtful. The modesty of the amount is a good point, but its temperature is risky."

As amply demonstrated, the New York soda fountain has had many parasitical affiliations; probably its strangest tent-mate was a saloon formally inaugurated with the blessing of the church four weeks after a non-fanfareous launching. The front page of the *New-York Daily Tribune* of August 3, 1904 described this unusual event: "New-York has seen many 'grand openings' which were astonishing for one reason or another, but never until yesterday has a bishop assisted here at the dedication of a drinking place, and drinking places do not often have 'dedications.' The bishop was the Right Rev. Dr. Henry C. Potter, of the Protestant Episcopal Diocese of New-York; the place, the Subway Tavern," christened in honor of the city's newest rapid transit form (to be in operation from City Hall to West 145th Street on October 26) and located within audibility of its rumblings, at Bleecker and Mulberry Streets. "There was an audience of more than a hundred about evenly divided between persons interested in social reform . . . and 'drifters' from the neighboring Bowery. . . . Back of the speakers' chairs over the doorway leading into the soda and beer room in the front, was a large sign," "THIS WAY TO THE WATER WAGON." This in the main philanthropic "poor man's club"—based on the model family taverns established under the Earl Grey system in England—survived the much criticized canonical dedication by only thirteen months, but its unorthodox initiation had a strange peroration: "Mr. [Joseph] Johnson [Jr., President and Manager] announced that the congregation would sing 'Praise God from Whom All Blessings Flow.' . . . The selling of drinks, mixed or otherwise [from bar and soda fountain as well] anything you liked, began as the hymn ended. . . . Later in the afternoon the Bowery chuckled over the antics of several who declared they had 'consecrated jags.' "

The Free Lunch and the Swinging Doors (page 401), 1905
(While Elmrich R. Wessels' Saloon—"The Magnet"—was
located at 119 Newark Avenue, Jersey City, it is typical of
similar establishments found throughout the metropolitan area
at this time.)

.... *The throne is built of barrel staves*

LIKE YOUNG LOCHINVAR, and in a direction contrary to the Course of Empire and Horace Greeley's borrowed injunction, the free lunch came out of the West. J. Ross Browne (in the December, 1860 number of *Harper's New Monthly Magazine*) told of days of gold in California, whither he first went in 1849, and of how "After the Kern River Exchequer had been exhausted [in 1855] . . . even the gentlemen of elegant leisure [known as "Bummers"], who had gone off so suddenly in search of small change for liquors and cigars, could now recuperate their exhausted energies at the free lunch establishments of San Francisco." And so, across country the custom of the laden counter—all its savories gratuitously given for the price of a drink—rolled into the City of the Three Rivers and made its home in every bar, from that of the sawdusted floor to those of the gilded hotel and gambling house.

"All signs seem to point now to the temporary triumph of the saloon over the forces of Christian civilization in America," read an exercitation by the Rev. Thomas Dixon, Jr., published in *Frank Leslie's Weekly* of March 3, 1892. "The saloon is master of every important city. . . . In New York City the saloon is the power behind the throne, before the throne, under the throne, and on top of the throne. In fact, the throne itself is built of barrel staves. . . . In 1889 we had nine thousand three hundred and sixty-nine [liquor] licenses in force. . . ." (Jacob A. Riis, in *How the Other Half Lives*, New York, 1890, cites more conservatively from police statistics of the previous year, fixing the number of saloons at 7,884.) "I am able to state that nine thousand five hundred and six . . . were issued in this city in 1891. . . . The number of unlicensed drinking-places is estimated at from two thousand to three thousand. . . . The saloon to-day appeals first to man's sense of the beautiful. . . . In crowded, dingy tenement roosts, the soul cries in vain for anything to satisfy this divine aspiration. The saloon on the corner hastens to meet this want of man's inmost immortal being. In flashing crystalline glass, polished wood, hammered brass, beautiful frescoes, brilliant lights, warmth and cheer he is bidden welcome." The Rev. Dixon illustrated his sermon with an account of the glories of the Hotel Vendome bar at Broadway and Forty-first Street, which he called "A Poem in Decoration." "At the extreme end of the room, and separated from the bar by twenty or thirty feet, stands the free-lunch counter, built of African marble and Mexican onyx! It is loaded with the most tempting food cooked by master hands." Looking over the Rev. Dixon's shoulder, we study the "Buffet" menu of the establishment, with its thirty-three varietal salivating delights, from Mulligatawny soup through cold cuts, sandwiches and salads of lobster and chicken, caviar and crackers—an uncomplaining and inexhaustible board from which "A man is served anything he calls for, to the utmost limit of his appetite." The first of these free banquets was dispensed in New Orleans in 1838.

On September 9, 1893 *The Illustrated American* paragraphed: "Exit The Free Lunch.— The saloon keepers of New York city are agitated about their luncheon counters. The American and Irish-American liquor dealers, in particular, are anxious to abolish the pickled onion and the cold corned beef which have hitherto filled the vacuum of many a lone bachelor who perforce must seek that solace in the bar which he cannot find elsewhere. So we are threatened with a return to the old days when a bowl of crackers and another of cheese used to ornament the bar." In the question of "cheese versus beef," the weekly was of the opinion that since the dairy product would drive the dyspeptic to the drugstore and send ravening souls racing to a restaurant, the publicans "had better hold on like grim death to that alluring luncheon counter."

On March 23, 1896 New York State enacted the Raines Law, with its provisions for a high license fee on retail trade in intoxicants; its Sunday closing of saloons (which resulted in their subterfugal conversion into the exempted inn and hotel class, often houses of assignation); its specifications bearing on barroom visibility from the street and its ban on the free lunch. In anticipation of the enforcement of this bill, sponsored by John Raines (prominent Republican in the Legislature at Albany) the *New-York Daily Tribune* of March 20 canvassed the trade. " 'I have been in the . . . business all over the Union for over thirty-five years,' said a popular downtown caterer. . . . '[This measure] will certainly make a revolution in the retail liquor traffic. Why, as matters now stand, millions of money are annually expended in this seeming gratuity, and over fifty thousand regulars depend upon what they can gather from our counters for their daily subsistence. . . . I know by face . . . over twenty-five regulars who eat of my hot lunch six days in the week. . . .' 'What will become of this class in the city?' 'The Lord knows; it is the actual uprooting of a fixed institution. . . .' 'Billy' Proctor . . . one of the oldest proprietors of bar and restaurant in the Wall-st. region . . . said to the reporter: 'Yes, this free lunch business has been an expensive luxury for me. The various dishes I set out in those blazers every day as a free lunch to my patrons cost me $35 a day' [$10,000 a year]. . . . 'Do you do it for philanthropy?' 'Not much! I serve it because it is the thing to do for a first-class restaurant. . . .On holiday occasions my free "lay-out" will cost me $200 . . . but this free lunch institution is a part of our legitimate expense, as our gas or ice bills.' 'And what will become of your regulars?' 'Don't speak of it,' 'Billy' said, with a sad face and a gesture of profound sympathy. 'I pity them! I pity them!' "

The hardihood of this convention, however, insured its survival. An instructive article on "Living in New York on Nothing a Year" is to be found in *The New York Herald* of Sunday, April 14, 1907: "In the course of a day many thousands of dollars' worth of free food are given away on Manhattan Island. There are several hotels on Broadway whose free lunch costs each upward of one hundred dollars a day. Tens of thousands of people are fed, many of them making a full meal of it. The variety of dishes offered and the care with which they are cooked and served are astonishing. The free lunches of several such hotels in a single day would fill an elaborate menu. The man who would live on nothing a year could actually become something of a connoisseur. He could study the cooking of the various chefs and learn where to find the best chicken or salad or roast, fish or oysters, and by carefully selecting his courses he could make an excellent dinner within a radius of a few blocks. Incidentally, he would enjoy the cooking of the best chefs in America."

William Dean Howells (in the "New York Streets" essay terminating *Impressions and Experiences*, 1896) found "scarcely a block of any of the poorer avenues which has not its liquor store, and generally there are two; wherever a street crosses them there is a saloon

on at least one of the corners; sometimes on two, sometimes on three, sometimes even on all four. I had the curiosity to count the saloons on Sixth Avenue. . . . In a stretch of some two miles I counted ninety of them, besides the eating houses where you can buy drink with your meat; and this avenue is probably far less infested with the traffic than some others. You may therefore safely suppose that out of the hundred miles of shops, there are ten, or fifteen, or twenty miles of saloons. They have the best places on the avenues, and on the whole they make the handsomest show. They all have a cheerful and inviting look, and if you step within, you find them cosy, quiet, and, for New York, clean. There are commonly tables set about in them, where their frequenters can take their beer or whiskey at their ease, and eat the free lunch which is often given in them."

The New Metropolis, edited by E. Idell Zeisloft (1899), is corroborative: "In 1897 there were 8,316 liquor licenses issued in New York. . . . In Brooklyn in the same year there were 4,129 licenses issued. . . . It is estimated that $250,000 a day passes over the polished counters of New York saloons. If all the saloons in Greater New York were placed side by side they would line both sides of a street extending from the Battery to King's Bridge."

I have the reminiscent word of a benedict of 1900 that during a hansom ride he set himself the alluring task of kissing his blushful bride each time they passed a pair of swinging doors, and soon fell so far behind the count that he was obliged to abandon his attrite amorousness.

"Its popularity is somewhat of a puzzle," Maxfield Parrish in his eighty-fifth summer wrote to me in 1954, when I questioned him about this happy mural held affectionate in the annals of convivial art, "but I dare say any painting hanging over a famous bar is bound to be that."

One in manifest destiny with Bouguereau's *Nymphs and Satyr* of the Hoffman House and the earlier vanished memory of the mammoth mirror in Broadway's mid-nineteenth century Gem Saloon—a blank canvas on which each man painted a fleeting self-portrait—*Old King Cole* was commissioned by Nicholas Biddle, then manager of the Astor Estate, to decorate the Flemish oak bar of the Knickerbocker Hotel. Within a year of the opening of this caravanserai, the *Metropolitan Magazine* of July, 1907, made glowing appraisal: "Mr. Maxfield Parrish grasped his opportunity . . . and rose to the present summit of his art. No man ever more thoroughly avoided the commonplace. The first evidence of his skill lies in the manner in which he has caused the warm shadows of the pine boughs and the like, which harmonize with the dull finish of the . . . wall, to lead the eye to the brighter center of the composition and to his treatment of dry, yellow ground at the castle foot. . . . He disposes his masses with a rich dignity. He creates a cool, fresh atmosphere, which, though often subdued, never brings somber reflections. He deals with objects that seem permanently natural and familiar, though at the same time fantastic and poetic. He may lack here the many little conceits and oddities so often found in his work, but his whimsical imagination and sense of homely fun never vanishes for a minute."

A pupil of Howard Pyle, Maxfield Parrish—sometimes referred to as "a Barrie with a palette"—did much to raise the standard of color illustration, poster design, and lettering as a fine art; the crisp, joyful, sunlit blue that bears his name once sparkled on magazine covers, scene designs, and the artifacts of daily living, and seems to permeate even those of his book illustrations treated in black and white. For the Knickerbocker assignment—completed the year he became a National Academician—he drew upon one of the earliest nursery rhymes of England, dating back (in its original form) to the sixteen hundreds, and, forswearing its various mutations, adapted the gentle traditional satire of the third century Monarch of Mirth who, some chroniclers say, fathered a saint (Helena, mother of the Roman Emperor Constantine).

When Rollin Kirby's forbidding Prohibition figure came to symbolize an era, the Knickerbocker quietly closed its doors on May 27, 1920, and transformed its gaiety into an office building. In 1935, after a loan engagement at the Racquet and Tennis Club, the "merry old soul" was brought to the Astor-owned St. Regis to decorate a room specially designed in his honor; the following year this retreat became the Iridium Room, and the demanding sovereign was exiled to more modest quarters across the lobby—to return in triumph to the earlier setting, lovingly known since 1948 as the "King Cole Bar."

402

"This old relic," its creator wrote to me, "has not traveled far but often, and may be some day will come to rest for good. . . . There will no doubt be an impulse to move it again, and it ought to be on casters. That's all I can think of."

"Old King Cole," over the Bar of the Knickerbocker Hotel, 1906
Southeast corner of Broadway and Forty-second Street

MOST BIOGRAPHIES begin with antecedence and birth; but the life story of the Park Avenue Hotel best ranges in reverse from a banal epilogue back in time to a strange prelude.

On September 15, 1926, a week after the structure was vacated, its once populous lobby was littered with *meubles* and movables and the tables of the favored court restaurant stacked high with lots of linen, draperies, and rugs awaiting the finality of the auctioneer's descending hammer. By December of the following year, the completed Two Park Avenue Building reared its twenty-eight commercial stories on the site of the hotel famed for quiet luxury, al fresco dining, and evening concerts since its second incarnation, as of June 10, 1878.

The first flash-back sequence begins with 1869. In that year—far to the vanward of England's "Garden City movement," initiated by Ebenezer Howard in 1898—A. T. Stewart of dry goods réclame purchased some 7,000 acres on Long Island's Hempstead Plains, to establish an *urbs in rure* for the workingman, and gave it the name later used by town planners to describe an ideal of living. Concurrently, this stern disciplinarian, whose low wage scale and harsh fines for deviations in personnel behavior imposed genuine hardships on his employees, conceived the mollificatory idea of building a non-profit-making hotel for breadwinning women. John Kellum—the designer of his vast Broadway and Ninth Street retail emporium (later John Wanamaker's) as well as of his barren marble dwelling at Fifth Avenue and Thirty-fourth Street—was charged with the execution of this neo-philanthropic monument to misplaced altruism. Both architect and patron had passed away before Mrs. Stewart brought the scheme to delayed fructification with a monster preview of its innovative iron-fronted marvels on April 2, 1878. Three million dollars had been lavished on what the *New-York Daily Tribune* of February 27 described as "one of those great pale structures, having countless wide windows with deep casements . . . [that] look coldly massive during the day, but light up at night magnificently." In tone, pearl-gray topped the lower story "darkened to the color of brown stone"; and the "numerous pillars and pilasters" were "in imitation of red Scotch granite." The eight reception rooms, the parlors and the dining rooms, as well as the 502 "sleeping rooms" were an Eastlakian illustration of "the most modern ideas on the subject of house-furnishing." They imaginatively surrounded "a large sized court," with "pavements in various colors like mosaic," and a medial fountain with a forty-foot central jet supplemented by "a thousand smaller jets, filling a wide and deep basin," flanked at the four corners by "ornate bronze candelabra, manufactured in Paris, to order, each supporting five lamps, of ornamental design." The rates—$6 to $10 a week—were thought to be at variance with the $5–$15 earnings of New York's working girls, but it was anticipated that patronage drawn from the professional and skilled labor categories would be sufficient to fill many hotels of this nature. Nevertheless, the immediate failure of the scheme sprang from its high tariff and the disciplinary regulations reflected in a mordant cartoon which appeared with slight variations in both the German and English editions of

404

Puck on April 3, 1878, over the caption "A. T. Stewart's Women's Home, and the True Inwardness thereof." A view of the façade on "Flirtation Paradise" shows the cloistered tenants leaning from the elaborate fenestration, communicating with their prohibited swains in the language of the handkerchief, the fan, the fluttering note and even the short distance "telephone." A long bill held by an inmate appears over the tag

"The *dearest* spot on earth to me
Is Stewart's Woman's Home!"

Another vignette depicts a maiden reading one of the library's 3,000 volumes attached to a chain; elsewhere a slovenly servant reproaches a guest: "Hi, there! Yez can't undress in the bath rooms." Furthermore, in the same issue, a play on the actual house rules proclaims that the price of ablution varies "according to length of bather's sojourn." In obvious but unnamed caricature, *Puck* ventures to suggest Henry Ward Beecher—his career by then

The Palm Garden and Court of the Park Avenue Hotel, 1901
(Originally A. T. Stewart's "Women's Hotel")
West side of Park Avenue, Thirty-second to Thirty-third
Streets

scandal-blasted—as "a Chaplain and a sort of Inspector in General." These and other parodies had a factual basis, since it was forbidden to interject individuality into the closely supervised matched cells; pianos, sewing machines, pets, knick-knacks and personalia of any description were contraband. Small wonder that announcement of the failure of the experiment and plans for conversion into a regular hotel appeared in the *New-York Daily Tribune* of May 27, 1878! *Puck*, in editorial indignation, spoke fearlessly: "The late A. T. Stewart was a man of cold disposition and frigid manners. These little things come in handy, now. Between the two, it is difficult to say whether Stewart or Hilton deserves more gratitude for generous instincts." (The latter, one of the executors of the great merchant's estate, was generally regarded as the profiteering villain of the piece.) "But Stewart did one thing more than the other man to win our esteem—he died. Stewart and Vanderbilt are both dead, and presumably appropriately located." (Even *Puck* could not foresee that the mercantile prince's mortal remains—irrespective of his spiritual whereabouts—were to be stolen from the family vault in St. Mark's Churchyard on the November 7th following.) "But in one thing the dry-goods man has the advantage of the Commodore. His executors are men after his own heart. If the old Philistine were alive to-day, he couldn't suggest one additional item of meanness and petty tyranny in the arrangements of the 'Woman's Home.'"

. . . . Always filled with people

"BUT THE German, with his love of music and song, with his joy in God's free nature, with his inclination toward companionship and *Gemütlichkeit,* with all his recollections of a Sunday in the old homeland, what has he got?" queried Karl Theodor Griesinger, the liberal editor and historian from Baden, as he contemplated the plight of his transplanted Landsmänner, in the distillation of his five dissatisfactory years here (*Lebende Bilder aus Amerika,* Stuttgart, 1858). "Dear reader, I'll tell you what he has—lonely homesickness. . . . Of course, nothing of this appears in the letters home. . . . There is not a hint that your Sunday's recreation is 'stealthily and secretly, mutely, deep in silence, without songs or the clink of glasses, without sunshine or promenade, to drink your high-priced beer.' . . . But New York is quite different. If the Americans have discovered the Sunday law, the New York Germans have discovered the 'Sacred Concert'; God bless the discovery. At the 'Sacred Concert' pure church music is performed. The Sunday papers carry long announcements of such concerts in German restaurants. Even the German theater presents a sacred concert. If you go to the theater you will find that the sacred music never gets to be presented. In fact it will seem to you that a comedy is being offered, with perhaps some pleasant music between the acts. And in the restaurants it will sound as if there were Strauss waltzes issuing forth from the trumpets. It may be a little difficult to recognize the church music in the billiard games, the target practice with air guns, the amusing performance of the yodelers, the gymnastic leaps of an acrobat, even the tinkling sounds of the beer glasses. The whole place is thick with people, men and women all sit with full glasses before them, munch on bread and cheese, and do their souls good. This sacred music is certainly worth its twelve-cent admission fee. Let the American saints grumble over this German Sunday; let them

406

send for the police because the place is open. New York is a cosmopolitan city and will not fall into the hands of the preachers."

To gratify this gregarious fondness for good music and foaming mugs, this thirst and *Heimweh,* there were a variety of resorts with summer speckled tree shade scattered about town, prominent among them the Terrace Garden, frequently mentioned here and there from the mid-1860's until its demolition in May of 1927. George C. D. Odell, in *Annals of the New York Stage,* traces its history (parallel with the connective Lexington Avenue Opera House) through the successive seasons with faithful if admittedly languid care, inventorizing a medley of warm-weather diversions and winter wares, performances by German companies, operas, operettas, benefits, concerts (here Theodore Thomas found rising fame), Sommernachtsfests, masked balls, and banquets. Although many nationalities figured in the roster of entertainments, the resort was heavily flavorous of Teutonicism always—"Klein-Deutschland," the dramatic historiographer braceleted it and its ilk. *King's Handbook of New York* (1892) referred to Terrace Garden and its Siamese twin, the Lexington Avenue Opera House, as "two names by which an establishment which extends from East 58th Street to East 59th Street, near Lexington Avenue, is known," consisting of "a theatre, fronting on 58th Street, a ball-room and an open-air garden. Properly speaking, the first title applies to the entire establishment, and the second to the theatre only. Performances of comic opera in German are given in the theatre, and concerts in the garden in the summer, and both theatre and ball-room are used for social affairs in winter. The place is greatly in favor among the Germans."

The *New-York Daily Tribune,* June 9, 1901, makes comparison not altogether odious: "It is a pretty far cry in many respects from Kroll's, in Berlin, to the Terrace Garden . . . and yet persons familiar with the two places will note points of resemblance. . . . What it [the Prussian retreat] is like now deponent saith not . . . but some years ago the old theatre stood in an illuminated garden in which bands provided music for the diversion of the visitors who sauntered through the green alleys or sat at tables in the enjoyment of creature comforts. Wearied of this, or curious about the performance in the theatre, one might saunter in and mayhap hear one of the world's greatest singers in an opera by Mozart, Meyerbeer, or a charming old Singspiel by Lortzing. . . . Terrace Garden is a replication of Kroll's on a small scale. There are trees and arbored tables and music; much to eat and drink, and opening from the Garden is the old theatre."

Samuel Swift, in *The New Metropolitan* (May, 1903) takes us indoors for culinary odors: "German cooking, with dishes as Teutonic as raw beef, flourishes at Terrace Garden . . . and the walls and ceilings are decorated in quaint mediæval style. Here and at Luchow's . . . Americans are numerous, but you may also see German family parties."

All of this circumambiency has found its way into one of the best of Byron's photographs—another work that rememorates the tenderness which Jean-Eugène-Auguste Atget turned on his adored city of Paris. In "The Maw Of The Monster" chapter of *New Cosmopolis* (New York, 1915), James Huneker—filled with *Weltschmerz* and *"Kennst Du das Land"*-ism —caught the refrain when he questioned his *lecteur* along memory-searching lines of delightsome whileaways, ending with "and Terrace Garden when Michael Heumann was in charge?" He sighs: "Some of these places still exist, but there is one that does not. Where Proctor's Theatre now stands in East Fifty-eighth Street was a small brewery operated by Peter

Byron. n.y
21784

Terrace Garden, 1906
North side of East Fifty-eighth Street,
near Lexington Avenue

Buckel. Big trees pierced the floor of the piazza, and under them you could sit and enjoy yourself; opposite was Terrace Garden—it is still the same old Terrace Garden—always filled with people. The street then reminded me of a street in Vienna."

. . . . *A journey of some twenty years' duration*

"SHERRY, BY the way, has been distanced in the race as regards the erection of his new buildings [*sic*] by Delmonico, who now expects to open his new restaurant . . . on Nov. 15, while Sherry's building, on the corner diagonally opposite, will hardly be finished before next April, if then." So *Town Topics,* on September 30, 1897, informed the patrons of these rival establishments.

Both veteran restaurateurs, however, shared a common defeat, for on November 2 the *New-York Daily Tribune* described two social events of the previous day. At Mills House No. 1 (Bleecker, Sullivan, and Thompson streets—a site formerly occupied by once fashionable Depau Row), "men of moderate means," benefiting from D. O. Mills' desire to provide them with "pleasant, clean and comfortable hotel quarters" (designed by Ernest Flagg), sat down to a 15-cent regular dinner, "and when night came . . . the reading-rooms, the . . . courts and the cosey corners . . . were alive with . . . [those] who had paid 20 cents for the privilege of being there." Meanwhile, on Fifth Avenue and Thirty-fourth Street, at the Astoria—added to the north side of the Waldorf by hyphen and by Hardenbergh (the architect)—"The guests . . . displayed quite as much interest in inspecting the decorations and appointments . . . as in the entertainment. . . . They roamed at will over the whole vast structure, examining in turn the grand ballroom, the Astor Gallery, with its mural decorations; the west foyer, containing Benzoni's statue, *The Flight from Pompeii* [see pages 112 and 113]; the myrtle room, the east room, the Colonial room, [and] the east foyer, containing Story's statue of Cleopatra. . . ."

Two weeks later, on November 15, while Stanford White was still supervising the shaping of the physical aspects of Sherry's (the outer shell today survivant as the Fifth Avenue office of the Guaranty Trust Company of New York) "Delmonico's entered upon another epoch of its career" as the *New-York Daily Tribune* of the 16th said, pronouncing its new home, designed by James Brown Lord, "one of the most striking buildings in the city. The top is capped with a row of blazing electric lights. . . . The style of architecture is Renaissance, and white limestone is the material used. . . ." Within were "A number of patrons who have followed the fortunes of Delmonico's ever since the first eating house was started in William-st. [seventy years and nine family-owned incarnations away]. . . . The front in Fifth-ave. is unbroken by any entrance. . . . The entrances [on Forty-fourth Street] . . . are protected by handsome wrought-iron coverings. The main entrance leads to the office. The Palm Room is between the restaurant and café. A long wall of glass doors separates this room from the main hall. The balcony, which overlooks the [white and pale yellow decorated] Palm Room, is finished in light natural-colored, highly polished woods. . . . The dining-room on the Fifth-ave. side is decorated in Louis XVI style. Panels of satin in alternate stripes of green and yellow are set in the wall and the windows are heavily draped with satin.

The ceilings are delicately tinted in light yellow and bronze, and are divided into five rectangular panels from each of which hangs an ornate candelabrum. . . ." The café, to the east of the Palm Room "has a high wainscotting of carved black oak, and the frieze is finished in grayish tints. . . . The prevailing tints in the dining-room upstairs are white and red. The whole appearance . . . is rich but subdued. Avoidance of anything that savors of mere glare and color has been successful. The same idea has been carried out in the private supper-rooms, and especially in the ballroom suite, which is exceptionally handsome. The bachelor apartments are on the top floors and the roof will be used as an open-air restaurant."

Anomalous were the environs of all this muted elegance: Tyson's Fifth Avenue Market— an élite butcher shop—is listed at No. 529 in the city directories from 1881–1882 to 1902–1903; "Ye Olde Willow Cottage," with its name-giving tree an interruption to pedestrian traffic,

Delmonico's, 1898
Northeast corner of Fifth Avenue and Forty-fourth Street

figures almost mythologically in the chronicles of the years as an objective for sleighing parties, a place of refreshment (once, according to hearsay, operated by the pugilist, Tom Hyers)—an eyesore to some and the unworthy object of nostalgic sighs to others. The threnody of these anachronisms was forecast in the spring of 1902, when the plot (part of the Paran Stevens estate) changed hands to the tune of $1,000,000. On January 13, 1905, the *New-York Daily Tribune* reported the resale of the "corner parcel," and untidiness soon gave way

The kitchen at Delmonico's, 1902

to the marble splendor of the building in which The Night and Day Bank opened on April 30, 1906. To the south, in 1898, was one of the stables of the New York Cab Company. Only three and a half decades before, on July 13, 1863, during the four-day Reign of Terror of the Civil War Draft Riots, a frenetic mob had set total fire to the Colored Orphan Asylum on the west side of the Avenue, where the sophistication of the new Sherry's was now to make social history.

At the century's end, a less sanguinary feud was being waged on this selfsame battle-ground. "The fight is on between Delmonico's and Sherry's," (ultimately opened on October 10, 1898), declared *The Illustrated American* of October 21st. "Their splendid new establishments, so near together that they can scowl at each other, have been thrown open on upper Fifth Avenue. It will be a fight to the death, with the odds in favor of Delmonico's." In the still prejudiced issue of January 6, 1899, "The Captious Critic" keeps us informed of developments on the battlefront: "New York is very much interested in Sherry's attempt to introduce to upper Fifth Avenue the 'table de luxe' which in other places flourishes under the more hackneyed title of table d'hote. Mr. Sherry's fine repast . . . costs only a modest three dollars—a figure so low in the annals of Sherry pricedom that the discreet are likely to think twice before trying one . . . [while] the frequenters of the older and more plebian resorts [serving a fifty-cent meal "with a remarkable bottle of something purplish-red thrown in"] are hardly able to understand how it is possible to spend three dollars on a table d'hote without wine. For after all, a table d'hote under any other name must taste the same. Society has taken up the Sherry table de luxe as if it were an entirely new gastronomic contrivance. . . . Charles Delmonico still continues to more than hold his own. He is not resorting to any of the cheaper methods of gaining favor, feeling secure in the thought that his patrons are amply able to pay the right price for the right thing."

The chefs of these gastronomic rivals were vocal, too, but not belligerent, and proudly conscious of their white-capped responsibilities, for Pascal Grand of Sherry's, billed in *Munsey's Magazine* of February, 1902, as "One of The Great Cooks of The Twentieth Century," stated that "From vegetable boy to chef, in the kitchen of a Sherry or a Delmonico, is a journey of some twenty years' duration." Charles Ranhofer, Delmonico's chef from 1862–1876 and from 1879–1899, writing from the Twenty-sixth Street establishment in the December, 1896 issue of the *Metropolitan Magazine*, was not lacking in the drama and pride of his calling: "The culinary art should be the basis of all diplomacy; it may be said to be the distinguishing thing of civilization, and in its perfection it is the inspiration of genius. . . . The chef of a large establishment must possess at least two essential qualifications: he must be an epicurean by nature, and this natural gift must be enhanced by long years of training in his profession. . . . All my men are excellent cooks. . . . I have only to direct them, and they consult me should the least difficulty arise. My staff of assistants numbers forty-two." Of the owners of the gilded gullets through which the end result of all this concentered effort was to pass, he wrote: "The man of wealth who does not know how to feel the delight of giving a good dinner to his friends fails to appreciate the blessings of his fortune, and no man who desires to possess perfect health and long life should be without a devoted physician and a wise cook. . . . The regular customers of Delmonico's establishment [gratefully able to pay from $4 to $10 and more a plate, depending on "the quality of the accompanying wines"] are by taste and breeding epicureans. . . ."

413

The glory that was Sherry's and the grandeur that was Delmonico's vanished within a few years of each other. On May 7, 1919, *The New York Times* factually informed its readers: "Louis Sherry announced yesterday that on May 17 he will abandon his restaurant . . . [on] Fifth Avenue. Prohibition and war-born Bolshevism, Mr. Sherry declared, were two things largely responsible for his determination to leave the restaurant business." The same paper, on May 22, 1923, became more emotional: "There were a few moist eyes among the diners at 9 o'clock last night when the orchestra at Delmonico's struck up 'Auld Lang Syne.' . . . Last night was Delmonico's last." Two years later, however, on August 19, 1925, fifty of the faithful foregathered once more, to partake of a ghost-ridden feast amid the ruins, "While bricks and lumber crashed within a few feet of them," wrote the *Times* of the 20th. "There were left yesterday only the walls of the first story, a few iron girders sticking up to about where the third floor used to be, gaunt and covered with plaster dust, and the walls of . . . [the] main dining room on the Fifth Avenue side." There, "Despite the dust, the clang of bells and the crash of bricks in chutes outside, the luncheon was served with all the embellishments of former days," by the catering firm of Maresi-Mazzetti and waiters who had received their training in the old Delmonico's at Twenty-sixth Street. The brave walls, their starkness partially concealed by American flags, still pathetically preserved "a little of their green coloring."

. . . . *The garden party school of millinery*

"ALL KINDS OF HATS"—a headline in the *New-York Daily Tribune* of April 9, 1902—might well serve as a caption for this photograph. "The striking feature of hats this season is their picturesqueness. Sweet simplicity is a pose much affected, but even the simplest styles have the 'picture' quality strongly in evidence. . . ." This garden party school of millinery was favorable to a new version of "the old fashioned yellow Leghorn," the same newspaper had announced three weeks earlier, in its issue of March 20: "It is not in the texture alone that the Leghorn has been improved, for it is now to be had in all the most beautiful of light colors, such as Pompadour pink, forget-me-not blue, light shades of flax and soft toned greens [sometimes in "two shade" combination with brown], on which the delicate floral effects of this year may be displayed to the greatest advantage." The horticultural theme, according to *The New York Herald* of April 6, was carried out by the use of "fairy like . . . roses, in the palest pink or pure white . . . field flowers . . . scattering themselves in artistic profusion . . . Bluets, buttercups, daisies . . . wood violets, cowslips, daffodils and mignonette," along with the Paris-sponsored hyacinth, while the fad for orchard-inspired trimming was on the wane. Shapes—if one followed the *Herald* gospel—had "little variety, for everything is flat—extremely flat—and with a rather broad brim." Exceptions to the "plateau" were the Tricorne, Marquis, Campion and Watteau. The *Tribune* of April 9 spoke for the "stateliness" of the "amazon shape, . . . well suited to the semi-low coiffure that is so generally worn," as further evidenced by A. Simonson's advertisement, advocating the "Lover's Knot" as a fashionable back hair arrangement. "Dress hats were never gayer in color than now, although quiet tones are preferred for ordinary wear. . . . It seems certain that large

414

hats, rather than the extremely large, will be worn. . . . Toques and turbans of malines, tulle and chiffon are as high in favor as ever." The advance report (in the *Tribune* of March 20) had mentioned "complexion veils" of "light meshes . . . [with] open effects nearly as fine as cobwebs."

Beneath all these expensive frivolities, maquillage was at a practically non-existent minimum, as borne out by the humorous anecdote of a "philosopher" (quoted in the *Tribune* of March 20) who had observed a woman—"handsomely but conspicuously dressed . . . [with] the most brilliant complexion imaginable . . . on the platform of a crowded car," so terror-stricken by an abrupt jounce that "she turned perfectly white, excepting a large spot on each cheek, which stood revealed in the most unmistakable manner as paint."

While a report read before the Women's Christian Temperance Union of Kings County on April Fool's Day of 1902 (and duly reported in the *Tribune* of the 2nd) "alleged that in New-York City alone there are one hundred thousand women who smoke" even a powerful magnifying glass fails to reveal evidence of this vice being practiced by any of the luncheon guests. Mrs. Emma Graves Dietrick, author of this paper, found the habit common to all

Ladies' Luncheon at Delmonico's, 1902

classes from "the women of the slums" to those "of wealth and social standing"; and lamented the effect on the next generation, for "the sons of the rich and poor alike will be voters, and their daughters will be mothers of American citizens." She saw "The number of smokers among our cultured women . . . increasing. Worn with late hours and dissipation . . . [they] seek for relief from an overtaxed nervous system." Repeated passages [I noted four] in *The House of Mirth* by Edith Wharton (New York, 1905) give insight into the stigma attached to this hungry indulgence. For instance: ". . . Having finally discovered that the seat [on the late afternoon train bearing her to a house party] adjoining Miss Bart's was at her disposal, she [Mrs. George Dorset] possessed herself of it . . . explaining . . . that she had come across from Mount Kisco in her motor-car that morning, and had been kicking her heels for an hour at Garrisons without even the alleviation of a cigarette, her brute of a husband having neglected to replenish her case before they parted. . . . 'And at this hour of the day I don't suppose you've a single one left, have you, Lily?' she plaintively concluded. Miss Bart caught the startled glance of Mr. Percy Gryce, whose own lips were never defiled by tobacco. 'What an absurd question, Bertha!' she exclaimed, blushing at the thought of the store she had laid in at Lawrence Selden's [bachelor apartment]." And again, seventy-three pages later: "He [Selden] had drawn out his cigarettes as he spoke, and she [Lily Bart] reached her hand toward the case. 'Oh, do give me one—I haven't smoked for days!' 'Why such unnatural abstinence? Everybody smokes at Bellomont' [the scene of the houseparty]. 'Yes—but it is not considered becoming in a *jeune fille à marier.*'"

While the ladies here shown are not—for the moment at least—living "in a bath of nicotine" (another bit from the Wharton novel of manners) many of their number doubtless shared in equally reprehensible distractions. For example, an editorial in the *New-York Daily Tribune* of April 4, 1902 is devoted to an athletic diversion: "The craze for ping pong has spread so swiftly as almost to surpass every previous record. All the clubs are putting in tables for this game. Manufacturers are working day and night to supply the demand for the balls and the tools of the sport. Brokers forget to look at the tape while they smite the little spheres in their offices. . . . Women and men alike have fallen victims to this fascination by the thousands. . . . The jesters, both amateur and professional, make this game one of their chief subjects for skits and bits of wit and humor. . . . It has a language of its own [not to mention ailments of eye and ankle named in its honor], and street urchins as well as club members are beginning to use its technical phrases with fluency and freedom. Moreover, ping pong books are issuing from the press so copiously that they will soon fill large spaces on library shelves, and even the Shakespeare—Baconian controversy is giving way to the more fascinating contentions of ping pong." And, if further evidence of depravity and addiction is needed, we learn with horror from the *New-York Daily Tribune* of March 16, 1902 that the " 'Bridge' Craze [is]Still 'On.' ": "He proved a false prophet who said a few months ago that bridge whist was on the wane. Instead of losing, it seems to gain in popularity, and the ranks of its devotees are swelling to really an alarming extent. It is no exaggeration to say that there are to-day hundreds of women in New-York who are afflicted with 'bridge mania,' as it has come to be called, and who spend their afternoons, and frequently their evenings, regularly at the card table. . . . Physicians have found it necessary seriously to remonstrate with some of their patients, and in many cases to prohibit them entirely from playing a game which they cannot do in moderation." At a luncheon of the

National Society of New-England Women (at Delmonico's also, and I have reason to suspect possibly even the gathering here depicted, although the coverage in the *Tribune* of April 12, 1902—*The New York Times* and *The New York Herald* having passed up the opportunity—does not give sufficient detail for positive identification) Mrs. Edward Addison Greeley spoke with feeling and mixed metaphor: "While I believe in getting all the pleasure we can while passing through this vale, I think we should plant a few acorns for the future oaks as well as pick daisies all the time. This applies to the card table and other entertainments of that kind. We come to the month of April tired out, with a few luncheon favors and prizes won at euchres to show, and wonder what it all amounts to. What a power we might exert in this city if we would meet to discuss important subjects as we rush to whists and euchres! We could revolutionize the thoughts of New-York women toward higher things."

. . . . *The Chinese Delmonico's*

"EVEN THE glitter of the St. Regis failed to spur their jaded appetites," declared *The New York Herald* of Sunday March 11, 1906, in which this, the 19,359th photograph taken by the Byron Company, is reproduced in a magazine section feature describing the pathetic plight of two "noted epicures, sated with the foods served at the high class cafés and hotels. . . . In fact, it was at the St. Regis that they formed the decision to go out in search of something new," and set forth on a "gastronomic globe trotting" expedition that came to a bilious end. "After three days spent in . . . repairs" to their alimentary tracts they celebrated their convalescence by meeting in the lobby of the point of origin, where the "promoter" (the party of the first part in this engrossing travelogue) and his subdued "victim" agreed unanimously to "remain in . . . [their] old haunts." In their exotic *pèlerinage*—circumventing the aromatic delicacies of the Magyar, Russian, Turkish and other foreign restaurants in "cosmopolitan Manhattan," where, according to E. Idell Zeisloft (in *The New Metropolis*, New York, 1899) were "to be found samples of the cookery of nearly every nation under the sun"—they had paid digestive penalty in resorts Kosher, Italian, Spanish, Greek, French and Chinese.

Their port of call in Chinatown was not by any means a "fly by night" affair, for from the early 1890's through the gustatory Baedekers and *vade mecums* of the beginning 1930's it earned mention and popular continuity. A disserving paragraph appeared in an article— "Some Oddities Of Chinatown" by the dyspeptic John Hubert Greusel—in the July 1, 1893 issue of *Once A Week:* "Through a narrow hall and up a dirty stairs brings one to the Chinese Delmonico restaurant. A good dinner consists of nine courses, served on bare wooden tables and eaten with chop-sticks. The meal begins with sweets, half a dozen bits of sugared ginger heaped on a small egg-shell compote; the ginger is dyed a brilliant scarlet. In rapid succession follow dried nuts, candied apricots and other delicacies . . . ; tea is offered in cups no bigger than a thimble; a tin teapot is at hand, from which the diner replenishes his diminutive cup as often as need be. Some of the patrons have before them huge bowls of steaming rice, which they eat by bringing the dish to their lips, and then literally shoveling the food into the open mouth. . . . As the dinner proceeds, some of the natives kick off

Restaurant in Chinatown, 1905; 24 Pell Street

their slippers, their bare stockings peering through the rungs of their stools. The odor of fuming cigarettes fills the air; an incessant babble prevails; every few moments you will see a Chinese pick up a bone or a bit of refuse food and deliberately send it flying under the table to the dirty floor! A greedy cat munches away under one of the tables. Were it not for the red banners on the walls, the eating-house would be as bare as a barn; and, assuredly, it is as uninviting as a pig-sty. Yet the visitors to Chinatown love it dearly, and laugh and chatter there in a corner; the ladies, especially, on their first visit, cannot prevent themselves going into ecstacies over the tiny teacups. Thus, to-day, the 'slummers' eat, drink and are merry in their new experience with strange dishes." Harriet Quimby, devoting a half dozen pages to "Epicurus in Chinatown" in *The New Metropolitan* of July, 1903 (including an illustration of the Oriental Restaurant at 3 Pell Street, captioned "Chinatown's Waldorf-Astoria"), evidently had a happier flow of gastric juice. After describing the Quarter's fixed colony and the Sunday and holiday convergence of Chinese laundrymen from other parts of the city, she states that for the tourist trade the "perennial attraction of Chinatown" lay not in "the red radiance of the decorations and signs," nor in "the curious garb of the denizens," nor in the mysteries of the joss house, the quaintly stocked shops or the strange theatre, but in "Chinese cookery." Chinatown, she tells, "maintains several restaurants," each with

418

its American customers. She gives the native prandial timetable (breakfast at ten, dinner at four, and light fare close to midnight) and recommends "the dining hour" as "the most interesting time . . . for a visit to this picturesque locality. . . . [Then] the scene is varied by the appearance of waiters who pass hither and thither bearing trays of assorted bowls . . . balanced on their heads. They are carrying dinner to merchants who cannot leave their shops. . . . The American who enters one of these restaurants for the first time may be surprised at finding that the way to the tables leads through the kitchen. . . . The idea is to give the patron evidence that everything is done in a cleanly manner. . . . In Chinatown good cooking is a part of religion—the cook is a priest."

. . . . *The father of more art children*

"THE ONLY thing I've got against you, Chase," exclaimed the carping James Abbott McNeill Whistler, "is that you are a teacher." The target of this critical barb, however, took paternal pride in the artistic "laying on of hands": "I believe I am the father of more art children than any other teacher," he once said.

William Merritt Chase's career as "The Painter of Precept"—a title bestowed by J. Walker McSpadden in *Famous Painters of America* (New York, 1907)—began at the end of his six-year-long student days in Munich, when he refused an appointment in the Royal Academy to become Professor of Drawing and Painting at the Art Students' League of New York, the first independent school of its kind in this country, founded in 1875 and then in its fourth season. During its first quarter century, which saw many vibrant changes in our native art, Chase (according to Charles de Kay in *The Illustrated American* of March 12, 1898, possessed of "more medals than a bicycle chief") occupied a favorite place. Elizabeth Bisland, who visited him in his Tenth Street studio (see page 422) in behalf of *The Cosmopolitan* (May, 1889) gives insight: "The personality of the artist is an interesting one. Short and squarely built, with a kindly self-reliant face, a strongly cast, intellectual head, and the manner of the successful, competent man—a competency that appears to be the key-note of his work and character . . . Chase has been a strong influence with the younger artists, . . . being sought by them with the impression that no other American could give an equal training in technique, and so teach them the painter's side of their art."

By the 1892–1893 season enrollment at the League's quarters in the newly opened Fine Arts Building at 215 West Fifty-seventh Street reached about 1,000 under a faculty of nine; and Chase—in addition to his own creative work and the conducting of daily classes in portraiture and still life—had found time to take charge of a summer school (the first of his many such ventures here and abroad) mainly for landscape painting, in the Shinnecock Hills of Long Island. New York, then as now the cultural mainspring of the country, offered the competition of several other recognized centers of similar instruction (The National Academy of Design; the Art Schools of the young Metropolitan Museum; and the Cooper Union Art School) attracting a yearly average of 4,000 neophytes, indicative of the trend away from the earlier, almost prerequisite years of study abroad, in the old masterly climate of Munich and the headier atmosphere of Paris.

419

Life Classes at the Chase School of Art, 1896; 57 West Fifty-seventh Street

In those days it was not considered *au fait* for men and women students to gaze upon the nude simultaneously in a single instant of time, so that when in 1896 (Mrs. Kenneth Hayes Miller told me) a group of boys—including her future teacher and husband—took advantage of their model's rest period to burst in upon the girls' life class, expulsion inevitably followed. The sinners sought out the progressive Mr. Chase (then in temporary secession from what he regarded as the confining principles of the League) to become the nucleus of the new Chase School of Art. Helen Pendleton Miller identified the young man in the white shirt, with the black tie, standing at the easel to the left of the bearded master himself, as the twenty-one-year-old Miller (first pupil and later instructor at the school, 1900–1911). The *Metropolitan Magazine* of May, 1897, devoted seven profusely illustrated pages to Chase's independent and flourishing atelier, a place for serious application (happily not without its moments of traditional horseplay), which in its first year attracted forty to fifty new pupils every month, about 60 per cent of them women. Despite Chase's outspoken winnowing, which eliminated about a laggard half of this influx within each thirty days, the rooms were filled to capacity; and the innovation of an advanced night class attracted many. The article made apparently unfair and superficial comparison with Julian's Academy in Paris, which impressed Robert Henri (in *The Art Spirit*) as "a great cabaret with singing and huge practical jokes . . . a factory, too, where thousands of drawings of human surfaces were turned out." In 1901, Chase expressed his pedagogic credo in a "Thumbnail Editorial" on "The Danger of Art Schools" in the February issue of the *Metropolitan Magazine:* "I came home [from Munich] . . . and tried to forget what I had learned. When

420

my own students leave me—I have three hundred of them—I say to them: 'Now shake off the influence of the school as quickly as you can. Cultivate individuality. Strive to express your own environment according to your own lights, in your own way.' Many students stay too long in the art school. . . . The school is necessary . . . but it ceases to be anything but detrimental after it has given . . . the mechanical facility, the technique. . . . I should say that the average period of study is about three years. . . . Not more than one-tenth of the art students follow art as a life career, and this, perhaps, is just as well."

By a series of transmutations (as the New York School of Art, 1902–1909; the New York School of Fine and Applied Art, 1909–1941) the Chase School of Art is the lineal predecessor of the present day Parsons School of Design, so designated since 1941. Chase retired in 1907 at the age of fifty-eight, in the wake of a disagreement with the wider latitudes of Robert Henri, whom he had added to his faculty, and returned to The Art Students League in the interest of his own self-expression. J. Walker McSpadden, in the book already cited, allows us vignetted glimpses of him through the pens of his pupils. One student remembered him as "A Beau Brummel with the vitality of ten men—feet spread well apart and firmly planted on the floor—glasses [with their "wide black string"] firmly and constantly shoved in one place—Chase stands before his students and opens his big heart of the best that is in it." Another describes the master's passage: "Chase is full of mannerisms, yet he has had them so long that they have become as much a part of himself as his—carnation. He will interlard his talk with 'ehs' and 'ahs' and little shrugs and gestures, and nibbling at his fingers, and sometimes you will understand his criticism and sometimes you won't. It may be something very practical, or again it may be something delightfully vague which goes right over your head—smack! against the canvas. When you come to your senses the destroyer has passed by and is laying waste at the other end of the room."

"I LIKE a painter who will leave his door half-open," ruminated "Ishmael" in the May 16, 1891 issue of *The Illustrated American*. His visit to John George Brown must have been practically synchronous with that of Joseph Byron, for he describes the painting the photographer has recorded in progress and preserved in the album of his American beginnings: "On two easels, standing side by side . . . two pictures, one in oil and one in water-color, of the same subject—a little, cross-legged vagrant, seated, playing silent serenades on a dumb broom with which he imitates a mandolin. The face, the pose, the spirit of the lad are true as life. And if you mark them, you will get the key to the success of the painter. Technically, I doubt whether either of the two works (I prefer the water-color, myself) would have contented such men as Pelez or Bastien Lepage ["I can't bear French art," snarled the combative Brown with his strong North of England accent], who have handled the same class of subject; but there is no question that the art they reflect is popular and pleasing. This may not be the highest kind of praise, but it is something, and, indeed, much."

The depreciatory "scribbler" cast an eye about the "square room" (once occupied by George H. Boughton) on the top floor of the Tenth Street Studios, where Brown had already passed about thirty of the fifty-three years he was to spend in this building so centripetal in the history of American art from 1857—when James Boorman Johnson commandeered the freshly acquired Beaux-Arts training of Richard Morris Hunt to fashion the first New York structure exclusively devoted to the needs of men of the brush and chisel—until the diminuendo of its sentimental latter days and reluctant demolition in 1954. Urban aerie of the Hudson River School, fortress of Academicians (on more than one occasion over a hundred canvases passed through its doors to hang in a single Academy annual), it might well serve as protagonist in several acts of the drama of American art, with a stellar cast including such figures as John LaFarge, Frederick E. Church, J. F. Kensett, Sanford R. Gifford, Albert Bierstadt, Winslow Homer, Homer D. Martin, J. Alden Weir, Emanuel Leutze and an infinitude of others. A glimpse of the "Artist Receptions" held there has come down in a double-page spread of wood engravings in *Frank Leslie's Illustrated Newspaper* for January 23, 1869, just as they later overflowed into Mrs. Thomas Bailey Aldrich's *Crowding Memories* (1920). The splendor of the accoutrements of William M. Chase's peremptory confiscation of what was originally purposed as the main exhibition gallery inhabits his own painting, *Chase's Tenth St. Studio*, also forever lingering in F. Hopkinson Smith's word image of the Tile Club party, novelized in a chapter of *The Fortunes of Oliver Horn*. In sober contrast to the opulence of this artistic overflow are the "diggings" into which "Ishmael" guides us on an early spring noon of 1891: "There was not much in the room to distract the eye from the easel at which Mr. Brown stood painting. A square room, hung with faded brown and purple curtains, furnished with well-worn cabinets and odds and ends, old chairs, old stools and benches; a platform in the centre of one wall, lighted by such light as could creep in through the panes of a wide and dusty window; old palettes, pendent in one corner near a big portfolio of sketches; a table, littered over with innumerable tubes and brushes. Wherever they could possibly be piled or stacked together, scores and more scores of studies."

The artist—"Of medium height, gray-haired and bearded, quick and particularly warm of speech, impetuous, simple and unassuming, both in dress and manner"—was a native of Durham, England, and even as an infant gave evidence of drawing ability. After an apprenticeship as a glass-cutter, he managed to secure sound art training at the School of Design in Newcastle, studying under Robert Scott Lanier and later with Orchardson in Edinburgh. In 1853 the twenty-two-year-old Brown—obligated to his mother's support—came to America and secured prompt employment in the Brooklyn glassworks of William Owen, whose daughter became the first of his three wives. From portraiture he soon turned to his own highly personal genre idiom, to which he remained more or less constant, with certain successful but less popular divagations, to the end of his eighty-one years, often producing as many as two dozen canvases in a twelvemonth. An apparently interminable procession of urchins—newsboys and bootblacks, "the children of the poor, the disinherited, the waifs and strays, the orphans"—trudged up the studio stairs to become his models, his subjects, and his friends.

J. G. Brown, N.A., in his studio, 1891; 51 West Tenth Street
(From Joseph Byron's album)

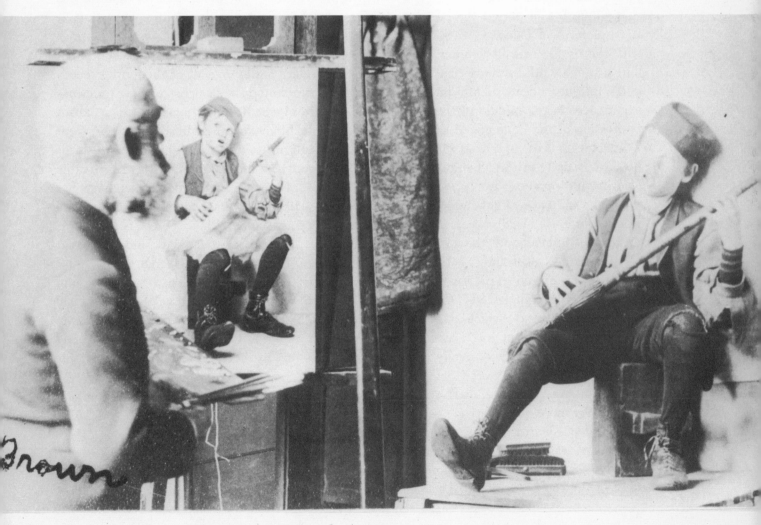

THE "PHOTO-JOURNALISTIC" team (to borrow a tag from Wilson Hicks) of Byron and Henry Warcom Newton collaborated on a "word-and-picture" story of Eastman Johnson for the *Metropolitan Magazine* of July, 1895. The septuagenarian artist (an alumnus of the Royal Academy at Düsseldorf, where he shared the atelier of Emanuel Leutze—then engaged in painting his oversize *Washington Crossing the Delaware*) was very much in the news because of his commission to execute a portrait of ex-President Harrison for The White House.

The interviewer waited on the artist at the Fifty-fifth Street home to which he had moved in 1872 from the old University Building on Washington Square; and as host and writer ascended the three flights to the top-floor studio glimpses were afforded of rooms "plainly but tastefully furnished, and the walls . . . covered with hundreds of pictures, nearly all . . . evidently the work of Mr. Johnson's brush." Midway, the party paused—not for recuperation, but to permit the passage of "a couple of 'movers'" engaged in transporting "a large picture" of General Miles out of the house. At the top of the climb was a chamber with the usual north-lit window, in front of which were "a number of cabinets and small bureaus, many others being scattered around the western wall . . . ; all of them are exceedingly antique and artistically finished, as becomes the studio of an artist of Mr. Johnson's experience. In the middle of the studio is a cross arrangement of gas jets." The journalist's impression of the famous and successful genre painter and portraitist bears quotation, too: "Mr. Johnson is as chipper as Russell Sage and is as full of life and go as any man two-thirds his age. In spite of the affection in his right knee [gout] he moves about with considerable alacrity, and converses freely and easily while he works. He is about five feet and eight inches in height and has a slight suggestion of a 'presence.' His hair is gray; his pointed beard is a bright white. He usually wears a pair of spectacles, and he smokes a heavy meerschaum pipe, or keeps it in his mouth the greater part of the time. . . . His eyes are dark and snappy. A short working jacket and a pair of leather slippers are features in his personal description."

The artist—inured to painting on his feet, frequently from nine or ten in the morning and as long as the light lasted—posed with the Harrison portrait (one of two of this national figure from his hand) which, so he said, had required eight or nine sittings of unequal length. He found his subject an "excellent poser," with a "charming manner" belying the cold reserve and taciturnity generally believed characteristic: "in short, an ordinary and amiable gentleman."

Johnson was not unfamiliar with the "great" (a word from which he shied away, preferring the more qualificative "well known" by way of compromise), for, as John I. H. Baur wrote in *An American Genre Painter Eastman Johnson 1824–1906* (the fine definitive monograph and catalogue of the great retrospective exhibition held at The Brooklyn Museum in 1940), ". . . the list of his portraits, stretching from the sixth to the twenty-fourth president of the country, reads like a Who's Who of nineteenth century America." His life in art

Eastman Johnson, N.A., in his studio, June, 1895; 65 West Fifty-fifth Street

began as a painter of likenesses, but he is perhaps most cherished for his prized genre pieces, from which he started to turn away in the early 1880's, his last dated narrative subject being *The Nantucket School of Philosophy* of 1887. In the more lucrative field of the commissioned portrait, his work commanded impressive remuneration: in the case of the Hatch Family Group (now owned by The Metropolitan Museum of Art) $1,000 for each one of the fifteen members of this felicitously composed domestic scene; about $5,000 for a full-length portrayal and around $1,500 for a head and shoulders. The Harrison likeness (H. 59½ × W. 39½ in.), now in a Reception Room on the ground floor of The White House, brought him $2,500, frame included.

With the aid of a magnifying glass and the generous and expert eye of Mr. Baur (now Curator of Paintings and Drawings at the Whitney Museum of American Art), it has been possible to identify several of the works in the studio. Resting against the wall is the strong three-quarter face of William M. Evarts; to the right of the canvas of the small girl on the mantel is half hidden the Boston Museum of Fine Arts' *The Little Convalescent;* just beyond it, *Not At Home* (in the collection of The Brooklyn Museum); next in line, one of the series painted in his sister's Kennebunkport barn; and behind the easel appears the playful boy atop *The Old Stage Coach* (or a study for this subject) first inspired and sketched in the Catskills, and finally painted in Nantucket in 1871, with a lively group of young islanders serving as models.

. . . . *More days inside that horse*

THERE WERE those who thought he bore a physical resemblance to the great Buonarroti. This probably did not please him, for in an interview published in *Harper's New Monthly Magazine,* June, 1878, he said: "Michael Angelo, Thorwaldsen, Canova, Flaxman—why should you stop to talk with them when you can listen to Phidias and Praxiteles?" Despite this conversational lack of interest, he admitted with certain reservations that the Florentine "was a mighty intellectual force, who emancipated art from some of its harder and more timid conditions; but he was not true enough to nature, and he was not the founder of a school."

John Quincy Adams Ward, born on an Urbana, Ohio, farm in 1830, preferred the local clay as the medium of his childhood modelings, rather than as an agricultural agent. The mature man who spoke wistfully—"I want to see every statue that has ever been made"—first gazed upon a piece of sculpture when he journeyed to Cincinnati in 1848 to study Hiram Powers' *Greek Slave,* subject of a sonnet by Elizabeth Barrett Browning and the artistic miracle of an age. "I would have gone through any imaginable privation," he later said, "had I been able to speak to the sculptor that day!" Forswearing, after trial of each, the family imposed professions of farmer and physician, he came east and at the age of nineteen, with the utmost diffidence, entered the Brooklyn atelier of Henry Kirke Brown, where he spent seven years, first as paying pupil, then as remunerated assistant. In this capacity, he had a part in his master's chef-d'œuvre, the equestrian statue of George Washington unveiled in Union Square on July 4, 1856. "I spent more days inside that horse than Jonah did inside the whale," he reminisced. Of his beginnings, Adeline Adams (in *John Quincy Adams Ward   An Appreciation,* written for The National Sculpture Society, 1912)

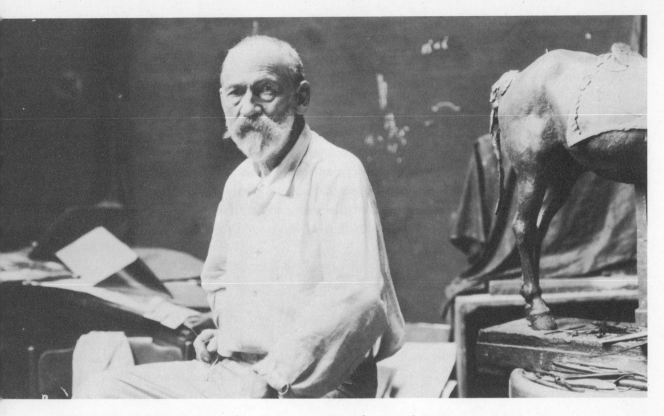

J. Q. A. Ward, N.A., in his studio, 1899; 119 West Fifty-second Street

said "he had modeled with Cellini-like distinction and charm many small objects to be cast in precious metal."

By 1861 he was ready to open his own studio, from which came the bronze *Indian Hunter*, in progress from 1857 to 1864, to be accepted by the Commissioners of Central Park as the first of four of his works to find a green background there, including the Shakespeare of 1873, for which his friend Edwin Booth is said to have posed, giving instructions the while as to the disposition of the Bard's cloak. "I am always afraid to ride or to drive near one of my statues," he said in 1878; "I don't believe I have stopped in front of one of them since it was put up." The squares and public places of New York bear testimony to his great-handed talent in the imperishable masculinity of his tributes to illustrious citizens, statesmen, and soldiers (although the spirited quadriga, *Naval Victory*, surmounting the Dewey Arch of 1899 was made of less stern stuff). The pedimental composition of The New York Stock Exchange on which Paul W. Bartlett worked as associate—in juxtaposition to the near-by colossal Washington of the Sub-Treasury steps—shows the range of his art. Other cities, too, share with ours the force that made him the sculptor's sculptor. A horseman himself, of the three equestrian statues which were his very special passion, the one of his middle age—that of General Thomas in the Nation's Capital (1878), often considered his masterpiece—was hailed by Saint-Gaudens as the finest of its kind in the world, while Herbert Adams spoke for his last unflinching stand, the monumental Fairmount Park General Hancock on his charger (the heroic model of which was completed as the sculptor lay dying in 1910).

Byron's camera (that so often seems to carry longevity in its focus) shows Ward in the

427

second of two home studios built for him in friendship by Richard Morris Hunt—seated in the vast, long, well equipped twin-skylighted room in which he did so large a part of his virile life's work from 1882 until within less than two years of the end of a career that brought him early honors and consistent rewards. Elected to the National Academy at thirty-three, he became its president in 1874, serving The National Sculpture Society in the same capacity from 1893 on; he was a beloved Centurion, a member of the National Institute of Arts and Letters (1898) and many kindred organizations.

Wholly American-trained himself, he was a fine and generous preceptor. All unknowing, he anticipated the admiring and affectionate valediction of his kinsmen in art as he wept for Adonais—his one-time pupil, Charles Albert Lopez, suddenly turned aside from great promise in 1906: "I will say adieu. And when the waste mold that encloses my personality shall have been broken, I ask no greater honor than to have my brother sculptors meet here, and say a kind word in my memory."

. . . . *Lady with a lampshade*

MISS CATHLEEN GEBHARD NEILSON, soon to become the bride of Reginald Claypoole Vanderbilt (fourth and youngest son of Cornelius Vanderbilt II and great-grandson of "The Commodore") is here shown somewhat morosely facing the double battery of a forthright camera and a considerably more charitable brush.

This particular particle in recorded time is fully documented in *The New York Herald* of March 15, 1903: "When Miss Cathleen Neilson . . . was posing for the portrait of her by Mr. Richard Hall, Mr. Vanderbilt conceived the idea of having a flashlight photograph taken of one of the sittings. The necessary arrangements were made with Mr. Joseph Byron, and a reproduction of the picture which resulted is given above. It shows Miss Neilson herself as she posed for the portrait, the painting almost finished and Mr. Hall, palette and brushes in hand. Giving as it does, the opportunity of comparing the photographic likeness of Miss Neilson with the painter's work, the picture is highly interesting and quite unusual. Mr. Hall's portrait is said by friends of the young lady to be an exceptionally good likeness. Mr. Vanderbilt, on whose order the picture was painted, is understood to be particularly pleased with it. He attended most of the sittings and suggested the pose, which exhibits Miss Neilson's characteristic grace and dignity so well. The coloring, which, unfortunately, cannot be reproduced in the photograph, is soft and adds much to the beauty of the picture, as well as to the truth of the likeness. A larger reproduction of the portrait itself is shown on another page of to-day's *Herald* [a pardonable plethora, since the nuptials were but a month away]. Mr. Vanderbilt is said to have paid $6,000 for the portrait, which will probably be exhibited at the Paris Salon before it is finally hung in the home of the owner."

The fashion-favored forty-two-year-old artist, born in Finland of English and French parentage, was court painter to the society of two continents. Three Vanderbilts (Mr. and Mrs. Alfred G., and Mr. William K.), suitably surrounded, looked down from the walls of M. Knoedler & Company's galleries, then at 355 Fifth Avenue, as part of Hall's first one-man show there (January 2–15, 1902). An article by Perriton Maxwell in the *Metropolitan Maga-*

428

zine for May, 1904, dealt with his work and that of Theobald Chartran: "In New York the breed of artists that dabbles on canvas their too obviously counterfeit presentments of social celebrities is plentiful and prosperous. The galleries are full of their pictorial inanities: their lives are a round of little gaieties, smug pretenses and pink teas, with painting as a gentle avocation. . . . In vigorous opposition to the type described are such masterful painters as John S. Sargent, John W. Alexander and William M. Chase. In the middle ground are . . . two interesting men . . . Theobald Chartran and Richard Hall . . . who portray fashionable womankind as they would . . . a sunset or a street scene, with some knowledge and much facility. The thing that makes these two artists interesting is their more or less workmanlike presentation of frequently uninteresting persons. An *ennuied* society woman is not the most engaging model in the world, unless the artist presents in an engaging manner her ennui with her hat and gown. Let it be said to the credit of both these painters [who attracted manly patronage as well as more impressible female favor] that they put down upon canvas wittingly or otherwise, the poverty no less than the fullness of character written in the faces of their sitters."

The press was all approval for Hall's recalcitrant lady with a lampshade. At the time of

Richard Hall at work on his portrait of Cathleen Neilson, fiancée of Reginald Claypoole Vanderbilt, 1903; in the Bryant Park Studio (Beaux Arts Studios), 80 West Fortieth Street

the announcement of her betrothal, the *New-York Daily Tribune* of August 5, 1902 described her as being "of medium height, with wavy brown hair and brown eyes, and an adept in all outdoor games." The "notification" did not come as a surprise, as the "attachment between the young people" had been "a matter of comment for more than a year," during which time of trial—and, as it turned out, error—the bridegroom-to-be had managed to celebrate his majority by reputedly dropping $70,000 in a single gambling session at Richard Canfield's and had failed to graduate from Yale with the Class of 1902—a blot eliminated from the family escutcheon the following fall. On the day before the Newport wedding ceremony of April 14, 1903, he was arrested and convicted for "fast driving" in an automobile. While these newsworthy weaknesses did not deter his fiancée (prenuptially accredited by an admiring journalism as being "a girl with a considerable amount of determination and tact"— sterling qualities not altogether revealed on Mr. Hall's understandably sugar-coated canvas) they may have led her to divorce the sportsman in 1919. As Mrs. Sidney J. Colford, Jr., she died prematurely in Paris on June 4, 1927.

. . . . *Years of my life and thought*

"Scribbled in pencil, ink, water color, anything; smirched with the blood of victims sacrificed on the altar of the knowledge-hunger; burned with sparks of the campfire; greasy with handling by unwashed, hasty, eager hands; badly written; at times badly illustrated with hasty sketches—hasty, but meaningful. . . . They represent more than anything else those sixty years of my life and thought, my strivings and my joy." So Ernest Thompson Seton, in *Trail of an Artist-Naturalist* (1940), described "the Journal of my Travels and Doings . . . on my desk before me—fifty fat leather-clad volumes." These registers are now in the possession of his widow as part of the collection to be known as the Seton Foundation, at Seton Village, Santa Fe, New Mexico. The opening entry—"the first step into a glorious kingdom"—was made in Toronto, Ontario, on November 13, 1881, when the lifelong student of nature (then just three months past his majority) "Saw three robins over the White Bridge." On the shelf above him, in this portrait, eighteen recorded years are in alignment. They stretch back to his prairie apprenticeship as a "frontier naturalist" on the plains of western Canada; to the earliest of the countless stories and of the forty-two books he was to write and illustrate; to his drawings for *The Century Dictionary;* to his art education in the ateliers of London and Paris; to his marriage on June 1, 1896, to Grace Gallatin, who during courtship days abroad had assisted in the preparation of his *Studies in the Art Anatomy of Animals,* published in that year of his return to America. We come on him here not long after the appearance of his greatest popular success—*Wild Animals I Have Known* (1898) of which he said in his autobiography: "There can be no doubt that this book founded the modern school of animal stories, that is, giving in fiction form the actual facts of an animal's life and modes of thought"—a form he had first initiated, with the poetry of a youth of sixteen, in "The King Bird A Barnyard Legend." And far ahead the account was to stretch, until two months short of his death on October 23, 1946, annotating the rest of his eighty-six-year span. The years were to include a wide variety of triumphs and accomplishments, among them his "most ambitious undertaking," *Lives of Game Animals*

(1925–1928); successes on the lecture platform; service as the founder of Woodcraft Indians and chief of the Boy Scouts of America. He was to be the recipient of honors of all kinds in the field he had chosen in his childhood. Always the Journals were with him; around this log of a lifetime the room seems to rotate.

Ernest Thompson Seton in his studio, 1899
144 Fifth Avenue

In this citified domain so permeated with wilderness, mine is the decided advantage: for I have before me a set of photographs by Byron showing all sides of this studio, and, guided by the charming Mrs. Gallatin Seton (divorced from the naturalist in 1935) I have just walked with her in memory up the steep flights in the converted brownstone residence, past the mounted peacock that stood in unsuperstitious welcome on the newel post, into the skylit third-floor apartment, consisting of the artist's livable workshop with its open fireplace, a dining room, two hall-connected bedrooms, a makeshift bathroom (geyser-heated), and a kitchen inhabited by a succession of "extra maids." One, her mistress (still as reminiscent of Julia Marlowe as when she sat to Robert Henri and Anders Zorn) recalls with merriment: the "Lily" (of the field-like proclivities) who squandered most of her first week's three-dollar wage on a gay ribbon for her sailor, and who left because a heap of spent towels convinced her of the unsanitary ways of her employers, she being accustomed to "clean people."

The Ernest Thompson Setons (for he had reverted from Seton Thompson to the name illustrious in his Scottish paternal ancestry) were "At Home" on winter Wednesday evenings, when society and Bohemia shared "good music or entertainment by talented guests." Distinguished steps crossed the Bokhara rug, and trod upon the big brown Rocky Mountain grizzly bear skin that bore the mark of the bride's bullet. ("My husband never shot anything except with a camera," Mrs. Seton said, explaining that she had used her gun in the tall Wyoming timber to free the trapped animal from hunting dogs in training for Theodore Roosevelt's visit.) Some of the assemblage doubtless studied Mr. Seton's paintings and begged him to retell the famous tale of Lobo the Wolf, whose portrait drawn by the artist-naturalist hung just to the left of the row of Journals, and who became a four-footed immortal in *Wild Animals I Have Known*, following his initial short story appearance as "the King of Currumpaw" in 1894. All about were possessions still cherished by Mrs. Seton, for the young pair early collected such permanencies as the eight Chippendale chairs acquired in Chelmsford, Essex. Among the through-the-years company reinvoked by their hostess were Senator Jacob H. Gallinger of New Hampshire; Congressman Stephen G. Porter of Pennsylvania; John Burroughs, "The Sage of Slabsides," naturalist and essayist; Kate Douglas Wiggin, of *The Birds' Christmas Carol* and other fame; Hamlin Garland, scribe of the Prairie and the Middle Border, with Mrs. Garland; the authoress Juliet Wilbor Tompkins; Charles Dana Gibson and the bride he was forever drawing (once under the title of "If the Old Goddesses Were Still Alive"); the painters William M. Chase and Irving R. Wiles; Isaac F. Marcosson, city editor of the Louisville *Times;* and Mabel Choate, daughter of the great lawyer and diplomat. It is doubtful that any of these suffered the verse-inscribed penalty the host had carved on the back of a prize captured in the Thieves' Market in Paris (a seat here unseen, but placed before the dark blue and white African-woven woolen drapery of the cosey corner):

> "Who takes this chair
> Of Dagobert
> Must raise a laugh
> Or pay to quaff."

A PERIOD poses for its portrait here: the pellucid prose of Henry James speaks again; the glass reflection of Glackens' *Chez Mouquin* is reaffirmed; the poised perfection of Edith Wharton's Lily Bart ("Everything about her . . . at once vigorous and exquisite, at once strong and fine") steps out of *The House of Mirth* into Byron's focus (page 434).

The three women were authors all. Caroline King Duer (seated beside the desk)—vivacious poet, essayist and playwright—wrote to me not long before her death on January 21, 1956, that she well remembered the recording of this study in subtlety, this fine-spun document that bears—as I shall tell—astonishing continuity with our own disordered age; is, in fact, a sort of transfluence between two disparate worlds, linking the Civil War with the Atomic Age in strange sequence. Mrs. Duer (née Elizabeth Wilson Meads, and married during the year before silence fell at Appomattox), novelist of *The Prince Goes Fishing*, died in 1908, in her own quietly framed time. The aloof tallness of her youngest daughter—rebirth of one of Seurat's Conté crayon studies for *La Grande Jatte*—standing so classically erect and in all appearance so inviolately sheltered, had brought a courage out of context with her, as she crossed the threshold of her parents' home, next door to her own, on that summery day to become the hauntingly dominant chord of this family piece. Staten Island born in 1874, Alice Maude Duer, whose eventless childhood had been spent on the ancestral estate of "Hauxhurst," overlooking the Hudson from a stern Weehawken cliff, already a professional writer and tutor during her student days at Barnard College, married Henry Wise Miller on the October 5th following her graduation in 1899. The *New-York Daily Tribune* of the next day was profuse in its apologies for the small simplicity of the Grace Church Chantry wedding, the lovely bride all in lace and unattended, and the reception, according to a journalistic reprise on the following Sunday, "thoroughly informal, partaking more of the character of an afternoon tea." The "limited space" in the East Fifty-third Street home to which Mr. and Mrs. Duer had moved during the previous season was called to account for this restricted tabulation of heads high in the New York social scale. The young pair were off to a tropical bungalow in Costa Rica, where it was hoped the cultivation of rubber trees would bring fair fortune. Three years later, fever and failure returned the Millers to New York, and while the husband—later to become a member of the Stock Exchange—worked as a runner for a brokerage firm, rising to an order clerkship, the many-sided housewife and mother taught English composition and mathematics, and produced paying fiction. Henry Wise Miller relates in his affectionate *All Our Lives* (1945): "When I got home from Wall Street Alice helped me to send out circulars and to keep books for a retail coffee business I had started on the side, and we wrote book reviews and potboilers far into the night." By the time Mrs. Miller met Byron's camera—her "fine glaze of beauty and fastidiousness" (to filch a phrase from Edith Wharton) belying a dynamism all un-Edwardian—she had two published titles. The *New-York Tribune Illustrated Supplement* of September 13, 1903 pro-

Byron, N.Y.
21762

nounced *The Modern Obstacle,* her first novel, "a clever book." On December 6th, the same paper emphasized her resourcefulness "in giving an unexpected turn to her plot" in *Calderon's Prisoner,* which included another less "well constructed" novelette, *Cyril Vane's Wife,* nevertheless "like its companion . . . throughout interesting." On February 19, 1927 *The New Yorker,* in its second anniversary issue, ran a laudative "Profile" entitled "A Lady Who Writes," in which Harvey O'Higgins marveled: ". . . She can manage a household, a dinner, a costume, a servant, a social appearance, or any other item of reality in the smarter circles of New York life as efficiently as she can participate in a meeting of the trustees of Barnard, preside over a luncheon of the Authors' League, conduct a witty newspaper column like 'Are Women People?', make a suffrage speech . . . or put across on the readers of the *Saturday Evening Post* a story that is a poisonous satire of some of their most sacred cows. . . ." Several of her novels—among them *Come Out Of The Kitchen!* (1916) and *The Charm School* (1919)—met with equal success in stage and screen versions. This duo, and *Gowns by Roberta* (published in 1933 and happily made into a Broadway musical), were cited in *The New York Times* editorial of August 24, 1942 (two days after their author's death) because they "added to the enjoyment of countless men and women of all ages even if, as literature, they were too light and gay to become what we ponderously call classics." Speaking of her long narrative war poem of 1940, *The White Cliffs,* the *Times* commented that even "if she did not become a great poet she at least achieved what all true poets strive for. She stirred emotions and the mind at a time when there was need for such a stirring. And to do that is to approach greatness." To millions, over the tense air, during Britain's "Shining Hour," Lynn Fontanne gave unforgettable voice to Alice Duer Miller's plea for a civilization at bay:

> "But in a world where England is finished and dead,
>   I do not wish to live."

Mrs. James Gore King Duer and her daughters, 1906
at 60 East Fifty-third Street

435

. . . . The homeless, tempest-tost

THE INTERNATIONALLY known poetess Emma Lazarus (1849–1887) wrote these lines of compassion and hope for the benefit of the American campaign to raise funds for the base of the Statue of Liberty, that great symbolic gift of the people of France to the citizens of the United States. The sonnet—first read by the many-talented F. Hopkinson Smith on the opening night of the Bartholdi Statue Pedestal Art Loan Exhibition at the National Academy of Design (December 3, 1883)—was inscribed on a bronze tablet twenty years later (through the good offices of Miss Georgina Schuyler) and placed within the monument that heroically dominates the entrance to a free world.

Original manuscript in the Collection of the Museum of the City of New York

(*Overleaf*) Immigrants in the Steerage of the S.S. *Pennland* of the Red Star Line, 1893

The New Colossus.

Not like the brazen giant of Greek fame,
  With conquering limbs astride from land to land;
Here at our sea-washed, sunset-gates shall stand
A mighty woman with a torch, whose flame
Is the imprisoned lightning, and her name
Mother of Exiles. From her beacon-hand
  Glows world-wide welcome; her mild eyes command
  The air-bridged harbor that twin-cities frame.

"Keep, ancient lands, your storied pomp!" cries she,
With silent lips. "Give me your tired, your poor,
Your huddled masses yearning to breathe free,
The wretched refuse of your teeming shore,—
Send these, the homeless, tempest-tost to me,
I lift my lamp beside the golden door!"

Emma Lazarus.

November 2 nd 1883.

AT A time when the Atlantic was wide and ships were silent and kept their own counsel along spacious sea lanes under an inviolate sky, the S.S. *La Gascogne* of the French Line steamed out of Le Havre on January 26, 1895, with the expectation of reaching New York on the 2nd or 3rd of February. When the 5th came and went without a happy landing, mounting despair began to haunt the city, broken only on the afternoon of the 11th, when the anxious telescope of the Fire Island observer sighted three steamships close together, one of them showing the international code signals making the letters "J.K.D.Q.," the *Gascogne*'s own. She was going at a speed of about 5 knots and displayed three balls in a perpendicular line at her pennant, conveying in the sign language of the deep that she was not under control. On all that lonesome way, swept northward from the traveled tracks by giant waves and westerly hurricanes, she had not spoken a single steamer until the previous day and had seen only one four-masted schooner as her crew worked around the clock to repair machinery four times broken.

". . . the news of her arrival," reported the *New-York Daily Tribune* of February 12th, "came like a sweet message from the sea. The confidence of the ability of the great ocean liners to battle successfully against all the seas that roll and all the storms that blow was restored." Downtown, outside the company offices at 3 Bowling Green, hats were swung wildly into an air vibrant with lusty cheers and strong men wept out of relief and joy; in the uptown restaurants and cafés there was universal jubilation.

The next morning (the 12th) the brave commander, Captain Baudelon, refused proffers of assistance as his crippled but gallant lady made her way alone and with slow dignity through the icebound Narrows, and would not permit her lines to be taken until the very last moments of this epic passage from shore to shore. More than two thousand people along the water front, from the windows and house-tops on West Street and at the French Line pier, frenetically bellowed their welcome to the conquering heroine as her black hull and tall red funnels broke through the fog of tugboat steam and she was warped into her berth at 11:15. "The marine prodigal had returned."

The S.S. *La Gascogne* of the French Line arriving in New
York, February 12, 1895

ON NOVEMBER 4, 1825, a wedding was celebrated in New York. On that day, Governor DeWitt Clinton poured a keg of Lake Erie water into the Atlantic Ocean, marking the opening of what Marshall B. Davidson, in *Life in America,* calls one of the young Nation's "artificial rivers to fortune," the Erie Canal. By this symbolic act, New York was joined to the mainland of the United States in a maritime *mariage de convenance* which went further than the "Big Ditch's" 363-mile length in establishing the commercial supremacy of our city washed by the waters of three rivers through three centuries.

Seven decades later, a less imposing alliance—the culmination of an interrupted eleven-year courtship—took place when the opening of the Harlem Ship Canal created a more efficient union of the Hudson River and Long Island Sound, previously related by the picturesque winding humility of Spuyten Duyvil Creek and finally the East River through the courtesy of the Harlem (elevated to new dignity in its transition from a boatmen's sporting paradise into a link of the circumferential watery highway around Manhattan). This short cut spared small vessels the weary necessity of rounding the Battery. Subsequent dredging of the Harlem Channel (now 350 to 400 feet wide and 15 deep), not only accented New York's insularity, but also added to its qualifications as the port of ports.

On this sunny anniversary of the Battle of Bunker Hill, the by-passed Battery—so often the welcoming background and beginning of New York celebrations—was forsaken in favor of the "North End," where the starting cannonade from the men-o'-war echoed through the aboriginal Indian caves at Inwood. Financed by voluntary subscription, a magnificent land parade wound through the crowd-bordered streets of Harlem and the Bronx, while the great marine pageant sailed past gay, vocal throngs afloat and ashore, as far as City Island, to include the generous slice of Westchester County newly annexed in an extension of the city limits. Heading the Reception Committee was the Honorable John T. Agnew (son of a participant in the Erie Canal Celebration arrangements and himself a forerunner of Grover Whalen, meriting the title of "Veteran Civic Celebrator" bestowed by *The Illustrated American* of June 29, 1895) while Captain Osbon—who had served as Farragut's flag officer—was the Admiral in command. The national importance of the occasion was underscored by the presence of President Cleveland and other notables. A barrel of water from Lake Champlain was ritually mingled with the salt of the Sound just before the banquet at Sulzer's Oak Point Pavilion, where tribute was paid to the late General John Newton (famed for his 1876–1885 operations of clearing the Hell Gate Channel) planner of the present project, and to Lieutenant Colonel George L. Gillespie of the U.S. Army Corps of Engineers, and Augustus Doerflinger, who with their staffs of government and civil engineers, carried it through. The celebration closed in pyrotechnical glory from the master hand of Pain, who had devised portraits of Governor Morton, Mayor Strong, and General Egbert L. Viele (chairman of the committee of arrangements) in outlines of flame.

The opening of the Harlem Ship Canal, June 17, 1895
Scene near Macombs Dam Bridge (Central Bridge) at 155th
Street

Three days later, remote in space and spirit, another and more portentous union, combined with a simultaneous christening, gave continental diplomatists a premature trembling fore-taste of the scantily veiled terrors that lay not too far ahead. *The New York Herald* of June 21 pointed a warning editorial finger: "The destinies of Europe . . . may hinge on incidents and accidents of the celebration" of the inauguration of the 61-mile state-owned canal linking the North Sea and the Baltic. Kaiser Wilhelm II in his Admiral's uniform stood like an elevated ship's figurehead of old on the high bridge behind the mainmast of the *Hohen-zollern* (see page 445) as she led the many-flagged visiting warships through the Holtenau locks into Kiel—nerve center of the German Navy and source of the name by which the new waterway became commonly known. With assurance and reassuringly, the words on which a world waited were spoken: "In memory of Emperor William the Great, I christen this canal, . . . in the name of God, in honor of Emperor William I., for the weal of Germany and the welfare of nations."

The Imperial Yacht *Hohenzollern* visits New York, 1902
Photograph taken by the Byron Company at the cabled command of Kaiser Wilhelm II

A MERE sixteen years before the Commander of a German U-Boat first peered at the New York sky line through his periscope, a handsome narrow vessel—white-sided, with salmon-pink underbody and the black eagle of Germany surmounted by a gilded crown on her bow—steamed up New York's hospitable Bay to serve as a floating residence for Prince Henry of Prussia, due to represent his king and brother at the launching of the Kaiser's American-built yacht, *Meteor*.

The *Hohenzollern* (4,400 tons burden; 378 feet in length; 900 horsepower; fitted with electricity and light armament) ranked as a Cruiser in the German Navy. Her crew on this friendly mission totaled 400. After lying at the new Hoboken pier of the North German Lloyd Line for eight busy days of nautical housecleaning in preparation for the Prince's arrival, the ten-year-old ship crossed the Hudson on February 20, 1902, to her berth at the foot of West Thirty-fourth Street. Here she was inspected by capacity audiences and expensively pillaged by souvenir hunters, who stole tassels and fringe from the costly tapestries and bargained with the sailors for crockery stamped with the imperial crest. The easily discernible sightseer of Teutonic origin, according to the *New-York Daily Tribune* of March 2, "strutted about the ship, delivered panegyrics upon the Kaiser, but dropped his voice to a very respectful whisper when the officers went by." The curious peered into the dining saloon from the promenade deck, were guided across the reception hall and gaped at the six-room royal suite through roped doorways.

Meanwhile, according to a press dispatch relayed by the *New-York Daily Tribune* of March 2, newspapers in the Vaterland were handling accounts of Prince Henry's American reception "as though they were installments of a serial romance," while politicians abroad speculated on whys and wherefores, and the German Socialists, reading of their Prince's "unaffected bearing," scoffed at "democracy for export," sneering that "royalty at home is never so amiable." The good-will emissary was royally fêted, dispensed regal hospitality, and stood by while our own "Princess Alice" (President Roosevelt's daughter) gracefully christened the *Meteor*, the largest schooner yacht afloat, built by the Townsend & Downey Shipbuilding Company for the pacific pleasure of William II, ruler of the world's leading military state. The visiting Prince's entourage included Admiral von Tirpitz, Secretary of the Imperial Admiralty since 1898, and in no small measure responsible for the already initiated programme that would make the German Navy second only to that of Great Britain by the outbreak of World War I, when its submarines were for a time dread sovereigns of the sea.

However, all this *Sturm und Drang* was seemingly remote on March 19, 1902, when the *Tribune* spoke of the yacht *Hohenzollern*'s peaceable mission as an earnest of the Kaiser's "solicitude that his brother's visit should be interpreted as conclusive proof of goodwill and promote as far as possible such a state of feeling between the two nations [America and Germany] as would render misunderstanding difficult hereafter."

The Empress' sitting-room on the *Hohenzollern*
Photograph taken by the Byron Company at the cabled command of Kaiser Wilhelm II

A week before this editorial gladdened New York's breakfast tables, the *Hohenzollern* had slipped quietly downstream in advance of the liner that carried Prince Henry back to "Deutschland über Alles" and his kingly brother, who was even then evidencing a growing identification with his strange God.

ON SATURDAY July 3, 1880, "the *ALBANY* left her landing in New York nine minutes late, with over 2,000 passengers aboard and against a strong head wind and ebb tide, made West Point and Newburgh on time. By the time the boat reached Rhinebeck, she was about an half hour late, caused by some slight difficulty with her new machinery. By this time the crowd of people had swelled to immense proportions and at this landing fully 500 disembarked, and when Catskill was reached fully as many more got off there. From Catskill to this city [the State capital] tows and other hindrances caused the vessel to lose time, and she did not reach here until half-past seven o'clock. All along the river, residents had their houses decorated, and with cannon and other explosives welcomed the advent of the *ALBANY*. At Hudson, the dock and hills were crowded with people despite the fact that quite a rain prevailed at the time. When she hove in sight of the city, the greatest excitement prevailed, and, amid the booming of cannon, the screeching of steamboat whistles, the ringing of bells, the playing of Austin's band, and the shouts of a thousand people assembled on the docks and piers, the *ALBANY* steamed into port and touched her dock. It was a scene long to be remembered, and we doubt if ever before a new boat met with such a royal reception at any place on the Hudson. A happier man than the genial Captain Dave Hitchcock will be seldom seen. He was very enthusiastic, and stated that the *ALBANY* was a marvelous boat, making such time as she did under adverse circumstances. . . . Saturday was indeed a gala day in the history of the Albany Day Line, and the proprietors have every reason to feel proud of their new boat, and Albanians of their namesake." This account—found in the Hallenbeck Collection at Albany, and quoted in part by Thomas A. Larremore in his elegiac article, "Muffled Drums For Albany–Potomac," in the *Steamboat Bill Of Facts* Journal Of The Steamship Historical Society Of America. June and December, 1949.—is from one of those unidentified, undated clippings that lay people file away with love and without regard for curatorial curiosity. According to Mr. Larremore, the *Albany* was a shy creature, who shunned publicity, possibly feeling—along with Miss Alice Brayton, the socially prominent Newport spinster (as paraphrased by Cleveland Amory in *The Last Resorts*, New York, 1952)—"that a lady's name should appear in the papers three times—when she is born, when she marries and when she dies." The birth of this steamboat took place in the yards of Harlan and Hollingsworth, at Wilmington, Delaware in 1879–1880, and the engine (built and installed by the W. & A. Fletcher Company) was placed in her iron hull (a new departure for her owners' fleet) in the latter year. A paddle-wheeled "three piper," her young dimensions were 295 × 40 × 11½ feet, with a gross tonnage of 1,415, as she slid down the ways at her launching in January, 1880. She was duly christened by Charles T. Van Santvoord, the Treasurer of the Albany Day Line (later the Hudson River Day Line), which first unostentatiously advertised its $187,318.58 investment on Sunday July 11, 1880, in a factual insert in *The World*: "*ALBANY* and *C. VIBBARD* daily (Sundays excepted) leave

447

Vestry st. pier 8.35 and 24th st. at 9 A.M. (Brooklyn by Annex at 8 A.M.), landing at Nyack Ferry, West Point, Newburg, Poughkeepsie, Rhinebeck, Catskill and Hudson. Passengers landing at West Point or Newburg can return by down boat. Connect at Rhinebeck (by ferry) with the 2.45 P.M. train on the Ulster and Delaware R.R. Tickets sold and baggage checked NORTH and WEST. Tickets or coupons good on the Hudson River R.R. received for passage. Special Trains to and from SARATOGA." The *Albany* superseded the *Daniel Drew* on this run. In her infancy, she appeared on page 1 of *The Evening Post* of July 16, 1880, as the subject of a letter to the ever patient editors dated July 13 and signed "B": "Taking passage in the new boat Albany at Catskill last Friday, I at once sought the captain or clerk, asking where the life-preservers were kept, as none was in sight. He replied that plenty were to be found in the baggage room and in the closets on the several decks. This I found to be true, but there was no indication on any of the doors to show that life-preservers could be found within. Now, in case of a fire forward, or amidships, and of course a panic among the passengers, it would be difficult to reach these means of safety even if every person on board knew where to find them. Is it not the duty of the officers to keep these distributed all over the boat, as the passengers are. This of itself should go far to allay excitement and enable all to help themselves. This distribution, would not, it is true, add to the decoration so lavishly displayed on this boat, but in case of accident might save many lives." It should be pointed out that "B" was not a victim of anxiety neurosis, for steamboat accidents were epidemic, almost diurnal occurrences at the time.

The *Albany's* first wedding with the waters has been duly recorded above. In 1892–1893 she underwent extensive alterations which increased her length to 325 feet, 6 inches and her gross tonnage to 1,415.42, added feathering paddle wheels; and, as Mr. Larremore (who was faithful to her from his boyhood through her old age) points out, "her paddle boxes assumed the oblong, streamlined shape that set the fashion."

On May 26, 1900 the *Albany* celebrated another marriage (again rain-clouded), as told in the *New-York Daily Tribune* of the following morning: "A large party of guests enjoyed a trip up the Hudson yesterday afternoon on the steamboat Albany, of the Hudson River Day Line. The occasion was the extensive refitting and improvement . . . undergone since last summer. She is almost a new boat this year. Her grand saloon and hurricane deck have been extended thirty feet, a new mahogany staircase to the upper deck has been put in, two drawing rooms forward have been added, a beautiful bronze fountain has been placed near the band stand, and the steamboat has been liberally replenished throughout in plate glass, carpeting, furniture and decoration." It was "the decoration so lavishly displayed" in this third incarnation that Byron was invited to record. The river had long been accustomed to sumptuousness. As early as October 7, 1849, the visiting Swedish lady of letters, Fredrika Bremer, in an epistle addressed to "My sweet sister, my sweet friend!" (published in *The Homes Of The New World; Impressions Of America,* New York, 1853) wrote of "the great steam-boat, the 'New World,'" on which she had sailed up the Hudson, as "really a little floating palace, splendid and glittering with white and gold on the outside, splendid and elegant within: large saloons, magnificent furniture." Moreover, an earlier *Albany* built in 1826, is described by George W. Murdock (engineer emeritus of these inland water liners) in his unpublished, faithfully illustrated *History of Hudson River Steamboats* in the collection of The New-York Historical Society: "The 'Albany' was owned by Messrs Stevens, of

Hoboken, N.J., who had spared no expense . . . she was splendidly fitted up, the panels in the cabin were decorated with several highly-finished paintings by the best artists in the country. The Messrs Stevens deserved great credit for thus pointing out a new source of employment to the artists." On the staircase of the later floating art gallery here shown is seen the appropriate marble *June* of Erastus Dow Palmer (1817–1904), known as "The Albany Sculptor" (after the city of his affiliation), famous for his unabashed nude, *The Indian Girl,* and *The White Captive* (rival of *The Greek Slave*). The narrative canvases, from left to right are: *Fairy Tales,* by the German Zuber-Bühler; *The Pride of the Family* by Emil Auguste Pinchart, native of Cambrai, pupil of Gérôme, and specialist in historical and genre subjects as well as portraiture; and the demure, often reproduced *Evangeline*—by Thomas Faed, R.A. (1826–1900), famed for his homely delineations of Scottish life.

With her consorts, the *Chauncey Vibbard* and the *New York,* the *Albany* saw a quarter of a century of service in the Hudson River Day Line to and fro between the Empire City and the capital of the Empire State, but with the advent of the *Hendrick Hudson* in 1906 her service was limited to daily round trips to Poughkeepsie; in 1913 even this reduced

The Grand Stairway of the Hudson River Steamer *Albany,*
Fall of 1900

glory was taken from her, and for four years she plied on the New York-Roundout route. During this chapter—in 1916—her boilers were replaced and her passenger capacity increased to 2,000. By 1918 she was being chartered for excursions—with a compensating Saturday run to Albany—and gave grateful assistance to the more modern vessels of the fleet when needed. In 1931 she was pastured at Athens; on March 6, 1934 she was literally "sold down the river" to B. B. Wills at an auction held at New York's new County Court House; and at 2:50 on the afternoon of April 19, bound for Washington, D.C., she steamed away from the West Forty-second Street Pier, bidding farewell forever to the Highlands, to the towering Palisades, to the companionable, landlocked locomotives of the New York Central, to the summer waters her prow had parted so often in swift whiteness, in the gay company and haunting memory of such illustrious dead as the sweet-voiced *Mary Powell* of the magic bell. Even her name was changed, but she lived on in bravely borne exile. Then, in 1949, Mr. Larremore laments threnodially, came an AP dispatch, with the date-line "WASHINGTON, MAY 16—THE POTOMAC RIVER LINE ANNOUNCED TODAY ITS 69-YEAR-OLD EXCURSION STEAMER, THE POTOMAC, IS HEADED FOR THE SCRAP HEAP. THE SHIP . . . ORIGINALLY KNOWN AS THE S. S. ALBANY . . . WILL BE SCRAPPED AT BALTIMORE. IT WILL BE TOWED THERE SOMETIME NEXT WEEK, OFFICIALS OF THE LINE SAID." It was not until 1950 that she was shorn of her once white and yellow beauty, thenceforth to wander unkempt over the rivers as a barge. Today, on the grounds of The Mariners Museum at Newport News, Virginia, the lift and lilt of her walking beam, as she proudly skimmed the waterways, pulses even in immobility.

. . . . *A rare and wonderful thing in a floating lady*

"WE FLOATED proudly and smoothly on the broad, magnificent Hudson. . . . The shores, with their boldly wood-covered heights . . . and the dark clouds which hung between the hills in heavy draperies above the river were in perfect harmony with the gloomily beautiful passes through which we swung, and which presented at every turn new and more magnificent pictures. The river was full of life. Wooden-roofed steam-boats, brilliant as ours [the *New World*], with gold and white, passed up and down the river. Other steam-boats drew along with flotillas of from twenty to thirty boats, laden with goods from the country to New York, while hundreds of smaller and larger craft were seen skimming along past the precipitous shores like white doves with red, fluttering neck-ribbons." So Fredrika Bremer (see *The Homes Of The New World; Impressions Of America*) wrote to her sister on October 7, 1849, as part of the recountal of a visit to Andrew Jackson Downing in his prototypic Gothic villa at Newburgh. The great landscape architect—with William Cullen Bryant one of the instigatorial voices that led to the creation of Central Park—was to perish in fire and water on July 28, 1852, when the steamer *Henry Clay* lost her race (along with her life) against the *Armenia*, along the very river on which the staff of M. Witmark & Sons celebrated early success of a summery day in 1897.

It is doubtful that any of this gay party aboard the *Bay Queen* wrote to their relatives in the consonance of the Swedish authoress. Far more likely, their thoughts would have

A Company Excursion to Newburgh, 1897

ebulliated in verses sung to catchy melodies, for the company hailed from Manhattan's latest non-geographical sector, "Tin Pan Alley," where the new-fashioned songs of a nation were being turned out. It was the young firm of M. Witmark & Sons that was helping to propel the current revolution in popular music. Marcus, the prideful father, held an honorary sort of presidency because his quintet of boys were minors back in 1885, when they started the enterprise sold to Warner Brothers for $1,000,000 in cash close to the end of another era (December, 1928–January, 1929). As narrated by Isidore Witmark and Isaac Goldberg in the absorbing history of the House, *From Ragtime To Swingtime* (New York, 1939), it all began in 1883, with a toy, a trademark and a personal declaration of independence. It was then that Jay at eleven—adjudged too rambunctious to receive a school medal for arithmetical excellence—acting on fraternal advice, chose a "printing press" with the brand name "Challenge" in preference to the proffered juvenile temptations of a chest of tools, a velocipede or baseball equipment. On the same day fourteen-year-old Isidore, smarting under unjust dismissal from a job, vowed that he would never again work for another man while life lasted. So the beardless mathematician and his brothers Isidore and Julius P. (thirteen) started an amateur job printing establishment in their home, 402 West Fortieth Street, on the fringe of Hell's Kitchen. The Witmark boys were richly talented. Julius, precociously by way of minstrelsy, was already on the march to featured billing in top Broadway musicals; Frank was to become known as "The American Waltz King," Adolph S. (Ed) a concert singer of renown, and Isidore a noted composer. In fact, it was "President Cleveland's Wedding March" (1886), dashed off by Isidore in a few thumping hours, that brought the young firm—converted to music publishing in 1885—its first abundant success. Jay's contribution was of a more practical nature; his the business head. During the initial decade the Witmark catalogue included such tuneful triumphs as "He Was A Pal Of Mine" (M. J. Cavanagh and I. Witmark, 1890), "The Picture That Is Turned Toward The Wall" by the English Charles Graham (1891), Andrew Mack's "The Wedding of The Lily And The Rose" (1892), and John T. Kelly's "I Long To See The Girl I Left Behind" (1893), so favored by quartets, and many another remembered refrain. In the melodic future lay an age of operettas— those of Victor Herbert, Julian Edwards, Gustav Luders, Karl Hoschna, Sigmund Romberg and others—all to be published by M. Witmark & Sons; the association with George M. Cohan, Chauncey Olcott and many another of the musicianly illustrious; the great operatic and musical comedy productions; the instrumental hits; the songs of laughter and lacrymae. Expansion, including the establishment of the Witmark Entertainment Bureau and the development of what was to become the amateur minstrel center of the country, brought about nautilus-like changes of habitat; and at the time of this carefree absentation from rhythmical routine the increasing staff of the House (later dubbed by Sam S. Shubert "The Tiffany of the Music World") deserted its 49–51 West Twenty-eighth Street headquarters for a day aboard the *Bay Queen*.

Their aqua-borne playground had earlier answered to a martial name—*Gen¹. Sedgwick*, in honor of the gallant soldier who was defending the Union in The Seven Days' Battle and bleeding from two wounds at Antietam in 1862, the year that she was born in Jersey City. Graceful and swift, the sidewheeler made short diurnal runs at first, and then became an excursion boat about the bustling harbor, on Long Island Sound, or up the Hudson, until she wearied in 1902, when her engine was removed and her once handsome hull broken up at Tottenville. Five years short of this humiliating end, she was a happy choice for the melodious cruising company posed on her deck, for she carried a steam calliope—a rare and wonderful thing in a floating lady on New York waters.

"I MUST now give a brief account of Greenwood Cemetery, which we visited the other day," wrote Lady Emmeline Stuart Wortley in *Travels in the United States, Etc. During 1849 And 1850* (London, 1851). "The views from the heights of the cemetery were sublime. I admired the one from Ocean Hill the most. There is a lovely variety of valleys, elevations, plains, groves, and glades, and paths. When will London have anything even *approaching* to this magnificent cemetery? The ocean rolling and moaning, with its fine melancholy, organ-like sounds, so near, like a mighty mourner, she cannot have."

This *campo santo*—a flight from New York's overpopulated central churchyards—filled the anxious necessity expressed by George Templeton Strong in his diary entry of July 27, 1839, after a visit to the new burial ground: ". . . in this city of all cities some place is needed where a man may lay down to his last nap without the anticipation of being turned out of his bed in the course of a year or so to make way for a street or a big store or something of that kind." Chartered on April 11, 1838, following the leadership of Boston's Mount Auburn (1831) and Philadelphia's Laurel Hill (1836) its original 175 landscaped acres were the objective of many a stroll, and carriage drive following the four-and-a-half-mile road construction known as "The Tour." Its early scenic glories and monuments are detailed in a six-partite section of *The Rural Cemeteries of America* (with "Picturesque And Monumental Views, In Highly Finished Line Engraving, From Drawings Taken On The Spot, By James Smillie, Esq." and "Descriptive Notices By N. Cleaveland," published in New York by R. Martin, 1846–7)—a threnodic opus highly recommended by the *New York Christian Messenger* (August 22, 1846) as a "gift-book, or an ornament to the centre-table" comparing favorably with "any of the superb English annuals," while the *New York Sun* gave endorsement on December 16, 1846: "Lonely and solemn Green-Wood may now live in its chastening influence in the drawing-room, and by the family fireside."

Henry R. Stiles, who includes a careful tracery of this Island of the Dead in his three-volume work, *A History Of The City Of Brooklyn* (1870), guides us through the mid-century years: "As the fame and attractiveness of Greenwood increased, its throngs of visitors grew larger, and, as a natural consequence, places of entertainment began to cluster around its only entrance. To escape this great inconvenience a new and better guarded avenue to the grounds was placed at the southwestern corner of the cemetery, and every precaution possible was taken to protect its approaches from objects and scenes inconsistent with the sacredness and decorum which befitted the place. This entrance, completed in 1850, together with the lodge, offices, etc., accompanying it, were of a higher order of architectural effect, worthy of the dignity and the improving finances of the institution. In 1860, after many years of tedious negotiation and patient waiting, the embarrassments resting upon a portion of the north-western part of the cemetery ground were so far removed, as to give full possession and convenient access. Steps were immediately taken for the opening of a northern gate, destined, hereafter, to be the main entrance. . . . Every precaution possible has been taken to guard this new approach, and to give it, as far as may be, an air of quiet and seclusion."

The Green-Wood Cemetery, May 30, 1899
Fifth Avenue and Twenty-fifth Street,
Brooklyn

The firm of R. Upjohn & Son began work on the Nova Scotia sandstone Arch (seen in the background of this photograph) in 1861, and completed it during the three following years. Reflecting the strong influence of the style of Richard M. Upjohn, it is described by Stiles as "monumental in form and character." He goes on to say: "None who know the gospel narrative will need an interpretation of the stories told in stone over the gateways. The entombment of the Saviour, and his resurrection, the raising of Lazarus, and the restoration of the widow's son, are happily embodied in these well executed groups and life-like forms, wrought in olive tinted sandstone, the designs, as well as the four allegorical figures on the shields of each gable, being conceived and executed by Mr. John Moffit [sic]."

On Decoration Day, 1899—when Byron chose this elegaic theme—Green-Wood already embraced its present 478 acres, traversed by some twenty miles of roadway, with twenty to twenty-five miles of footpaths. By this time 302,762 burials had been made in the world-famous necropolis, of which Joseph L. Chester, under the pseudonym Julian Cramer, wrote in the *Knickerbocker Magazine* (January, 1843):

> "Oh! if the parted soul have aught of care
> For what has been its tried companion long,
> Methinks it could not choose a fitter spot
> For its long dreamless sleep—than this!"

. . . . *In a newer city in a younger world*

GENERATION AFTER generation of artisans and peasants, season after season for centuries, toiled up the steep incline of Mont-Saint-Michel to build—with their hands and prayers, with the bread and salt that kept their hearts and minds and bodies alive in worship—the Fortress-Abbey-Church, a radiant temple to the glory of the Archangel whose name means "Like unto God." Within all the great cathedrals of an older world are felt the sufferings and the supplications, the thanksgiving and the solace, the continuity of devotions without end for days without number; countless candles lit by son after father and father after son; the incense and the echoing chants of praise; the groping of a million human faces made beautiful by the beauty all about—beauty of the spirit, of carvings in stone, of the jewel-light of stained glass windows, of the Psalms and of the Word. And even before the arms had raised the arches of support and the spires that soared in the strength of delicacy, before the naves stretched the length of many steps, altars were set in crypts, so that people could come that much closer to what they were seeking.

So it was to be with the Cathedral of Saint John the Divine in a newer city in a younger world, where a Church has been building through the years for the centuries. It was on January 8, 1899 (twenty-seven times four seasons after the Right Reverend Horatio Potter's founding thoughts; seven twelvemonths after the first devotions held in the Close on the opening afternoon of 1892, six times around the sun from the laying of the cornerstone on St. John's Day, near the following December's end) that people first came to worship in the Crypt. "Every Sunday afternoon from 4 o'clock to 5 o'clock there is a service [there]. . . . Every Sunday thousands are attracted to Cathedral Heights," *Leslie's Weekly* tells on

December 5, 1901. "After each service in the crypt a free lecture is delivered by Mr. Barnard, of the vestry, explaining the structure. . . . For instance, the first stupendous arch [145 feet in height at the keystone], which is now finished, and toward which the eyes of pilgrims . . . turn in wonder . . . is one of four . . . which will support three other arches, to tower 300 feet. These three will . . . support the spire. . . . The columns for the three arches like that in the illustration [and in Byron's photograph, page 458] are finished, and the arches will soon be under construction. None of these four arches, when the cathedral is completed, will be seen from the outside. They will form a part of the great arched ceiling under the spire. The three arches supporting the spire will, of course, be in view from without. . . . The extreme east end of the building . . . is what will be known as the Belmont Chapel. In front of it will stand the eight granite monoliths. . . ."

The transportation of these great columns, Druidical in their stark nobility, is described in *The Mail and Express Illustrated Saturday Magazine*, August 22, 1903: "It was a long and tedious job to move the monoliths from the barge to the specially constructed truck which was brought alongside [a dock on the North River Shore at 135th Street, under the viaduct], and further delay has been caused by the non-arrival of the traction engine to haul the truck to Cathedral Heights. . . . The first anchor for the winch has been made fast at the wharf, and anchors will be placed every two hundred feet along the route." The specially constructed truck, reputedly the largest in the world and weighing more than 100 tons with its majestic load, was to be moved by means of the steam winch alone. *Munsey's Magazine* for September, 1904, told of the rearing of the first of the giants into the sky: "On the 27th of June, six men, with a set of steel pulleys, twenty-four strands of three-quarter-inch steel rope, and a stationary engine, gathered at the Cathedral . . . on Morningside Heights—the Acropolis of New York . . . and in forty-five minutes lifted into place a ninety-ton pillar of polished granite. With the exception of the Obelisk in Central Park, it was the largest and heaviest stone ever set in the United States." This mighty task had to be repeated seven times, before the last of the Titans was set in place on November 25. "For four or five years," the article continues, "the huge central piers of masonry have stood, bare, gaunt and unfinished, upon the ridge that overlooks the northern part of the metropolis. There was a long delay in procuring the great granite pillars. . . . Only at a cost of twenty-five thousand dollars for each column were they finally obtained from quarries at [Bear Island near] Vinal Haven, Maine. . . . It was found necessary to bring a special ship-load of huge pine-trunks from Oregon, by way of Cape Horn, in order to make a derrick tall and strong enough to lift them into place. Add to the original cost of each pillar five thousand dollars for transportation, and about a quarter of a million dollars is represented in this . . . row of lofty granite sentinels." Further details are furnished by Edward Hagaman Hall in *A Guide to the Cathedral Church of Saint John the Divine in the City of New York* (10th ed., New York, 1931): "The Eight Great Columns . . . among the marvels of the Cathedral . . . were quarried as monoliths and turned on a specially constructed lathe. When the first two were subjected to the pressure of polishing they broke, and the contractor asked permission to make the shafts in two pieces. The lower stone in each shaft is 38 feet high and weighs 90 tons, and the upper stone is 17 feet high and weighs 40 tons, the total height between base and capital being 55 feet and the weight 130 tons."

Cathedral builders for the most part have been men, but the placing of these colossi among the columns of the world was directed by a woman—Mrs. Carrie A. Howland, "the

The Cathedral of Saint John the Divine under construction,
1904

wife and partner of the contractor for the erection of the choir columns," the *Illustrated
Supplement* of the *New-York Tribune*, August 14, 1904, related. "She is the contractor's
assistant in all stages . . . of the enterprise. Mrs. Howland is quietly energetic, very methodical, and quick to discern danger to the men employed, or to remedy any hitch in the
work. Many new methods have been devised by her, and in an emergency she selects the
tools and implements required with a promptness that belongs only to the initiated, experienced and also inventive mechanic. She usually wears while at work a black straw hat,
light colored shirtwaist, a black woollen skirt, and on cool days a black woollen jacket. She
carries a parasol or umbrella on hot days. Her complexion is fair, she has blue eyes and
dark brown hair, she is of medium height, but of slight build, and is womanly and naturally
graceful in speech and manner . . . cables, ropes, pulleys, levers, scaffolds, hammers and
drills are as familiar to her as teaspoons or scissors are to other women."

Behind her were the original architects, Heins and LaFarge. Father John LaFarge (born
into one of America's most illustrious families in the arts) tells of their collaboration in *The
Manner Is Ordinary* (New York, 1954): "The incidents of my brother Grant's relation to the
Episcopal cathedral of St. John the Divine . . . deserve recording. With . . . George L.

458

Heins, husband of our aunt, Aimée LaFarge, he had been the original architect of the cathedral. Heins's work had been more in the administrative line, and Grant's in that of the designing itself. The understanding was that the contract would expire with the death of either partner, and so when Heins passed away in 1907 the trustees, who were dissatisfied with the original plans, refused to renew the contract and instead placed the work in the hands of Ralph Adams Cram." (Dr. Hall states that LaFarge remained the architect until the completion of the Choir in April, 1911—the consecration being held on the 19th of that month—when Cram & Ferguson took over.) "Grant's design was one of four chosen in a national competition in the year 1890 and . . . later selected from the four. It was . . . more or less in a Romanesque or pre-Gothic style. One of the factors in the design was the Cathedral of Gerona in Spain which Grant had visited in his youth. . . . Its [St. John's] chief feature was a tremendous four-sided tower over the transept, and the magnificent monoliths flanking the main altar. But Grant always said he refused to be bound down by any particular designations of styles. . . . As it was, one or two of the original trustees became enamored of the Gothic idea and were convinced that an Anglican cathedral in this country would not be perfect unless it were expressed in Gothic terms. . . ." From the hour when Christopher Grant LaFarge "was notified of the non-renewal of the contract until his death [on October 11, 1938], he never discussed the matter, and only very rarely did any of his friends or family realize how severe a blow he had absorbed."

The "monoliths," too, have kept their vow of silence.

. . . . The Lady And The Tiger

"There was a Young Lady of the Niger
Who Smiled As She Rode on a Tiger,
They returned From the Ride
With the Lady inside
And the Smile on the face of the Tiger."

quoted the Infanta Eulalia in the course of after-dinner conversation in her suite at the Savoy on May 27, 1893, expressing the pious hope that she was not destined to share the sad fate of the ingested damsel. This recitation and comment followed her amused study of an unsigned cartoon on the front page of *The Evening Telegram* of that date, captioned "The Lady And The Tiger," showing the Princess herself riding the Tammany symbol. Her grasp of the implications, a member of the party explained, stemmed from the perusal of a Thomas Nast classic (published in *Time*, January 11, 1890) hanging in the cabin of the dispatch boat *Dolphin*, which, "decked like a page," served as the Royal Yacht during the Infanta's sojourn here. So taken was she with the limerick accompaniment (attributed to William Cosmo Monkhouse), that she had committed it to memory. She added, however, the *New-York Daily Tribune* of the 29th hastened to report, that "she had no fear, if the smile of the tiger which was bearing her in the picture was as pleasant as that of the Mayor [Thomas F. Gilroy] who had been so courteous and polite to her since her arrival." She had been received by him on the afternoon of the 25th, when she was escorted up Fifth Avenue in procession to the newness of Ralph S. Townsend's architectural triumph (dating from 1892) where her path through the lobby was over a flower-strewn tapestry freshly laid by immaculately white-cotton-gloved hall boys.

The entire second floor was given over to the pretty, blue-eyed, brown-haired aunt of Alfonso XIII, King of Spain, on her tour of inspection just four hundred and one years in the wake of Columbus' mission. The fourteen-room state suite—according to *King's Handbook of New York* (Second Edition, 1893), "one of the most sumptuous and enchanting apartments on either continent"—was described in the *New-York Daily Tribune* of May 25: "The main parlor . . . is divided into three parts by a simple arrangement of columns, pilasters and embroidered curtains. One of the parts is finished in striped yellow satin panels, with furniture coverings of the same material; another in red and yellow and the third in green. All are in the Louis XVI style. The ceilings have been painted to give them the effect of circled skies. A mirror extends from the ceiling to the floor, the full width of the rear parlor, in front of which are two beautiful candelabra about eight feet high. Electric lights twine about the columns. . . . The walls and ceilings [of the bedroom] are of raised modelwork placed upon an enamelled wooden base. The curtains, portieres and decorations are elaborate in the extreme, with the colors white and pink prevailing. The walls of the alcove are

The 7th Regiment passing in review in honor of the Infanta
Eulalia, June 3, 1893. Scene at Fifth Avenue and Fifty-ninth Street

finished in heavy satin, and the bed is of inlaid satinwood, with a pink satin canopy and pink satin and lace coverlet. . . . Off the private parlor of the Infanta is the bathroom, whose walls are of enamelled decorated tiling, with facing of Mexican onyx." Adjoining the Louis XV dining room was "the English breakfast-room, . . . capable of holding about 100 people."

On the afternoon of June 3, a multitude of 15,000 gathered about the Plaza, to cheer the royal party on the occasion of the review of New York's "crack" Regiment. The Infanta, in "a light green gown and a turban hat," occupied a specially built box at the north end of the Hotel Savoy, with her husband, Prince Antonio Maria d'Orléans—wearing the uniform of a colonel of the Spanish Hussars—at her side, General Fitzgerald at the right, the Duke of Tamames at the left, and Mayor Gilroy, Commander Davis, General Porter, and the rest of the party in the background. "The regiment had turned out almost its full strength, about 950 men being in line," stated the *New-York Daily Tribune* of the next morning. "They were in full dress uniform, including white belts and trousers, and never did they make a better showing."

The Princess—often on the verge of fainting from fatigue, and with the prospect of the World's Columbian Exposition ahead—smiled bravely through the hardships of an eleven-day round of sightseeing and ceremony (see page 463), and even found feminine time to order a "royal gown" (from Ehrich Brothers, at Sixth Avenue and Twenty-third Street) described in the *Tribune* of May 28: "It is made of a rich shade of eminence brocaded satin. The waist is semi-decollete, the entire front and back being covered with black net on which butterfly points are artistically embroidered. . . . On the top of each [elbow-length] sleeve is a large jet butterfly. The skirt is made with a deep flaring ruffle, the top of which is edged with two rows of rosebud jet embroidery." But real adventure came on Friday afternoon, June 2 (and again we are obligated to the *Tribune,* this time of June 3 and 5) when the royal visitor (wearing a yachting costume topped by a red sailor hat) and her husband, "finding themselves alone, stole out of the Savoy for a stroll. They walked first through Fifty-ninth-st. as far as the Columbus statue. . . . Then returning, they took a Broadway cable car at Seventh-ave. . . . for a ride downtown. At Fiftieth-st., the Infanta and the Prince were transferred to an ordinary horse-car, the little red, every day transfer tickets being sufficient to give them passage further on. At Twenty-third-st. they got out and walked. A short distance below Twenty-third-st., on Broadway, they noticed a crowd before a window. It was the entrance to the photograph studio [Pach Brothers, at No. 935] where a few days before [on May 31] the Infanta and her party had sat for their pictures [following a session at the gallery of the Moreno Co. on the 30th]. The crowd was looking at a large picture of the Infanta." Was it perhaps the one taken in a "tan-colored street costume, with gloves and bonnet to match," or the yellow silk, or maybe the "beautiful garment" described in the *Tribune* of June 1 as "a yellow satin court dress with a train, with white sleeves, lace yoke and ribbon and lace on the shoulders," in which "While posing . . . she reclined on a sofa"? In any event, "Elbowing their way to the entrance of the studio, the Princess and her husband stood unrecognized for some minutes. . . . In telling the story to her caller yesterday the Infanta laughed heartily over the little adventure, and said that for once she was sure she had heard people express themselves freely and as they thought about her."

. . . . In way of victory and suffering

"When Abraham Lincoln was shoveled into the tombs,
  he forgot the copperheads and the assassin . . .
  in the dust, in the cool tombs.

And Ulysses Grant lost all thought of con men and Wall
  Street, cash and collateral turned ashes . . . in the
  dust, in the cool tombs."

Carl Sandburg (Cornhuskers)

"Let us have peace," wrote he who was to have so little, in his letter accepting the Republican Party's nomination for the Presidency in 1868. In eight bungling White House years the military "savior of the Union" lost in peace the prestige that had been his in war, and then in restlessness toured a world in which he found nor rest nor beauty. A hero's welcome home faded in defeat at the Republican National Convention of 1880; the following year—his $5,000 income supplemented by that from a $250,000 fund admiringly raised—he settled down in unappealing red-brick ugliness at 3 East Sixty-sixth Street and joined the banking and brokerage house of Grant & Ward, newly formed by his unbusinesslike namesake and Ferdinand Ward, a parvenu of Wall Street. Ignorant in finance as he was innocent in politics, Grant—along with his sons—was victimized by the partnered scoundrelism, and the ex-President who on May 1, 1884 calculated himself almost two and a half times a millionaire, six days later—with the closing of the Marine National Bank and the associated failure of his own firm—found himself in dishonored ruin. Then came the collapse of the trust fund, and even his brave swords—along with all his real and personal property—were given as security to the reluctant William H. Vanderbilt, who had lent him $150,000 to stave off the inevitable. As if unwarranted disgrace and poverty were not enough, illness struck, and battling pain he wrote of his battles for the *Century Magazine.* On February 21, 1885 he started his two-volume *Personal Memoirs* (to be posthumously published at that year's end by Charles L. Webster & Company—the firm of which Mark Twain, his sponsor, was chief owner—and to yield a $450,000 royalty). He wrote against time and it ran out about a week after the last chapter was agoniously pencilled. The first full General of the Army of the United States since Washington's command died fortitudinously on July 23 at Mount McGregor, New York.

A month before, he had indicated his burial wishes in a note to his son, Frederick Dent Grant, expressing a preference for West Point, cancelled out by the impossibility of sharing this soldier's grave with his wife; mentioning "Galena, or some place in Illinois," since it was there that he had received his first commission as General; and finally suggesting "New York—Because the people of that city befriended me in my need." On July 28, after a Manhattan inspection tour of various possible sites, Colonel Grant telegraphed to Mayor William R. Grace, "Mother takes Riverside Park. Temporary tomb had better be at the same place." The plans of Jacob Wrey Mould, architect of the Park Department, were immediately thrown

The Infanta Eulalia of Spain and Mayor Gilroy leaving the
temporary burial place of Ulysses S. Grant, where the royal
visitor had placed a floral tribute, May 30, 1893
This photograph marked Percy C. Byron's initial sale of a
news picture

into execution. By August 7, the arched and buttressed red and black brick vault, bluestone
trimmed with granite base and lining of white enameled brick, stood ready to shelter the
heroic dead in hemlock shade, overlooking the nobility of the palisaded Hudson as it moved
solemnly toward the sea. The following morning a reporter gazed down from the Tribune
Building, across from City Hall (where during three nights and two days a quarter of a
million people in double line—sometimes mile-long in waiting—had passed the bier) and
saw the sombre car, " 'dark as a funeral scarf,' an object of majestic gloom with its twenty-
four sable horses with their sable trappings" leave the plaza. Among the pallbearers were
Sherman and Sheridan, who had been Grant's comrades in arms, and Johnston and Buckner,
who had borne arms against him. Led by General Hancock, the melancholy procession of
sixty thousand men, including the President of the United States and two former Presidents (Hayes and Arthur) moved dirgefully up Broadway, between massed, silent spectators
and raven-draped buildings; up Fifth Avenue from Fourteenth Street to Fifty-seventh; westward and then along the Boulevard to Seventy-second Street and by way of Riverside Drive
to leave a soldier, lonely in his glory,

"in the dust, in the cool tombs."

Meanwhile, plans for a permanent mausoleum, a hero's sepulcher, had been set in immediate motion; but a dozen delayed years passed before John H. Duncan's "White Temple"—

463

The Dedication of Grant's Tomb, April 27, 1897

built by popular subscription—was ready to receive its dead. On April 17, 1897, it was the sorrowing filial duty of Colonel Frederick D. Grant and Ulysses S. Grant, Jr., to walk once more behind their father's coffin, as it was quietly borne the short way from its humble brick repository into the great domed edifice and placed in the massive dark red porphyry sarcophagus on its square pedestal of bluish-gray Quincy-quarried granite. Again General Grant lay lonesome

"in the dust, in the cool tombs."

Overhead on the morning of April 27, according to *The New York Herald* of the next day, there was "another war between the gray and the blue," for a gale raced across the island like a conquering host, as the city celebrated "the day of the apotheosis of Grant—not a funeral, but a festival." Again there was the sound of marching as 53,000 men moved northward in step from Madison Square, while this time over half a million people cheered; again saluting ships lay at anchor in the Hudson. "Many thousand persons gathered at the tomb [where Mayor Strong presided] to witness the ceremonies and the review. . . . The President and Vice President of the United States, the members of the Cabinet, the Speaker of the House of Representatives, former President Cleveland, the representatives at Washington of all the foreign countries, the family of General Grant and distinguished Union and Confederate Generals were conspicuous in the main stand. There was music by a carefully selected chorus, led by Frank Damrosch, and Bishop J. P. Newman . . . offered a prayer." In his oration, President McKinley said: "Great as he was in war he loved peace, and told the world that honorable arbitration of differences was the best hope of civilization." So at nightfall they left Ulysses S. Grant alone in his wisdom,

"in the dust, in the cool tombs."

On the evening of December 20, 1902, Julia Dent Grant's coffin was carried to the waiting twin sarcophagus close to that of her husband, and they who had shared so much in way of victory and suffering were together

"in the dust, in the cool tombs."

. . . . *A man out of the common*

IN ALL the Western World, Li Hung Chang had but two heroes. One, "Chinese" Gordon, his comrade in arms as the British commander of the "Ever Victorious Army" that supported the Emperor's cause in the Taiping Revolt, had (although later conciliatory) leveled a rifle at him because of his breach of faith in ordering the execution of the rebel princes promised security in return for the surrender of Suchow on November 29, 1863. The other, Ulysses S. Grant, the viceroy's guest at a seventy-course Cantonese banquet in 1879, declared that during his globe-encircling tour he had met only four men touched by true greatness: Disraeli, Bismarck, Gambetta, and Li Hung Chang. In 1896 the seventy-three-year-old statesman of the Celestial Empire, sent to represent his country at the coronation of Czar Nicholas II, paused on his way from East to West and back again, to mourn at the graves of his two warrior friends. On August 30, over twenty thousand New Yorkers gathered around Grant's temporary resting place on Riverside Drive to watch "the greatest foreigner and most powerful ruler that has ever visited the United States" (as *The New-York Times* of August 29 described him) pay votive tribute to one of the nation's soldier Presidents. Li Hung Chang's $500 contribution toward the great marble tomb then building close by had been one of the first received.

The day before, His Excellency—clad in the Yellow Jacket (his country's most important decoration) and wearing the four-eyed peacock feather of honor in his cap—had sailed into the city on board the S. S. *St. Louis*. His was a tremendous presence, and "It was not merely on account of his height, well over six feet . . . that he would be deemed a man out of the common," (according to a Britisher quoted in the *New-York Daily Tribune* of August 23). "His attitudes are dignified and natural. The hand, concealed as he generally keeps it in the loose sleeves of his jacket" except when extended for the pleased inspection of a large diamond ring, "is well formed, and with much prehensile power, and above all things worthy of note is the fact that the nails . . . are cut as short as our own. . . . The Viceroy's eye is larger and rounder than most of his countrymen. . . . Its hue is . . . hazel . . . and the gleam in it is most genial, and at times almost merry."

The occidental press devoted column after column to descriptions of the visitor's retinue and entourage, down to his bodyguards and sentries and servants and cooks (all protectively salaried for life, even after dismissal); to his suite at the Waldorf; to his dietary habits and abstinences at banquets to which he came replete; to his silver-mounted pipe of opium, his long cigarettes and their holder; to his early hour of retirement and the days which began prematurely with sleep-interrupting "breakfasts" of gruel and a soothing drink at 3:30 A.M.; to his pleased amazement at New York's tall buildings, which seemed to him "so well con-

Li Hung Chang outside the Waldorf, 1896
Scene on West Thirty-third Street, off Fifth Avenue

structed that they would resist any wind, perhaps"; and to the six-day round of festivities and functions in his honor.

On August 29, the Ambassador was received by President Cleveland at the 2 West Fifty-seventh Street home of the former Secretary of the Navy William C. Whitney. On this occasion, according to the *New-York Daily Tribune* of the following morning, he left his Waldorf apartments and "came downstairs leaning upon the arm of Secretary Olney on one side and his adopted son, Lord Li, on the other. . . . Following him came the official interpreter, two members of his suite and several servants, carrying rugs and shawls. The big umbrella was brought forth and hoisted to protect [him] from the rays of the sun. . . . An attendant opened the [carriage] door for him. Another lifted his foot and placed it on the step. Two others assisted him to get in. Once inside the carriage, he raised the umbrella over his head and sank back contentedly." All went off according to protocol; but tucked away on an inside page of the *New-York Daily Tribune* of September 12 are several astonishing and undiplomatic revelations quoted from an interview granted by the Ambassador to William Eleroy Curtis of *The Chicago Record:* "It pleased His Excellency to make some rather sarcastic comments upon the foreign policy of the present administration"—because of its non-intervention in the Chino-Japanese War of 1894—"and to express his personal dislike for President Cleveland." Still smarting under his country's defeat, Li Hung Chang warned of our defenselessness in case of possible Nipponese aggression (at a time when the Western Hemisphere was just vaguely beginning to think of the later exploited Yellow Peril) and stated that his recent enemy's war machine could annihilate "every city on Puget Sound . . . in a week" and "throw shells of dynamite into San Francisco [from ten miles off at sea] until the city was entirely destroyed."

On September 2, the day before leaving New York for Philadelphia, Li, who had asked so many unwittingly embarrassing questions (including expressed curiosity about the ages of the ladies who were presented to him and the salaries of the officials who were his hosts) himself voluntarily invited questioning. "What does Your Excellency think of the pictures of Your Excellency that have appeared in the papers of this city?" asked a reporter. The Viceroy replied through an interpreter: "They are not good. They are very poor representations of their original."

. . . . *The Charge of The Four Hundred*

"ANY WAR would be disastrous to New York, more so, indeed, than to any other city in the world," said Prince Louis of Battenberg (grandson-in-law of Queen Victoria and grandfather of H. R. H. Prince Philip, Duke of Edinburgh, consort of Queen Elizabeth II of England) on November 10, 1905, in an interview in his white-fitted private cabin on board H. M. S. *Drake,* the day after his arrival here. "This is impressed upon me," he continued, with occasional accentual traces of his German origin, "by the tremendous amount of bustle and traffic that one sees in coming up the harbor. What New York wants above all things is peace. The two fleets [six visiting British men-'o-war and twelve warships of the United States Navy] now in the harbor could, I think, reduce the city to atoms in the time it takes my cook to fry an omelet."

467

Prince Louis of Battenberg arriving at West Point, November
11, 1905
Disembarking from the Steamer *C. W. Morse* of the People's
Line

While, according to the press, the primary activation of the "Admiral Prince's" visit to
North America was to consolidate Canada's then faltering relationship with the mother
country and to serve as a good-will ambassador to the United States, Miss May Leslie—in
the chorus of the *Wonderland* company playing at the Majestic Theatre—felt that he had come
"all the way over from England just to make a poor little Irish girl lose most of her week's
pay" as penalty for her refusal to carry a British flag in the "Nature Song" number of that Victor
Herbert musical. Prince Louis himself gave a tertiary and not invalid reason: "I have been
saving my teeth until I could come to an American dentist, because I have heard that they
were so good." Five lengthy sessions—accorded due publicity in the New York papers—at
the 30 West Thirty-ninth Street offices of Drs. Wilbur M. and Washington Dailey were
required to bring about this $1,000 molar salvation.

The Prince hurried back and forth from the dental chair to the banquet seat, in a mad
round of official and social activities, the end result of which—prognosticated a British tar—
was bound to be an attack of the gout. Frederick Burr Opper's cartoon, "The Charge of
The Four Hundred" (now in the collection of the Museum of the City of New York),
mirrored the hapless victim beset by a wildly scrambling mob of matrons and monocled
clubmen, holding out invitations to "A Swift Little Dinner," a "Pink Tea," "A Little Lunch,"

a "Bachelor Blow-out," etc., with ballooned beseechments such as "Come Out In My Auto," "It'll Be *So* Dear Of You To Come," and "Aw Prince, Don't Say No."

The Byron shutters clicked furiously as they followed His Serene Highness—a smiling, solidly built, six-foot-plus figure, with a full brown beard and the diminishing hair of his fifty-one years—to the reception at Governors Island and the following day up the Hudson to West Point. The first of these functions was a luncheon attended by one hundred representatives of both Army and Navy and a distinguished civilian contingent. The host, General Frederick D. Grant (son of Ulysses S. Grant), in command of the Department of the East, greeted the Prince as he stepped ashore to the customary Admiral's salute of thirteen guns, while the Eighth Infantry Band gave the military ruffle; and arm in arm the pair walked up the hill between lines of soldiers at attention, to the flag-bedecked Officers Club, where according to *The New York Herald* of November 11, "Autumn foliage and yellow chrysanthemums were conspicuous in the scheme of decoration, and the banks of flowers on the tables, gold braid and shining swords of the officers, and the elaborate costumes of the women, made the spectacle a brilliant one." After informal terminal toasts, Mrs. Grant, the hostess, subjected Prince Louis to a two-hour ritual handshaking ordeal, following which he went on to a reception at the Navy Yard, and a dinner given by the Naval Alumni at Delmonico's.

The Luncheon for Prince Louis of Battenberg, November 10, 1905 at the Officers Club, Governors Island
Mrs. Frederick D. Grant (the hostess, hatless) with Lieutenant General Adna R. Chaffee, Chief of Staff of the United States Army, and other guests

So, through the days and nights until he sailed away on November 20, the royal visitor (who preferred to be known as a sailor in the British Navy he had entered as a cadet in 1868 and in which service he was to die an Admiral of the Fleet in 1921) was fêted at entertainments public and private; witnessed the gala opening of the Horse Show; attended a matinée at the Hippodrome and a performance of *Her Great Match* at the Criterion Theatre (a selection possibly activated by Edward VII's kingly predilection for Maxine Elliott, the star of this Clyde Fitch vehicle); reveled into the dawn at the Lambs' Gambol; visited the phenomena that are Coney Island and Chinatown; and listened to Negro melodies. His most unusual adventure in democracy, however, lay beneath the surface of the city, for on November 17, escorted by August Belmont and a party of friends, he rode up and down in New York's year-old subway.

. . . . A handsomer body of men

"ONE OR two beavers for candles and two to three hundred pieces of fire wood," in addition to the wage of 24 stuivers (presently equivalent to about 48 cents) a night, were promised to the nine men engaged by the Burgomasters of New Amsterdam on October 4, 1658, to serve as the "Rattle Watch"—the city's first paid police force.

With magnifications and mutations, what was known as the Watch Department persisted until May 7, 1844, when this legacy from the days of Dutch rule was abolished and a Day and Night Police established. On the following November 27, the Municipal Police came into being, to be supplanted in 1857 by the Metropolitan Police.

"New York's Finest" (a title first bestowed about 1850 by George W. Matsell, Chief of Police from 1845 to 1857 and Superintendent from 1873 to 1875) were in great disrepute in the early 1890's; and as a result of various reform movements in general and the agitations of the Reverend Dr. Charles H. Parkhurst in particular, the State Senate appointed the seven-man Lexow Committee "to investigate the police department of the City of New York." A five-volume report, running to 5,766 published pages of testimony, told a tale of corruption beyond the wildest imagerial tabloidery, accusing sixty-seven men of crime; but, as late as January 1, 1896, not one of the band had begun a prison sentence. On May 6, 1895, with the generally popular appointment of Theodore Roosevelt as president of the Police Board, and Colonel Frederick D. Grant, Andrew D. Parker and Avery D. Andrews as the other members of the "Reform Quartette," the tide of demoralization was stemmed. After ten months of "Teddy's" hard-hitting policies ("I have always been fond of the West African proverb: 'Speak softly and carry a big stick, you will go far,'" he was to declare in 1900) Mrs. Burton Harrison wrote in her chapter on "Externals Of Modern New York" in *History Of The City Of New York* By Mrs. Martha J. Lamb and Mrs. Burton Harrison, New York, 1896) that "there is now nowhere to be found a police force better prepared for the duties laid out for such an establishment. . . . For a present population of nearly two millions, we now have one chief of police, 23 captains, 154 sergeants, 37 detective sergeants, 174 roundsmen, 3,651 patrolmen, 73 doormen, 15 surgeons, and 28 matrons."

Because of the blight on the "bluecoats," the popular annual Police Parade had been tact-

"The Police on Parade," June 1, 1897

fully omitted in 1895. Therefore, when the event was resumed in 1896 *The New-York Times* of June 2 noted that "more than usual interest was manifested," the crowd hissing the villains of the investigation and cheering its heroes. The parade here shown was the last before the consolidation of 1898, which melded the New York, Brooklyn, Long Island City, Staten Island, Park and Bridge Police into a single department. On the afternoon of June 1, 1897, preceded by a roundsman and six mounted patrolmen as skirmishers, and by the Bicycle Squad (organized in 1895 "for the better protection of pedestrians against careless bicycle riders") Chief Peter Conlin rode his favorite bay horse Prince like a centaur at the head of 2,800 men—the "Largest Body a Chief of Police Ever Led in This City," according to *The Evening Post*. The *New-York Daily Tribune* of the next morning commented that nearly 1,000 of the participants had "been appointed . . . under the reform administration, and their slender but muscular bodies contrasted somewhat sharply with the bulky and fat bodies of policemen who have been in the service for years. . . . There were many crooked lines . . . although the police generally made a creditable appearance on the march." To the blare of regimental bands, the parade swept up Broadway from Bowling Green to Twenty-third Street, swung over to Madison Avenue and then west to Fifth by way of Twenty-ninth Street, for the descent on the reviewing stand at the Worth Monument. It is here seen passing "the cosy home of the younger social element"—the wisteria-and-ivy-covered Calumet Club on Fifth Avenue at the northeast corner of Twenty-ninth Street, founded in 1879, "by

471

men of pleasure for men of pleasure," so Robert Stewart wrote in *Munsey's Magazine* of October, 1899. On the right, according to Jay Irving (ardent student and authority on "Our Police Protectors") is Inspector Moses W. Cortright of the Chief's Staff—who had joined the force as a Patrolman in 1867 and was to become Chief Inspector—accompanied by his Sergeants. The tracks underfoot are those of the horsecar railroad completed in 1896 by the Twenty-Eighth and Twenty-Ninth Street Crosstown Railroad Company, running along those latitudes from First Avenue to Eleventh, to the Twenty-third and Thirty-fourth Street ferries. Operated in later years by storage battery, this line was discontinued on August 8, 1919.

The photograph here shown was used to decorate the cover of a music sheet (to be found in the all-embracing collection of J. Francis Driscoll, of Brookline, Massachusetts) entitled "The Mounted Metropolitan Police. An Incident Of The Big Parade," with music by Lyn. Udall and words by Karl Kennett, published in 1898 by Howley, Haviland & Co. The verse deals with the dramatic episode of an Independence Day procession, when "a laughing baby girl" fell from a window ledge and "dropp'd as neat as could be, in the arms of Officer Rafferty," who had courageously maneuvered his steed into the tiny form's plummeting path, and who then bore the little one triumphantly up Broadway, "The baby's sunny hair, on his bosom like a fleece." According to the lyricist—and why doubt his veracity?—"the ladies said they didn't know when they'd seen a handsomer body of men than the Mounted Metropolitan Policemen."

. . . . *The cobwebs out of our civic brain*

PROMINENT AMONG New York's pioneer street cleaners were the self-appointed four-legged porcine delegates whose omnipresence was a source of constant annoyance to the citizenry and a recurrent theme in the accounts of the stranger in Manhattan. During the winter of 1817–1818 William Cobbett, the English politician and writer, found an index of our local prosperity in the "*calves' heads,* large bits and *whole joints* of meat . . . left on the shambles . . . [to] fall to the share of the *street hogs,* a thousand or two of which are constantly *fatting* . . . on the meat and fish flung out of the houses." The Swedish scientist Baron Axel Klinkowström recounted that in 1819 these early perambulant garbage collectors "have often caused ridiculous situations. Once during the fashionable promenade hour on Broadway I saw some of these animals rush on the sidewalk, making a sharp contrast with the elegant clothes, and one filthy pig bumped into a well-dressed woman. Often they trip people who are not sufficiently observant." And in 1842 Charles Dickens in his *American Notes* warned: "Take care of the pigs. Two portly sows are trotting up behind this carriage, and a select party of half a dozen gentlemen hogs have just now turned the corner. Here is a solitary swine lounging homeward by himself. . . . He is in every respect a republican pig, going wherever he pleases, and mingling with the best society on an equal, if not superior footing. . . . They are the city scavengers, these pigs."

Until March 5, 1866, when outdoor orderliness became one of the functions of the State-controlled Metropolitan Board of Health, the situation had changed very little from that

472

described by Baron Klinkowström in 1819: "As the care of the streets is not by the property owners, but by contract, you can well imagine the dust that is raised when twenty to thirty sweepers at once clean the large streets." *Harper's Weekly* of November 14, 1868 devoted two wood engravings to the early-morning line-up of the street-sweepers, whose nine to ten hours of more or less dilatory quotidian effort was supplemented by the advance visitations of rag-pickers averaging an independent income of from thirty to fifty cents a day. In 1872, what passed for the Bureau of Street Cleaning was transferred from the two-year auspices of the New York City Board of Health to the jurisdiction of the Board of Police. It was not until May 26, 1881 that the legislature placed a single commissioner in charge of the newly created Department of Street Cleaning (to become the Department of Sanitation on December 1, 1929).

It remained, however, for Colonel George E. Waring (appointed Commissioner during the reform administration of Mayor Strong in 1895, at a time when our thoroughfares were black with slush and grip was epidemic) to garb his newly disciplined force in the conspicuous duck suits at first evocative of ridicule and protest and calling forth the appellation "White Wings," but soon to earn the respect of a cleansed city. On May 26, 1896 (the fifteenth anniversary of the department) this brilliant sanitary engineer marshaled his uniformed cohorts and equipment—the two thousand-odd men on foot, the 750 horses, the carts and the

The first parade of the Department of Street Cleaning,
May 26, 1896
The reviewing stand in front of the Croton Distributing Reservoir, at Fifth Avenue and Forty-first Street
Colonel George E. Waring giving instructions

sweeping machines and their drivers, needed to purify 450 miles of streets each day—in their first parade, an impressive monster column of marchers that at one point covered Fifth Avenue from the Fifty-ninth Street Plaza to Madison Square.

Of the three valiant years before a new regime saw fit to dispense with the service of this expert sanitarian, Jacob A. Riis wrote in *A Ten Years' War* (1900): "It was Colonel Waring's broom that first let light into the slum. That which had come to be considered an impossible task he did by the simple formula of 'putting a man instead of a voter behind every broom.' . . . the streets that had been dirty were swept. The ash barrels which had befouled the sidewalks disappeared. . . . The trucks [more than 60,000 strong] that obstructed the children's only playground, the street, went with the dirt. . . . His broom saved more lives in the crowded tenements than a squad of doctors. It did more: it swept the cobwebs out of our civic brain and conscience, and set up a standard of a citizen's duty which . . . will be ours until we have dragged other things than our pavements out of the mud."

. . . . *With the green of the "Gem of the Sea"*

THE ANNIVERSARY of "the Tutelar Saint of Ireland" was commemorated in 1779 "by the Natives of that Kingdom with their accustomed Hilarity," we are informed by *The New-York Gazette: And The Weekly Mercury* of March 22. Following their band, "*The Volunteers of Ireland* . . . marched into the City, and formed before the House of their Colonel, Lord Rawdon, who put himself at their Head, and, after paying his Compliments to his Excellency General Knyphausen, and to General Jones, accompanied them to the Bowery, where a Dinner was provided, consisting of five hundred Covers; after the Men were seated, and had proceeded to the Enjoyment of a noble Banquet, the Officers returned to Town, and dined with his Lordship."

On a later celebration, *The New York Herald* of March 18, 1895, commented: "Here's a St. Patrick's Day which began in the middle and celebrated itself both ways. That's the New York of it. . . . Saturday was the prelude, yesterday a series of symphonies in green, last night the interlude and to-day is the finale and grand march."

The sun shone, but the high winds of the month of Mars did not unfurl the "Sunburst of Erin" from its customary holiday place at City Hall, for the new Lawson Act prohibited the display of foreign banners on public buildings, but else and everywhere the emerald folds fluttered from pole and window in green glory. Numerically the 1895 show (according to *The New York Herald* of the 19th) was ". . . the smallest St. Patrick's Day parade ever seen here" for under two thousand marchers were in line, "and not ten per cent were young men." This fractional demonstration, as compared with the muster of from ten to fifteen thousand celebrants of years gone by, was attributable to the fact that half the membership of the Ancient Order of Hibernians had decided that funds were better spent in benevolence than on pageantry. "Yet many thousands . . . lined the route, and it was noticeable that the young and stalwart who wore a green ribbon or a shamrock were on the sidewalks cheering the gallant veterans of the A.O.H., who still cling pertinaciously to this mode of honoring . . . their patron saint."

474

St. Patrick's Day Parade, Monday, March 18, 1895

Two fresh departures—the afternoon hour and the west side route—also differentiated this particular parade from precedent. Companies A and C of the Hibernian Rifles, forty-eight divisions of the Ancient Order of Hibernians, the United Irish Societies and members of the county societies of Derry, Monaghan, Sligo, and Limerick lined up on Fifth Avenue, between Fortieth and Forty-second Streets, and at two o'clock—to the beat of homeland, Italian and German airs from the Catholic Protectory and other bands—marched north to Fifty-seventh, turning Hudsonward to pass Mayor Strong, huddled in his overcoat on the stoop of his home at No. 7, past Calvary Church and the Osborne, by Henry J. Hardenbergh's American Fine Arts Society façade (at the left of the photograph) and the Central Presbyterian Church (at the extreme right); before the reviewing stand at Broadway, then up the Boulevard as far as Ninety-sixth Street; along Amsterdam Avenue for half a mile and over to Columbus Avenue as far as the popular picnic ground, Lion Park at 108th Street, close to the thirty-year-old brewery of the leonine name. There were speeches, "a series of evolutions and a musical drill" by the Catholic Protectory Band and dancing to "old Irish airs, jigs and reels," stated the next morning's *New-York Times*.

There were celebrations all about. At Sulzer's Harlem River Park and Casino, at 127th Street and Second Avenue, from two in the afternoon once around the clock, a section of the Ancient Order of Hibernians held athletic contests, dealt harshly with oratory, and danced into the dawn. The 111th anniversary dinner of the Friendly Sons of St. Patrick took place at Delmonico's, Fifth Avenue and Twenty-sixth Street, and, according to the *New-York Daily Tribune,* "jolly as have been the crowds of men who have assembled in the big ballroom to 'dine at different dates,' no jollier crowd ever met in the room than the men who gathered last night and paid homage to the man who drove the snakes from Ireland in bygone ages." There were festivities at Rogers' Restaurant on Park Place, where the Friends of Ireland held their fifteenth annual banquet; the entertainment, reception, and ball of the uniformed Irish-American Volunteers filled Adelphi Hall at Fifty-second Street and Broadway; the Commercial Department of the De La Salle Institute gave a programme for relatives and friends. On East Fourteenth Street, at Tammany Hall (bedecked "with the green of the 'Gem of the Sea,' entwined with the Stars and Stripes . . . "), "supper was served a little before breakfast time, . . . but a happier crowd has seldom left the portals . . . [of the "Wigwam"] than the members of the [St. Patrick's] alliance as the sun burst through the clouds this morning."

. . . . *The bone and the sinew of the municipality*

"You shall not press down upon the brow of labor this crown of thorns, you shall not crucify mankind upon a cross of gold." These words, spoken by William Jennings Bryan at the Democratic National Convention in Chicago on July 8, 1896, perorated the oration that made him the Presidential nominee of his party in a bitter campaign for the free coinage of silver as opposed to the Republican platform of a protective tariff and the Gold Standard (sound money) championed by William McKinley. Once again, sectionalism came into the arena—the agrarian South and West pitted against the industrial and commercial Northeast.

On October 31, the Saturday preceding McKinley's election, the Business Men's Republican and Sound Money Association marched, over 110,000 strong, in a seven-and-a-half-hour demonstration, up Broadway, past the reviewing stand at Madison Square and on to Fifth Avenue and Fortieth Street, led by General Horace Porter, the Grand Marshal, on his "graceful bay horse, whose dainty feet"—according to the *New-York Daily Tribune* of November 1—"seemed light as air as he capered proudly up the avenue." The Legions of Gold "came by companies and battalions, and brigades and regiments," sixteen abreast, in "the most stupendous array of marching men ever assembled in a like space in the New World. . . . From the grandstands the coming hosts stretched away in plain view far down the avenue, which was a mass of waving flags . . . a field of red, white and blue, that faded away in the distance until the colors blended." A hundred and fifty-three bands played airs of patriotism that stirred the sidewalk throngs, and at one point the melody of *America* "seemed to extend along the entire line of march and up and down the avenue and over on Broadway, and swing in from the side streets with massed strains that ebbed and flowed."

The Wholesale Dry Goods Republican Club, with its 25,000 members, was in the vanguard, followed by the Central Dry Goods Division and representatives of the Wool Exchange; the Merchant Tailors' Sound Money League; the Railway and Steamship Sound Money Club; the Paper and Associated Trades; the Coal Trade Sound Money Club, the miners "in their besmirched canvas overalls and blouses, . . . pickaxes or shovels on their shoulders, and in their hats . . . the [burning] miner's torch"; the Wine and Spirit Traders' Society of the United States; the Produce Exchange Sound Money League; the Architectural Division, led by Bruce Price (designer of the American Surety Building and the St. James Building, and father of Emily Post), "one of the most striking figures in the parade . . . some six feet two inches tall . . . with his tall hat, magnificent physique and handsome face"; the Cotton Exchange Sound Money Club, with badges of yellow ribbons and cotton bolls; the Coffee Exchange and Lower Wall Street Business Men's McKinley and Hobart Sound Money Club; a delegation from the College of the City of New York, and more than 600 Columbia students; the Leaf Tobacco Sound Money Club, bedecked with "long bunches and streamers of

The Great Sound Money Parade, October 31, 1896
Scene on Broadway, looking north from Murray Street

tobacco"; the Bankers' and Brokers' McKinley and Hobart Club—"among the most kittenish of all the paraders" with their "varied assortment of cheers and yells, one of which was a play on the ratio of silver to gold in the dollar: '1, 2, 3, 4, 5, 6-teen to 1—nit!'"; the Lawyers' Sound Money Campaign Club; the Publishers' and Advertisers' Sound Money Club, with one side of their gigantic banner showing a silver dollar "Marked Down to 49 Cents"; and so on and on—the trades and the crafts, the commercialists and the professional men, side by side—"the bone and sinew of the municipality—the life and strength of the city" united in a commonality of cause.

Yellow, the color of the championed monetary standard, shone everywhere under the sun and the flag: in ribbons worn by marchers and spectators alike; on hatbands, as neckties, and in the form of gold bugs. "But the yellow chrysanthemums outdid all the rest. Almost every man wore one in the lapel of his coat. As line after line of yellow chrysanthemums went by the wonder grew. Where did they all come from?" *The New York Herald* of November 1, describing the "Grand Army of Gold," commented: "Yellow was the predominating color. . . . A man with a bad attack of jaundice would have been cheered, and a well developed case of yellow fever would have been regarded as a most excellent thing. Indeed, everybody seemed to have yellow fever."

. . . . *The latest styles in spring war paint*

"As FAR back as the oldest living votary of fashion in New York can remember, Fifth Avenue has on each Easter Sunday afforded a spectacle similar to that of yesterday," generalized *The New York Times* of April 11, 1898, descriptive of the "Dress Parade" of the previous day, laboring the point that "Succeeding generations have supplied the processions of fashion and of beauty on this famous avenue, and eager thousands have hastened thither from the four quarters of Manhattan Island to gaze upon it."

Just how immemorial was the secularity of Easter is difficult to establish. As long ago as March 29, 1869, the *Times* added a worldly note to the catalogue of worship: "The day being so pleasant, the streets and parks were filled with pedestrians. . . . The ladies were out in full force, looking doubly charming under the influence of those genial skies." A page of caricatures by Thomas Worth (one of the most successful of the Currier & Ives artists) appeared in *Harper's Weekly* of April 26, 1873, poking period fun at the "Cracking Of The Easter-Egg [to permit the emergence of a handsomely over-bedecked lady], And Budding Forth Of The Spring Fashions." We are allowed a modestly intimate glimpse of "Mr. Bantam As Nature Made Him," below a vignette showing his tailor's improvements on this lamentable state. An uncensored view of Mr. Sprat's valet struggling with corset strings strips the mystery of how the master achieved the "Beautiful Form Which Some Of His Friends Admire So Much," while distaff vanity, hemmed in by two mirrors, speculates: "I Wonder If My Back Hair Will Suit Those Critical People In The Pew Behind Us." Meanwhile, "Miss Uppercrust" swoons on her puzzled escort's arm, as she "Discovers Her Dressmaker With A Dress On Like Her Own." The *New-York Daily Tribune* of Easter Monday, 1874, concerning itself with "the proper celebration of the sacred day," seems disappointed that "the lingering March

478

The Easter Parade, April 10, 1898
Scene on Fifth Avenue, looking north from below Forty-first Street

winds forbade any very general adoption of Spring toilets, . . . usually a noticeable feature." In 1883, when H. A. Ogden contributed a page of anticipatory pen-and-ink holiday
impressions to *Frank Leslie's Illustrated Newspaper* of March 24, including a crowded
glimpse of "Easter-Sunday morning on Fifth Ave." the *Times* of the 26th gave official veri-
fication, telling of how ". . . early in the forenoon . . ." the golden pathway from Twenty-
sixth Street to the Park "blossomed into a splendor of elegantly clad men, women and children, and of prancing horses, glittering harness, and shining carriages." In 1886, the *Times*
of April 26, in its description of the Avenue as "a moving, living fashion plate," made happy
coupling of two words that have remained concordant: "It was altogether a brilliant picture
. . . and country cousins who had come to see the Easter parade gazed lovingly and longingly
at the costumes of such cunning fancies as their own village dressmaker never dreamed. . . ."
Two years later the accepted designation was headlined on April 2. Of uncatalogued vintage
is the oft told tale that the pageant owes its origin to the first bearing of floral decorations
from St. Thomas's Church to bring primaveritude to the wards of nearby St. Luke's Hospital.

Byron's celebrants of 1898 are promenading opposite the Croton Distributing Reservoir, a
landmark reared in 1837–1842 and about to give reluctant way (1899–1901) to The New
York Public Library. North of the massive masonry, across Forty-second Street, is the Hotel

Bristol, first found in the city directory of 1878–9 and holding its own as "an aristocratic and elegant house" in *King's Handbook Of New York* (Second Edition, 1893). Of this fin-de-siècle Easter Day we have divergent accounts: the *New-York Daily Tribune* of April 11 claiming that "Society itself" led a parade favorably lacking in resemblance to anything "on the earth, nor under it, nor over it, . . ." as that morning's *Herald* held that "Democracy ruled the great thoroughfare of the metropolis," while aloof "At the [lily-decked] parlor windows sat milady and the buds of the household, between the half drawn curtains, looking at the throngs in the avenue," who stared back in impertinent and awed reciprocity. "There was the subtle roll of the carriage over the smooth asphalt [newly replacing the noisesome Belgian blocks], which gave an ease and grace to those who sat in the vehicles." The *Tribune* felt that Easter had never been "More Generally Celebrated in New-York," with such "enthusiastic unanimity." Hotels were crowded with out-of-town visitants; florists were "overworked"; churches offered "elaborate musical programmes" and "appropriate sermons, some of which had been prepared for years, yes, and preached more than once before." In hats, the *Tribune* asked rhetorically on its Easter Sunday woman's page, "What colors predominate?" Echo answered: "Purple, of course, and gray, and delicious shades of geranium red, running into pink; but, beyond and above all else, indeed, the latest cry of the hour is a certain rich, intense shade of turquoise blue. . . . Entire hats of this blue are shown at the best shops, composed of wonderfully shirred silks, spotted gauzes, chenille, plumes, bits of yellow lace, pink or scarlet roses, and purple violets with heaps of foliage." Miniature but unmuted celebrations were held in other sections of the city, according to the Monday *Tribune:* "In the colored quarters the exhibition was stentorian, and there were hundreds of cakewalks in all but name. Little Italy was vivid with brilliant shawls and sashes, while lower Second-ave. [with its Hungarian tide] blossomed as the red, red rose."

The *Tribune* account alone touched on the Spanish-American hostilities, to break openly eleven days later: "A number of Buffalo Bill's Indians [part of his "Wild West" show at Madison Square Garden] appeared in lower Fifth-ave. on their way to the Fourteenth-st. station of the elevated road. They exhibited the latest styles in spring war paint, which, by the way, may be in great demand before the end of the present week."

. . . . *Depend almost entirely on the Journal*

"YESTERDAY AFTERNOON the new tent of the Eagle's headquarters at Camp Black flung its big banner to the breeze, welcoming the Brooklyn soldiers and their visitors to the cosy interior. It is not only the largest and most comfortable tent in camp," averred the May 6, 1898 issue of the newspaper once edited by Walt Whitman, "but commands a fine view of the white, cone shaped canvas homes of the boys which stretch in a bright line for over a mile and a half on Hempstead Plains. . . . The tent is white and occupies a considerable area in comparison to those surrounding it. . . . Yesterday the interior was decidedly picturesque and looked like the stage setting of a war drama. Four cots were ranged along the back, the sleeping quarters of the Eagle correspondents. . . . Big swinging lamps will be put in in a short time, so that the officers who may wish to glance at the war news, may come in at night and take advantage of the files, where not only the Eagle, but the illustrated weeklies may be had. . . . Just as soon as the visitor steps from the train and looks toward newspaper row, the big red banner and the large, white, square tent attracts his attention."

The *New York Journal* boasted a more far-flung empire, stretching octopus arms from its headquarters in metropolitan "Newspaper Row" beside City Hall Park (where the "Park Row Patriots" of the *New-York Daily Tribune*'s phrase watched anxiously for the latest word) to remote hamlets. On May 6, the Hearst organ proclaimed: "The bulletin service of the Journal is now perfected to such an extent that the news is posted on all the Journal boards in and out of the city at the same time it appears on the board at the main office. The men at the military camps depend almost entirely on the Journal bulletins for their information."

To return to the account from the "big white canvas home of the Eagle": "Between [the] tent and the camp is the drill ground where the raw recruits are taught the intricacies of tactics, are howled at and nagged while drums beat and bugles blow and trained companies parade to and fro just to shame the awkward squads into something like military order. Every moment or so, as the visitor looks at the rows of white hives"—seen in the background of the photograph—"across the broad field, a dark object dashes out from the white cloud and grows rapidly larger as it approaches. It is an orderly with some message for the General [Charles F. Roe], whose tent surmounts the brow of the hill. His horse gallops madly up, the sentry salutes and a moment afterward the orderly has darted off in another direction. . . . All is excitement, yet all is methodical and the disagreeable details of camp life are lost when the brilliant scene is enjoyed from the Eagle tent."

"Newspaper Row" at Camp Black, May 18, 1898
Hempstead Plains, Long Island

The "details" were more than "disagreeable." On April 29, when Company H of the 71st Regiment—"the first infantry organization of the National Guard of this State to go into service in the present war"—opened the camp, named after the Governor of New York, "the broad, level fields of Hempstead . . . presented a decidedly dreary view" according to the *New-York Daily Tribune* of the following morning. Every conceivable creature discomfort was the lot of the pioneers and those who followed them. Charles Fuller of Squadron A wrote, in *What a New York Trooper Saw of the War* (1900), that "few places ever looked more uninviting, than did Camp Black on the night of our arrival [May 2nd, when more than 6,000 soldiers shared misery]. . . . my first night of guard duty in 'Uncle Sam's' service is the most disagreeable recollection I have of the late war. . . ." With the resilience of America and of youth, there appeared, the *Tribune* of the 5th relates: "Fantastic names . . . on the tents. . . . 'The Suicide Club,' 'Waldorf-Astoria,' 'Metropolitan Museum of Art' are good samples of the signs seen on the field." On the first Sunday of Camp Black's brief, ungorgeous life (the beginning of its end was announced in the *Tribune* on June 10, and it ". . . became a thing of the past . . ." on December 16) 25,000 visitors descended on the post, via the Long Island Railroad, awheel, and—in the case of the contingent from the nearby Meadow Brook Club—in "swell four-in-hands." On May 21, *Harper's Weekly* reproduced a wash drawing by its "Special Artist," Thuré de Thulstrup, entitled "Repelling Invaders At Camp Black."—the enemy band in this frontal attack being two comely girl cyclists. A bottle of whiskey was considered the most acceptable gift and drinking the fashionable refuge of the soldiery. Accounts of pillaging, pranks and disorderly conduct seeped out. Throughout the month of May the elements trained the ill-prepared troops for the tropics as far as precipitation, if not temperature, was concerned; over the week end of the 7th a gale of fierce intensity "swept over the vast expanse of Hempstead Plains," the *Eagle* reported, "with terrific force, ripping up the tents of the soldiers and nearly all of the tents in newspaper row. . . . One of the Eagle tents was split to shreds and another damaged. . . ."

On the parade ground, too, took place the solemn mustering in. "On our return from the interesting ceremony which made us pawns to be played upon Uncle Sam's mighty chessboard," Charles Fuller recounted, "our stout colored cook 'Tom' eyed us quizzically as we lined up for mess, and sagely remarked: 'Well, yes'day you was gemmen—to-day you'se nobody.'"

. . . . *We have had our glory*

". . . GAUNT AND yellow images of the men they had been, some of them so weak that they wept because of the kindness of their reception, while others stared at the cheering crowds with the wild strange look of men to whom the things of earth are of little moment. . . ." So *Harper's Weekly* of September 10, 1898 described the ragged victorious heroes of the 71st Regiment, conquered by fever and lack of food, and, as one of their number (the artist, Charles Johnson Post, Private, Co. F.) told me not long before his death in 1956, a logistic breakdown that paralleled the Crimean War. "There was not much exuberance about the boys . . ." reported the *New-York Daily Tribune* of August 30. "As a whole, the regiment

The home-coming of the 71st Regiment, August 29, 1898
Scene outside the Armory, at the southeast corner of Thirty-
fourth Street and Park Avenue

looked weak and worn. Most of the men wore unkempt beards, and their cheeks were gaunt and their eyes deep set in their heads. . . ." The remnant of a regiment, ". . . too weary to grow enthusiastic . . ." "marched" from the Battery to the Park Avenue and Thirty-fourth Street Armory it had left—1,043 strong—scarcely four months-without-end before. Fourteen had died on the field of battle during the Santiago Campaign; a far greater number (80) from tropical and other diseases; 68 (of whom 5 later perished) had bled in combat; many lay shivering in yellow fever and malaria-ridden beds in Cuba, or prostrate in typhoidal Camp Wikoff at Montauk; some were on recuperative furlough. A bare 350 veterans were in line, with the demi-living—weak beyond walking—transported in cable-cars, in pathetic parade led by a Police squad and a detachment from the 171st Regiment. "The route . . . seemed through a three-sided tunnel of stars and stripes . . ." (along Broadway). "There were not wanting inscriptions of welcome on many buildings, and some of the friends of the soldier boys exhibited placards calling them by name. On one building was the sign in homemade letters, 'Welcome to Sergeant Staudermer, Company K, 71st Regiment,' and there were plenty of signs welcoming the entire regiment without giving names." The chimes of Trinity played "Home, Sweet Home," "Yankee Doodle" and "America," as the white bene-diction of ticker tape descended from brokerage offices. At Waverly Place some of the in-valided alighted to join their comrades for the march through the "huge red, white and blue canyon" that was Fifth Avenue. About a hundred men, transferred to waiting carriages, drove in the sad procession of triumph. Among those in line was "Billy-Be-Damm" of Company M—a Central Park goat who had unflinchingly faced enemy fire during the Battle of San Juan, and who later received an honorable discharge as a non-commissioned officer. The valiant mascot was cheered along with the decimated regiment, which turned east on Thirty-fourth Street to the tune of "When Johnny Comes Marching Home" from the Waldorf-Astoria's musicians, and the Armory gates swung wide to receive their war-torn own. "We have had our glory, and are finding out the terrible cost of it," editorialized *Harper's Weekly*.

A penetrant commentary on the civilian attitude toward the veteran of this imperialistic war appeared in the October 6, 1898 issue of *Life*, translated into line by Charles Dana Gibson's agile mind and pen from an anecdote in the *New-York Daily Tribune* of September 25, under the heading "Stories Of Camp Wikoff": "As the train was leaving for New-York last evening . . . a couple of young women entered the car with a basket of fruit tied with ribbons. 'Oh, there is a poor soldier, one of our heroes; let us give him some fruit!' exclaimed one of them, and rushing up to one of the men, she said: 'Won't you have some fruit? You have been such heroes we want to do something for you.' 'You are mistaken, miss; I belong neither to the 71st nor to the Rough Riders. I am only a Regular, consequently not a hero!'"

. . . . *A barrel of red, a barrel of white and a barrel of blue*

"It was on one of the Fifth avenue grand stands during the wait for the parade. A travelling salesman for a printing ink house in a big Ohio city was telling his New York friend how it was that he left his route and travelled all night to be here in time for the parade. 'This is what decided me,' said he. 'Business in Buffalo yesterday had been bad. I was discouraged and had about given up the idea of coming. Toward evening I struck a customer who ordered of me a barrel of red, a barrel of white and a barrel of blue ink. That meant Dewey to me. I took the next train, and here I am.'"

Apparently a great many people followed the example of this itinerant, whose stimulus was annotated in *The New York Herald* of October 1, 1899, for that paper reported: "Three millions of persons saw the parade yesterday. . . . Of these, one million were residents of Manhattan and the Bronx. Nearly a million more came from the populous suburban districts across both rivers, and the rest were poured into New [York by] the railways."

"Real Dewey weather," so General Miles was the first to adjectivize, beamed upon the "Multitudes Stretch[ing] from Ground to Housetop to the Uttermost Point of View" to cheer "the one figure without a flaw," as the correspondent of the London *Daily Mail* described the Admiral.

His Saturday began in the early hours, when he left the deck of the cruiser *Olympia* (on whose bridge he had stood in victory at the Battle of Manila Bay on that history-made May first morning of 1898) and went by water to the Battery, passing the vessels of the "White Squadron" gayly afloat along a spaced two-mile stretch of the Hudson (fluid avenue of the great naval parade of September 29). Escorted to City Hall by the official committee and two troops of Squadron A, he accepted the gift of the City of New York—a loving cup

484

of gold, "Roman in design," from Mayor Van Wyck, who hailed him as "chief among the naval heroes of the world." The waiting carriages bore the Admiral and his officers to the specially chartered steamboat *Sandy Hook*, aboard which breakfast was served on the way to Grant's Tomb, the point of departure for the land parade to Washington Square (see pages 486–487), one continuous salvo shared with Governor Theodore Roosevelt (whose administrative genius as Assistant Secretary of the Navy had gone so far to make our sea strength) and Rear Admirals W. S. Schley and William T. Sampson, the victors of Santiago. "As if to lend brightness to a scene already bright, the air was full of red Autumn butterflies which seemed to have selected New York as a meeting place and chosen particularly Fifth Avenue for their flight, as if they mistook the flags and colored kites for flowers," marveled *The New York Times* of October 1. On the Madison Square reviewing stand close to the Worth Monument "the Admiral's booth . . . [was] surmounted by a canopy of blue and white. . . . At each corner was a wreath of laurels, and at intervals bronze eagles with outstretched pinions had been placed . . . ," so Sunday's *New-York Daily Tribune* tells. "Over twenty thousand pink roses were used in banking the rail. The Admiral's chair was cushioned with blue plush, and had the added comfort of large arms. . . . When the seats in this stand were filled it looked from afar like a huge bouquet of many colors. Many of the women wore scarlet golf jackets." Here the man who had carried on the naval tradition of John Paul Jones and of Stephen Decatur, of Perry and of Farragut, picnicked on sandwiches and sparkling wine, as, according to *The New York Herald*, "his eyes wandered in admiration toward the white fabric which had been reared in his honor. From the base to the wings of the Victory, a hundred feet above him, the Admiral gazed at the Dewey Arch. He started forward a little when he caught a glimpse of his own face on a medallion held by one of the figures. His air was that of a man who wondered if such a tribute were really meant for him. He looked across at the white pillars" of a colonnade stretching from Twenty-fifth to Twenty-third streets, leading to and away from the glistening monument to triumph patterned after that of Titus, which, "outlined against the green of the trees, gave the impression that he was in some classic grove." Suggested and designed by the architect Charles Rollinson Lamb and garnished with the work of thirty fellow members of the National Sculpture Society, these temporary symbols of "staff," which crumbled and disappeared by the end of 1900, were the voluntary offering of the forefront of the city's sculptors (only one out-of-town talent participating). The surmounted quadriga, *Naval Victory*, was the work of J. Q. A. Ward (see page 427); such master hands as those of Daniel Chester French, Herbert Adams, George E. Bissell and Karl Bitter were of the number. Along this *Via Victoris* and through the great Arch passed close to 31,000 men of the United States Navy, Army and the militia of various states.

Thus New York in three-day jubilee—with illumination and fireworks by night—answered Governor Roosevelt's triggering message to the State Legislature urging a welcome to "the man who at the close of the nineteenth century has added fresh renown to the flag that has already so often been borne to glorious triumph in the land and on the sea," a welcome to the hero who, with "The thunder of . . . [his] guns in Manila Bay raised in a moment's time the prestige of American arms throughout the world."

And so, at long parade's end, the weary Admiral was driven away, again under the escort of the "superbly caparisoned" Hussars. "Squadron A," he exclaimed. "How splendid!"

Byron N.Y.
7460

The Dewey Parade,
September 30, 1899
Members of
Squadron A in front of the
Croton Distributing Reservoir
Fifth Avenue, south from
Forty-second Street

Acknowledgments

To Percy C. Byron, who placed the labor of two lifetimes in my hands;

To Captain Edward Steichen, the greatest photographer of all, who has given this small book his large blessing;

To the late Lloyd Morris, distant cousin and close friend, who sent me on my way;

To M. S. Wyeth, Jr., the first to listen to the story;

To A. L. Hart, Jr., of The Macmillan Company, who has exercised his editorial prerogative by blue-penciling what I wrote about him;

To Alfred Manso, also of The Macmillan Company, whose creational genius imparted to this volume its physical shape and substance;

To my colleagues at the Museum of the City of New York—Hardinge Scholle, my first Director, and to his successor, John Walden Myer, under whom I have served for over a quarter of a century; to Patricia Pulling, Assistant *sans pareil;* to Albert K. Baragwanath, my "alter editor," and to my other co-workers, May Davenport Seymour, V. Isabelle Miller, Susan E. Lyman, Janet Pinney, Lawrence Beattie and William M. Williamson—each one a specialist;

To Samuel Grierson, Erich Hartmann, John Harvey Heffren and Beaumont Newhall (Curator, George Eastman House, Rochester, New York) for advice in connection with problems relating to Photography;

To my friends, very particularly and most especially Ruth and Marshall B. Davidson, who were always there; to John A. Kouwenhoven, who taught me new ways of seeing;

To Cleveland Amory and Oliver Jensen, who voluntarily subjected themselves to the ordeal of reading the text in galley form;

To such institutions as The New York Society Library, The New York Public Library, The New-York Historical Society and The Library of Congress, and the staff members who give them greatness;

To those many helpful firms and experts and individuals who have answered my many questions;

To Grace Windsor Teed, of The Macmillan Company, who deciphered illegibility and typed my manuscript;

To Warren H. Potter, of The Macmillan Company, who compiled the index;

To Kathleen McMullan, who brought patient skill to proofreading;

And mostly to my Mother;

   To all these, and many more, who have done so much for so little, I give my thanks.

                              G. M. M.

Index

Boldface numbers refer to photographs

492

494

502

Pitt Street, 136
Plant, Morton F., 303
Players, The, xi
Playgrounds, **142**, **143**, 474. *See also* Streets as playground
Plaza, Central Park and 59th St., 1, 4, 26, **27**, **28**, **32–33**, 182, **460**, **461**
Plaza Art Galleries, 119
Plaza Hotel, 31, **32–33**, 34
Plaza Operating Company, 34
Pleyel, Ignaz, 331
Poems of Passion (Wilcox), 99
Police Commissioners, Board of, 47. *See also* New York City Police Department
Police Parade, **470**, **471**, **472**
Polla, Patron Saint of, 138
Polo Grounds, 177, **178**, **179**
Pond, J. B. (lecture bureau), 22
Pond, William A., & Company, 158
Pool, Thomas, 180
"Poorhouse Bill," 61
Poorhouse Quartet, 61
Pope Leo XIII, 138
Pope Manufacturing Company, 150, 153
Porter, H. H., 341
Porter, Horace, 152, 153, 461, 476
Porter, Stephen G., 432
Porter, William S. (O. Henry), 23, 44, 125, 229
Portrait of Madame Sophie (Drouais), 120
Portrait of Mrs. Penrose (Hoppner), 120
Post, Charles Johnson, 482
Post, Emily, 477
Post, George B., 6, 31, 388, 392
Post Office (1878), 6, **9**, 10
Postal Telegraph Company, 76
Posters, **130–131**, 150, **151**, 237, **238**, 239, 240
Potomac (steamboat), 447, 450. *See also Albany* (steamboat)
Potomac River Line, 450
Potter, E. C., 53
Potter, Henry C., 397
Potter, Horatio, 456
Potter, Isaac B., 152
Potter, Paul M., 386
Powers, Hiram, 426
Powers, James T., 247
Pranishnikoff, I., 158
Pratt, S. H., 47
Praxiteles, 426
Preece, John, 66
Presbyterian Hospital, 50, 337
"President Cleveland's Wedding March" (Witmark), 452
Price, Bruce, 477
Prices, 78, 238, 273, 290, 300–301, 394, 395, 400, 404, 410, 413, 468, 470; for paintings, 120, 226–227, 426, 428; for sculpture, 112, 377. *See also* Salaries; Wages
Pride of the Family, The (Pinchart), **449**
Prince Goes Fishing, The (Duer), 433

Princeton University, 144, 218, 303
Printing-House Square, 389
Printing-out paper, xii
Prisoner of Zenda, The (Hope), 239, 277
Prize fighting, 147
Proctor, Billy, 400
Proctor's Theatres: 23rd St., 272, 273, **274**; East 58th St., 407
Produce Exchange Sound Money League, 477
Prohibition, 402, 414
Prospect Union, Harvard University extension school, 363
Prostitution, 46, 47, 363–364
Pryor, Mrs. Roger A., 354
Public Record Office of Northern Ireland, 28
Publishers' and Advertisers' Sound Money Club, 478
Puck, 405, 406
Pulitzer, Joseph, xii
Pullman Company, 284
Pump Room, Equitable Building, **390**
Purdy and Henderson, 1
Pure Food and Drug Act, 393
Purple Passage The Life of Mrs. Frank Leslie (Stern), 99
Pursuit of Pleasure (Myers), 82
Pushcarts, 79, 132, **133**, **134–135**, 137
Putnam's Monthly, 12
Pyle, Howard, 402
Pyne, Mrs. Grafton H. (Leta C. Wright), 197
Pyrography, 105

Quand Les Cathédrales Etaient Blanches (Le Corbusier), 4
Quarantine, 209
Queen's Lace Handkerchief, The, 245
Queensborough, Lord (Almeric Hugh Paget), 206
Quick lunch, 298, 391–394
Quimby, Harriet, 418
Quimby, J. M., & Company, 303
Quito (steamer), 370, **371**

Racetracks, 296
Raceward, Thomas (Percival-Hodges-Irwin), 255
Racquet and Tennis Club, 402
Rafferty, Officer, 472
Ragtime, 250, 451
Rail-Road Journal, 295
Railway and Steamship Sound Money Club, 477
Raines, John, 400
Raines Law, 47, 324, 400; hotels, 69, 324
Rainy Daisies, 75, 104, 245
Rainy Day Club, 71, 74–75
Rainy-day costume, 71, 74–75
Rambler bicycles, 153
Randall property, 12
Randall's Island, 339; ferry, 339
Ranhofer, Charles, 413

Ransome, John, 279
Raphael, 315
Rathskeller restaurant, 13, 389
"Rattle Watch," 470
Rauh, Ida, 358
Rawdon, Lord, 474
Rebecca of Sunnybrook Farm (Wiggin), 221
Reception Hospital (Harlem), 339
Reception rooms, 96
Recreation Pier, 138, **139**
Rector's, **5**, 6, 34, 250
Redheaded Outfield And Other Baseball Stories, The (Grey), 177
Reed, Marietta (Mrs. Paran Stevens), 112, 114
Regattas, 167, 170–171
Rehan, Ada, 277
Rehearsal (ballet), **262**, 263
Reid, Robert, 53, 60
Reilly, William, 246, 247
Réjane, Madame, 213, **215**
Relyea, Marjorie (Mrs. R. D. Holmes; Mrs. Albert Stokes), 250
Rembrandt, 255
Reminiscences of Augustus Saint-Gaudens, The, 28, 58
Reno, Jesse W., 379
Renoir, Pierre, 125
Rents in Our Robes (Leslie), 99
Renwick, James, 12, 26
Le Repos (Breton), 227
Republic, The (Daniel Chester French), 377, **378–379**
Republican Party, National Convention of the, 462
Restaurants, 6, 19, **384**, 388, 389, **393**, 402, 410–411, 413–414, **415**; foreign, 389, 406–407, **408–409**, 410, 417–418, 419
Reszke, Edouard de, 94, 206
Reszke, Jean de, 94, 263
Return of the Fishermen (Isabey), 120
Reynolds & Engel, 116
Rhodes, Harrison, 239
"Rialto, The," **5**, 13, **14**, 41, 236
Rice, Fanny, 245
Rice Electric Display Company, 13–14
Richard Savage, 253
Richards, T. Addison, 184
Richardson, H. H., 50
Richepin, Jean, 257
Richter, C. L., 182
Ridge Street, 136
Riffraff, 45, 46, 47, 156, 287, 336. *See also* Gangs
Riggs, Mrs. G. C. (Kate Douglas Wiggin), **220–221**
Riis, Jacob A., 128, 132, 138, 140, 143, 368, 399, 474
Riis, Roger William, 128
Riley, R. W., 287
Ring, Blanche, 247
Ringling, John and Mable, Museum of Art, 227
Riverside Drive, 152, 153, **156**, **160–161**, 163, 185, 273, **463**, **464**, **465**

505

506

510